STANDARDS-BASED REFORM AND THE POVERTY GAP

STANDARDS-BASED REFORM AND THE POVERTY GAP

Lessons for No Child Left Behind

ADAM GAMORAN

Editor

BROOKINGS INSTITUTION PRESS
Washington, D.C.

ABOUT BROOKINGS

The Brookings Institution is a private nonprofit organization devoted to research, education, and publication on important issues of domestic and foreign policy. Its principal purpose is to bring the highest quality research and analysis to bear on current and emerging policy problems. Interpretations or conclusions in Brookings publications should be understood to be solely those of the authors.

Copyright © 2007
THE BROOKINGS INSTITUTION
1775 Massachusetts Avenue, N.W., Washington, D.C. 20036
www.brookings.edu

Library of Congress Cataloging-in-Publication data
Standards-based reform and the poverty gap : lessons for No Child Left Behind / Adam
  Gamoran, editor.
    p.   cm.
  Summary: "With latest data and research, scholars study what lessons can be drawn
from earlier efforts to help NCLB achieve its goals. Authors show that standards-based
reform has had some positive effects and some of the critics' greatest fears have not been
realized. Recommendations offered for implementation of impending reauthorized
NCLB"—Provided by publisher.
Includes bibliographical references and index.
  ISBN-13: 978-0-8157-3032-3 (cloth : alk. paper)
  ISBN-10: 0-8157-3032-2 (cloth : alk. paper)
  ISBN-13: 978-0-8157-3033-0 (pbk. : alk. paper)
  ISBN-10: 0-8157-3033-0 (pbk. : alk. paper)
  1. United States. No Child Left Behind Act of 2001. 2. Educational accountability—
United States. 3. Educational change—United States. 4. Poor—Education—United
States. 5. Academic achievement—United States. I. Gamoran, Adam, 1957– II. Title.
  LB2806.22.S736 2007
  379.1'580973—dc22   2007033616

9 8 7 6 5 4 3 2 1

The paper used in this publication meets minimum requirements of the
American National Standard for Information Sciences—Permanence of Paper
for Printed Library Materials: ANSI Z39.48-1992.

Typeset in Adobe Garamond

Composition by Kulamer Publishing Services
Potomac, Maryland

Printed by R. R. Donnelley and Sons
Harrisonburg, Virginia

To Joel, Daniel, and Naomi

Contents

PART I

The Context
of Contemporary
Education Reform

1

Introduction: Can Standards-Based Reform Help Reduce the Poverty Gap in Education?

ADAM GAMORAN

Pervasive inequality is the most pressing problem facing U.S. education. While average achievement levels in some U.S. school districts equal those in the world's high-achieving nations, other districts rank among the world's low performers. Inequality is evident not only between districts but also within districts and within schools, where students of different social backgrounds attain widely varying outcomes. The problem is particularly pronounced for students who face economic disadvantages. While students from disadvantaged racial and ethnic groups made noteworthy progress over the last forty years (mainly from around 1970 to 1990), gaps among students from families with varied economic resources remained stable and wide throughout that period. Achievement differences between students living in poverty and their more privileged peers, often called the "poverty gap," have shown little sign of diminishing.

The current federal program designed to reduce inequality in education, the No Child Left Behind Act of 2001 (NCLB), is the latest in more than two decades of federal efforts to raise educational standards. From *A Nation at Risk* in 1983 to the National Goals Education Panel of 1990 and the Goals 2000 Act in 1994, federal policy had attempted to increase standards and better align curriculum, instruction, and assessment in the nation's schools. NCLB is unique among the government's efforts in that it focuses not only on raising standards overall but also on increasing the achievement of students in a variety of demographic subgroups, including those from racial and ethnic minorities, disabled students, English language learners, and students faced with economic disadvantages. NCLB also is much stronger and more far-reaching than previous federal efforts to raise education standards. For example, to receive federal education aid, states must set standards for student performance and every year assess reading and mathematics achievement for students in third through eighth grades and in high school. In selected grades, science achievement must also be assessed. In addition, at least 95 percent of students in each school and district must take the tests; no more than 3 percent of disabled students may take an alternative assessment; and English language learners must take the assessments within two years of arrival in the United States. Those measures prevent schools from "hiding" their low achievers and thus inflating their results. Failure to meet the achievement targets (known as "adequate yearly progress," or AYP) results in sanctions that range from requiring districts to offer students tutoring and transfer options to closure and reconstitution of schools.

There are many reasons to expect that NCLB's approach to increasing standards and holding schools accountable for student performance will boost the chances for poor children to succeed in school. First, by requiring schools to report test results separately for students in different demographic subgroups, NCLB shines a spotlight on social inequalities in school performance that sometimes have been obscured in the past, perhaps increasing the political will to address this profound problem. Second, in principle, the transfers and supplemental services offered to students in schools that are not making AYP should help disadvantaged students to obtain better opportunities. Third, NCLB requires districts to place a "highly qualified teacher" in every classroom. Teaching out of field or with provisional certification is more common in schools with large proportions of low-income students than elsewhere, so that requirement also may improve opportunities for the disadvantaged. Finally, NCLB requires districts participating in the Reading First program to choose curricula and teaching methods for which there is scientific evidence of success. If those methods are more effective than untested alternatives, the move to evidence-based teaching of reading may be especially important for poor children, who are overrepresented among struggling readers.

Yet there are many challenges to reducing inequality under NCLB. More diverse schools may be more likely to be labeled as not making adequate yearly progress simply because their larger number of population subgroups means that they have more targets to hit. The massive level of improvement required by 2014 also suggests that schools with high concentrations of disadvantaged students may be unable to succeed. NCLB sanctions such as transfers and supplemental services draw resources *away* from struggling schools, so students who are not fortunate enough to transfer may find their opportunities getting worse, not better. Indeed, the students least likely to transfer when their schools are failing may be those living in poverty whose parents have low levels of education. Moreover, even if districts provide extra resources to schools with low-income students (for example, through the Reading First program), those resources may not be enough to compensate for a disadvantaged home and community environment. Also, many districts are passing accountability for meeting standards to students themselves, and some (but not all) research suggests that students living in poverty are disproportionately burdened with sanctions when accountability systems are put in place. Finally, NCLB confronts a variety of political challenges, including resistance to implementation and bias in implementing Reading First (as revealed by the U.S. Department of Education's Office of Inspector General in reports such as *The Reading First Program's Grant Application Process*, which appeared in September 2006). Resistance and bias in implementation may prevent NCLB from reducing inequalities even if the theories behind the legislation are valid.

Many of the questions raised in this volume are amenable to empirical analysis. While it is too soon to assess outcomes under NCLB, standards-based reform by states and school districts has been in place long enough to allow researchers to measure its impact, and their findings can be used to guide the implementation and possible revision of NCLB. To address the possibilities, the Institute for Research on Poverty and the Wisconsin Center for Education Research sponsored a conference at the University of Wisconsin–Madison in February 2006. Participants came from a variety of disciplinary backgrounds, including economics, political science, psychology, and sociology, and their presentations included syntheses of work to date and new empirical studies. Through careful analysis and lively debate, speakers, discussants, and audience members sifted through the evidence to assess the relation between NCLB and the poverty gap. Though complex and sometimes contradictory, the findings pointed toward modest improvements for poor children, but at nowhere near the rate of improvement demanded by NCLB—or by anyone who views low educational outcomes among disadvantaged youth as a major impediment to the advancement of American society.

Schools, Standards, and Gaps in Achievement

NCLB is no doubt flawed by its assumption that schools alone can eliminate achievement gaps in the face of powerful social inequalities in the wider society. Yet while that assumption is surely unrealistic, the question of what schools *can* do is unresolved. How much gap-closing can be expected from standards-based reform? What lessons can be learned from past reform efforts that will lead to greater progress, if not fully accomplish NCLB's ambitious goals? On one level, NCLB creates incentives for improving student performance and reducing gaps in achievement, and on that level, the policy appears to be succeeding. To an extent never before attained in the United States, educators, politicians, and the general public have been alerted to the problems of inequality, including inequality between students in poverty and their more advantaged counterparts. Incentives, however, are unlikely to suffice. Instead, specific strategies are needed to improve students' learning opportunities in schools, such as strategies to improve teacher and instructional quality and to promote evidence-based practices. Moreover, to make a difference in achievement gaps, those strategies need to target the most disadvantaged students. To what degree has standards-based reform led to improvements in the quality of teachers and teaching? If improvements are evident, have they occurred in schools with disadvantaged student populations? Those questions are addressed in chapters 2 through 4 in this volume.

The main targets of NCLB sanctions are school districts and schools. In response, many states and districts are targeting students, reasoning that if principals, teachers, and support staff are working hard to raise standards, students should respond with greater efforts of their own. Common sanctions include not promoting students who perform poorly on assessments to the next grade and not allowing them to graduate from high school if they fail the exit exam. While grade retention and graduation testing are not included in NCLB, they are increasingly being employed alongside NCLB. What can be learned from recent experiences with sanctions of students that will aid understanding of the prospects for reducing achievement gaps under NCLB? Chapters 5 and 6 address that question.

School choice and supplemental tutoring are among the key sanctions that NCLB places on schools that fail to bring students to the required level of achievement. While those sanctions clearly are galvanizing attention, the empirical question is whether they make a difference in student achievement. Given the experience before and during the early implementation of NCLB, should achievement gaps be expected to narrow as schools and districts implement the sanctions, as required under NCLB? To answer that question, which is addressed in chapters 7 and 8, one must attend both to the impact of the strategies when they are implemented well and to the extent and quality of their implementation as NCLB moves forward.

To draw lessons for NCLB from recent experiences under standards-based reform, it is essential to understand the political context of NCLB and to examine the early implementation of the legislation. Those topics are addressed in chapters 9 and 10, which look to NCLB's future. NCLB is scheduled for reauthorization in 2007, but many observers predict that it will be delayed until after the 2008 presidential election. The findings in this book are intended to inform the debate over reauthorization, whether immediate or delayed.

Findings on Standards-Based Reform and Inequality

Following this introduction, chapter 2 provides a background for understanding the relation between standards-based reform and the poverty gap. Barbara R. Foorman, Sharon J. Kalinowski, and Waynel L. Sexton draw attention not only to NCLB and its immediate predecessors in federal education policy but also to the civil rights movement, the War on Poverty, and the broader recognition of the rights of all students to a quality education as a means of ameliorating social disadvantages. With her coauthors, Foorman, who brings special insight to research-based understanding of NCLB from her recent service as first commissioner of education research at the Institute of Education Sciences, shows that the same milieu that gave rise to standards-based reform also stimulated the right to education movement, which supports quality education for students with disabilities. Until recently, laws regarding general education improvement and laws regarding special education have been implemented separately. With the passage of the 2004 Individuals with Disabilities Education Act (IDEA), however, the possibility emerged of a coordinated approach to ensuring high-quality schooling for all children, regardless of their social background or disability. Foorman and her colleagues recognize the tensions between IDEA and NCLB, but they maintain that those tensions can be resolved.

While IDEA and NCLB offer important new opportunities to reduce the poverty gap, Foorman and her colleagues argue that they represent only the first step. The quality of the implementation of the measures is crucial to their success. In the view of the authors, key aspects of implementation include the use of instruction based on scientific evidence of effectiveness, the alignment of instruction with standards and assessment, and the application of effective measures early in children's lives.

Findings on Accountability Reforms and the Quality of Teachers and Teaching

Among the major elements in NCLB's strategy for raising test scores and reducing test score gaps is improvement in the quality of teachers and of teaching. In chapter 3, Meredith Phillips and Jennifer Flashman set the tone for the empirical work in this book with their examination of NCLB-like policies during the 1990s. Recognizing that it is too soon to evaluate NCLB directly, they focus on how changes during the 1990s in state accountability policies were linked to changes in teacher and instructional quality within states. They consider not only potential positive consequences, such as those anticipated by the designers of NCLB, but also unintended, negative consequences, such as the possibility that the rigors of stricter accountability may drive the best-qualified teachers away from the profession, or, in the case of the 1990s, to states with weaker accountability regimes. They use accountability reports from the Council of Chief State School Officers to assess changes in state policies and the Schools and Staffing Surveys of 1993–94 and 1999–2000 to measure state changes in teacher and instructional quality. They estimate state fixed-effects models to rule out changes attributable to fixed, unobserved attributes of states.[1]

Overall, Phillips and Flashman find that variation in state accountability policies was not consistently linked to changes in teacher and instructional quality. Their evidence offers little basis for the concern that accountability policies may be detrimental to teacher quality. They observe that sanctions directed at teachers tend to reduce perceptions of autonomy among teachers in high-poverty schools but that that tendency might indicate that teachers are being pushed to align instruction with standards, as intended under standards-based reform. They also find, not surprisingly, that in states that increased the use of student testing for accountability, teachers participated more often in professional development devoted to student assessment; teachers also devoted more instruction time to subjects that were more heavily tested. Both findings illustrate the power of standards-based reforms to affect teachers' behavior. Phillips and Flashman further observe that accountability measures directed at teachers were associated with a variety of positive

---

1. State fixed-effects models eliminate all variation associated with fixed characteristics of states by including an indicator variable for each state or by subtracting the state mean value from each data point. Such models require data on states at more than one point in time.

changes, including increases in teacher experience, certification, college quality, and rates of teachers holding advanced degrees and remaining in the profession. However, those findings did not hold for all types of schools. Some were evident in schools attended mainly by disadvantaged students, while others appeared in schools with more advantaged populations; there was no clear pattern. Moreover, while the findings seem promising, it is striking that the most persistent effects were associated with policies directed at teachers, not schools, whereas NCLB mainly targets schools and reaches teachers only indirectly. Consequently, it will be important to monitor NCLB's impact to determine whether it needs to aim more directly at teachers to affect the quality of teachers and teaching.

Teacher and instructional quality also are central to chapter 4, by Laura M. Desimone, Thomas M. Smith, and David Frisvold. The authors draw on teacher data from the 2000 and 2003 National Assessments of Educational Progress (NAEP) to examine changes over a slightly later, albeit shorter, period of time. The NAEP teacher data, which are representative of participating states, include information not only on background and training but also on approaches to instruction, as reported by the teachers themselves. The authors consider whether teacher characteristics and practices differ in high-poverty and low-poverty schools and, within schools, for students who receive free lunches and those who do not. They also examine whether the differences observed changed from 2000 to 2003 and whether any changes were linked to state accountability policies, which they measured using a variety of data sources on the dimensions of power, authority, consistency, specificity, and stability of standards. After a series of descriptive findings, they also estimate models with state fixed effects.

Consistent with past research, the findings of Desimone and her colleagues show that in 2000, low-poverty schools tended to have teachers with better credentials and math backgrounds than high-poverty schools. Within-school gaps also were evident: disadvantaged students had less access to qualified teachers in both high- and low-poverty schools. The gaps changed little between 2000 and 2003. Moreover, most of the state policy variables were not linked to changes in teacher quality. One exception, however, was that states that increased their alignment of standards and assessments (consistency) witnessed small increases in the percentage of certified teachers and of teachers with mathematics majors. Finally, the authors report two notable changes in teacher quality related to school poverty levels. On the one hand, states that began ranking schools (an indicator of power) narrowed the gap between high- and low-poverty schools in the likelihood of having certified teachers. On the other hand, states that introduced more specific standards saw *increases* in the gap between high- and low-poverty schools in teacher certification levels. Because of the short time frame, the findings are tentative, but they suggest that publicizing schools' success or failure in reaching standards may help bring schools attended by students in poverty closer to their more advantaged counterparts—as intended by the designers of NCLB— whereas excessive specification of standards may make it more difficult for high-poverty schools to recruit certified teachers.

Findings on Sanctions for Students: Grade Retention and Exit Exams

Although NCLB sanctions are aimed at schools, many states and districts are responding by holding students accountable for their own success or failure to meet performance targets. Proponents of that strategy hold that greater accountability gives students an immediate stake in their own progress and thus increases incentives for students to perform well. Among the major strategies for ensuring student accountability are the retention of students who fail to pass standardized tests at key grade levels and the use of exit examinations as a prerequisite for high school graduation. Those strategies are not elements of NCLB, but many states and districts are employing them in an effort to include students themselves in the spectrum of parties to be held accountable for student performance, and the testing requirements of NCLB create the mechanisms that enable these sanctions.

In chapter 5, Robert M. Hauser, Carl B. Frederick, and Megan Andrew examine trends in grade retention from 1996 to 2005. They use census data to examine national trends and data from fourteen state education agencies to consider state-specific patterns. A major concern regarding the relation between NCLB and poverty is that if school districts hold back students who fail assessments, the proportion of students below age-appropriate grade levels is likely to increase, particularly among students from minority and low-income backgrounds who tend to have lower test scores. Based on a cogent review of the existing literature, Hauser and his colleagues note that retention is associated with higher dropout rates and has rarely been effective as a means of boosting achievement. Consequently, the question of whether NCLB has resulted in a rapid rise in retention rates takes on great urgency. What the authors find, however, is no spike in retention. In fact, retention rates peaked in 2001, the year before NCLB was implemented. The national data show a consistent increase in retention from 1996 to 2001, likely reflecting the standards-based reform movement, but that trend was consistent with an older pattern going back at least to the 1970s. Thus, whereas stan-

dards-based reform probably has resulted in more use of retention, the early implementation of NCLB has not accelerated that practice. However, both national and state data show increased rates of retention in the earliest years of schooling—those not covered by NCLB—and the available state data show substantial variation in retention rates from year to year.

Hauser and his colleagues offer a tantalizing finding concerning social background and retention under NCLB: from 2001 to 2003, the overall degree of inequality in retention declined. Does that mean that under NCLB, retention decisions have become more "objective"—that is, less dependent on social background and more dependent on test scores (to the degree that background and test scores are independent)? Regardless of the cause, it is not yet clear whether the reduction in inequality will be sustained. In 2004, the relation between retention and social background jumped back to its pre-NCLB level, but it declined again in 2005. Hence, the relation between NCLB, retention, and inequality remains an open question that demands continued close scrutiny.

The use of high-stakes tests for high school graduation is another incentive for students under standards-based reform. In chapter 6, Thomas S. Dee and Brian A. Jacob examine the impact of high school exit examinations on high school completion, college enrollment, employment, and earnings. Also using census data, they estimate state fixed-effects models for the period 1980–98. In addition, they draw on the Common Core of Data to estimate district fixed-effects models for one state, Minnesota, from 1993 to 2002. An important feature of Dee and Jacobs' study is that the authors distinguish between "minimum competency exams," basic skills tests that have long existed, and more rigorous exit examinations that reflect the more recent standards movement. They also distinguish effects for different population subgroups, an approach that is essential for understanding the implications of exams for inequality.

Dee and Jacob find that states that introduced high school exit examinations between 1980 and 1998 tended to reduce their rates of high school completion, particularly among African American students. In light of the relation between race and poverty in the United States, that finding implies that exit exams may help perpetuate poverty rather than provide a way out. The finding held for both minimum competency exams and more rigorous testing schemes. For Whites and Blacks, exit examinations were unrelated to college enrollment or employment, but for Hispanic females, exit exams led to higher rates of college enrollment and employment. The coefficient for exit exams on high school completion also was positive for Hispanics, though nonsignificant. Consequently, while exit exams may have exacerbated Black-White inequality, they seem to have mitigated inequality between Hispanics and non-Hispanic Whites. Dee and Jacob further observe that while minimum competency examinations were unrelated to earnings, more rigorous assessments contributed to higher weekly wages for employed African Americans but lower wages for Whites and Hispanics. That finding highlights the importance of considering labor market as well as education outcomes and hints that members of disadvantaged groups who succeed can benefit from high-stakes testing but that those who fail may fall further behind.

Findings on Sanctions for Schools: Supplemental Educational Services and School Choice

One way that NCLB differs from past standards-based reforms is that it includes not only standards but also serious sanctions intended to create better learning opportunities for students whose schools fail to reach their achievement targets. One of the primary sanctions is the mandate to provide "supplemental educational services" (SES)—that is, free after-school tutoring—to low-income students in schools that fail to meet their AYP targets for three years in a row. That requirement is expected to narrow the poverty gap by elevating the achievement levels of low-achieving, low-income students. In chapter 7, George Farkas and Rachel E. Durham examine what is known about SES and whether it is likely to achieve its goals. Drawing on a combination of past research, new government-sponsored case studies, and their own investigations, they address several questions about tutoring programs and whether they are likely to reduce the poverty gap.

Across the country, fewer students are receiving SES than might be expected on the basis of the large number of schools that have failed to achieve their AYP goals. The best recent estimate is that only 20 percent of eligible students are receiving supplemental services. Moreover, while the effects of SES are not being tested directly, there is good reason for concern about the benefits of this costly strategy for gap-closing, at least as it currently is implemented. Past research has provided convincing evidence of the benefits of one-to-one tutoring (one student per tutor), but tutoring under NCLB occurs mainly in small groups, for which there is much less evidence of effectiveness. Moreover, a nationwide randomized trial indicates no achievement benefits of after-school programs; at best, such programs are effective for elementary student achievement only when they are of high quality, as often is not the case. Farkas and Durham conclude that as currently designed, supplemental educational services are likely to have little impact on achievement overall or on the poverty gap. To attain better results, tutoring needs to occur in smaller groups. Programs also must be more accessible, and students need to attend more regularly. Competition among providers might stimulate improvement, but only if sound information becomes available about which providers and types of programs are effective and only if parents act on that information at the local level.

School choice is yet another sanction that is mandated by NCLB and envisioned as a remedy for low test scores. Students whose schools fail to meet their AYP targets for two years in a row have the option to transfer to another public school, including a charter school, that has not failed AYP. The benefits of school choice for reducing inequality presumably work in two ways. First, obviously, it is supposed to give low-achieving students the chance to move to better schools. Second, it is expected to create incentives for districts and schools to elevate the quality of schools that are vulnerable to losing their students under school choice, thereby improving quality for all students and especially for those in schools with heavily disadvantaged populations.

In chapter 8, Paul T. Hill takes a hard look at the prospects of school choice under NCLB for reducing the poverty gap. He identifies both possible risks and potential benefits and gleans from existing evidence new ideas for how the risks can be managed and the benefits attained. Even though much has been written about the effects of both public and private school choice, Hill shows that there is little basis for firm conclusions. Implementation of NCLB is too recent to permit direct findings; moreover, very few students have exercised choice under NCLB. Even when previous work is considered, the evidence is so weak that it is difficult to predict what will happen under NCLB. That weakness is especially evident in the case of charter schools, which have generated a flurry of studies but few solid findings. Hill's strongest conclusion is that choice needs to be subjected to rigorous research, not only about whether the effects are positive or negative but also about the conditions under which school choice under NCLB can raise achievement and reduce inequality—and for whom. The evidence so far suggests that choice effects will be contingent on implementation, and understanding the contingencies will be the key to predicting the effects of choice on inequality.

The last section of the book looks toward the future of standards-based reform by drawing lessons from recent history and current practice. Understanding the politics of NCLB is one key to anticipating its future course. As Tom Loveless explains in chapter 9, NCLB was distinctive, in an era of polarized politics, in the level of bipartisan support that it initially enjoyed. While support from across the political spectrum is still evident, so is criticism from all sides. According to public opinion polls, general support for NCLB has eroded to the point that now supporters and opponents are about evenly balanced. Still, the lines of support for and opposition to NCLB continue to confound convention. For example, supporters are found more often among Republicans and opponents among Democrats, but African Americans and Hispanics tend to be the most supportive demographic subgroups. Moreover, middle-income groups tend to be more supportive of NCLB than either low- or high-income respondents, who express more skepticism. Nor do views of NCLB at the state level conform easily to well-known patterns. Perhaps the most provocative of Loveless's findings concerns the relation between state performance on NAEP and state resistance to NCLB. The most resistant states tend to be those in the middle of the performance range; both high- and low-performing states tend to be less defiant. Moreover, states with the largest Black-White achievement gaps (and states with the smallest black populations) tend to be among the most resistant to NCLB. Whether NCLB can survive, Loveless reasons, depends on whether the members of the original coalition that supported the law—which Loveless characterizes as representing "conservative ideas . . . wrapped in liberal clothing"—continue to see advances from their various perspectives.

In chapter 10, the concluding chapter, Andrew C. Porter takes stock of the evidence presented in the volume on past practices of standards-based reform and offers insights for the reauthorization of NCLB. Porter begins, however, by focusing on aspects of NCLB that were not touched on elsewhere; in particular, he demonstrates dramatic differences among states in implementing NCLB. In light of Foorman and her colleagues' assertion in chapter 2 that the effects of standards-based reform depend on its implementation, the wide variation among states raises questions about NCLB's chances for success but also offers prospects for research, since variation is required in order to identify policy effects.

Porter's advice is drawn from a combination of evidence to date and a theory about how standards-based reform can be effective. According to that theory, an accountability system will succeed only if it sets a good target and if it is symmetric and fair. Using his theory, Porter points out a number of key strengths of NCLB, as well as some ways it might be improved. For example, he argues that assessment targets could be strengthened by attending to scores throughout the range of achievement instead of focusing on a particular proficiency target. Assessment targets could also be improved by addressing student mobility and by considering alignment between content standards and assessments. The fairness of NCLB could also be strengthened; at present, neither supplemental services, nor school choice, nor highly qualified teachers are provided consistently or well. Without these resources, schools lack much chance of raising the achievement levels of their students, particularly students from the most disadvantaged backgrounds.

Forecast for Improvement

Will NCLB help reduce the poverty gap? While our crystal ball remains cloudy, the evidence and analyses in this book portend as much rain as sunshine. On the one hand, many of the greatest fears commonly expressed by opponents of NCLB have not materialized. Good teachers have not been driven away from the classroom by standards-based reforms; retention has not shot upward; and while high school graduation may be threatened by exit examinations, there is at least a hint that such exams may contribute to higher wages for African Americans in states that introduce them. NCLB clearly has brought attention to the inequality in achievement faced by students from racial, ethnic, and linguistic minorities; by those with economic disadvantages; and by those with disabilities. Moreover, there are some signs of progress related to standards-based reform, even if it is too early to judge NCLB. Certain aspects of teacher quality have improved, and some students are no doubt benefiting from new opportunities such as free tutoring and the chance to transfer to a different school.

On the other hand, the positive developments fall far short of the degree of change envisioned under NCLB. As Foorman and her colleagues point out, identifying inequalities, setting standards, and developing strategies are only the first step toward closing achievement gaps. When it comes to implementation, much work needs to be done, and some trends are troubling. While retention rates have not spiked, they rose steadily during the standards-based reform period, to the disadvantage of African American, Hispanic, and low-income students in particular. The few benefits to teacher quality seem to be related to teacher accountability rather than school accountability, which is the target of NCLB; moreover, those benefits accrued to schools with advantaged populations at least as often as to those in disadvantaged environments, so little reduction of inequality can be seen. Use of the school choice and tutoring options, two key strategies for improvement, has occurred at such low rates and with such inconsistent and poorly monitored quality control that even the relatively few students who have participated may not have obtained the expected benefits. Nor, as Porter notes, have the teacher quality provisions of NCLB been fulfilled, so the modest improvements identified by Phillips and Flashman and by Desimone, Smith, and Frisvold probably are not widespread.

Most of the debate and commentary that one hears and reads about NCLB has to do with its system of test-based accountability, as states, districts, and schools struggle to cope with seemingly unrealistic expectations of how fast test scores should rise. The findings in this book, however, suggest that an even greater problem with NCLB may lie in the inadequate implementation of strategies to respond to test score gaps. With attention focused on achievement inequality and with NCLB sanctions providing a strong motivation for change, a unique window of opportunity now exists to bring new resources and strategies to bear on the education of poor children.

Can NCLB's implementation be improved, and if so, will improvement mitigate achievement inequalities? That is the question that future work must address. At this point, four comments are in order. First, according to the findings in this book, the strategies promoted by NCLB remain promising. That is, improving teacher quality, offering choice and supplemental services, and promoting evidence-based practice have not been ruled out as strategies for addressing the poverty gap. They remain largely untested, but available evidence does not reject them. Second, in contrast, the strategy of extending accountability to students is dubious. Both retention and high school exit examinations have negative consequences for at least some students. It falls on proponents of these strategies to demonstrate their benefits before they can justifiably be extended. Tellingly, they are *not* part of NCLB; rather, they reflect the response of many states and districts to NCLB requirements. In this instance, NCLB seems to have gotten it right: sanctions directed at students are not likely to reduce inequality. Third, more resources need to be devoted to extending supplemental services and to studying its effects. That is not only an implementation challenge; it is also a major research task. Little is now known about even the most basic questions concerning tutoring under NCLB, such as whether participants are coming closer to proficiency over time. Fourth, more rigorous research on a wider variety of educational practices is needed, and the research must be designed explicitly to identify effective instruction for disadvantaged children. It is well to call for evidence-based practice, but as long as the evidence remains in short supply, the call will go unanswered.

2

Standards-Based Educational Reform Is One Important Step Toward Reducing the Achievement Gap

BARBARA R. FOORMAN
SHARON J. KALINOWSKI
WAYNEL L. SEXTON

The 2001 passage of the No Child Left Behind Act (NCLB) represents the high-water mark of the movement toward standards-based educational reform. The goal of NCLB is "to ensure that all children have a fair, equal, and significant opportunity to obtain a high-quality education and reach, at a minimum, proficiency on challenging State academic achievement standards and State academic assessments."[1] As many analysts have observed, this legislation reflects two powerful currents that have driven U.S. education policy over the past fifty years: the pursuit of educational excellence and the effort to ensure that all students, regardless of ethnicity or income, have equal access to education. Less widely recognized is a third policy stream that converged with the pursuit of excellence and equity in NCLB: the right-to-education movement for individuals with disabilities. This movement is particularly important in any discussion of the poverty gap because poor students are disproportionately represented within the special education population.

    This work is supported by the Interagency Education Research Initiative (IERI; grant R305W020001 from the U.S. Department of Education), funded by the Institute for Education Sciences (IES). We would like to thank Jack Fletcher and Sharon Vaughn for their helpful comments on issues pertaining to implementing IDEA 2004 and RTI models in schools.
    1. See 20 *U.S. Code* (*U.S.C.*) 6302 § 1001.

In addition, the lessons researchers have learned about what works in special education can help promote learning for all disadvantaged students.

In this chapter we examine the historical development of each of these movements so that we can provide a fuller context for standards-based reform. We describe the key provisions of the legislation governing general education (NCLB) and special education (the Individuals with Disabilities Education Improvement Act [IDEA] of 2004).[2] And, most important, we show how integrating and coordinating general education and special education within the context of standards-based reform can help reduce the poverty gap. Imposing standards-based reform is but the first step toward this goal. With this step must come an implementation plan that provides layers of instructional interventions whose intensity and duration are determined by teachers' (and often administrators') assessments of students' progress. In the final part of this chapter, we discuss interventions that have been shown to reduce inequalities among children and conclude by highlighting the challenges and opportunities facing efforts to implement these research findings at scale within the context of NCLB and IDEA 2004.

Equal Access, the Pursuit of Excellence, and the Road to NCLB

The roots of standards-based educational reform can be traced back to the beginnings of American history—to the push for equality proclaimed by the Constitution in 1776, restated by Lincoln in the Emancipation Proclamation in 1864, and demanded by Martin Luther King, Jr. in his "I Have a Dream" speech in 1963. In education, the Supreme Court affirmed the importance of equal access in its landmark ruling in *Brown* v. *Board of Education*. This 1954 decision, which stated that "separate educational facilities are inherently unequal," provided the spark for the Civil Rights Act of 1964, which prohibited discrimination based on race, color, sex, religion, or national origin.[3]

In that same year, President Lyndon B. Johnson created an education commission chaired by John Gardner to formulate new approaches to federal aid for education. The Gardner Commission recommended linking federal education aid to the War on Poverty by focusing on improving learning opportunities for children from low-income families. President Johnson adopted this approach and signed the Elementary and Secondary Education Act (ESEA)

---

2. See Individuals with Disabilities Education Improvement Act of 2004 (IDEA), Public Law (PL) 108-446, 118 *U.S. Statutes at Large* (*Stat.*) 2647–2808 (2004).

3. See *Brown* v. *Board of Education*, 347 *U.S.C.* 483 (1954, p. 495); Civil Rights Act of 1964, PL 88-352, 78 *Stat.* 241 (1964).

into law in April 1965.[4] The largest financial component of ESEA was Title I, which was intended to help local education agencies serve the educational needs of children from low-income families. Services commonly provided under Title I were supplementary reading instruction and summer school for low-performing students and professional development for teachers.

Although there was broad consensus about the primary objective of ESEA, there was concern about the expanded role of the federal government in education. As a result, the legislation included a provision that the federal government could not "exercise any direction, supervision, or control over the curriculum, program of instruction, administration, or personnel, or over the selection of any instructional materials in any educational institution or school system."[5] There was also debate about whether Title I services should be provided to all poor children or only to those at risk for academic failure regardless of socioeconomic level.[6] In theory this debate continues, but in practice Title I is a schoolwide designation based on the percentage of students participating in the federal lunch program.

Spending under Title I grew from $1 billion in 1965 to $2.7 billion in 2000. During this period, accusations of fiscal abuses of Title I funds prompted Congress to amend ESEA four times.[7] During the Reagan administration in the early 1980s, expenditures for Title I were cut back, and increases in appropriations were curtailed, leading to a decline in the purchasing power of Title I dollars.[8]

Ironically, at the same time, corporate leaders in the United States were voicing concern about the poor performance of the education system. Similar concerns, within a geopolitical context, had created pressure for educational reform during the cold war. Following the Soviet Union's launch of Sputnik in 1957, the United States put increased emphasis on science and math education and invested in technological projects such as the race to the moon. But with the demise of the Soviet Union in 1989 and the growth of a global economy, the focus shifted from strategic to economic competition. Corporate leaders began to warn that the United States was losing its competitive edge. This concern was first articulated in 1983 in the National Commission on Excellence in Education's report, *A Nation at Risk*.

4. See Elementary and Secondary Education Act (ESEA) of 1965, PL 89-10, 79 *Stat.* 773 (1965).
5. See Elementary and Secondary Education Act of 1965, PL 89-10, 79 *Stat.* 27 (1965), section 604.
6. Stein (2004).
7. Murphy (1991).
8. Jennings (2001, p. 13).

Under the commission's banner, Secretary of Education Terrel H. Bell had assembled a group of educators, business leaders, and public officials to address "the widespread public perception that something is seriously remiss in our educational system." Its report warned that U.S. schools suffered from "a rising tide of mediocrity that threatens our very future as a nation and a people," and the group claimed further that because of inferior teaching Americans had engaged in "unilateral disarmament" in the economic war for markets with other industrial nations whose students outperformed ours on international mathematics and literacy tests.[9] To remedy this situation, the commission called for more rigorous and measurable standards and higher expectations for academic performance on standardized tests, along with more time devoted to "the New Basics" and improved teacher preparation and educational leadership. These recommendations led many states to strengthen requirements for high school graduation, develop curriculum standards, and establish teacher licensure tests.

Nonetheless, concern about the state of U.S. education continued to build. By the 1990s, despite massive expenditures under Title I, scores on the National Assessment of Educational Progress (NAEP) showed no reduction in achievement gaps between majority and minority students. For example, among high school seniors, 43 percent of African Americans, 36 percent of Hispanics, 35 percent of American Indians and Alaska Natives, and 25 percent of Asian Americans or Pacific Islanders were below the basic level of proficiency in reading on the 1998 NAEP, compared with 17 percent of Whites.[10] The evidence also indicated that neither the U.S. Department of Education nor the states had done much to implement the provisions and deadlines of the Improving America's Schools Act (IASA) of 1994, which included an aggregate measure of school progress to determine whether state proficiency goals were met.[11]

In response to these concerns, on January 8, 2002, President George W. Bush reauthorized ESEA as the No Child Left Behind Act of 2001. Although very similar in purpose to ESEA, NCLB takes the commitment to disadvantaged students a step further by raising the bar of academic standards and holding state and local education agencies accountable for student achievement. Even more drastic, NCLB links federal funding to student achievement and imposes sanctions for failure to close achievement gaps.

9. U.S. Department of Education (1983).

10. National Center for Educational Statistics (NCES) (1999).

11. Improving America's Schools Act of 1994, PL 103-382 (1994); see Shaul and Ganson (2005) for aggregate measures of school progress.

Historically, Republican presidents have cut federal funding to education. Instead, President Bush made increased federal funding for education contingent upon student achievement and quality teaching. By adopting this approach, he both tackled the teachers unions, as Democrats were reluctant to do, and mollified conservative members of the Republican Party who were displeased with NCLB's mandatory testing requirements in third through eighth grades and its restrictions on parental choice. Just as it took a Republican president, Nixon, to open relations with communist China, it may have taken a Republican president to put teeth into the federal role in education. Having said this, it is important to recognize the critical roles played by Senator Edward M. Kennedy and Representative George Miller, two Democrats who negotiated compromises within their own party and with the White House to achieve passage of NCLB.[12]

The Right-to-Education Movement

The 1954 *Brown* v. *Board of Education* decision was a giant step toward ensuring equal protection under the law for African American and other minority students. However, children with disabilities did not have their right to public education protected by law until 1975, when Congress passed the Education for All Handicapped Children Act (EAHCA).[13] EAHCA not only guaranteed the right to education for all students with disabilities, but it also established the mechanisms through which parents and children could exercise that right. By approving EAHCA, Congress assured students with disabilities between the ages of five and twenty-one the right to a free appropriate public education (FAPE) in the least restrictive environment (LRE) based upon an individualized education plan (IEP), and the right to due process.[14] Additional integral requirements of EAHCA were the use of nondiscriminatory evaluation procedures, parent participation in making instructional decisions for their child, and a Child Find system to ensure that all children who were in need of early intervention or special education services were located, identified, and referred.

In 1990 EAHCA was reauthorized as the Individuals with Disabilities Education Act (IDEA). In 1997 IDEA was amended, and federal financial

12. Cross (2004); see also Loveless, chapter 9 in this volume.
13. See Education for All Handicapped Children Act of 1975, PL 94-142, 89 *Stat.* 773 (1975).
14. Katsiyannis, Yell, and Bradley (2001).

assistance was linked to state compliance in developing and implementing early intervention services for infants with disabilities and their families.

The year 2004 brought the latest reauthorization of IDEA, renamed the Individuals with Disabilities Education Improvement Act, the intent of which is "to help children with disabilities achieve to high standards—by promoting accountability for results, enhancing parental involvement, and using proven practices and materials; and, also, by providing more flexibility and reducing paperwork burdens for teachers."[15] IDEA 2004 emphasizes high-quality, data-driven instruction, as well as early identification of and intervention for learning problems before they significantly impact student learning.[16] To achieve high-quality instruction, IDEA 2004 calls for scientifically based instructional practices and a data collection system to inform the instructional process. In addition, IDEA 2004 provides the opportunity for a student's response to intervention (RTI) to become part of the criteria for identification of a specific learning disability. Before 2004, students were identified with a learning disability when their low achievement was discrepant with their normal intelligence. The IQ-achievement discrepancy model evolved into a wait-to-fail model that delays treatment to later grades when persistent achievement problems are more difficult to resolve.[17] Under the RTI approach, students who struggle to learn academic content may receive supplemental instruction within general education. RTI has promise not only for providing earlier identification and intervention, but also for decreasing misidentification.

To achieve the educational goals of IDEA 2004, local districts may now use up to 15 percent of their federal IDEA allotment for professional training and to develop and coordinate early intervention services for students not currently in special education but in need of additional academic or behavioral support to succeed in the general education environment. In both principle and funding, IDEA 2004 encourages a collaborative relationship between general education and special education to ensure early intervention for students with learning difficulties.

This approach may also help reduce the poverty gap, given the disproportionate representation of poor and minority students within the special education population. Poor children are overrepresented in the high-incidence categories of mild mental retardation (MMR), emotional disturbance (ED),

15. See *Federal Register* 70, no. 118, Proposed Rules (Tuesday, June 21, 2005): 35782–783.
16. See Individuals with Disabilities Education Improvement Act (IDEA) of 2004, PL 108-446, 118 *Stat.* 2647–2808 (2004).
17. Fletcher and others (2004).

and, to a lesser extent, learning disabilities (LD). (At the same time, many poor children are excluded from the LD category because the criteria exclude those whose unexpected underachievement can be attributed to economic, cultural, or economic disadvantage.)[18] However, they are *not* overrepresented in low-incidence categories (deaf, blind, orthopedic impairment, and so on) that are observed outside school and typically diagnosed by a medical professional. Such patterns of disproportionate representation in special education have led Congress to ask the National Research Council (NRC) twice—once in 1982 and again in 2002—to examine underlying causes and make recommended changes. The 2002 NRC report found the disproportionate representation of minority students in special education most apparent for American Indians (13 percent) and African Americans (14 percent). The percentages for other groups were 12 percent for Whites, 11 percent for Hispanics, and 5 percent for Asians or Pacific Islanders. The disproportionate representation is expected to increase because of the dramatic increase in minority students in the school-aged population from 14 percent in 1950 to 35 percent in 2000 and the increase in the numbers of children served in special education (now one in ten, an increase of 35 percent since the initial passage of IDEA in 1990).

In explaining the disproportionate representation of minority students in special education, the NRC (2002) addressed three areas: biological, social, and contextual factors; schooling; and the referral and assessment process. Conditions associated with poverty were identified as major reasons for lower performance at school entry (for example, exposure to toxins such as lead, alcohol, and tobacco; low birth weight; poor nutrition; and lack of a stimulating and supportive home and child care environment). The NRC report pointed out that high-poverty schools tend to have fewer qualified teachers, fewer resources, and less support for high academic achievement, and thus they perpetuate or even widen the learning gaps poor children bring to school. The report concluded that the referral process is seen as subjective, assessments are seen as having conceptual and procedural shortcomings, and placements into special education are made too late to be effective or efficient. The 2002 NRC report's major recommendation to resolve the disproportionate representation of minority students in special education is to integrate regular and special education services in an early identification and

18. Identification of learning disabilities is based on unexpected underachievement as indicated by a significant discrepancy between achievement and intellectual ability. This discrepancy cannot primarily be the result of a visual, hearing, or motor handicap; mental retardation; emotional disturbance; or an environmental, cultural, or economic disadvantage.

early intervention model; "one in which no child is judged by the school to have a learning or emotional disability or to lack exceptional talent until efforts to provide high-quality instructional and behavioral support in the general education context have been tried without success."[19]

What Do NCLB and IDEA Mean for Schools?

As indicated by its very name—No Child Left Behind—NCLB was to merge with the reauthorization of IDEA to ensure that *all* children, regardless of race and ethnicity, income, language, or disability status, had the opportunity to be successful in school. However, because their histories differed and the terrorist events of 2001 intervened between the passage of NCLB in April 2001 and the reauthorization of IDEA in December 2004, the two acts have yet to realize their intended integration.

Key Provisions of NCLB

NCLB emerged out of decades of attempts by Congress to make Title I funding more responsive to the educational needs of low-income students. During the 1990s, states worked on developing content standards, and by 2001 forty-nine states had content standards and testing in place. However, these standards and tests were rarely aligned so that tests reflected the content taught.[20] NCLB's accountability provisions are best understood within this context of past inefficiencies and misalignment of content and testing. Key new requirements under NCLB are the following:

—A deadline by 2014 of 100 percent proficiency was set for all students, and disaggregated data were used to determine adequate yearly progress (AYP) toward that deadline.

—Testing was increased with more grades tested in language arts and math (third through eighth grades and some time testing between tenth and twelfth grades), and a science assessment was added, beginning in the 2007–08 school year.

—Graduation and participation rates were included in determining AYP to ensure high levels of student participation in testing.

—States are required to participate in the National Assessment of Educational Progress (NAEP) in reading and math in fourth and eighth grades.

—Sanctions such as transfer, tutoring, and reconstitution are required when Title I schools do not meet AYP.

19. National Research Council (2002, p. 6).
20. Citizens' Commission on Civil Rights (2001).

—Instructional strategies must be based in scientifically based research.

—Teachers are required to meet the federal definition of *highly qualified* as having at least a bachelor's degree and certification in the subject area in which they teach.

Although responsibility for education remains under the purview of the states, NCLB expanded the federal role beyond guidance and technical assistance to include approval of state proposals for NCLB funding, enforcement of accountability provisions, and specification of requirements for teacher qualifications. The NCLB requirement that all teachers be highly qualified for each core subject they teach by the 2005–06 school year has primarily been interpreted by the states that have set their certification and degree requirements. Thus, with respect to teacher qualifications, the federal government has still left significant discretion to the states.

MEETING AYP. The requirement that 100 percent of students be proficient by 2014 had bipartisan support and reflected Congress' frustration with the slow progress made under the Improving America's Schools Act of 1994. Likewise, the requirement that schools report disaggregated data was rooted in the failure of IASA, which relied on aggregate measures, to reduce achievement gaps. Under NCLB, state proficiency goals also have to be met for students who are economically disadvantaged, who represent major racial and ethnic groups, who have disabilities, and who have limited English proficiency.[21]

Most states aggregate district data as if the district were one big school. In other words, data from all schools are combined, and then the state determines if the district as a whole and all subgroups meet targets. If students as a whole or any subgroups do not meet the targets, then the district does not achieve AYP. A curious twist is that a district may fail to achieve AYP even though all of its schools achieve AYP because the district is held accountable for subgroups too small to be counted at the school level. Most states set minimum sizes for subgroups at thirty to fifty. For example, Public School 48 in the South Bronx failed to achieve AYP in 2005 because of the low average performance of the English language learners' group.[22] When the principal, Mr. Hughes, looked at the names of the thirty-one students, he realized that six of the students in this group had not been in English language develop-

21. Students with limited English proficiency are given three years to learn English before being tested in English, unless the district demonstrates that testing in the native language will be more reliable.

22. Michael Winerip, "Bitter Lesson: A Good School Gets an 'F'," *New York Times*, January 11, 2006, p. B7.

ment classes for several years and instead were qualified for special education. After these students were moved to special education, the English language learner subgroup became too small to count for AYP, and Mr. Hughes thought his school was saved. However, his special education subgroup now did not have adequate proficiency.

Before 2005 special education was a major reason schools were failing to achieve AYP.[23] In an analysis of Illinois data, the *Chicago Sun-Times* reported that "disabled students were the sole reason 142 schools and 201 districts were listed as in need of improvement under the No Child Left Behind law. The second-highest was low-income students, at 57 schools and five districts."[24] In North Carolina, only 37 percent of special education students reached AYP in reading and 41 percent reached AYP in mathematics compared with 93 percent of all students in both subjects.[25] In an analysis of why more than 200 Washington area schools failed AYP during the 2004–05 school year, the *Washington Post* found that targets were not met in one or more of the following subgroups: special education, economically disadvantaged, or African American.[26] Pressured by districts and states to provide more flexibility in special education testing, Secretary Spellings increased the cap on students allowed to be tested with modified achievement standards from 1 percent to 3 percent (or about 25 percent of all special education students) in 2005. These are primarily students with severe cognitive disabilities. The critical point is that under NCLB no student in special education is exempt from AYP. However, since 2005, about a quarter of students in special education are tested and evaluated with modified achievement standards because of severe disabilities. These changes in the cap may make poverty rather than special education the primary reason schools do not achieve AYP.

Measurement experts caution that the NCLB requirement that all subgroups meet the same mean proficiency scores disadvantages racially diverse schools.[27] This is because the initial abilities students bring to the school, largely a product of their socioeconomic background, strongly predict their academic growth and outcomes. These experts suggest alternative accountability systems that include multiple measures of achievement, measuring gains in students' reading and math skills, and taking into account state

23. Packer (2004).

24. Kate N. Grossman, "Special Education Performance Trips Up Many Districts," *Chicago Sun-Times*, December 15, 2004, p. 6.

25. Nealis (2003).

26. Reginald Ballard, "Why Is Your School on the List?" *Washington Post*, March 12, 2006, p. B1.

27. Kim and Sunderman (2005); Linn (2003); Raudenbush (2004).

accountability ratings of school performance.[28] The U.S. Department of Education has responded to some of these concerns by allowing several states to pilot test a growth-based accountability model that gives schools credit for student improvement over time by tracking individual student achievement year to year. For states that do not have the assessment systems or data collection capabilities to use a growth model, an index model will be allowed that gives schools credit for moving students from "below basic" to "basic" even if they are not yet proficient.

HOW ARE DISTRICTS IDENTIFIED FOR IMPROVEMENT? In most states, a district is identified as being in need of improvement if it fails to make AYP for two consecutive years in the same subject area. In 2005 states were allowed to amend accountability plans to identify districts only if they fail to achieve AYP for two consecutive years across all grade spans—elementary, middle, and high school. In North Carolina, for example, there are two grade spans (third to eighth and high school), and districts are identified only if *both* grade spans fail to meet targets in the *same* subject for two years in a row. States that divide into three grade spans may be able to avoid improvement status because of low-performing high schools by having their elementary and middle schools achieve AYP.

CONSEQUENCES FOR SCHOOL DISTRICTS. Schools and districts identified for improvement must create an improvement plan that, among other things, incorporates scientifically based research strategies to strengthen the core academic program, devotes 10 percent of Title I funds to professional development, includes specific measurable achievement goals and targets for each subgroup, includes the possibility of extending the school day or year, tries to include parents in the improvement process, and specifies the responsibility of the state in providing technical assistance. The requirement that schools identified for improvement provide supplemental services (tutoring) in the second year of improvement has now been changed to allow for these services during the first year of improvement. Districts identified for improvement must select a provider from a list of providers identified in their state grant and approved by the U.S. Department of Education, unless the plan to provide their own supplemental services has been approved.

If a district that was identified for improvement does not achieve AYP after implementing its own improvement plan, the state comes in with "cor-

28. Kim and Sunderman (2005).

rective action" and parents of the children in the district are informed. Such actions must include at least one of the following:

—deferring program funds or reducing administrative funds

—instituting a new curriculum

—replacing the district personnel who are relevant to the failure to achieve adequate yearly progress

—removing particular schools from the jurisdiction of the district and establishing alternative arrangements for public governance and supervision of these schools

—appointing or replacing a trustee to administer the district in place of the superintendent and school board

—abolishing or restructuring the district

—allowing students to attend a school in another district and providing for their transportation[29]

In summary, NCLB has major consequences for school districts that fail to achieve adequate yearly progress. However, NCLB allows states more flexibility in dealing with *districts* identified for improvement than it does for dealing with *schools* identified for improvement.

Key Provisions of IDEA 2004

Since the enactment of EAHCA in 1975, research and experience have validated methods of teaching and learning, the positive effect of high expectations, and the benefit of access to the general education curriculum in the general education classroom for students with disabilities.[30] Ironically, the education of students with disabilities has been impeded by low expectations, inadequate attention to replicated research, and only a basic level of access to the general curriculum.[31] IDEA 2004 deals directly with these issues by addressing the development and implementation of research-based interventions provided by highly qualified teachers to ensure that students with disabilities have access to and make progress in the general education curriculum. This one statement carries with it numerous implications: scientifically based instruction must be schoolwide to ensure access to the general curriculum; student progress must be monitored; general and special education staff must work collaboratively; and students with disabilities must be included in a meaningful way in accountability assessments. To accomplish these goals,

29. Center on Education Policy (2005).
30. *Federal Register* 70, no. 118 (Tuesday, June 21, 2005): 35782–783.
31. U.S. Department of Education (2002).

IDEA 2004 provides incentives for whole-school approaches that incorporate scientifically based academic programs, positive behavioral interventions and supports, and early interventions. Specifically, IDEA 2004

—provides an alternate identification model for students with learning disabilities that promises a shift from research on specific conditions and their causes to early intervention and intervention effectiveness;[32]

—requires evidence that the child was provided appropriate instruction when determining special education eligibility, thereby emphasizing the importance of implementing high-quality, research-based instruction in the general education setting;

—defines a *highly qualified special education teacher* as one who has at least a bachelor's degree, is certified by the state in special education, and demonstrates competence in the core academic subjects taught;

—requires school districts to provide summaries of students' academic achievement and functional performance, including recommendations on how to meet postsecondary goals;

—aligns performance goals and indicators with states' definitions of adequate yearly progress;

—requires inclusion of students with disabilities in district and state accountability assessments—with appropriate accommodations and alternate assessments when necessary—aligned with the state's challenging academic content standards and challenging student academic achievement standards;

—provides funding to support the development and provision of appropriate accommodations for children with disabilities or the development of valid and reliable alternative assessments;

—requires each student's individualized education plan to reflect why a student cannot participate in the state's or district's assessment program and why the particular alternate assessment selected is appropriate and contains benchmark or short-term objectives aligned to alternate achievement standards for those who take alternate assessments;

—requires states to report to the public with the same frequency and in the same detailed manner for students with disabilities as it does for nondisabled students;

—provides more flexibility in IEP requirements and reduces paperwork to allow staff time to focus on direct instruction.

In addition to these critical instructional components, other important IDEA 2004 changes concern procedural safeguards, due process, and student

---

32. Fletcher and others (2004); Danielson, Doolittle, and Bradley (2005).

discipline as it relates to the manifestation of a disability. IDEA 2004 provides parents and schools with increased opportunities to resolve disagreements in a timely, positive, constructive manner.

Integrating NCLB and IDEA 2004

The connection between IDEA 2004 and NCLB is clearly stated in the background section of the *Federal Register*'s proposed rules for IDEA:

> Enactment of the new law provides an opportunity to consider improvements in the current regulations that would strengthen the Federal effort to ensure every child with a disability has available a free appropriate education that (1) is of high quality, and (2) is designed to achieve the high standards reflected in the Elementary and Secondary Education Act of 1965, and as amended by the No Child Left Behind Act of 2001 (NCLB) and its implementing regulations.[33]

In general, the two acts work in concert to ensure high-quality instruction that closes the achievement gap. Both place an emphasis on prevention and early intervention and rely on whole-school approaches and multitiered instruction that incorporate scientifically based academic programs and positive behavioral interventions and supports. Both require highly qualified teachers, as defined by federal law. Both require alignment of performance goals and indicators with states' definitions of adequate yearly progress. Both require progress monitoring, data collection, and data evaluation to inform the instructional process. Both mandate high expectations for students with disabilities by including them in district and state accountability systems and assessments, counting the numbers participating in each assessment condition, and reporting detailed results to the public with the same frequency as is done for nondisabled students. To help accomplish the integration of these two acts, funds from NCLB and IDEA may be shared.

Challenges and Potential Solutions to Implementing the Research Base for NCLB and IDEA

NCLB and IDEA share a common goal: a single, well-integrated system that connects general, remedial, and special education and considers the learning needs of *all* students. Certainly there are inherent incompatibilities in the implementations of these two laws, such as the targets for improvement, defi-

---

33. *Federal Register* 70, no. 118 (Tuesday, June 21, 2005): 35782–783.

nitions of teacher quality, and curriculum for students with cognitive impairments, but these tensions are resolvable, especially when the focus is kept on what is best for children. For example, special education targets *individual* children through the IEP, whereas AYP targets mean proficiency levels of subgroups that include special education students. In this case, many states want to move general education toward a focus on individual targets by measuring individual growth as a means to determine AYP. Likewise, the requirement that teachers be certified in the subjects they teach places an extra burden on secondary-level special education teachers who must be certified not only in special education but also in the core academic subjects they teach. This is a burden, but it is the right thing to do if special needs children are to have qualified teachers. Another tension in integrating special and general education is the expectation that students with cognitive impairments meet grade-level standards. Schools may eliminate life-skills classes in an effort to focus resources on special education children when, in fact, the achievement of functional behaviors may be the most realistic and best education for these students. The increase in the cap on the percentage of students assessed under modified standards and alternate tests may encourage schools to keep life-skills curricula for those students who are unable to achieve grade-level standards.

Assuming that these tensions between general education and special education can be resolved, there are hopeful signs that the emphasis by NCLB and IDEA 2004 on evidence-based practices, prevention and early intervention, and teacher quality will in fact result in reduced inequalities among students. We will briefly review some of this research and then point out the challenges and potential solutions to bringing this research to scale within the context of NCLB and IDEA 2004.

Research on Prevention and Early Intervention in Reading

In the past two decades researchers made the case that the reading gap widens over time; that once beginning readers fall behind, they tend to stay behind; and that even intensive intervention cannot turn them into fluent readers.[34] Early intervention research, however, shows that the numbers of children needing supplementary services can be reduced to less than 5 percent with the introduction of quality classroom instruction.[35]

34. See Stanovich (1986) concerning the reading gap widening over time; Francis and others (1996); Juel (1988) concerning readers remaining behind; Torgesen and others (2001) concerning intensive intervention not improving reading performance.
35. Foorman, Breier, and Fletcher (2003); Foorman and others (1998).

The best practices of quality classroom interactions are complex interactions between student characteristics and classroom-level variables. Only a few research teams have examined how classroom-level variables based on observations of instruction moderate the relationship between student reading ability at the beginning of the year and student reading achievement at the end of the year.[36] To do so requires multilevel analyses where student data are nested within classrooms.

Barbara Foorman, David Francis, Jack Fletcher, Christopher Schatschneider, and Paras Mehta found that students' ability in phonemic awareness interacted with instructional approach in predicting reading outcomes in 285 first and second graders in sixty-six classrooms in eight schools served by Title I. The instructional approaches consisted of direct code instruction, embedded code instruction, a research version of implicit code instruction, and an unseen control of the district's implicit code approach. Teachers received ongoing professional development in the approach they delivered, and more than one approach existed in each school. After a year of instruction, students receiving direct code instruction improved in word reading at a faster rate and had higher end-of-year scores than students in the implicit code group, and this growth was moderated by initial ability in phonemic awareness. That is, explicit instruction in the alphabetic principle lessened the effect of low initial abilities in phonemic awareness on reading success.

In another study of first and second grade classrooms, Foorman and others obtained ratings of teaching effectiveness and time allocation in 107 classrooms in seventeen high-poverty schools.[37] Twenty time allocation variables were reduced using exploratory factor analysis to seven literacy patterns that became predictors, along with effectiveness ratings, of reading and spelling outcomes. For example, higher-rated teachers in both grades had students with higher reading comprehension achievement, and more highly rated second grade teachers spent more time teaching vocabulary. Students' word attack outcomes were higher when teachers spent more time reading books than preparing to teach or giving directions and when highly rated first grade teachers taught more phonemic awareness and alphabetic skills and wasted less instructional time.

In a study of first grade classrooms, Carol Connor and others found that students with lower fall decoding and vocabulary scores exhibited greater decoding growth in classrooms that spent more time on teacher-managed

36. See Connor, Morrison, and Katch (2004); Connor, Morrison, and Slominski (2006); Foorman and others (1998); Foorman and others (2006); Taylor and others (2003).
37. Foorman and others (2006).

explicit decoding activities, with small amounts of child-managed activities in the fall that increased across the year.[38] However, for students with higher fall decoding and higher vocabulary scores, time allocated to explicit decoding instruction had little effect; rather, it was time allocated throughout the year to child-managed, meaning-focused activities that fostered greater decoding growth. To test whether teachers could use computer-generated algorithms to differentiate instruction, in a separate study, Connor and others examined the effect of teachers' use of web-based software on first graders' gains in achievement.[39] Forty-seven first grade teachers in ten Florida schools were randomly assigned to treatment ($n = 22$) or control ($n = 25$) groups. Teachers in the treatment group were provided professional development on how to use the software to assign students to instructional groups based on their reading skills and how to implement this individualized instruction on a daily basis. Controlling for fall vocabulary and reading scores, students in the treatment classrooms had higher reading growth compared with the growth of students in control classrooms. Additionally, students had higher reading outcomes if their teachers spent more time using the software. Finally, in classrooms where teachers used the software with high fidelity, students with low fall vocabulary scores achieved reading outcomes comparable with those of students with high fall vocabulary scores.

In addition to research showing the benefits of improving classroom-level instruction, recent research has also shown that the numbers of children needing special education services can be reduced further by daily small-group instruction with a knowledgeable reading teacher.[40] Funding for these secondary and tertiary layers of intervention is available through both the Reading First component of NCLB and IDEA 2004. According to IDEA 2004, up to 15 percent of special education funds may be used for prevention, and response to intervention (RTI) can be a process for evaluating students' eligibility for special education services. The legislation states that local educational agencies "shall not be required to take into consideration whether a child has a severe discrepancy between achievement and intellectual ability" and "may use a process that determines if the child responds to scientific, research-based intervention as a part of the evaluation procedures."[41]

38. Connor and others (2004).

39. Connor and others (2007).

40. Denton and others (2006); Mathes and others (2005); Vaughn and others (2006); Vaughn and others (2007).

41. See Individuals with Disabilities Education Improvement Act (IDEA) of 2004, PL 108-446 § 614 [b] [6] [A]; § 614 [b] [2 & 3] (2004).

Implementation Challenges

Although problem-solving and RTI as standard treatment protocols are both developed from sound theory and a growing database, some suggest a lack of data and some disagree with the interpretation of the data.[42] All agree that the problem-solving and standard treatment protocol approaches to RTI will be a challenge to implement in underresourced schools with educators steeped in a silo mentality and new to the concept of assessment-driven instruction.

CHANGING ADULT BEHAVIOR. In spite of the victory at the policy level, early intervention and response to intervention models are being implemented with difficulty at the school level. There are several reasons for this but the most fundamental is that we are asking adult educators to change—in some cases to change what they do, such as school psychologists no longer giving IQ tests—and in all cases to change how they think about learning. Rather than thinking of students as learning *disabled*, from a *deficit* perspective, we are asking them to think of students as learning *enabled*. From a *risk* perspective, we know the importance of identifying children at risk of learning difficulties and of intervening early to prevent failure. This new way of conceptualizing learning and instruction places the general education teacher in the front lines of prevention. A hallmark of school improvement should be the *reduction* of the number of students served in special education so that only those with serious cognitive, physical, or emotional impairments are included.

CHANGING ROLES FOR SPECIALISTS. What about the changing roles for special education teachers, English language development teachers, Title I teachers, and, in some states, dyslexia teachers? NCLB and IDEA 2004 encourage the coordination of the funding streams for these specialists to serve students in an integrated fashion. Rather than subjecting students to multiple interventions taught by different adults using different strategies and materials, the goal should be to organize instruction into the RTI notion of layered or tiered intervention, with adequate professional development and coaching resources put into tier 1—classroom instruction—to reduce the numbers needing tiers 2 and 3. Specialists can be critical to success at all three levels, working with the classroom teachers in small-group instruction in the classroom as well as staffing supplementary interventions. Special edu-

---

42. *Problem-solving and RTI as standard treatment protocols:* Burns, Vanderwood, and Ruby (2005); Burns, Appleton, and Stehouwer (2005); *suggestion of lack of data:* Fuchs and others (2003); *disagreement with the data interpretation:* Naglieri and Crockett (2005).

cation teachers have been involved in prereferral intervention and consultation models in the past without much success.[43] What is needed are specialists with content knowledge of how to teach reading and math, who can provide additional doses of instruction, monitor student progress to evaluate learning, and signal the need for reteaching or further intervention.

TARGETED PROFESSIONAL DEVELOPMENT. In our zeal to have instructional decisions informed by data, it is critically important to provide teachers with professional development that links assessment with instruction.[44] In the past, specialists conducted the testing to see whether students qualified for special services. Teachers used a variety of informal inventories or selected from among a plethora of publishers' curriculum-based tests to note student progress. However, rarely were these informal assessments selected for their reliability and validity or for their alignment with state standards and tests. In the era of high-stakes testing, districts and schools have purchased or developed "test prep" curriculum materials and practice tests that exist in addition to the teachers' classroom curriculum, rather than having worked to improve classroom instruction to target students' learning needs.[45]

Professional development is also needed on the selection of curriculum materials. In a rush to meet Reading First's requirement of curriculum based on scientifically based reading research (SBRR), districts have purchased new reading curricula and intervention programs that often are questionable with respect to their empirical base, their alignment with each other, and teacher buy-in. It is not surprising that teachers prefer programs with which they are familiar and tend to resist program change, especially if the change supplants their prerogative to teach what they want to teach. Furthermore, there is confusion about what SBRR means. The concept of basing curriculum and instruction on scientifically based reading research has been reduced to the acronym SBRR, which has little more meaning than materials published after 2001 when NCLB was passed.

Potential Solutions

Successful implementation of NCLB and IDEA 2004 requires massive professional development of educators at all levels and technical assistance from the federal level. Federal, state, and local efforts are under way to meet imple-

---

43. See Gersten and Dimino (2006).
44. See Connor and others (2007); Mathes and others (2005).
45. Foorman and Moats (2004); Foorman, Breier, and Fletcher (2003).

mentation needs in such areas as SBRR; alignment of standards, instruction, and accountability; and early prevention models.

SBRR

Instantiating the concept of scientifically based research into the field of education will require changes in preservice and in-service teacher education. In 2005 Congress appropriated funds for a report on teacher preparation programs in the United States that is due in fall 2007. The study will focus on K–12 teachers with an emphasis on reading, mathematics, and science. The National Research Council (NRC) of the National Academy of Sciences was asked by Congress to undertake this study:

> To synthesize data and research on the academic preparation and educational characteristics of candidates in pre-service, graduate, and alternative certification programs; the specific content and experiences that are provided to candidates for degrees and alternative certification in education; the consistency of the required course work and experiences in reading and mathematics across teacher preparation programs; and the degree to which the content and experiences are based on converging scientific evidence . . . . The NRC is also asked to develop a model for collecting information on content knowledge, pedagogical competence and effectiveness of graduates from teacher education programs and teachers trained in alternative certification programs, and review the needs of schools for high quality teachers, as called for in the No Child Left Behind Act.[46]

The intention in this congressional mandate to delve more deeply into the content knowledge and pedagogical skills required to make teachers highly qualified is welcome because the reliance on bachelor degree and state certification in the current federal definition is inadequate. More promising predictors of student achievement gains are the following: number of years teaching, scores on national licensure examinations, and interactions between geography (urban and rural versus suburban) and student poverty and teacher quality.[47] However, it is when gains in content knowledge and teach-

46. See House of Representatives No. 108-401 (2003, p. 851). (This is a conference report that accompanies H. R. 2673, available upon request.)

47. See. Hanushek and others (2005) for number of years teaching as a predictor; Tuerk (2005) for scores on national licensure examinations; Desimone, Smith, and Frisvold, chapter 4 in this volume; Tuerk (2005) for geography and student poverty and teacher quality.

ing skill translate to gains in student achievement that professional development can be seen as effective.[48]

Another federal effort under way to promulgate the notion of scientifically based reading research is the What Works Clearinghouse (WWC).[49] The WWC is funded by the Institute of Education Sciences in the U.S. Department of Education to prepare, maintain, and disseminate high-quality, systematic reviews of studies of effectiveness in education. It is modeled after similar international efforts in the behavioral sciences (the Campbell Collaboration) and in medicine (the Cochrane Collaboration). So far the WWC has identified few scientifically rigorous studies of educational interventions and curriculum products. The hope is that researchers and publishers will work together to conduct randomized field studies of curricula to better understand the conditions under which core and intervention materials can be implemented with fidelity by teachers to positively affect student learning and achievement. The results of this research would go a long way toward helping schools meet the SBRR requirement in NCLB and IDEA 2004 and would also help inform state adoption of curricula.

Alignment, Benchmarks, and Curriculum-Based Assessment

Many districts have recognized the need to align their curriculum with state standards, but the ones that have been successful in reducing the achievement gap have gone a step further and have established grade-level benchmarks and curriculum-based assessment to meet those benchmarks. A school district that has put benchmarks and curriculum-based assessments in place and has a track record of reducing the achievement gap is Aldine Independent School District in Houston, Texas. Aldine ISD has 56,255 students in sixty-one schools. Sixty percent of its student body is Hispanic, 32 percent Black, 6 percent White, and 2 percent Asian or Pacific Islander. Seventy-eight percent of its students are economically disadvantaged (state average is 55 percent), 27 percent are limited English proficient (state average is 16 percent), and 10 percent are in special education (state average is 12 percent). Aldine has matched or exceeded state averages on the state accountability test in reading and math at almost all grade levels in the 2005–06 school year.

Multiple Tier Models

The response to instruction model coming out of IDEA 2004 and the three-tier model popular in Reading First are both preceded by effective school

48. Foorman and Moats (2004); McCutchen and others (2002).
49. What Works Clearinghouse (www.whatworks.ed.gov).

reform models such as Success for All, direct instruction, and Comer's School Development Program.[50] When implemented well, schools in these reform models and other high-poverty and high-achievement schools have similar characteristics: outstanding instructional leadership, more time on task with high-performance standards for all students, ongoing assessment that informs instructional decisions, focused and ongoing professional development, and involved and supportive parents.[51] Principals at these schools rearrange budget priorities to ensure sufficient textbooks, other teaching aids, and ongoing professional development. These schools tend to have someone onsite—a mentor, a coach, or a facilitator—who can work with all teachers on the effective instructional delivery of core and intervention programs. They also work with new teachers on classroom management and lesson planning and help coordinate and interpret assessment data. Additional time on task is typically structured as small-group tutoring before, after, or during school and student homework is corrected and returned promptly. Curriculum is aligned within and across tiers of instruction, within and across grades, and with state standards. Grade-level benchmarks are clear, and progress is continually monitored so that specialists can provide more intensive intervention to small groups of students when needed. Teachers at these schools engage in limited "test prep" because the vast majority of the students pass the state accountability tests. Few students in these schools are in special education.

In summary, the RTI model can be the glue that integrates general and special education. Classroom teachers and specialists—whether Title I, dyslexia, English language development, or special education teachers—need to work as a collaborative team in determining whether students are responding adequately to instruction offered in the classroom and when supplementary instruction is needed. RTI is not simply a problem-solving model of assessment for the identification and evaluation of children for special education; it is also the empirically based process for making decisions within general education. RTI's success depends on the ability of classroom teachers and specialists to work together to serve *all* students from a preventative, data-driven perspective. To achieve this success, serious commitments to professional development and technical assistance will be required.

---

50. See Haager, Klingner, and Vaughn (2007) for a discussion of Reading First; Borman and others (2003) for other reform models.

51. See Denton, Foorman, and Mathes (2003); Taylor and others (2000).

Conclusion

Education has been moving toward standards-based reform for the past twenty years. Yet it is only recently, with the bipartisan passage of the No Child Left Behind Act of 2001 and the reauthorization of the Individuals with Disabilities Education Improvement Act in 2004, that schools are held accountable for quality instruction and proficient outcomes for *all* students. As a result, new products and tests are being sold to fill the vacuum created by the requirement that materials be based on scientifically based reading research. Schools are paying more attention to the requirement that teachers be certified in the subject they teach. What is needed most, however, is a focus on implementing systemic reform at the school level. Drawing on lessons learned from effective educational reform models and successful response to intervention implementations, districts can provide professional development to build capacity at the school level for systemic change. Administrators need to work with teachers to create replicable models of school improvement. Once innovative practices are proven effective in improving student outcomes, school and district leaders need to work to sustain the innovations over time. Once sustained and effective innovations are adopted into organizational routines, the promise of NCLB and IDEA 2004—a reduction in the achievement gap—can begin to be realized.

References

Borman, Geoffrey D., and others. 2003. "Comprehensive School Reform and Achievement: A Meta-analysis." *Review of Educational Research* 73, no. 2: 125–230.

Burns, Matthew K., James J. Appleton, and Jonathan. D. Stehouwer. 2005. "Meta-analytic Review of Response-to-Intervention Research: Examining Field-Based and Research-Implemented Models." *Journal of Psychoeducational Assessment* 23, no. 4: 381–94.

Burns, Matthew K., Mike Vanderwood, and Susan Ruby. 2005. "Evaluating the Readiness of Prereferral Intervention Teams for Use in a Problem-solving Model: Review of Three Levels of Research." *School Psychology Quarterly* 20, no. 1: 89–105.

Center on Education Policy. 2005. "Identifying School Districts for Improvement and Corrective Action." Washington.

Citizens' Commission on Civil Rights. 2001. *Closing the Deal: A Preliminary Report on State Compliance with Final Assessment and Accountability Requirements under the Improving America's Schools Act of 1994.* Washington (www.cccr.org/ClosingTheDeal.pdf).

Connor, Carol McDonald, Frederick J. Morrison, and Leslie E. Katch. 2004. "Beyond the Reading Wars: Exploring the Effect of Child-instruction Interactions on Growth in Early Reading." *Scientific Studies of Reading* 8, no. 4: 305–36.

Connor, Carol McDonald, Frederick J. Morrison, and Lisa Slominski. 2006. "Preschool Instruction and Children's Emergent Literacy Skill Growth." *Journal of Educational Psychology* 98, no. 4: 665–89.

Connor, Carol McDonald, and others. 2007. "Algorithm-guided Individualized Reading Instruction." *Science* 315, no. 5811: 464–65.

Cross, Christopher T. 2004. *Political Education.* New York: Teachers College Press.

Danielson, Louis, Jennifer Doolittle, and Renee Bradley. 2005. "Past Accomplishments and Future Challenges." *Learning Disability Quarterly* 28, no. 2: 137–39.

Denton, Carolyn A., and others. 2006. "An Evaluation of Intensive Intervention for Students with Persistent Reading Difficulties." *Journal of Learning Disabilities* 39, no. 5: 447–67.

Denton, Carolyn, Barbara Foorman, and Patricia Mathes. 2003. "Schools that 'Beat the Odds': Implications for Reading Instruction." *Remedial and Special Education* 24, no. 5: 258–61.

Fletcher, Jack M., and others. 2004. "Alternative Approaches to the Definition and Identification of Learning Disabilities: Some Questions and Answers." *Annals of Dyslexia* 54, no. 2: 304–31.

Foorman, Barbara R., and Louisa C. Moats. 2004. "Conditions for Sustaining Research-based Practices in Early Reading Instruction." *Remedial and Special Education* 25, no. 1: 51–60.

Foorman, Barbara R., Joshua I. Breier, and Jack M. Fletcher. 2003. "Interventions Aimed at Improving Reading Success: An Evidence-based Approach." *Developmental Neuropsychology* 24, nos. 2–3: 613–39.

Foorman, Barbara R., and others. 1998. "The Role of Instruction in Learning to Read: Preventing Reading Failure in At-risk Children." *Journal of Educational Psychology* 90, no. 1: 37–55.

Foorman, Barbara R., and others. 2006. "The Impact of Instructional Practices in Grades 1 and 2 on Reading and Spelling Achievement in High Poverty Schools." *Contemporary Educational Psychology* 31, no. 1: 1–29.

Francis, David, and others. 1996. "Developmental Lag Versus Deficit Models of Reading Disability: A Longitudinal, Individual Growth Curves Analysis." *Journal of Educational Psychology* 88, no. 1: 3–17.

Fuchs, Douglas, and others. 2003. "Responsiveness-to-Intervention: Definitions, Evidence, and Implications for the Learning Disabilities Construct." *Learning Disabilities Research & Practice* 18, no. 3: 157–71.

Gersten, Russell, and Joseph A. Dimino. 2006. "RTI (Response to Intervention): Rethinking Special Education for Students with Reading Difficulties (yet again)." *Reading Research Quarterly* 41, no. 1: 99–108.

Haager, Diane, Janette Klingner, and Sharon Vaughn, eds. 2007. *Evidence-Based Reading Practices for Response to Intervention.* Baltimore, Md.: Brookes Publishing.

Hanushek, Eric A., and others. 2005. *The Market for Teacher Quality.* Working Paper 11154. Cambridge, Mass.: National Bureau of Economic Research.

Jennings, John. 2001. "Title I: Its Legislative History and Its Promise." In *Title I: Compensatory Education at the Crossroads,* edited by Geoffrey D. Borman and others, pp. 1–24. Hillsdale, N.Y.: Erlbaum.

Juel, Connie. 1988. "Learning to Read and Write: A Longitudinal Study of 54 Students from First through Fourth Grades." *Journal of Educational Psychology* 80, no. 4: 437–47.

Katsiyannis, Antonis, Michael L. Yell, and Renee Bradley. 2001. "Reflections on the 25th Anniversary of the Individuals with Disabilities Act." *Remedial and Special Education* 22, no. 6: 324–34.

Kim, James S., and Gail L. Sunderman. 2005. "Measuring Academic Proficiency under the No Child Left Behind Act: Implications for Educational Equity." *Educational Researcher* 34, no. 8: 3–13.

Linn, Robert L. 2003. "Accountability: Responsibility and Reasonable Expectations." *Educational Researcher* 32, no. 7: 3–13.

Mathes, Patricia, and others. 2005. "The Effects of Theoretically Different Instruction and Student Characteristics on the Skills of Struggling Readers." *Reading Research Quarterly* 40, no. 2: 142–47.

McCuchen, Deborah, and others. 2002. "Beginning Literacy: Links among Teacher Knowledge, Teacher Practice, and Student Learning." *Journal of Learning Disabilities* 35, no. 1: 69–86.

Murphy, Jerome T. 1991. "Title I of ESEA: The Politics of Implementing Federal Education Reform." In *Education Policy Implementation*, edited by A. R. Odden, pp. 65–80. Albany: State University of New York Press.

Naglieri, Jack A., and Deborah P. Crockett. 2005. "Response to Intervention (RTI): Is It a Scientifically Proven Method?" *NASP Communiqué* 34, no. 2: 38–39.

National Center for Educational Statistics. 1999. *NAEP 1998 Reading: A Report Card for the Nation and the States*. Washington: U.S. Department of Education.

National Commission on Excellence in Education. 1983. *A Nation at Risk: The Imperative for Educational Reform*. Washington: U.S. Government Printing Office (www.ed.gov/pubs/NatAtRisk/).

National Research Council, Division of Behavioral and Social Sciences and Education. 2002. *Minority Students in Special and Gifted Education*. Committee on Minority Representation in Special Education, M. Suzanne Donovan and Christopher T. Cross, eds. Washington: National Academy Press.

Nealis, Libby K. 2003. "No Child Left Behind? AYP and Students with Disabilities." *NASP Communiqué* 32, no. 4: 30–31.

Packer, Joel. 2004. "No Child Left Behind and Adequate Yearly Progress Fundamental Flaws: A Forecast for Failure." Paper prepared for the forum on Ideas to Improve the NCLB Accountability Provisions. Center on Education Policy, Washington, July 28.

Raudenbush, Stephen W. 2004. *Schooling, Statistics, and Poverty: Can We Measure School Improvement?* Princeton, N.J.: Educational Testing Service.

Shaul, Marnie S., and Harriet C. Ganson. 2005. "The No Child Left Behind Act of 2001: The Federal Government Role in Strengthening Accountability for Student Performance." In *Review of Research in Education*, edited by L. Parker, pp. 151–65. Washington: American Educational Research Association.

Stanovich, Keith E. 1986. "Matthew Effects in Reading: Some Consequences of Individual Differences in the Acquisition of Literacy." *Reading Research Quarterly* 21, no. 4: 360–407.

Stein, Sandra J. 2004. *The Culture of Education*. New York: Teachers College Press.

Taylor, Barbara M., and others. 2000. "Effective Schools and Accomplished Teachers: Lessons about Primary-grade Reading Instruction in Low-income Schools." *Elementary School Journal* 101, no. 2: 121–65.

Taylor, Barbara M., and others. 2003. "What Matters Most in Promoting Reading Growth? Toward a Model of Reading Instruction Maximizing Cognitive Engagement in Literacy Learning." *Elementary School Journal* 104, no. 1: 3–28.

Tilly, W. David, III. 2006. "Diagnosing the Learning Enabled: The Promise of Response to Intervention." *Perspectives* 32, no. 1 (Winter): 20–24.

Torgesen, Joseph K., and others. 2001. "Intensive Remedial Instruction for Children with Severe Reading Disabilities: Immediate and Long-term Outcomes from Two Instructional Approaches." *Journal of Learning Disabilities* 34, no. 1: 33–58.

Tuerk, Peter W. 2005. "Research in the High-stakes Era: Achievement, Resources, and No Child Left Behind." *Psychological Science* 16, no. 6: 419–25.

U.S. Department of Education. 2002. *National Longitudinal Transition Study*. Washington: U.S. Government Printing Office.

Vaughn, Sharon, and others. 2006. "Effectiveness of Spanish Intervention for First-grade English Language Learners at Risk for Reading Difficulties." *Journal of Learning Disabilities* 39, no. 1: 56–73.

Vaughn, Sharon, and others. 2007. "Effectiveness of an English Intervention for First-grade English Language Learners at Risk for Reading Problems." *Elementary School Journal* 107, no. 2: 154–80.

PART II

Looking Back: Standards-Based Reforms and Opportunities for the Disadvantaged

3

How Did the Statewide Assessment and Accountability Policies of the 1990s Affect Instructional Quality in Low-Income Elementary Schools?

MEREDITH PHILLIPS
JENNIFER FLASHMAN

In 2005 a mere 16 percent of low-income fourth graders could read proficiently (as measured by national tests) compared with 42 percent of their middle-class counterparts.[1] The math gap was even larger.[2] The No Child Left Behind Act (NCLB) of 2001 represents an ambitious attempt to improve this situation. Critics of NCLB complain about vagaries in the law, its underfunding, and the leeway given to states to choose their own standards and tests.[3] But few can disagree with its ultimate purpose: "To ensure

We are grateful to Jessica Schraub Norman and Ananya Sengutpa for their help assembling the accountability data; Bea Birman, Tiffani Chin, Adam Gamoran, Gloria Ladson-Billings, Andrew Porter, and three anonymous reviewers for their comments on this chapter; and the UCLA Council on Research and especially the Russell Sage Foundation for their grants in support of our work with the Schools and Staffing Survey.

1. NCES (2005b). For the purposes of this chapter, we define low-income students as those who qualify for subsidized school meals. Students qualify for either free or reduced-price meals if their family income falls below 185 percent of the poverty line (U.S. Department of Agriculture 2002).

2. In 2005, 19 percent of low-income fourth graders scored at or above proficient in math compared with 49 percent of middle-class fourth graders (NCES 2005a).

3. Nanette Asimov, "37 Schools Forced to Make Changes; Improving or Not, They Failed U.S. Goals," *San Francisco Chronicle*, September 20, 2005, p. B1; Michael Dobbs, "New Rules for 'No Child' Law Planned," *Washington Post*, April 7, 2005, p. A13; Bob Schaffer, "U.S. Education Reform and the Role of the States," *Denver Post*, December 25, 2005, p. E-05.

that all children have a fair, equal, and significant opportunity to obtain a high-quality education and reach, at a minimum, proficiency on challenging state academic achievement standards and state academic assessments."[4]

NCLB aims to accomplish its goals by holding public schools accountable for their students' achievement. Under NCLB, public schools must test all students annually in math and reading in third through eighth grades. Schools face corrective action or complete restructuring if their students fail to meet state standards for academic progress several years in a row. NCLB also makes it easier for students in low-performing schools to attend better schools or obtain free tutoring.

Yet the law wisely gave states several years to comply with its most critical requirements. Not until the 2005–06 school year, for example, did states need to have a "highly qualified" teacher in every classroom and reading and math testing in third through eighth grades. Consequently, it is still too early to assess the effects of NCLB on the nation's educational system.

Accountability before NCLB

Fortunately, however, the assessment and accountability provisions of NCLB build directly on assessment and accountability policies begun a decade earlier. During the 1990s, spurred in part by the Improving America's Schools Act of 1994, many states increased the number of tests they required students to take, and some states began imposing consequences on schools or school districts when students performed poorly on those tests.[5] This chapter examines the effects of these statewide reforms to provide a glimpse of the probable effects of NCLB and to generate ideas about how to improve NCLB when it comes up for reauthorization. Because other scholars have already examined the impact of state accountability policies on student achievement, we focus instead on how such policies influenced teachers and school administrators— especially those who work in schools that serve low-income students.[6]

Possible Consequences of Accountability Policies

Proponents of accountability reform suspect that teachers and administrators have not been doing as much as they could to improve academic achieve-

---

4. No Child Left Behind Act of 2001, 107 Cong., 2d sess., Public Law 107–110, sec. 1001, Statement of Purpose.

5. Improving America's Schools Act of 1994, 103 Cong., 2d sess., Public Law 103-382.

6. For evidence about student achievement, see Carnoy and Loeb (2002); Hanushek and Raymond (2005).

ment, especially among traditionally low-performing students. Their solution is to attach positive and negative sanctions to students' test results, hoping that these incentives will stimulate teachers and administrators to focus more assiduously on increasing academic achievement and equity.[7] If this solution works, we should find empirical evidence that accountability reforms motivate teachers or administrators to focus additional resources on improving academic achievement. For example, accountability policies may motivate teachers to work harder or longer to ensure that children master important concepts and skills. Such policies may also motivate administrators to substitute instructional expenditures for noninstructional expenditures, thereby improving teacher quality, reducing class sizes, or providing more effective professional development.

Critics worry, however, that accountability policies have unintended negative consequences. One concern is that accountability reforms may reduce teacher quality by creating working conditions that good teachers (who have other job options) find unbearable.[8] Some studies show that mandated tests cause at least some teachers to cover skills at different paces, at different times, and in a different order than they otherwise would.[9] Other studies argue that accountability policies take the joy out of teaching by forcing creative teachers to replace their innovative teaching strategies and materials with a lockstep curriculum focused solely on improving tested skills.[10] These studies imply that accountability reforms may compel the best teachers to leave the profession or transfer to the private sector, or these reforms may dissuade potentially good teachers from entering the teaching profession (or at least public school teaching) in the first place.

Critics also worry that test-based accountability policies encourage teachers and administrators to focus too much on improving tested skills to the detriment of other types of skills that the tests do not measure.[11] A number of studies suggest that mandatory assessments cause teachers to shift their instructional time toward tested subjects and skills and away from untested subjects and skills.[12] The effects of this shift may actually be positive if the tested subjects are more important than the untested subjects or if the tested

7. See, for example, Robert Gordon, "What Democrats Need to Say about Education," *New Republic*, June 6–13, 2005; Jay Mathews, "Let's Teach to the Test," *Washington Post*, February 20, 2006, p. A21.

8. See, for example, Chenfeld (2006).

9. Chin (2002).

10. See, for example, McNeil (2000).

11. Gallagher (2004); Marshak (2003).

12. Hamilton, Stecher, and Klein (2002); Jacob (2005); Koretz (2002).

subjects provide an important foundation for learning the untested subjects. But the effects may be negative if narrow tests lead teachers to neglect important skills that lie beyond the scope of the tests.

It is, of course, also possible that both the proponents and critics of accountability reform assume too much about the power of test-based incentives to change public education.[13] Perhaps administrators tinker only at the margins—attempting to improve students' test performance by strategically reallocating their best teachers to tested grades or by reducing class sizes in those grades. Perhaps teachers modify their practices only superficially and wait out the reform, knowing that their students' needs are far more persistent than any particular education reform ever seems to be.[14]

Accountability and Equity

Proponents, critics, and skeptics agree, however, that if accountability reforms influence educational practice they will have their largest effects on schools that serve low-income or minority students. Low-income students and African American and Latino students score considerably lower on tests, on average, than do their middle-class White and Asian American counterparts, and schools remain remarkably segregated by ethnicity and social class.[15] Consequently, both the positive and negative incentives created by test-based accountability policies should affect predominantly poor and predominantly minority schools the most. Yet it is impossible to know a priori whether such policies will have net positive or negative consequences.[16]

Relevant Literature

Previous research on the effects of pre-NCLB accountability reform on student achievement has generally found that stronger accountability policies are associated with improved test scores. For example, using cross-sectional data on accountability systems in 2000, Martin Carnoy and Susanna Loeb found that fourth and eighth graders in states with strong accountability systems gained more in math than did their counterparts in states with weak or nonexistent accountability systems.[17] Likewise, using panel data on state

13. Wilms (2003).
14. Tyack and Cuban (1995).
15. See Phillips and Chin (2004) for an overview.
16. See the excellent discussion in Clotfelter and others (2004).
17. Carnoy and Loeb (2002).

accountability systems during the 1990s, Eric Hanushek and Margaret Raymond found that students gained more in math and reading between fourth and eighth grade when they lived in states that adopted accountability systems.[18] And, using data on school districts rather than states, Brian Jacob found that a policy that threatened to retain students and put schools on probation (with the additional threat of reconstitution if they did not improve) led to improved reading and math scores among third, fifth, and eighth graders in the Chicago Public Schools, at least on the test that the district used to judge academic skills.[19]

These studies and others have also examined a range of likely explanations for these effects on student achievement—from increased special education placements or preemptive retention to changes in teachers' instructional practices or teacher quality. The evidence on special education placements or retention is mixed, with some studies showing effects of accountability reforms and others finding no effects.[20] A number of studies have concluded, however, that teachers respond strategically to accountability pressures by focusing their instruction on tested material.[21]

A final set of studies has examined whether accountability policies influence class size, teacher quality, or teachers' attitudes, especially in schools that serve disadvantaged children. Two studies, based on data from two different states, yield somewhat different answers about the impact of accountability on teacher quality. Charles Clotfelter and others found that the introduction of an accountability system in North Carolina (or the official labeling of schools as "low performing") increased teacher turnover in low-performing schools but did not cause a statistically significant decline in the proportion of high-quality teachers (as measured by experience and the selectivity of the college that the teacher attended) in low-performing schools.[22] In contrast, Donald Boyd and others found that the introduction of mandatory testing in fourth grade in New York, combined with school-level consequences for poor test performance, *reduced* the relative turnover rate of fourth grade teachers.[23] In addition, teachers who entered fourth grade after the reform tended to be

18. Hanushek and Raymond (2005).

19. Jacob (2005).

20. See Cullen and Reback (2002); Deere and Strayer (2001); Figlio and Getzler (2002); Hanushek and Raymond (2005); Jacob (2005).

21. For reviews, see Hamilton, Stecher, and Klein (2002); Koretz (2002). Also see suggestive evidence based on test score gains in tested and untested subjects in Deere and Strayer (2001) and Jacob (2005).

22. Clotfelter and others (2004).

23. Boyd and others (forthcoming).

more experienced and, in the lowest-performing schools, were more likely to have attended selective colleges.

Two other studies used the same national data that we use in this chapter, from the Schools and Staffing Survey (SASS), to investigate the relationship between accountability policies and changes in teachers' attitudes and quality between 1994 and 2000. Jaekyung Lee and Kenneth Wong found that differences among states in their accountability policies during the 1990s were not associated with changes in class sizes or in-field teaching.[24] Similarly, Susanna Loeb and Felicia Estrada found that differences among states in accountability policies in 2000 were not associated with changes in teachers' academic skills (as measured by the selectivity of their undergraduate institutions) or with changes in teachers' reports about their job satisfaction or control over the curriculum.[25] And neither of these studies found different effects of accountability in poor schools relative to their nonpoor counterparts.

Our chapter builds on this past research. Like Lee and Wong, we examine the effects of state accountability policies on class size, and like Loeb and Estrada, we examine the effects of accountability on teachers' academic skills (as measured by the selectivity of the colleges they attended) and their perceptions of autonomy. In addition, we estimate the effects of accountability policies on the time that teachers devoted to school-related activities outside of normal school hours, on teachers' exposure to several types of professional development, and on the turnover, experience, credentials, and educational attainment of teachers. Our methodology also differs from this prior work because we estimate the effects of *changes* in state accountability policies (rather than levels of state accountability policies) on various outcomes. This strategy allows us to control for any unchanging aspects of states that might be associated with differences among states in both their accountability policies and their teachers.

In contrast to Clotfelter and others and Boyd and others, we draw on evidence from many states rather than from just one. This multistate approach has one large disadvantage: we have less detailed and less precise data on the accountability policies in each state as well as on teachers' career paths. But our approach also has several advantages. First, states implemented different types of accountability policies during this time period. Some states mandated additional testing, while others also imposed consequences on schools, and still others imposed consequences on students or teachers. National data

24. Lee and Wong (2004).
25. Loeb and Estrada (2005).

allow us to examine the relative effects of these different types of accountability policies. Second, to the extent that other state education policies, such as teacher certification testing or class size reduction, changed over the same time period, our multistate analyses can better distinguish the concomitant effects of these policies from the effects of accountability policies. Third, and perhaps most important, our work provides a more general test of how accountability policies may have influenced schools and teachers in states across the nation. Thus our results may help policymakers predict how educators nationwide will respond to NCLB.

Methods

We constructed a dataset by combining data on state accountability policies from the Council of Chief State School Officers annual survey of State Student Assessments (hereafter referred to as CCSSO) for the 1993–94 and 1999–2000 school years with data reported by teachers in the Schools and Staffing Survey (SASS; conducted by the National Center for Education Statistics) for the same school years.[26] The CCSSO survey, which was filled out by the state directors of assessment, provides the best data for our purposes because it contains detailed questions about many different types of assessment and accountability policies and because it provides reasonably comparable data throughout the 1990s. SASS provides nationally representative data on teachers' characteristics, attitudes, instructional practices, class sizes, and exposure to professional development.

In contrast to previous studies that have used the SASS data, we restricted our sample to the teachers for whom we expected accountability policies to have the largest effects: full-time public school teachers who taught in regular schools or in schools with a "special program emphasis" (such as charter or magnet schools) and who taught English, math, science, history, or general elementary subjects. We excluded part-time teachers; teachers who taught in special education, vocational-technical, or alternative schools; and teachers who taught nonacademic subjects such as art, music, or physical education.[27]

26. Council of Chief State School Officers (2001a, 2001b); Council of Chief State School Officers, North Central Regional Education Laboratory (1995); Schools and Staffing Survey, NCES (1998, 2003).

27. Past studies have not restricted their samples to teachers of core subjects in regular schools; see, for example, Lee and Wong (2004); Loeb and Estrada (2005). Of the public school teachers in the pooled SASS sample, more than 40 percent listed a nonacademic subject as their main assignment field and another 10 percent taught in special education, vocational-technical, or alternative schools.

We also restricted our sample to teachers who taught in first through sixth grades. We decided to focus on elementary school teachers because we suspected that accountability pressures would be greatest for these teachers and because the majority of elementary school teachers teach multiple subjects, and we wanted to investigate whether accountability policies affected the percentage of time that teachers allocated to different subjects.[28]

Defining "Accountability"

States implemented various types of school accountability policies during the 1990s. All of these policies involved mandatory testing in some subjects and grades. In conjunction with testing, some states implemented *student accountability* policies that threatened to prevent students from being promoted to the next grade if they failed to meet certain performance standards on the tests. A few states developed *teacher accountability* policies that linked rewards and punishments for teachers to students' test results. Other states implemented *school accountability* policies that ranged from simply reporting schools' test results to school dissolution and takeover.

Most previous studies of state accountability policies have tried to capture this policy variation in their accountability measures, but no consensus has developed about the best way to measure accountability. Carnoy and Loeb and Loeb and Estrada used 1999–2000 data from Margaret Goertz and Mark Duffy's Consortium for Policy Research in Education (CPRE) report to create an accountability strength scale based on information about the extent of mandatory testing, the seriousness of consequences for schools, and the requirement of exit exams for high school students.[29] Kathryn Schiller and Chandra Muller, who examined the effects of state accountability policies on students' mathematics coursework, used several separate measures that they constructed from questions asked on the 1993 National Longitudinal Study of Schools survey.[30] Their measures included the number of mandated tests in math, reading, science, and social studies in high school; the consequences of testing for students (including retention, remediation, and high school graduation); and the number of positive and negative conse-

---

28. Note, however, that we restrict our sample to teachers of elementary grades (defined as first to sixth grades), not to teachers in elementary schools, and we include in our regressions a control for whether the teacher taught in an elementary school. Consequently, we can generalize our results to all full-time teachers of regular subjects who teach in grades 1 through 6, regardless of whether they teach in schools that also contain middle or high school grades.

29. Carnoy and Loeb (2002); Loeb and Estrada (2005); Goertz and Duffy (2001).

30. Schiller and Muller (2003).

quences for schools (including financial incentives; official recognition; accreditation; waivers from testing, reporting, and other regulations; negative publicity; or loss of control to a higher educational authority).

Lee and Wong combined data from three different policy surveys administered during the 1990s to characterize the overall strength of accountability policy in a state during the decade.[31] Their measure included testing, student accountability, teacher accountability, and school accountability data from the 1995–96 CCSSO survey, testing and school accountability data from the *Quality Counts 1999* report, and the CPRE policy index devised by Carnoy and Loeb for 1999–2000.[32]

Hanushek and Raymond used data from a survey and analysis done by Stephen Fletcher and Margaret Raymond that allowed them to characterize states as *report card* states, meaning that they publicly reported schools' test results, or as *consequential* states, meaning that they reported test results and attached at least one school consequence to those results.[33] Hanushek and Raymond then used those measures to describe the proportion of time that the state had the school accountability policies in place.

Like Schiller and Muller, we used multiple measures to capture potentially different aspects of state accountability systems.[34] We used the CCSSO data to create six different accountability measures for each state: the number of elementary grades in which a state mandated tests; whether the state required the use of assessments for student retention decisions; whether the state had any teacher accountability policy; the sum of positive and negative consequences for schools; an accountability strength measure that used Carnoy and Loeb's methodology to develop a scale that ranges from 0 to 5; and an indicator variable that approximates the current NCLB policy by combining rules about testing, score disaggregation, and consequences for schools.[35] Note, however, that our approximation to NCLB policy is quite imperfect because during the 1990s no states had policies that exactly resembled NCLB and very few states had accountability policies that required testing in many grades, score disaggregation, and serious school consequences. Moreover, our measure does not indicate whether students had access to supplemental educational services or school transfer options, nor does it contain information on whether states required test score disaggregation and reporting at the *school* level.

31. Lee and Wong (2004).
32. *Education Week* (1999); Carnoy and Loeb (2002).
33. Hanushek and Raymond (2005); Fletcher and Raymond (2002).
34. Schiller and Muller (2003).
35. See the data appendix for details on how we constructed these last two measures.

Table 3-1. *Changes in State Accountability Policies, 1994–2000*[a]

	1993–94		1999–2000		Change: 2000–1994	
	Mean	*SD*	*Mean*	*SD*	*Mean*	*SD*
Accountability measures						
Extent of testing	1.83	1.40	2.65	1.45	0.81	1.44
Student retention	0.13	0.33	0.19	0.39	0.06	0.43
Teacher accountability	0.04	0.20	0.13	0.33	0.08	0.35
School accountability	2.27	1.94	2.54	2.06	0.27	1.92
Accountability strength	2.05	1.47	2.39	1.46	0.33	1.35
NCLB accountability	0.06	0.24	0.23	0.42	0.17	0.38
State covariates						
Per pupil expenditures	6,070.99	1,450.52	6,829.90	1,349.22	758.91	378.13
Unemployment rate (percent)	5.38	1.22	3.74	1.00	–1.65	1.03
School enrollment (ln)	13.21	0.97	13.26	1.00	0.05	0.07
Class size legislation	0.15	0.36	0.40	0.49	0.25	0.44
Required teacher certification tests	0.73	0.45	0.81	0.39	0.08	0.35

Source: Authors' calculations.

a. The sample includes the forty-eight states for which we have data in both years. Florida did not respond to the 1999–2000 survey, and data from Nebraska are missing for 1993–94. See appendix table 3-A1 for descriptions of the variables, their coding, and their sources. All numbers are either means or proportions, except for the unemployment rate, which is a percentage.

Table 3-1 shows descriptive statistics for each of these measures (as well as for the state covariates that we included in our models). Appendix table 3A-1 describes the content of these measures in more detail. Although accountability policies became more prevalent in the late 1990s, table 3-1 shows that some accountability policies were already in place by 1994.[36] By 1994 the typical state required testing in nearly two elementary grades. The typical state also had slightly more than two school accountability policies already in place and ranked about a 2 on the 0 to 5 accountability strength scale. However, few states (only 13 percent) retained students on the basis of school performance in 1994, and only two of the forty-eight states in our sample (4 percent) had any teacher accountability policy.

By 2000, accountability had increased in all states, although the average change (at least as measured by the CCSSO data) was not dramatic. Between

36. Throughout this paper, all references to a particular year denote the last year of the school year (for example, 1994 refers to the 1993–94 school year).

Figure 3-1. *Assessment and Accountability Trends, 1994–2000*

Percentage of states

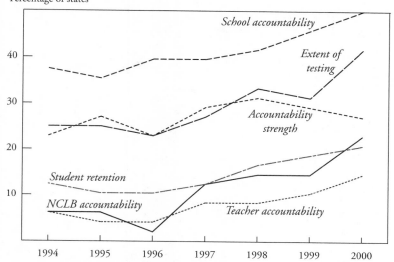

Source: Authors' tabulations of data from the Council of Chief State School Officers (1995, 1996, 1997, 1998, 1999, 2001a, 2001b). See text for more details.
NCLB = No Child Left Behind.

1994 and 2000, mandatory testing increased by nearly one more grade on average, an additional 6 percent of states based retention decisions on tests, an additional 8 percent of states adopted at least one teacher accountability policy, the number of school accountability policies increased by about a fourth of a policy, and the accountability strength index increased by about a third of a point on the 0 to 5 scale. Figure 3-1 displays these trends graphically, showing data for the intervening years as well.[37]

Even though table 3-1 and figure 3-1 show that all types of accountability increased between 1994 and 2000, states that adopted accountability policies in one domain were not necessarily the same states that adopted policies in another domain. Table 3-2 shows correlations among the changes in our accountability measures (as well as their correlations with other state covariates). Somewhat surprisingly, changes in mandatory testing were not correlated with changes in other types of accountability. In addition, although

37. For simplicity, we dichotomized the extent of testing, school accountability, and accountability strength measures before graphing them. We coded the first two variables (extent of testing and school accountability) as 1 if the state had a value of 3 or higher and the accountability strength variable as 1 if the state had a value of 4 or higher (because 4 or higher represents *strong* accountability).

Table 3-2. *Correlations among Changes in State Accountability Policies and Covariates, 1994–2000*[a]

Change in	1	2	3	4	5	6	7	8	9	10	11
1 Extent of testing	1.00										
2 Student retention	0.09	1.00									
3 Teacher accountability	-0.10	0.25	1.00								
4 School accountability	0.08	-0.02	0.12	1.00							
5 Accountability strength	0.08	0.04	0.10	0.78	1.00						
6 NCLB accountability	-0.10	-0.20	0.38	0.17	0.10	1.00					
7 Per pupil expenditures	-0.02	-0.14	0.12	-0.02	0.02	0.13	1.00				
8 Unemployment rate	0.21	0.07	-0.17	0.02	0.04	0.09	-0.03	1.00			
9 School enrollment	0.17	0.01	0.27	0.23	0.17	0.01	-0.27	-0.18	1.00		
10 Class size legislation	0.11	0.03	-0.14	0.17	0.22	0.00	0.06	0.17	-0.15	1.00	
11 Required teacher certification tests	-0.01	0.11	-0.06	0.06	0.08	-0.11	-0.22	-0.10	0.10	0.14	1.00

Source: Authors' calculations.

a. The sample includes the forty-eight states for which we have data in both years. Florida did not respond to the 1999–2000 survey, and data from Nebraska are missing for 1993–94. See appendix table 3-A1 and Data Appendix for more details on variables.

changes in student retention and teacher accountability were moderately correlated with each other, neither was correlated with changes in school accountability or changes in accountability strength. Changes in school accountability and accountability strength were highly correlated ($r = 0.78$), however, indicating that both reflect similar types of policy changes. Changes in NCLB accountability correlated modestly with changes in teacher accountability policies ($r = 0.38$).

SASS Outcomes

In 1994 and 2000, teachers in the SASS responded to numerous survey questions about themselves, their teaching, and their classrooms. Some of these survey questions measured the types of desirable consequences that accountability advocates hope will materialize in the wake of accountability reform; others measured the undesirable consequences that critics fear.

DESIRABLE CONSEQUENCES. SASS teachers reported the number of hours per week that they spent on school-related activities outside of school hours, both with and without students. We use these variables to try to identify how teacher effort changed in response to accountability policies. These variables are imperfect measures of time spent on achievement-related activities, however, because both questions asked about activities that are unrelated to student learning (for example, the question on time with students not only asked about time spent tutoring but also about time spent coaching, going on field trips, and transporting students). In addition, these variables do not allow us to capture any changes in the effectiveness or efficiency of instruction, even though teachers may respond to accountability pressures by covering more material and tolerating fewer distractions.[38]

We measured administrators' efforts to improve student achievement in two ways. First, we examined teachers' reports of how much professional development they received during the past year. Current evidence suggests that intense and content-focused professional development may help improve student achievement.[39] Second, we examined teachers' reports about the size of their classes. Research indicates that students learn more in smaller classes, at least in the early grades, and that smaller classes have their largest impacts on disadvantaged students.[40]

---

38. Chin (2002).

39. Angrist and Lavy (2001); Cohen and Hill (2000); Jacob and Lefgren (2002); for a review, see Kennedy (1999).

40. For reviews, see Ferguson (1998); Ehrenberg and others (2001).

UNDESIRABLE CONSEQUENCES. SASS teachers answered three survey questions about how much control they felt they had in their classroom over selecting instructional materials, content, and teaching techniques. They also answered a question about how much influence they perceived teachers at their school as having over establishing curriculum. We standardized these items within each year and then combined them to measure teachers' perceptions of their instructional autonomy.

We measured teacher stability with a question that asked whether teachers had taught at their current school the previous year. And we measured teacher quality using four variables: years of teaching experience, the average SAT scores of the teacher's undergraduate college, whether or not the teacher had a regular (or advanced) teaching credential (as opposed to no credential or a provisional, probationary, temporary, or emergency credential), and whether or not the teacher had at least a masters' degree. These measures of teacher quality are admittedly poor proxies for instructional practice, but most studies show that students learn less when taught by novice teachers and learn more when taught by teachers with stronger math and verbal skills (which we can only measure in the SASS data with the average test scores of the college that teachers attended).[41]

AMBIGUOUS CONSEQUENCES. We measured ambiguous consequences using data reported by both teachers and administrators. Teachers reported the amount of time they spent per week teaching reading/language arts, math, science, and history, and we investigated whether teachers spent a greater percentage of their time teaching a particular subject after their state mandated more testing in that subject. We also examined whether administrators responded strategically to mandatory testing by reducing class sizes in tested grades or by placing higher-quality teachers in those grades.

Analytic Approach

It is difficult to estimate the causal effect of state policies on educational outcomes because states adopt policies for a variety of reasons, and those reasons themselves may be correlated with educational differences among states. To take a simple example, suppose that states with higher per pupil expenditures are less likely than are other states to adopt accountability reforms. Suppose, too, that high-expenditure states tend to attract better teachers because those

41. See Clotfelter, Ladd, and Vigdor (2006); Ehrenberg and Brewer (1995); Ferguson and Ladd (1996); Greenwald, Hedges, and Laine (1996); Hanushek, Kain, and Rivkin (1998).

states pay more. If an analysis of the effects of accountability on teacher quality did not take educational spending differences among states into account, it would incorrectly conclude that stronger accountability reforms led to reductions in teacher quality. Studies that use only one year of data try to avoid these problems by controlling statistically for confounding variables.[42] However, it is difficult to control for a large number of state-level variables (because the total number of states is relatively small), and it is impossible to know whether confounding variables that have been omitted from the statistical model still bias the estimated policy effects.

State fixed effects models improve on cross-sectional models by eliminating the confounding effects of all state variables that do not change over time. We used such models in this chapter. We estimated the impact of accountability reform by pooling two cross-sections of the SASS (from the 1993–94 and 1999–2000 school years) and regressing our various outcome variables on teacher demographics, school characteristics, district characteristics, and measures of accountability policies in each state in a given year. We added to these models indicator variables for each state and an indicator variable for year. These models estimated the impact of within-state changes in accountability on within-state changes in teacher quality, class size, teachers' perceptions of instructional autonomy, and so on, holding constant the overall secular change in these outcomes. Fixed effects models do not, however, account for other within-state changes that may confound the effects of changes in accountability policies. We tried to deal with this problem by controlling for changes in other state-level variables that may have influenced changes in our outcomes.

Although the benefits of this within-state strategy outweigh those of cross-sectional strategies, the within-state strategy has its limitations. Although a six-year period is a reasonably long period in which to examine accountability changes, some state accountability policies changed only modestly or not at all during this time period. This lack of change limits our ability to detect statistically significant effects. Moreover, any mistakes we have made in measuring state accountability policies make it even harder for us to detect statistically significant effects. We caution readers that the standard errors in our tables, which we adjusted for dependencies among teachers within states, are often quite large. Thus we do not have enough statistical power to detect some potentially important effects of accountability policies.

42. See, for example, Carnoy and Loeb (2002).

Most of our models take the following form:

$$(1) \qquad y_{ist} = \lambda X_{ist} + \gamma LP_{st} + \beta A_{st} + \mu_s + \alpha_t + \varepsilon_{ist},$$

where y_{ist} is an outcome variable for teacher i in state s at time t; X_{ist} are teacher characteristics and the characteristics of teachers' schools and districts. These included teachers' gender, ethnicity, age (and a quadratic for age), and grade taught; the natural log of school size; the percentage of students in the school who were eligible for subsidized meals (and a quadratic for subsidized meals); the percentage of minority students in the school (and a quadratic for the percentage who were minority); indicator variables for whether the school was located in an urban, rural, or suburban area and whether the school was a charter school or a magnet school; the natural log of district size; the percentage of students in the district who were eligible for subsidized meals; and the percentage of minority students in the district.[43] LP_{st} are state characteristics that may influence teacher labor markets, including state per pupil expenditures, the state unemployment rate, and the natural log of state school enrollments, as well as state education policies that may also affect teachers, including class size reduction policies and test requirements for teacher certification. A_{st} are state accountability policies, and μ_s and α_t are state and year indicators.[44]

Near the end of this chapter, we use two additional models to examine whether teachers or school administrators reallocated resources within

---

43. We excluded teachers' age and age squared from our equations when we estimated the impact of accountability on teacher quality (that is, experience, education, credentials, college quality, and stability) because accountability policies may influence those outcomes through their effect on the age distribution of teachers. If, for example, accountability policies encourage older teachers to retire earlier than they otherwise would, those earlier retirements may leave schools with a less experienced, less well-educated teacher workforce. Under such a scenario, if we controlled for age, we would have risked understating the effects of accountability on teacher quality. Also, because the SASS data did not separately identify charter schools in 1994, our dummy for charters reflects a comparison between designated charters in 2000 and all other schools. Appendix table 3A-3 shows descriptive statistics for the teacher-level variables in our models.

44. For continuous outcomes, we estimated linear regressions. For dichotomous outcomes, we estimated logistic regressions. Although we report logit coefficients and standard errors in our logistic regression tables, we discuss odds and probabilities in the text. We weighted all our models with the teacher weights so that our estimates would be nationally representative of teachers in first through sixth grades who teach in regular or "special program emphasis" schools in each year, and we estimated robust standard errors. Because we estimated our models at the teacher level, but policy variation occurs at the state level, we adjusted our standard errors by clustering at the state level (Bertrand, Duflo, and Mullainathan 2004).

schools in response to assessment and accountability policies. To assess whether teachers spent more time teaching a subject if the state mandated more testing in that subject, we estimate:

$$(2) \quad y_{ist} = \lambda X_{ist} + \gamma LP_{st} + \beta \, TestSubject_{st} + \phi \, TestOtherSubjects_{st} + \mu_s + \alpha_t + \varepsilon_{ist}.$$

Equation 2 is analogous to equation 1, except that our dependent variables are the percentages of time that teachers reported spending on reading, math, science, or social studies instruction, and we replace the accountability policies, A_{st}, with $TestSubject_{st}$, which is the sum of the number of elementary grades with a mandatory test in a particular subject (for example, reading). We also add a control, $TestOtherSubjects_{st}$, for the number of mandatory tests in first through sixth grades in the other core subjects (that is, math, history, and science).[45] This model assesses whether teachers spent more time teaching a subject when a state mandated more testing of that subject, independent of testing changes in other subjects.

Our third model addresses the question of whether administrators reallocated classroom resources in response to testing and accountability policies. Specifically, we examined whether teachers who taught in grades that were subjected to mandatory state tests were more likely than were their counterparts who taught in grades without mandatory tests to have MA degrees, more experience, a regular teaching certificate, better academic skills, or smaller classes. These equations take the following form:

$$(3) \quad y_{ist} = \lambda X_{ist} + \gamma LP_{st} + \beta \, Test_{gst} + \phi \, Teachtestedgrade_{ist} + \alpha_t + \varepsilon_{ist}.$$

These models include the same variables in LP_{st} and X_{ist} that are in equations 1 and 2. Note that the teacher variables in all our models include indicators for the grade taught by each teacher. *Test* represents a set of six indicator variables for whether the state, in a given year, mandated a test in at least one core subject in first through sixth grades. *Teachtestedgrade* is a variable indicating whether a teacher teaches in a tested grade. We estimated these models separately for states with weak to moderate accountability policies (states that scored below 4 on the accountability strength index) and states with strong accountability policies (states that scored 4 or higher on the accountability strength index).

---

45. If a state mandated multiple tests in the same subject in any particular grade, we counted all tests in that subject and grade as one test.

For all our models, we assessed whether accountability reforms differentially affected teachers who taught in low-income schools by estimating the models separately by school type. Our first set of models compared teachers in schools in which less than 40 percent of the students qualified for subsidized meals (*nonpoor schools*) with teachers in schools in which at least 40 percent of the students qualified for subsidized meals (*poor schools*).[46] Our second set of models refined these classifications to also consider the percentage of minority students at the school. Specifically, we compared outcomes for teachers in nonpoor White schools, nonpoor minority schools, poor White schools, and poor minority schools.[47] These subsets of schools differed in predictable ways. For example, minority schools, regardless of their poverty status, were more likely than were their White counterparts to be located in urban areas. And poor White schools were much more likely to be located in rural areas.

Results

We first present results on the effects of assessment and accountability policies on teacher quality and teacher effort. We then examine effects on professional development, class sizes, and teachers' perceptions of autonomy. We conclude with evidence on whether assessment and accountability policies narrowed the curriculum or encouraged the reallocation of resources to particular grades.

Teacher Quality

We found mixed results about the impact of accountability policies on teacher quality. Table 3-3 shows no negative impact of accountability on teacher experience and shows possible positive effects of particular types of accountability policies on experience in nonpoor minority and poor White schools.

Table 3-4 shows that greater accountability may have caused a small (0.04 or 0.09 standard deviation) reduction in teachers' academic skills, as measured by the average SAT scores of the college they attended. Student reten-

---

46. We defined *poor schools* as those in which 40 percent or more of the students were eligible for subsidized meals because NCLB uses the same cutoff to define schools as having a "high concentration of low-income students."

47. We defined *poor schools* by the same 40 percent cutoff and *White schools* as schools that had less than 20 percent nonwhite students. The 20 percent White cutoff divides our weighted sample of teachers roughly in half.

Table 3-3. *Impact of State Accountability Policies on Teacher Experience*[a]

				Teachers in			
Policies	Public schools	Nonpoor schools	Poor schools	Nonpoor White schools	Nonpoor minority schools	Poor White schools	Poor minority schools
Extent of testing	-0.154	-0.162	-0.200	-0.142	-0.105	-0.323	-0.179
	(0.193)	(0.268)	(0.173)	(0.328)	(0.603)	(0.269)	(0.216)
Student retention	0.080	-0.650	0.403	-1.105	1.435	1.471	0.189
	(0.637)	(0.905)	(0.433)	(1.178)	(1.068)	(1.472)	(0.505)
Teacher accountability	-0.047	-0.502	0.302	-1.283	1.613	2.800+	-0.480
	(0.714)	(1.088)	(0.812)	(1.939)	(1.019)	(1.476)	(0.968)
School accountability	0.054	-0.017	0.188	-0.043	0.026	0.352+	0.135
	(0.162)	(0.173)	(0.175)	(0.288)	(0.286)	(0.201)	(0.227)
Accountability strength	0.034	-0.227	0.069	-0.372	0.275	-0.240	0.102
	(0.214)	(0.260)	(0.213)	(0.411)	(0.358)	(0.428)	(0.273)
NCLB accountability	0.379	0.818	0.215	0.104	2.590*	1.080	-0.297
	(0.701)	(0.788)	(0.865)	(1.129)	(1.225)	(1.235)	(1.105)

Source: Authors' calculations.

+$p < 0.10$; *$p < 0.05$.

a. Columns reflect different samples. Rows show regression coefficients and robust standard errors (in parentheses) for each accountability variable estimated in a model that includes no other accountability variables but does include teacher controls, school controls, district controls, a year dummy, state fixed effects, and state covariates. All models are weighted with the teacher weight. All standard errors are corrected for clustering at the state level. N in overall public school model for this outcome is 16,517. See text for details.

Table 3-4. *Impact of State Accountability Policies on Teachers' College Quality*[a]

				Teachers in			
Policies	Public schools	Nonpoor schools	Poor schools	Nonpoor White schools	Nonpoor minority schools	Poor White schools	Poor minority schools
Extent of testing	-0.834	-0.993	-0.612	-0.580	0.843	0.589	-1.666
	(1.760)	(2.757)	(1.903)	(3.166)	(3.551)	(1.891)	(2.520)
Student retention	-8.485*	-11.261	-10.048*	-12.744	-2.460	-3.832	-11.507*
	(3.923)	(6.728)	(4.418)	(7.942)	(9.639)	(8.029)	(4.446)
Teacher accountability	-5.648	-6.866	-2.746	-6.985	1.605	17.843**	-9.350
	(5.708)	(10.290)	(5.781)	(12.293)	(14.649)	(5.190)	(6.219)
School accountability	-1.103	-3.664+	1.421	-5.755*	-0.529	2.289	0.517
	(1.052)	(1.878)	(1.204)	(2.396)	(3.248)	(2.251)	(1.704)
Accountability strength	-4.287***	-8.332***	-0.445	-10.712***	-3.491	0.838	-1.263
	(1.139)	(2.163)	(1.721)	(2.667)	(3.529)	(2.559)	(2.250)
NCLB accountability	6.649	4.781	10.199	2.035	0.605	14.570*	3.699
	(5.476)	(8.203)	(6.410)	(7.597)	(19.595)	(6.879)	(10.165)

Source: Authors' calculations.

+$p < 0.10$; *$p < 0.05$; **$p < 0.01$; ***$p < 0.001$.

a. Columns reflect different samples. Rows show regression coefficients and robust standard errors (in parentheses) for each accountability variable estimated in a model that includes no other accountability variables but does include teacher controls, school controls, district controls, a year dummy, state fixed effects, and state covariates. All models are weighted with the teacher weight. All standard errors are corrected for clustering at the state level. N in overall public school model for this outcome is 15,294. See text for details.

tion policies seem to have reduced teachers' skills in poor schools, and probably in nonpoor schools as well (although the coefficient for nonpoor schools is not statistically significant at conventional levels, it is similar in magnitude to that for poor schools). But greater school accountability and increased accountability strength appear to have reduced teachers' skills primarily in nonpoor White schools.[48]

In contrast, table 3-5 suggests that most types of accountability policies increased the likelihood that public school teachers were certified, although the evidence of those effects in poor schools (and poor minority schools) is mixed. In those types of schools, student retention policies and stronger accountability polices appear to have increased the odds that teachers were certified, but NCLB-like accountability policies appear to have reduced those odds.

With respect to teacher education, we found that student retention and teacher accountability policies increased the odds that teachers held advanced degrees, especially in nonpoor minority schools (see table 3-6). Other types of accountability policies appear not to have influenced teachers' education, however.

Teacher Effort

Proponents of accountability reform hope that accountability policies will encourage teachers to work harder to raise student achievement. We found that teachers responded to a few of the accountability reforms of the 1990s by spending a little more time with students outside of normal school hours. For example, increases in teacher accountability and NCLB accountability were associated with teachers spending fifteen more minutes per week with students—the equivalent of nine more hours during a thirty-six-week school year.[49] We found no consistent evidence that these effects differed between teachers in poor and nonpoor schools, however. Other accountability policies, namely, greater testing and student retention, were associated with teachers spending more time outside normal school hours preparing lessons, grading, or in meetings. But these positive effects occurred largely in nonpoor schools.

48. We estimated these models for teachers with different levels of experience, as well, to investigate whether accountability reforms dissuaded recent graduates from more selective colleges (selectivity measured by the mean SAT/ACT of the college each teacher attended) from becoming teachers or whether they caused academically skilled, experienced teachers to exit the profession. We found that the decline in academic skills occurred only among experienced teachers (that is, those with more than four years of experience).

49. Because of space constraints, we have excluded some tables and footnotes from this chapter. Please consult our working paper (see Phillips and Flashman 2007) for additional information.

Table 3-5. *Impact of State Accountability Policies on Teacher Credentials*[a]

				Teachers in			
Policies	Public schools	Nonpoor schools	Poor schools	Nonpoor White schools	Nonpoor minority schools	Poor White schools	Poor minority schools
Extent of testing	-0.097	-0.120	-0.083	-0.226+	0.124	-0.100	-0.045
	(0.079)	(0.102)	(0.053)	(0.132)	(0.229)	(0.189)	(0.072)
Student retention	0.592**	0.297	0.850***	0.416	0.847*	-0.663	1.221***
	(0.204)	(0.304)	(0.194)	(0.467)	(0.387)	(0.925)	(0.274)
Teacher accountability	0.332*	0.524*	0.309	0.849*	0.482	1.349*	0.315
	(0.160)	(0.215)	(0.239)	(0.341)	(0.563)	(0.542)	(0.341)
School accountability	0.076+	0.083	0.042	0.111	0.100	0.319*	-0.041
	(0.040)	(0.066)	(0.063)	(0.083)	(0.203)	(0.161)	(0.092)
Accountability strength	0.189**	0.130	0.228**	0.227+	0.170	0.351	0.236+
	(0.068)	(0.092)	(0.079)	(0.118)	(0.211)	(0.229)	(0.120)
NCLB accountability	-0.224	0.411	-0.743*	0.575+	0.080	0.243	-0.911+
	(0.280)	(0.312)	(0.328)	(0.321)	(0.798)	(0.799)	(0.477)

Source: Authors' calculations.

+$p < 0.10$; *$p < 0.05$; **$p < 0.01$; ***$p < 0.001$.

a. Columns reflect different samples. Rows show logit coefficients and robust standard errors (in parentheses) for each accountability variable estimated in a model that includes no other accountability variables but does include teacher controls, school controls, district controls, a year dummy, state fixed effects, and state covariates. All models are weighted with the teacher weight. All standard errors are corrected for clustering at the state level. N in overall public school model for this outcome is 16,517. See text for details.

Table 3-6. *Impact of State Accountability Policies on Teacher Education*[a]

				Teachers in			
Policies	*Public schools*	*Nonpoor schools*	*Poor schools*	*Nonpoor White schools*	*Nonpoor minority schools*	*Poor White schools*	*Poor minority schools*
Extent of testing	0.041	0.024	0.028	0.012	0.102	-0.020	0.019
	(0.037)	(0.064)	(0.038)	(0.062)	(0.097)	(0.094)	(0.029)
Student retention	0.117+	0.039	0.196*	-0.116	0.672*	0.142	0.165
	(0.060)	(0.163)	(0.083)	(0.207)	(0.293)	(0.537)	(0.120)
Teacher accountability	0.222**	0.230+	0.186	0.121	0.769***	0.664	-0.029
	(0.083)	(0.132)	(0.113)	(0.195)	(0.209)	(0.458)	(0.111)
School accountability	-0.011	-0.016	-0.009	-0.005	-0.006	0.023	-0.017
	(0.028)	(0.043)	(0.040)	(0.037)	(0.094)	(0.073)	(0.030)
Accountability strength	-0.009	-0.041	-0.006	-0.041	0.024	-0.184	0.018
	(0.033)	(0.055)	(0.044)	(0.051)	(0.098)	(0.120)	(0.034)
NCLB accountability	0.025	-0.019	0.028	-0.110	0.429	0.429	-0.069
	(0.126)	(0.217)	(0.215)	(0.270)	(0.336)	(0.309)	(0.254)

Source: Authors' calculations.

+$p < 0.10$; *$p < 0.05$; **$p < 0.01$; ***$p < 0.001$.

a. Columns reflect different samples. Rows show logit coefficients and robust standard errors (in parentheses) for each accountability variable estimated in a model that includes no other accountability variables but does include teacher controls, school controls, district controls, a year dummy, state fixed effects, and state covariates. All models are weighted with the teacher weight. All standard errors are corrected for clustering at the state level. N in overall public school model for this outcome is 16,517. See text for details.

Professional Development

Accountability advocates also hope that school administrators will respond to accountability policies by providing teachers with additional professional development. We found little evidence that accountability policies changed the amount of time teachers spent in professional development that focused on the in-depth study of their content areas or on learning more about teaching methods, and any evidence we did find varied inconsistently across school type. In contrast, we found consistent evidence that additional state-mandated testing was associated with additional professional development focused on student assessment (that is, teaching teachers about assessment), especially in poor schools and in minority schools (see table 3-7).[50] These results show, for example, that when a state added testing in one additional grade, the odds that a teacher in a poor school received nine or more hours of assessment professional development that year increased by 21 percent.[51]

Class Size

Administrators might also respond to accountability pressures by reducing class sizes. Parents and teachers alike appreciate smaller classes, and research suggests that smaller classes (at least if they are small enough) raise achievement and reduce achievement gaps in the early elementary grades.[52] We found that student retention policies and teacher accountability policies were associated with class size reduction in both poor and nonpoor schools. Increased testing and stronger accountability policies may also have been associated with class size reduction. Because our models controlled for changes in states' policies on class size, a concurrent within-state trend in policies concerning class size reduction probably cannot explain these results. But a different unmeasured within-state trend might.

Instructional Autonomy

Critics worry that test-based accountability policies, with their relentless focus on improving tested skills, take much of the creativity and joy out of

50. Table 3-7 also shows that the adoption of a student retention policy may have been associated with increases in the amount of professional development in "assessment" that teachers in nonpoor schools received.

51. Recall that our tables for dichotomous outcomes report logit coefficients. Thus to obtain the percentage change in the odds, exponentiate the coefficient, subtract 1, and multiply by 100. In this example, $(e^{.193} - 1) \times 100 = 21$ percent.

52. See, for example, Ferguson (1998); Ehrenberg and others (2001).

Table 3-7. *Impact of State Accountability Policies on "Assessment" Professional Development*[a]

				Teachers in			
Policies	Public schools	Nonpoor schools	Poor schools	Nonpoor White schools	Nonpoor minority schools	Poor White schools	Poor minority schools
Extent of testing	0.138*	0.057	0.193***	−0.016	0.297***	0.134+	0.246***
	(0.058)	(0.072)	(0.046)	(0.068)	(0.090)	(0.078)	(0.042)
Student retention	0.180	0.275*	−0.088	0.230	0.336	−0.192	−0.075
	(0.163)	(0.135)	(0.231)	(0.156)	(0.243)	(0.288)	(0.245)
Teacher accountability	0.296	0.147	0.308	0.056	0.300	0.181	0.378
	(0.292)	(0.312)	(0.282)	(0.293)	(0.429)	(0.334)	(0.311)
School accountability	0.016	0.061	−0.009	0.077	0.062	−0.046	0.022
	(0.053)	(0.066)	(0.056)	(0.063)	(0.091)	(0.065)	(0.067)
Accountability strength	0.040	0.014	0.044	−0.009	0.126	−0.068	0.104
	(0.071)	(0.081)	(0.074)	(0.088)	(0.102)	(0.090)	(0.083)
NCLB accountability	−0.070	−0.334	0.203	−0.228	−0.529	0.270	0.257
	(0.246)	(0.310)	(0.255)	(0.294)	(0.420)	(0.351)	(0.311)

Source: Authors' calculations.

+$p < 0.10$; *$p < 0.05$; **$p < 0.01$; ***$p < 0.001$.

a. Columns reflect different samples. Rows show logit coefficients and robust standard errors (in parentheses) for each accountability variable estimated in a model that includes no other accountability variables but does include teacher controls, school controls, district controls, a year dummy, state fixed effects, and state covariates. All models are weighted with the teacher weight. All standard errors are corrected for clustering at the state level. N in overall public school model for this outcome is 16,517. See text for details.

teaching and thus may dissuade excellent teachers from teaching in disadvantaged schools. From that perspective, any reduction in teacher autonomy that results from accountability policies is negative. Accountability proponents counter, however, that the majority of teachers need the guidance and structure imposed by test-based accountability to provide a consistently high-quality education to disadvantaged students, who otherwise tend to experience low standards and unfocused instruction. From that perspective, a reduction in teacher autonomy might actually benefit students.

Our results provide evidence that at least some of the accountability policies of the 1990s reduced teachers' sense of autonomy and that these effects occurred largely in poor schools and in poor minority schools. These effects were not as large as one might expect from the qualitative literature on this topic, but critics and proponents of accountability will nonetheless disagree about whether these effects represent positive or negative consequences. The largest effects occurred in high-minority poor schools, where the expansion of state-mandated testing to an additional grade was associated with a 0.06 standard deviation decline in teachers' perceived autonomy. In those same types of schools, the adoption of NCLB-like accountability was associated with a 0.25 standard deviation decline in perceived autonomy (results not shown).

Because worries about teacher autonomy permeate discussions about accountability, we investigated these findings further. A case can be made that excellent teachers prefer to be told what to teach rather than *how* to teach it. Thus we compared the effects of accountability policies on two items in our index that reflect that distinction: teachers' perceptions of control over "selecting content, topics, and skills to be taught" and their perceptions of control over "selecting teaching techniques." The results for content mirrored those for the overall index (results not shown). For teaching techniques, we found weaker negative effects overall and a small (0.085 standard deviation) but interesting and statistically significant difference between teachers in advantaged and disadvantaged schools. Increases in mandatory testing appear to have caused teachers in poor minority schools to feel that they had slightly less control over their teaching techniques, while the same accountability changes seem to have caused teachers in nonpoor White schools to feel that they had slightly more control. These results provide some reassurance that accountability policies negatively affect teachers' control over content more than they negatively affect control over methods. But they also suggest that increased testing may cause teachers in the most disadvantaged schools to feel as though they have less autonomy over their teaching methods than do their peers in other schools, providing yet another reason for good teachers to prefer to teach in better-off schools.[53]

We also wondered if the negative effects of accountability on autonomy were largest for the best teachers. We cannot measure teacher quality directly, so instead we examined whether the effects differed for inexperienced and experienced teachers. Our results showed that increased testing was associated with a larger decline in autonomy among the most inexperienced teachers (those who had taught for four or fewer years) relative to their more experienced counterparts. These results are reassuring. They imply that administrators monitor inexperienced teachers more to ensure that they are following the curriculum, that inexperienced teachers feel less authority to ignore curricular impositions, or simply that inexperienced teachers are less adept (because of their inexperience) at integrating their own ideas and methods with the mandated curriculum.

Teacher Turnover

Critics worry that accountability reform makes teaching more unpleasant in schools where test scores are lowest, and thus it increases turnover at those schools. Turnover may negatively affect academic success if students suffer when their teachers are less familiar with a particular school's policies and practices. Greater turnover probably also correlates with greater teacher inexperience, at least in poor minority schools (because vacancies at schools tend to be filled based on seniority and experienced teachers tend to prefer to teach at more advantaged schools). On the other hand, increased turnover may improve student achievement if the weakest teachers respond to accountability pressures by exiting the profession.

We found that, if anything, accountability policies caused more teacher instability in nonpoor White schools than in minority schools (results not shown). For example, when a state increased its accountability strength by one unit on our index, the odds that a teacher in a nonpoor White school reported being new to his or her school increased by 31 percent. The effects of teacher accountability and NCLB-like accountability policies were even larger.

Unfortunately, our data could not tell us why accountability policies seem to have caused more instability in nonpoor White schools. It is possible that

---

53. See Lankford, Loeb, and Wykcoff (2002) for evidence on disparities in teacher quality in New York State. See Phillips and Chin (2004) for evidence on national disparities in teacher quality.

those schools reduced class sizes more than poor minority schools did, and thus they added more teachers (our estimates on the effects of accountability policies on class size reduction have large standard errors that make it impossible to rule out this theory). It is also possible that teachers in nonpoor White schools reacted especially negatively to accountability policies and left their jobs, creating vacancies for new teachers. Because we found no indication that teacher turnover increased in minority (poor or nonpoor) schools, however, our data do not suggest that teachers responded to accountability policies by leaving disadvantaged schools to teach in advantaged schools.

Ambiguous Consequences

Skeptics worry that teachers and administrators will respond to accountability pressures with marginal tinkering rather than important instructional changes. For example, previous research has found that accountability pressures motivate teachers to devote more time to teaching tested subjects.[54] The results in table 3-8 provide additional evidence of such changes. In both nonpoor and poor schools, teachers devoted more classroom time to a particular subject when their state required more testing in that subject. But these effects were small. For example, when states mandated testing in an additional grade in science or social studies, teachers increased the percentage of time they spent teaching science or social studies by less than 1 percentage point (or about a 0.10 of a standard deviation).

We also investigated whether administrators responded to accountability policies by reducing class sizes in tested grades or allocating their best teachers to tested grades, especially in states that had strong accountability policies (see table 3-9). The results suggest that administrators tried to assign teachers they perceived as more highly qualified to tested grades. For example, teachers who taught tested grades were more likely than were their counterparts who taught untested grades to have an MA. Similarly, in low-income schools located in "strong accountability" states, teachers who taught tested grades had more experience than did their counterparts in untested grades and were also more likely to be credentialed. However, there was no statistically significant difference between teachers from more selective colleges and their peers from less selective colleges in their likelihood of teaching in tested grades, regardless of the strength of the state's accountability policy. And classes were no smaller in tested grades than in untested grades, although the results hint that administrators may have

---

54. Hamilton, Stecher, and Klein (2002); Jacob (2005); Koretz (2002).

Table 3-8. *Impact of Testing Specific Subjects on Time Spent Teaching Those Subjects*[a]

Percentage of classroom time spent on:	Teachers in						
	Public schools	Nonpoor schools	Poor schools	Nonpoor White schools	Poor White schools	Nonpoor minority schools	Poor minority schools
Reading							
Number of grades with reading tests	1.156*	0.984+	1.014+	0.428	0.528	2.434*	1.211*
	(0.511)	(0.562)	(0.545)	(0.509)	(0.754)	(1.191)	(0.550)
Math							
Number of grades with math tests	0.053	0.395+	−0.138	0.941**	−0.081	−0.475	−0.243
	(0.185)	(0.234)	(0.275)	(0.348)	(0.447)	(0.340)	(0.311)
Science							
Number of grades with science tests	0.732**	0.849*	0.495*	0.832*	−0.131	1.344	0.659**
	(0.246)	(0.378)	(0.188)	(0.406)	(0.452)	(0.874)	(0.211)
Social studies							
Number of grades with social studies tests	0.651**	0.774**	0.544*	0.520+	1.354*	1.014	0.330
	(0.205)	(0.269)	(0.219)	(0.286)	(0.522)	(0.627)	(0.257)

Source: Authors' calculations.

+$p < 0.10$; *$p < 0.05$; **$p < 0.01$.

a. Columns reflect different samples. Rows show regression coefficients and robust standard errors (in parentheses) for the sum of grades tested in a given subject, estimated in a model that also includes number of grades tested in the three other core subjects, teacher controls, school controls, district controls, a year dummy, state fixed effects, and state covariates. All models are weighted with the teacher weight. All standard errors are corrected for clustering at the state level. N in overall public school model for all outcomes in this table is 11,051. See text for details.

Table 3-9. *Resource Allocations to Tested Grades, by Strength of State Accountability Policy and School Poverty*[a]

	Teachers in											
	Public schools				Nonpoor public schools				Poor public schools			
	Overall	Weak account-ability	Strong account-ability	Interaction statistically significant?	Overall	Weak account-ability	Strong account-ability	Interaction statistically significant?	Overall	Weak account-ability	Strong account-ability	Interaction statistically significant?
Masters degree												
Teach in tested grade	0.181* (0.073)	0.190** (0.066)	0.168 (0.141)	no	0.139 (0.099)	0.100 (0.081)	0.287 (0.310)	no	0.270** (0.101)	0.324* (0.126)	0.113 (0.184)	no
Teaching experience (years)												
Teach in tested grade	0.392 (0.345)	0.055 (0.355)	1.282+ (0.711)	no	0.384 (0.425)	0.321 (0.456)	0.216 (1.535)	no	0.637 (0.529)	-0.084 (0.554)	2.437* (0.920)	yes
Credential												
Teach in tested grade	-0.049 (0.171)	-0.167 (0.148)	0.323 (0.319)	no	-0.153 (0.159)	-0.081 (0.217)	-0.305 (0.621)	no	0.018 (0.215)	-0.279 (0.196)	0.869* (0.382)	yes
College quality												
Teach in tested grade	-0.536 (2.967)	-0.613 (3.407)	5.557 (6.625)	no	-2.876 (3.908)	0.409 (4.275)	-1.569 (7.237)	no	-2.399 (4.259)	-7.971+ (4.046)	9.150 (8.888)	yes
Class size												
Teach in tested grade	0.140 (0.200)	0.338* (0.161)	-0.653 (0.544)	yes	0.364 (0.225)	0.355 (0.262)	0.048 (0.573)	no	-0.025 (0.294)	0.425+ (0.241)	-1.299 (0.852)	yes

Source: Authors' calculations.

$+p < 0.10$; $*p < 0.05$; $**p < 0.01$.

a. Columns reflect different samples. "Weak accountability" states are defined as those with an accountability strength index of less than 4. "Strong accountability" states are those with an accountability strength index of 4 or 5. See appendix for more details on the construction of the accountability strength index. Rows show regression or logit coefficients and robust standard errors (in parentheses) for a dummy variable coded 1 if a teacher teaches in a tested grade and 0 otherwise. These coefficients are estimated from models that also include binary variables indicating whether or not each grade has a state-mandated test, binary variables for the grade each teacher teaches, as well as the other teacher, school, district, and state controls. The "Interaction statistically significant?" column indicates whether the interaction between "strong state" and "teach in tested grade" is statistically significant at least at the 0.10 level. All models are weighted with the teacher weight. All standard errors are corrected for clustering at the state level. Models that include state fixed effects produce substantively similar results.

made some effort to reduce class sizes in response to strong accountability pressures.

Conclusion

Our results offer support to both proponents and critics of accountability reform. On the one hand, accountability policies seem to have increased teacher credentialing and motivated teachers to spend a little more time working on school-related activities outside of school hours. Accountability policies may also have encouraged administrators to offer more professional development and to reduce class sizes. On the other hand, accountability policies seem to have reduced teachers' sense of autonomy and may have reduced teachers' academic skills. Skeptics would probably add, however, that most of these effects, whether positive or negative, were quite small. They would probably also argue that the clearest changes seem to have involved strategic decisions intended to improve students' scores in the short term.

One of our purposes in writing this chapter was to examine the effect of accountability policies on school inequality. We expected that teachers in low-income minority schools would bear the brunt of the effects of accountability reform.[55] And we worried that policies intended to raise achievement and reduce achievement gaps might have led, instead, to dramatic declines in instructional quality in schools that already faced the most challenges. But we did not find strong negative effects in disadvantaged schools. We did find that teachers in poor minority schools felt less autonomy over their curriculum and teaching methods after increases in state-mandated testing than did their counterparts in nonpoor White schools. We also found that teachers in poor or minority schools received more professional development about assessment after increases in state-mandated testing. But we found no consistent evidence that accountability policies differentially affected teacher quality in disadvantaged schools. And we also found some positive changes from which we would expect students to benefit, such as increases in the time that teachers spent doing school-related work outside of school hours and decreases in class sizes. These mixed results raise the crucial question of what will transpire as states comply with NCLB.

Although we cannot answer that question with certainty, both because NCLB is a federal rather than state policy and because none of the accountability policies adopted by states during the 1990s had the exact same compo-

---

55. Clotfelter and others (2004).

nents as NCLB, this chapter informs the debate in several ways. First, our results strongly suggest that accountability policies do, in fact, change educators' behavior. Consequently, policymakers at the federal, state, and district levels need to ensure that the incentives they create for administrators and teachers are aligned with the educational outcomes they desire.

For example, our results suggest that administrators try to concentrate resources on grades that are tested. NCLB does not mandate testing until third grade, and as a consequence, administrators may try to concentrate educational resources in the third grade or above. However, learning is a developmental process, and it is very hard for students to catch up academically after the early elementary grades.[56] Consequently, policymakers would be wise to add additional incentives at the federal, state, or district level that encourage schools to measure and remediate students' skill gaps earlier in the educational process.

To take another example, our results show that teachers spend more time teaching tested subjects, providing further support for the adage "You get what you test."[57] Consequently, policymakers need to ensure that testing requirements cover the subjects, knowledge, and types of skills that they want children to master. For instance, because NCLB currently excludes history testing, teachers will probably teach less history unless policymakers either mandate history testing as part of NCLB or create an additional policy that mandates history testing.

Second, our results suggest that different types of accountability policies have different effects. During the 1990s at least, accountability policies that imposed consequences on schools seem to have been less effective in changing educators' behavior than were accountability policies that imposed consequences on teachers or students. Although these results are tentative, because only a small number of states adopted teacher or student accountability policies during the 1990s, they nonetheless suggest that policymakers should consider adding teacher, and perhaps student, accountability components to NCLB when it comes up for reauthorization.[58] Policymakers should make such deci-

---

56. See, for example, Juel (1988).

57. See Linn (2000).

58. States' use of teacher accountability policies during the 1990s did not vary enough for us to distinguish the effects of negative teacher sanctions from the effects of positive teacher sanctions. We do know, however, that the states that adopted teacher accountability policies during the 1990s—which are the states that drive our results—typically had policies that included either only positive incentives (such as recognizing teachers for students' score gains or giving teachers monetary rewards) or both positive and negative incentives (such as both recognizing and evaluating teachers based on students' scores).

sions, however, only after carefully assessing the effects of student accountability policies, in particular, on students' academic success (see the chapters by Hauser, Frederick, and Andrew and Dee and Jacob in this volume).

Third, our results provide suggestive evidence that test-based accountability policies may make teaching in low-income, heavily minority schools even less desirable than it already is. For example, we found that increases in mandatory testing led teachers in low-income schools to feel less control over their teaching practices. These findings provide yet another rationale for policymakers to build strong incentives into NCLB that encourage our best teachers to teach in our most challenging schools.

Finally, our mixed and somewhat weak results imply that accountability reform will not be a panacea for our nation's educational problems. Significantly raising academic achievement or eliminating the achievement gap will undoubtedly require more than systemic school reform. Nonetheless, when NCLB comes up for reauthorization, legislators will have another opportunity to weigh in on the most significant federal education policy in decades. One question they should ponder is why we found such small effects of state accountability changes during the 1990s. A likely explanation is that these small effects reflect considerable heterogeneity in educators' responses to the incentives created by accountability reform. We suspect that these results signal that educators try to respond to accountability pressures but make widely varying and unequally effective choices about how to respond. If that is the case, policymakers should consider coupling accountability policies with the research-based programmatic support that educators need to improve their instructional practices.

Appendix

We constructed two accountability measures that require further explanation.

Accountability Strength

We tried to replicate the index that Martin Carnoy and Susanna Loeb used in their paper on the effects of accountability on student achievement.[59] Because we wanted to measure accountability in both 1993–94 and 1999–2000 and because Carnoy and Loeb's data source (CPRE) was not available for 1993–94, we tried to follow their classification rules yet still

---

59. Carnoy and Loeb (2002).

make an index based on the CCSSO data.[60] When we applied their schema to the CCSSO data and then correlated our 1999–2000 index with their 1999–2000 index, the two indexes were highly, but not perfectly, correlated ($r = 0.81$). Most states received either the same index score across the two data sources or received a score that differed by only 1 point. Six states differed by more than 1 point, however. Because these discrepancies concerned us, we tried to verify the CCSSO data for these states by consulting a third data source: *Quality Counts 2000*.[61] We assigned each state a new accountability index score based on the *Quality Counts* data and then compared the results with our CCSSO results. With the exception of Pennsylvania and Tennessee, the *Quality Counts* data largely confirmed our state accountability classifications.

NCLB Accountability

We intended to make a variable that reflected the requirements of the NCLB legislation. We did not have any items in both years that measured school transfer options or access to supplemental educational services, so we could not include those aspects of the legislation in our measure. NCLB requires testing in math and reading in third through eighth grades; requires score disaggregation by race and social class at the school level; puts schools on probation if they do not meet their adequate yearly progress targets; and then removes resources from these schools and takes them over or dissolves them entirely if they continue to fail to meet their performance targets. The CCSSO data did not allow us to measure whether states required test score disaggregation specifically at the school level. So, for a state to be classified as an NCLB state, we created a variable that required a state to have *all* of the following policies:

—mandatory math and reading tests in three elementary grades

—disaggregated test scores by race and socioeconomic status (SES) (reported at any level)

— a warning to *or* probation for schools on the basis of test scores

— a monetary penalty for schools *or* takeover *or* dissolution on the basis of test scores

However, very few states met these requirements in 1994 or 2000. Relaxing the test requirement—by requiring mandatory reading and math tests in

---

60. CPRE: Consortium for Policy Research in Education; CCSSO: Council of Chief State School Officers.

61. *Education Week* (2000).

at least two elementary grades—did not improve the numbers much. Thus we relaxed our rules further. Our final NCLB approximation required *all* of the following:

—mandatory math and reading tests in two elementary grades

—disaggregated test scores by race and socioeconomic status (reported at any level)

—a warning *or* probation *or* a monetary penalty *or* takeover *or* dissolution on the basis of test scores

This measure classifies three states as NCLB states in 1994 and eleven states as NCLB states in 2000.

Table 3A-1. *Description of Accountability Measures and State Covariates*

Variable	Description
Testing	
Grades tested	Sum of grades 1–6 requiring at least one mandatory test in a core subject
Consequences for Students, Teachers, or Schools	
Student retention	1 if state retains students based on test scores; 0 otherwise
Teacher accountability	1 if state has any of the following teacher accountability policies: awards or recognition, monetary rewards, monetary penalties, evaluation or certification
School accountability	Sum of the following school accountability policies: performance reporting, warning, probation, monetary penalties, dissolution, takeover, recognition, monetary awards, exemption from regulations, accreditation
Overall Accountability	
Accountability strength	Replication of Carnoy and Loeb (2002) Index: Index ranges from 0–5, where 0 = no state level testing; 0.5 = state level testing, no performance reporting; 1 = state level testing, performance reporting, no school accountability or exit exams; 1.5 = state level testing, performance reporting, weak accountability, no exit exams; 2 = state level testing, performance reporting, moderate accountability or exit exam; 2.5 = state level testing, performance reporting, weak accountability, exit exam; 3 = state level testing, performance reporting, moderate accountability, exit exam; 3.5 = state level testing, performance reporting, moderate-strong accountability, no exit exam; 4 = state level testing, performance reporting, strong accountability, no exit exam; 4.5 = state level testing, performance reporting, moderate-strong accountability, exit exam; 5 = state level testing, performance reporting, strong accountability, exit exam.
NCLB accountability	Dummy variable approximation of NCLB legislation, coded 1 if the state has mandatory reading and math tests in at least two elementary grades (out of grades 1–6), disaggregates test scores based on race and SES, and has at least one of the following test-based consequences: warning, probation, monetary penalty, school takeover, or school dissolution.

continued on next page

Table 3A-1. *Description of Accountability Measures and State Covariates—Continued*

Variable	Description
Labor Market Characteristics	
Per pupil expenditures	Current expenditures per pupil in fall enrollment in public elementary and secondary schools, by state, in 2000 dollars
Unemployment rate	Seasonally adjusted October unemployment estimate, by state
School enrollment	Natural log of public school enrollment, by state
Other State Education Policies	
Class size legislation	1 if state had implemented mandatory class size legislation in any grade at any level; 0 otherwise
Required teacher certification tests	1 if state legislation required teachers to take either a subject-specific or a general test to obtain a regular credential; 0 otherwise

Sources: All accountability data are from the State Student Assessments Annual Survey (Council of Chief State School Officers 2001; Council of Chief State School Officers/North Central Regional Education Laboratory 1995) for the 1993–94 and 1999–2000 school years. See text for more details. Per pupil expenditures and school enrollments are from NCES (2003). Unemployment rates come from the Bureau of Labor Statistics (1993–2000). Class size legislation data are from Pate-Bane (2004). Teacher certification testing data are from the American Association of Colleges for Teacher Education (1993) and the National Association of State Directors of Teacher Education and Certification (1999).

Table 3A-2. *Description of Teacher Outcomes*

Variable	Description
Teacher Quality	
Experience	Total years; sum of years taught at public or private schools (full- or part-time)
College quality	Mean SAT of undergraduate institution. Data from the Higher Education Research Institute (HERI) selectivity file, which is based on public reports of institutions' mean SAT and/or ACT scores. We infer year of college entrance from teacher-reported year of college graduation. HERI data are available for 1973, 1977, 1982, and 1999. We attach the HERI data from the year closest to the year of college entrance but exclude 1999 selectivity data because the 1999 scores reflect recentering of the SAT in 1995.
Credentials	Teacher reported: 1 if has regular, standard, or advanced teaching certificate in any state; 0 otherwise. Response options varied slightly between years. In 1994, respondents could report that they had a "certificate for persons who have completed an alternative program," but that option was not available in 2000. We coded respondents in that category as being certified.
Education	Teacher reported: 1 if has an MA or more than an MA; 0 otherwise (less than 1 percent of sample has less than a BA)

continued on next page

Table 3A-2. *Description of Teacher Outcomes—Continued*

Variable	Description
Time on School-Related Activities	
Time with students outside normal school hours	Teacher reported: hours per week. Teachers reporting 15 or more hours top-coded at 15 (approximately 3 percent of teachers); question text in 1994: "During your most recent full week, how many hours did you spend AFTER school, BEFORE school, and ON THE WEEKEND on each of the following types of activities? School-related activities involving student interaction (for example, coaching, field trips, tutoring, transporting students)?" The question text differs only slightly (and nonsubstantively) in 2000.
Preparation and meeting time outside normal school hours	Teacher reported: hours per week. Teachers reporting 30 or more hours top-coded at 30 (less than 1 percent of teachers); question text in 1994: "During your most recent full week, how many hours did you spend AFTER school, BEFORE school, and ON THE WEEKEND on each of the following types of activities? Other school-related activities (for example, preparation, grading papers, parent conferences, attending meetings)?" The question text differs only slightly (and nonsubstantively) in 2000.
Professional Development	
"Content" professional development	Teacher reported. Nine or more hours spent in "content" professional development over past year (1 = 9 or more hours; 0 otherwise). Question text in 1994: "Since the end of the last school year, have you participated in any in-service or professional development programs which focused on the following topics? In-depth study in your subject field." Question text in 2000: "In the past 12 months, have you participated in any professional development activities that focused on in-depth study of the content in your MAIN teaching assignment field?" Note that categories for reporting hours other than 8 hours or less differ across years so we cannot measure hours in other categories.
"Methods" professional development	Teacher reported. Nine or more hours spent in "methods of teaching" professional development over past year (1 = 9 or more hours; 0 otherwise). Question text in 1994: "Since the end of the last school year, have you participated in any in-service or professional development programs which focused on the following topics? Methods of teaching your subject field." Question text in 2000: "In the past 12 months, have you participated in any professional development activities that focused on methods of teaching?" See caveats above.
"Assessment" professional development	Teacher reported: nine or more hours spent in professional development on "assessment" over past year (1 = 9 or more hours; 0 otherwise); question text in 1994: "Since the end of the last school year, have you participated in any in-service or professional development programs which focused on the following topics? Student assessment (for example, methods of

continued on next page

Table 3A-2. *Description of Teacher Outcomes—Continued*

Variable	Description
Professional Development (continued)	
"Assessment" professional development (continued)	testing, evaluation, performance assessment). Question text in 2000: "In the past 12 months, have you participated in any professional development activities that focused on student assessment, such as methods of testing, evaluation, performance assessment, etc.?" See caveats above.
Class Size	
Class size	Teacher reported: total number of students enrolled in their class in the last full week of school for teachers teaching self-contained classes. Average number of students enrolled in one class period in the last full week of school for teachers teaching departmentalized classes. Restricted to teachers teaching self-contained or departmentalized classes. Teachers reporting classes with 65 or more students, or with fewer than 5 students, were excluded (less than 1 percent of the sample).
Perceived Instructional Autonomy	
Instructional autonomy	Average of four standardized, teacher-reported items about their perceptions of control over content and teaching methods. Question text for 1994: "At this school, how much control do you feel you have IN YOUR CLASSROOM over each of the following areas of your planning and teaching? Selecting textbooks and other instructional materials; Selecting content, topics, and skills to be taught; Selecting teaching techniques?" "At this school, how much actual influence do you think teachers have over school policy in each of the following areas? Establishing curriculum." The question text differs only slightly (and nonsubstantively) in 2000. However, the response set differs across years, with the 1994 SASS providing a scale from 0–5 and the 2000 SASS providing a scale from 1–5. Thus we standardized the items and created the standardized index within years before pooling the data across years. (Alpha = 0.746)
Teacher Stability	
Teacher is new to current school	Teacher reported: whether taught at same school last year; 1 if teacher is new to the school; 0 otherwise.
Time Allocated to Subjects	
Percentage of time on reading	Teacher reported: number of hours divided by the total number of hours for reading, math, history, and science combined. Restricted to teachers teaching self-contained classes. Teachers reporting fewer than 5 hours on all subjects or more than 40 hours on all subjects are excluded (approximately 1 percent of sample). Teachers who report teaching only one subject are excluded (N = 18). Question text in 1994 and 2000: "During your most recent FULL WEEK of teaching, approximately how many hours did you spend teaching each of these subjects at THIS school? English/Reading/Language arts"

continued on next page

Table 3A-2. *Description of Teacher Outcomes—Continued*

Variable	Description
Time Allocated to Subjects (continued)	
Percentage of time on math	Teacher reported: number of hours divided by the total number of hours for reading, math, history, and science combined. Restricted to teachers teaching self-contained classes. Teachers reporting fewer than 5 hours on all subjects or more than 40 hours on all subjects excluded (approximately 1 percent of sample). Teachers who report teaching only one subject are excluded (N = 18). Question text in 1994 and 2000: "During your most recent FULL WEEK of teaching, approximately how many hours did you spend teaching each of these subjects at THIS school? Arithmetic/Mathematics"
Percentage of time on history	Teacher reported: number of hours divided by the total number of hours for reading, math, history, and science combined. Restricted to teachers teaching self-contained classes. Teachers reporting fewer than 5 hours on all subjects or more than 40 hours on all subjects excluded (approximately 1 percent of sample). Teachers who report teaching only one subject are excluded (N = 18). Question text in 1994 and 2000: "During your most recent FULL WEEK of teaching, approximately how many hours did you spend teaching each of these subjects at THIS school? Social studies/History"
Percentage of time on science	Teacher reported. Number of hours divided by the total number of hours for reading, math, history, and science combined. Restricted to teachers teaching self-contained classes. Teachers reporting fewer than 5 hours on all subjects or more than 40 hours on all subjects excluded (approximately 1 percent of sample). Teachers who report teaching only one subject are excluded (N = 18). Question text in 1994 and 2000: "During your most recent FULL WEEK of teaching, approximately how many hours did you spend teaching each of these subjects at THIS school? Science"

Source: Schools and Staffing Survey (NCES 1998, 2003).

Table 3A-3. *Descriptive Statistics for Teacher Sample*[a]

	Mean	SD	N
Dependent Variables			
Time with students	1.54	2.96	16,517
Preparation and meeting time	10.01	6.36	16,517
Content professional development	0.38	0.49	16,517
Methods professional development	0.41	0.49	16,517
Assessment professional development	0.33	0.47	16,517
Class size	22.79	4.86	13,925
Instructional autonomy	0.00	1.00	16,517
New to current school	0.11	0.31	16,517
Years of experience	15.18	9.81	16,517
College quality	938.06	97.30	15,294
Credentialed	0.93	0.26	16,517
Education (MA or above)	0.43	0.50	16,517
Percentage of time on reading	48.12	11.47	11,051
Percentage of time on math	24.93	7.02	11,051
Percentage of time on history	13.98	7.12	11,051
Percentage of time on science	12.98	7.33	11,051
Teacher, School, and District Controls			
Male	0.11	0.31	16,517
Age	43.27	10.29	16,517
American Indian	0.01	0.09	16,517
Asian American	0.02	0.13	16,517
African American	0.08	0.27	16,517
Latino	0.05	0.21	16,517
Teach in grade 1	0.17	0.38	16,517
Teach in grade 2	0.16	0.37	16,517
Teach in grade 3	0.18	0.38	16,517
Teach in grade 4	0.15	0.36	16,517
Teach in grade 6	0.16	0.36	16,517
Elementary school	0.93	0.26	16,517
Urban	0.27	0.45	16,517
Rural	0.31	0.46	16,517
ln of school size	6.21	0.50	16,517
Percentage eligible for subsidized meals	43.46	29.47	15,959
Percentage minority	33.90	32.75	16,517
Charter	0.00	0.06	16,517
Magnet	0.06	0.24	16,517
ln of district size	9.08	1.74	14,443
Percentage in district eligible for subsidized meals	40.19	25.87	14,249
Percentage minority in district	33.22	29.80	14,443
1999–2000 school year	0.54	0.50	16,517

Source: Authors' calculations based on the Schools and Staffing Survey (NCES 1998, 2003).

a. All descriptive statistics are weighted with the teacher weight. Sample is limited to full-time teachers in first through sixth grades who teach academic (or general elementary) subjects and who work in regular or "special program" emphasis schools. Note that in addition to the variables shown above, statistical models also include quadratics for percentage subsidized meals and percentage minority, as well as a missing data indicator for the school-level subsidized meal variable, district-level subsidized meal variable, percentage minority in district, and district size. Most statistical models also include state fixed effects. Note that statistical models for the teacher quality outcomes do not include age or a quadratic in age. See text for more details.

References

American Association of Colleges for Teacher Education. 1993. *Teacher Education Policy in the States: A 50-State Survey of Legislative and Administrative Actions.* Washington.

Angrist, Joshua D., and Victor Lavy. 2001. "Does Teacher Training Affect Pupil Learning? Evidence from Matched Comparisons in Jerusalem Public Schools." *Journal of Labor Economics* 19, no. 2: 343–69.

Bertrand, Marianne, Esther Duflo, and Sendhil Mullainathan. 2004. "How Much Should We Trust Differences-in-Differences Estimates?" *Quarterly Journal of Economics* 119, no.1: 249–75.

Boyd, Donald, and others. Forthcoming. "The Impact of Assessment and Accountability on Teacher Recruitment and Retention: Are There Unintended Consequences?" *Journal of Public Finance.*

Bureau of Labor Statistics. Current Population Survey. October 1993–October 2000. "Civilian Labor Force and Unemployment by State, Seasonally Adjusted." Washington: Department of Labor (www.bls.gov/schedule/archives/laus_nr.htm [January 15, 2002]).

Carnoy, Martin, and Susanna Loeb. 2002. "Does External Accountability Affect Student Outcomes? A Cross-State Analysis." *Educational Evaluation and Policy Analysis* 24, no. 4: 305–31.

Chenfeld, Mimi Brodsky. 2006. "Handcuff Me, Too!" *Phi Delta Kappan* 87, no. 10 (June): 745–47.

Chin, Tiffani. August 2002. "The Accountable Classroom: How Assessment and Evaluation Influence Everyday Classroom Practices." Paper presented at the annual meeting of the American Sociological Association. Chicago, Illinois.

Clotfelter, Charles, and others. 2004. "Do School Accountability Systems Make It More Difficult to Attract and Retain High Quality Teachers?" *Journal of Policy Analysis and Management* 23, no. 2: 251–71.

Clotfelter, Charles T., Helen F. Ladd, and Jacob Vigdor. 2006. "Teacher-Student Matching and the Assessment of Teacher Effectiveness." *Journal of Human Resources* 41, no. 4: 778–820.

Cohen, David K., and Heather C. Hill. 2000. "Instructional Policy and Classroom Performance: The Mathematics Reform in California." *Teachers College Record* 102, no. 2: 294–343.

Council of Chief State School Officers. 1995. *State Student Assessment Programs Database, June 1995.* Washington: CCSSO, North Central Regional Education Laboratory.

———. 1996. *State Student Assessment Programs Database, May 1996.* Washington: CCSSO, North Central Regional Education Laboratory.

———. 1997. *Annual Survey of State Student Assessment Programs, Fall 1996.* Washington.

———. 1998. *Annual Survey of State Student Assessment Programs, Fall 1997.* Washington.

———. 1999. *Data from the Annual Survey of State Student Assessment Programs, Fall 1999.* Washington.

———. 2001a. *State Student Assessment Programs Annual Survey, Fall 2001.* Washington.

———. 2001b. *State Student Assessment Programs Annual Survey, Spring 2001.* Washington.

Cullen, Julie Berry, and Randall Reback. 2002. "Tinkering toward Accolades: School Gaming under a Performance Based Accountability System." Working Paper. Ann Arbor: University of Michigan, Department of Economics.

Deere, Donald, and Wayne Strayer. 2001. "Putting Schools to the Test: School Accountability, Incentives, and Behavior." Working Paper 113. College Station: Texas A&M University, Private Enterprise Research Center.

Education Week. 1999. *Quality Counts 1999:* "Rewarding Results, Punishing Failure," vol. 18, no. 17 (http://www.edweek.org/rc/articles/2004/10/15/qc-archive.html).

Education Week. 2000. *Quality Counts 2000:* "Who Should Teach?" vol. 19, no. 18.

Ehrenberg, Ronald G., and Dominic J. Brewer. 1995. "Did Teachers' Race and Verbal Ability Matter in the 1960's? Coleman Revisited." *Economics of Education Review* 14, no. 1: 1–21.

Ehrenberg, Ronald G., and others. 2001. "Class Size and Student Achievement." *Scientific American* 285, no. 5 (November 1): 78–85.

Ferguson, Ronald F. 1998. "Can Schools Narrow the Black-White Test Score Gap?" In *Black-White Test Score Gap*, edited by Christopher Jencks and Meredith Phillips, pp. 318–74. Brookings.

Ferguson, Ronald F., and Helen F. Ladd. 1996. "How and Why Money Matters: An Analysis of Alabama Schools." In *Holding Schools Accountable*, edited by Helen Ladd, pp. 265–98. Brookings.

Figlio, David N., and Lawrence S. Getzler. 2002. "Accountability, Ability, and Disability: Gaming the System?" Working Paper 9307. Cambridge, Mass.: National Bureau of Economic Research.

Fletcher, Stephen H., and Margaret E. Raymond. 2002. "The Future of California's Academic Performance Index." Stanford University, CREDO, Hoover Institution (April).

Gallagher, Chris W. January 2004. "Turning the Accountability Tables: Ten Progressive Lessons from One 'Backward' State." *Phi Delta Kappan* 85, no. 5: 352–60.

Goertz, Margaret E., and Mark C. Duffy. 2001. "Assessment and Accountability Systems in 50 States: 1999–2000." CPRE Research Report RR-046. Philadelphia, Pa.: Consortium for Policy Research in Education.

Greenwald, Rob, Larry Hedges, and Richard Laine. 1996. "The Effect of School Resources on Student Achievement." *Review of Educational Research* 66, no. 3: 361–96.

Hamilton, Laura S., Brian M. Stecher, and Stephen P. Klein. 2002. *Making Sense of Test-Based Accountability in Education.* Santa Monica, Calif.: RAND Corporation.

Hanushek, Eric A., John F. Kain, and Steven G. Rivkin. 1998. "Teachers, Schools, and Academic Achievement." Working Paper 6691. Cambridge, Mass.: National Bureau of Economic Research.

Hanushek, Eric, and Margaret Raymond. 2005. "Does School Accountability Lead to Improved Student Performance?" *Journal of Policy Analysis and Management* 24, no. 2: 297–327.

Jacob, Brian. 2005. "Accountability, Incentives and Behavior: The Impact of High Stakes Testing in the Chicago Public Schools." *Journal of Public Economics* 89, nos. 5-6: 761–96.

Jacob, Brian A., and Lars Lefgren. 2002. "The Impact of Teacher Training on Student Achievement: Quasi-Experimental Evidence from School Reform Efforts in Chicago." Working Paper 8916. Cambridge, Mass.: National Bureau of Economic Research.

Juel, Connie. 1988. "Learning to Read and Write: A Longitudinal Study of Fifty-Four Children from First through Fourth Grade." *Journal of Educational Psychology* 80, no. 4: 437–47.

Kennedy, Mary. 1999. "Form and Substance in Mathematics and Science Professional Development." *National Institute for Science Education Brief* 3, no. 2. Arlington, Va.: National Science Foundation.

Koretz, Daniel M. 2002. "Limitations in the Use of Achievement Tests as Measures of Educators' Productivity." *Journal of Human Resources* 37, no. 4: 752–77.

Lankford, Hamilton, Susanna Loeb, and James Wyckoff. 2002. "Teacher Sorting and the Plight of Urban Schools: A Descriptive Analysis." *Educational Evaluation and Policy Analysis* 24, no. 1: 37–62.

Lee, Jaekyung, and Kenneth Wong. 2004. "The Impact of Accountability on Racial and Socioeconomic Equity: Considering Both School Resources and Achievement Outcomes." *American Educational Research Journal* 41, no. 4: 797–832.

Linn, R. L. 2000. "Assessments and Accountability." *Educational Researcher* 23, no. 9: 4–14.

Loeb, Susanna, and Felicia Estrada. 2005. "Have Assessment-Based School Accountability Reforms Affected the Career Decisions of Teachers?" In *Measurement and Research in the Accountability Era*, edited by Carol Anne Dwyer, pp. 225–55. Mahwah, N.J.: Lawrence Erlbaum.

Marshak, David. November 2003. "No Child Left Behind: A Foolish Race into the Past." *Phi Delta Kappan* 85, no. 3: 229–31.

McNeil, Linda M. 2000. *Contradictions of School Reform: Educational Costs of Standardized Testing*. New York: Routledge.

National Association of State Directors of Teacher Education and Certification. 1999. *The NASDTEC Manual on the Preparation and Certification of Educational Personnel*. Dubuque, Iowa: Kendall/Hunt Publishing.

[NCES] National Center for Education Statistics. 2003. *Digest of Education Statistics, 2002*, by Thomas D. Snyder and Charlene M. Hoffman. NCES 2003–060. Washington: U.S. Department of Education, Institute of Education Sciences.

———. 1998. *Schools and Staffing Survey (SASS) and Teacher Follow Up Survey (TFS): Electronic Codebook and Restricted Use Data for Three Cycles of SASS and TFS*. NCES 98-235. Washington: U.S. Department of Education, Office of Educational Research and Improvement (March). CD-ROM.

———. 2003. *1999-2000 Schools and Staffing Survey (SASS): Restricted Use Data with Electronic Codebook*, rev. May. NCES 2002-315. Washington: U.S. Department of Education, Institute for Education Sciences. CD-ROM.

———. 2005a. *The Nation's Report Card: Mathematics 2005*, by Marianne Perie, Wendy S. Grigg, and Gloria S. Dion. NCES 2006–453. Washington: U.S. Department of Education, Institute for Education Sciences.

———. 2005b. *The Nation's Report Card: Reading 2005*, by Marianne Perie, Wendy S. Grigg, and Patricia L. Donahue. NCES 2006–451. Washington: U.S. Department of Education, Institute for Education Sciences.

Pate-Bane, Helen. 2004. "Reduce Class Size Now: State of the States." (www.reduceclasssizenow.org/state_of_the_states.htm [January 25, 2006]).

Phillips, Meredith, and Tiffani Chin. 2004. "School Inequality: What Do We Know?" In *Social Inequality*, edited by Kathryn Neckerman, pp. 467–519. New York: Russell Sage Foundation.

Phillips, Meredith, and Jennifer Flashman. 2007. "The Impact of Statewide Assessment and Accountability Policies on Instructional Quality in Poor and Non-poor Elementary

Schools." Working Paper CCPR-017-07, University of California–Los Angeles, California Center for Population Research.

Schiller, Kathryn, and Chandra Muller. 2003. "Raising the Bar and Equity? Effects of High School Graduation Requirements and Accountability Policies on Students' Mathematics Course Taking." *Educational Evaluation and Policy Analysis* 25, no. 3: 299–318.

Tyack, David, and Larry Cuban. 1995. *Tinkering toward Utopia: A Century of Public School Reform.* Harvard University Press.

U.S. Department of Agriculture, Food and Nutrition Services. 2002. "Child Nutrition Programs: Income Eligibility Guidelines." *Federal Register* 67: 8933–934.

Wilms, Wellford W. 2003. "Altering the Structure and Culture of American Public Schools." *Phi Delta Kappan* 84, no. 8 (April): 606–15.

4

Has NCLB Improved Teacher and Teaching Quality for Disadvantaged Students?

LAURA M. DESIMONE
THOMAS M. SMITH
DAVID FRISVOLD

Has NCLB improved teacher and teaching quality for disadvantaged students? The central impetus for the No Child Left Behind Act (NCLB) of 2001 was that many children were being "left behind" in our education system. Our analyses focus on how students from low-income families might be left behind in terms of teacher and teaching quality. How large were the teacher quality gaps between advantaged students (students who do not qualify for free or reduced priced lunch) and disadvantaged students (students who qualify for free or reduced price lunch) at the onset of NCLB? Has teacher quality for disadvantaged students improved? Can any improvements that have occurred be associated with NCLB-related policy changes?

To answer these questions, we estimate the relation between state-level implementation of recent standards-based reforms and subsequent improvements in teacher quality, as measured by several key indicators. Given the limits of available data, any conclusions we make must necessarily fall short of direct attribution of the federal NCLB legislation to changes in teacher and teaching quality experienced by disadvantaged students. However, we are

This research was supported by grants from the National Science Foundation's Research on Learning and Education (ROLE) (REC 0231884) and from the U.S. Department of Education's NAEP grant program (R902B040018-04). Opinions reflect those of the authors and do not necessarily reflect those of the granting agencies.

ʲvantaged students in states where
ds-based reforms, consistent with

ʲed students tended to rate higher on
ʲs of disadvantaged students, though
ʲvantaged students encountered better
ʲɪ in high-poverty schools (low-poverty
ɪents who qualify for free or reduced price
ʲ5 to 100 percent of students who qualify
ʲ), but disadvantaged students in affluent
scɪɪ   ɪ did advantaged students in poor schools.
There was ɪɪ   ɪge in overall teacher quality from 2000 to
2003, nor was there ɪɪ   ɔvement in mitigating gaps in teacher quality
between advantaged and disadvantaged students.

We found only occasional small improvements, and in some states a worsening, in the gap in teacher quality in states that were implementing standards-based reforms consistent with NCLB mandates. However, implementation of standards and assessments that are aligned with each other
(consistency), the number of sanctions a state can impose (power), and the
provision of professional development resources (authority) were associated
with better teacher quality for low-income students, but these did not eliminate the relation between poverty and teacher quality. We found that an
increase in power mitigated the negative relation between poverty and
teacher quality, while whether the state has clear and specific standards in
middle school mathematics (specificity) was associated with the worsening of
the relation between poverty and teacher quality.

State Implementation of NCLB

Our analyses tracked changes in teacher characteristics between 2000 and
2003. Although NCLB was passed in 2001, states were not required to complete full implementation until 2005–06. In working toward the deadline, it
was necessary for states to put many components of the law in place in 2003.
However, acting on their own accord, states had enacted many components of
the law since the early 1990s, as part of the standards-based reform movement.[1] In our analyses we examined the narrow window between 2000 and
2003 during which by most accounts implementation activity was quite high.[2]

1. Fuhrman (2001).
2. *Education Week* (2001, 2002, 2003).

Teacher and Teaching Characteristics

The No Child Left Behind Act calls for a highly qualified teacher in every classroom. According to the legislation, *highly qualified* is defined as full certification or licensure, a college degree, and demonstrated content knowledge in the subject that the teacher is teaching. The bar is set high in absolute terms, with the goal of 100 percent of teachers being highly qualified. NCLB includes provisions stating that all teachers in core academic areas must be highly qualified by the end of the 2005–06 school year. It also requires that newly hired teachers in Title I programs or schools be highly qualified immediately.[3]

Further, NCLB requires that states include in their compliance plans a section specifying what steps they will take to ensure that poor and minority children "are not taught at higher rates than other children by inexperienced, unqualified, or out-of-field teachers."[4] This provision reflects research that has shown that students from low-income homes are more likely to be taught by inexperienced teachers who are not certified and do not have a degree in the content area in which they are teaching.[5] Research also suggests that low-income students are more likely to have teachers who rely predominantly on basic and procedural instruction rather than on conceptual and higher-order instruction.[6]

This recent work is reflective of the opportunity-to-learn literature, which for decades has chronicled inequities in the quality of schooling experienced by low-income and minority students.[7] Carroll's (1963) original conception of opportunity to learn has been operationalized as the amount and quality of exposure to new knowledge, which includes the quality of teachers and their instruction.[8]

While there is no definitive consensus in the research on the extent to which teacher qualifications and teaching techniques affect student achievement, a substantial amount of research suggests that teachers with more than a few years of experience and those with strong content knowledge (for example, as reflected by a degree in the content area they are teaching) are more likely to foster gains in student achievement than are their less experi-

3. U.S. Department of Education (2003).

4. No Child Left Behind Act of 2001, sec. 1111, State Plans (www.ed.gov/policy/elsec/leg/esea02/index.html).

5. Ingersoll (2002); Goldhaber and Brewer (2000).

6. Barr and Dreeben (1983); Desimone and others (2005b); Gamoran (1986).

7. Gamoran and Mare (1989); Oakes (1985).

8. Conception of opportunity to learn operationalized: Carroll (1963); Hallinan (1987); Porter (1995); quality of teachers and their instruction: Stevens (1993).

enced, less qualified peers.[9] Similarly, use of conceptual teaching strategies in mathematics has been associated with gains in student achievement.[10] Certification status has mixed results in terms of its associations with good outcomes for students, and certification requirements vary substantially by state, so much so that some scholars believe certification is not a useful metric.[11] However, given that certification is one of the most explicit targets of teacher quality in NCLB, we include it as a key measure of teacher quality.

The reason for focusing on *teaching* quality is based on the belief that better instruction leads to improved student achievement; the focus on *teacher* quality is based on the belief that certain characteristics of teacher background are related to better teaching. In fact, one of the key underlying rationales for the NCLB provisions on teacher quality is that improving teaching quality will address the considerably wide variation in gains in student achievement that currently exists between classrooms. The emphasis on this rationale is reflected in the NCLB's *A Toolkit for Teachers*, which states:

> Recent studies offer compelling evidence that teacher quality is one of the most critical components of how well students achieve. For instance, studies in both Tennessee and Texas found that students who had effective teachers greatly outperformed those who had ineffective teachers. In the Tennessee study, students with highly effective teachers for three years in a row scored 50 percentage points higher on a test of math skills than those whose teachers were ineffective.[12]

Drawing on teacher quality research and its corollaries in the NCLB legislation, we focused our inquiry on conceptual and procedural teaching and on several teacher quality indicators: specifically certification, whether the teacher is inexperienced (less than two years of teaching experience), self-reported preparedness to teach mathematics topics, and whether the teacher has an undergraduate or graduate degree in mathematics. We focused on a single subject (mathematics) in a single grade (eighth) to allow us greater

---

9. Ballou (1996); Darling-Hammond (2000); Ferguson and Ladd (1996); Monk and King (1994); Murnane and Phillips (1981).

10. Carpenter and others (1989); Hiebert and others (1996).

11. Certification status association with good outcomes for students: Darling-Hammond, Berry, and Thorenson (2001); Goldhaber and Brewer (2000); certification not a useful metric: Ballou (1996).

12. U.S. Department of Education (2004), p.11; Tennessee study cited in extract: Sanders and Rivers (1996).

control over the potentially confounding effects of grade level and subject field. Further, a focus on mathematics is justified given that U.S. middle school students are achieving at alarmingly low levels in math and that teacher quality is a major contributor to the problem.[13]

Conceptual Framework: NCLB and State Policy

To characterize state implementation of NCLB, we grounded our study in a theory for analyzing the effectiveness of policy. The theory, developed by Andrew Porter and others and applied in several policy studies, posits five attributes that contribute to successful implementation of a policy:

—*Consistency*, the extent to which all components of the system are aligned with each other

—*Specificity*, the extent to which states provide clear and detailed guidance as to what teachers and students are to do

—*Authority*, the degree to which a policy has the support of relevant individuals or institutions

—*Power*, the rewards and sanctions attached to a policy

—*Stability*, the extent to which policies and practices remain in place over time.[14]

The policy attributes theory is a simple yet powerful framework for identifying and analyzing the policies that states have used to implement NCLB mandates. Ideally the relationship between changes in teacher quality and the policy environment would be studied by analyzing specific policies focused on teacher quality and the attributes of the larger policy system. However, comprehensive, longitudinal state-level data are not available on specific aspects of teacher quality policies. Thus we focus our policy measures on attributes of the larger policy system. The policy attributes framework suggests that the quality of attributes of the wider policy environment will affect the success of policy implementation in multiple areas, such as teacher quality. We relied on these hypothesized links between attributes of the policy environment and teacher quality outcomes to guide our study.

---

13. Low levels of math achievement: Porter (2005); Schmidt and others (2001); U.S. Department of Education (2003); teacher quality major contributor: Schmidt, McKnight, and Raizen (1997).

14. Porter (1994); Porter and others (1993); Porter and others (1988); Schwille and others (1988); Berends and others (2002); Clune (1998); Desimone and others (2005a); Desimone (2002).

Research Questions

We seek to shed light on two central questions related to understanding how NCLB policies may be affecting the quality of teachers and teaching for disadvantaged students in the United States:

—*What were the gaps in teacher and teaching quality between students in poverty and their more advantaged peers in 2000, and to what extent did those gaps narrow by 2003?*

—*Are improvements in teacher quality and the narrowing of gaps in teacher quality associated with state implementation of NCLB?*

Data and Measures

We use three sources of data for this study. The first is a database of state policies related to NCLB implementation. The other two sources are from the National Assessment of Educational Progress (NAEP), the national and state-by-state samples. Specifically, we use the national 2000 NAEP and the 2000 and 2003 state NAEP. Below we briefly describe each of these datasets.

State Policy Database

To develop state-level measures of the policy attributes described in our theoretical framework, we constructed our state policy database from existing national data sources employed by *Education Week*'s *Quality Counts* report, the American Federation of Teachers' report on states, the *Key State Policies* report published by the Council of Chief State School Officers, and the Thomas B. Fordham Foundation.[15]

We characterize the state NCLB policy system by its consistency, specificity, authority, and power.[16] In this analysis we do not measure *stability*, the degree to which policies remain in place over time, because the data available on the change in the content of standards and assessments are available for only a limited number of states.[17]

To address consistency, we focused on the characteristics of a state's standards-based reform environment that are consistent with policies called for in the NCLB legislation. Our consistency measure indicated whether the state

---

15. *Education Week* (2001, 2002, 2003, 2004); American Federation of Teachers (2001); Blank and Langesen (2001); Finn and Petrilli (2002).

16. The variables for the policy attributes in this analysis were based on indicators in the *Education Week*'s *Quality Counts* reports (*Education Week* 2001, 2002, 2003, 2004).

17. Blank and Langesen (2001).

used criterion-referenced assessments in middle school mathematics that had undergone an external alignment review in 2000 and in 2003. We measured specificity with an indicator of whether the state had clear and specific standards in middle school mathematics.

We had two authority measures. One was an indicator of whether the state provided assistance to low-performing schools; the second was a measure of whether the state provided resources for professional development. We categorize these two measures as authority, given that one way authority is realized is through the backing and support of institutions.[18] We consider the provision of assistance and resources to be mechanisms of institutional authority.

Finally, we measured power with two measures. Our first measure was an indicator of whether or not the state assigned ratings to all schools or identified low-performing schools. Because power in our framework is the rewards and sanctions associated with implementation of a policy, we consider the public identification of a school as successful or not successful as operating as a reward or sanction for the school and its teachers and students. Our second power measure was an additive composite representing six different sanctions that a state can legally impose on failing schools: closure, reconstitution, student transfers, withholding funding, conversion of the school into charters, and turning the school over to private management. Descriptive statistics for each of these measures is in the appendix, table 4A-1.

National Assessment of Educational Progress

We use the national and state student and teacher surveys and student mathematics assessment data from the National Assessment of Educational Progress (NAEP). The NAEP has a sample of fourth and eighth grades from the state and national levels, from which for the current analyses we use the eighth grade national sample.[19] The NAEP 2000 is based on a stratified national probability sample of approximately 16,000 eighth graders and their mathematics teachers at 744 schools. NAEP is one of the few nationally representative datasets that surveys teachers about their educational background, self-reported preparedness to teach mathematics topics, participation in professional development, and their use of a wide range of instructional strategies.[20] Although the NAEP sample was not specifically designed to estimate

18. Porter and others (1988).
19. U.S. Department of Education (1999, 2001).
20. Only the 2000 national NAEP asks about self-reported preparedness to teach mathematics topics, participation in professional development, and use of instructional strategies; these questions were dropped from the 2000 and 2003 state sample of NAEP.

the attributes of the teacher population, by using teachers' responses about each of their classes from which a student was sampled, we can examine the relationship between characteristics of the student and teacher and state policy.

Using the 2000 national NAEP, we created three measures of instruction that reflect two main approaches to teaching: conceptual and procedural. We measure *conceptual emphasis* with a series of questions that asked teachers how much they emphasized reasoning, communication, and an appreciation for mathematics. We included a measure of *conceptual strategies* that asked teachers how often students in their class wrote about mathematics and discussed and worked together with other students on solutions. Our measure of *procedural teaching* was composed of a series of questions that asked about how much emphasis the teacher gave to learning mathematics facts and solving routine problems. Table 4A-1 in the appendix lists the questions that make up each composite.

The measures of teacher quality we used were (1) years of experience, whether the teacher had fewer than two years; (2) certification, whether the teacher was fully or partially certified; (3) self-reported preparation to teach specific mathematics topics; and (4) mathematics degree, whether the teacher had a graduate or undergraduate degree in mathematics. Table 4A-1 in the appendix also provides details about how each of these measures was created.

The state-by-state National Assessment of Educational Progress, which began in 1990, is the only nationally administered, continuing state-representative assessment of what U.S. students know and can do in reading and mathematics. From each state participating in NAEP in a particular year, a representative sample of schools and students was selected. On average in 2000, approximately 2,000 students in sixty-five schools were selected per grade, per subject assessed in each state. In 2003, the number of students increased to approximately 3,000 students, on average, in about 100 schools. The selection of schools is random, within categories of schools with similar characteristics. We used the NAEP because it is comparable both across years and across the states that have participated and because it is the most current dataset on teacher qualifications by state. All fifty states participated and met the minimum guidelines for reporting their results in 2003, but in 2000, only thirty-nine states participated.[21]

21. Nonstate jurisdictions also participated in the 2000 state-by-state assessment, such as American Samoa, Guam, the Department of Defense Domestic Dependent Elementary and Secondary Schools (DDESS), the overseas Department of Defense Dependents Schools (DoDDS), and the Virgin Islands. We did not include these in our analyses because they do not necessarily operate under the same education reform environment as do the states.

Analysis

To answer our first research question, *What were the gaps in teacher and teaching quality between students in poverty and their more advantaged peers in 2000, and to what extent did those gaps narrow by 2003?*, we describe key teacher and teaching characteristics at the national and state levels in 2000 and 2003, both overall and by free lunch. For this we use national and state NAEP data. We identified national trends in teacher qualifications and instruction and in which states teacher qualifications increased, decreased, or stayed the same. Specifically, we examined the weighted sample means of teacher characteristics and instruction (that is, procedural or conceptual) to determine whether these attributes were different for teachers of students eligible for free lunches from those of teachers of noneligible students using the 2000 NAEP national sample of eighth graders. Data on instructional style are available only in the 2000 national NAEP; it was not included in the 2000 or 2003 state NAEP surveys.

To answer our second research question, *Are improvements in teacher quality and the narrowing of gaps in teacher quality associated with the implementation of NCLB?*, we sought to first understand whether states that were stronger on the policy attributes had smaller poverty gaps in teacher characteristics in 2000 than did states with weaker policy attributes. Since we do not have a random sample of students in each class from which to estimate class-level poverty, we are limited to examining teacher quality gaps across schools with different proportions of students who were receiving free or reduced price lunch. To examine these cross-sectional relationships between state policies, school-level poverty, teacher characteristics, and teaching style, we estimated a three-level hierarchical linear model on the NAEP 2000 national sample, focusing on teachers nested within schools, located within states. Our dependent variables were inexperienced teacher (that is, having two or fewer years of experience); certification status; level of preparedness to teach different mathematics topics; whether or not the teacher has a degree in mathematics, as well as use of different instructional strategies, including conceptual emphasis, conceptual strategies, and procedural teaching. School-level independent variables included the percentage of students receiving free or reduced-price lunches. State-level policy variables included power, consistency, specificity, authority1, and authority2).[22]

---

22. The equation for this analysis is the following:

(1) $$Q_{ijs} = \gamma_{000} + \gamma_{010}\%FreeLunch_{js} + \gamma_{001}POLICY_s + u_s + r_{js} + \varepsilon_{ijs},$$

We then examined the relationship between state policies and teacher characteristics over time, while controlling for change in state-level poverty.[23] The specific measures of teacher quality that we used were the percentage of teachers with zero to two years of experience; the percentage of teachers with an advanced, regular, or probationary teaching certificate; the percentage of teachers with any form of a teaching certificate (that is, advanced, regular, probationary, temporary, provisional, or emergency); the percentage of teachers with an undergraduate or graduate degree in math; and the percentage of teachers with a degree in math education or a math undergraduate or graduate degree. We estimated this as a state-specific fixed-effects model, so that the relation between state policies and teacher quality was determined from variation over time within states. Therefore, the estimates of β related the changes in state policy from 2000 to 2003 to the changes in the average teacher quality in the state during the same period, while accounting for the changes in percentages of middle school students in the state who were eligible for free lunch. These models allowed us to assess whether teacher quality had improved more in states with a higher implementation of NCLB-related policies between 2000 and 2003. Here we also examined whether the relationship between policies and teacher quality was different in wealthy schools (with 0 to 10 percent of students eligible for free lunch) than in poor schools (75 to 100 percent eligible for free lunch).

Finally, we tested whether the relation between state-level NCLB implementation and teacher quality changed between 2000 and 2003 and whether the implementation of policy between 2000 and 2003 was associated with a reduction in gaps in teacher quality related to student poverty.[24]

---

where Q_{ijs} represents teacher quality for teacher i in school j in state s, $POLICY_s$ represents each of the five state policies in the analysis (power, consistency, specificity, authority1, and authority2), $FreeLunch_{js}$ represents the percentage of students in school j in state s who are eligible for free or reduced-price lunches, u_s is a state-level random effect, r_{js} is a school-level random effect, and ε_{ijs} is a teacher-level random effect.

23. To do this we estimated the following model:

$$(2) \qquad Q_{st} = \alpha + \beta POLICY_{st} + \gamma FRL_{st} + \varphi_s + \varepsilon_{st},$$

where Q_{st} represents average teacher quality in state s at time t ($t = 2000, 2003$), $POLICY_{st}$ represents each of the five state policies in the analysis (power, consistency, specificity, authority1, and authority2), FRL_{st} represents the percentage of middle school students in the state eligible for free lunch, φ_s is a state-specific dummy variable, ε_{st} is a stochastic error term, and α represents the parameters to be estimated.

24. We estimated the following three-level models:

$$(3) \qquad Q_{ijst} = \alpha + \beta POLICY_{st} + \gamma FRL_{jst} + \delta 2003_t + \lambda POLICY^* 2003_{st} + \varphi_s + \eta_{ijst},$$

Table 4A-1 in the appendix provides the descriptive statistics (that is, mean, standard deviation, minimum and maximum values) from our national NAEP analysis; table 4A-2 provides descriptives for our state analysis, and table 4A-3 describes the variables in our teacher-level analysis. In our predictive models we control for whether the school is a regular or magnet school.

Results

What were the gaps in teacher and teaching quality between students in poverty and their more advantaged peers in 2000, and to what extent did those gaps narrow by 2003?

Answering our first research question requires examining differences between teachers of disadvantaged students and teachers of advantaged students in 2000 and in 2003.

National NAEP 2000 and 2003

We used national NAEP data to conduct a comparison of means of teacher and teaching quality characteristics by free lunch status of the school (not shown) in 2000 and 2003, with a follow-up Wald test to determine if mean differences were statistically significant.

We found that advantaged students were significantly more likely (at the 0.05 or less level) than their disadvantaged counterparts to have teachers scoring higher on each of our indicators of teacher quality, in 2000 and 2003.

$$(4) \quad Q_{ijst} = \alpha + \beta POLICY_{st} + \gamma FRL_{jst} + \delta 2003_t + \lambda POLICY^*2003_{st} + \theta FRL^*2003_{jst} + \varphi_s + \eta_{ijst},$$

$$(5) \quad Q_{ijst} = \alpha + \beta POLICY_{st} + \gamma FRL_{jst} + \delta 2003_t + \lambda POLICY^*2003_{st} + \theta FRL^*2003_{jst} + \rho FRL^*2003^*POLICY_{jst} + \varphi_s + \eta_{ijst},$$

where Q_{ijst} represents the characteristics of teacher i in school j in state s at time t, $POLICY_{st}$ represents each of the five state policies in the analysis as specified in equation 4-1, FRL_{jst} now represents the percentage of students eligible for free lunch (in school j in state s at time t), 2003 is a dummy variable = 1 for t = 2003 and 0 for t = 2000, and η_{ijst} is a random error term. In equations (4-2) through (4-4), the estimates of β describe the overall relationship between state policies and teacher characteristics; the estimates of γ describe the overall relationship between the school poverty status and teacher characteristics; the estimates of δ describe the overall change in teacher characteristics between 2000 and 2003; the estimates of λ demonstrate whether the relationship between state policies and teacher characteristics has strengthened or weakened in 2003 with the introduction of different policies associated with NCLB; the estimates of θ assess whether the relationship between school poverty status and teacher characteristics has strengthened or weakened over time; the estimates of ρ demonstrate whether the relationship between state policies and teacher characteristics has strengthened on the basis of school poverty status; and the estimates of φ represent state-level random effects.

Specifically, advantaged students were more likely to have a teacher with a regular teaching certificate (92 percent compared with 88 percent in 2000, 93 percent and 87 percent in 2003) and a BA or a higher degree in mathematics (57 percent compared with 49 percent in 2000, 32 percent and 30 percent in 2003) and were less likely to have an inexperienced teacher (13 percent compared with 16 percent in 2000, 13 percent and 17 percent in 2003).[25]

We also examined whether disadvantaged students in advantaged schools were better off or worse off than advantaged students in disadvantaged schools (mean comparisons not shown). Specifically, we compared students who were not eligible for free lunch (that is, advantaged students) in schools with 75 to 100 percent of students eligible for free lunch with students eligible for free lunch (disadvantaged students) in schools with 0 to 10 percent eligible for free lunch and followed up with a Wald test for significance.

Results showed that disadvantaged students in wealthy schools fared better than their advantaged counterparts in poor schools in 2000 and 2003 (see table 4-1). In both years significantly more disadvantaged students in wealthy schools than advantaged students in poor schools had teachers with certification (94 percent compared with 88 percent in 2000 and 94 percent and 83 percent in 2003) and with a major in mathematics (42 percent compared with 13 percent in 2000 and 23 percent and 19 percent in 2003). And in 2003 advantaged students in poor schools were more likely than were disadvantaged students in wealthy schools to have an inexperienced teacher (19 percent to 13 percent). Thus disadvantaged students do experience a teacher quality benefit when they attend lower-poverty schools.

Continuing to explore the contextual effects of schools on the teacher quality gap, we examined whether being in a high- or low-poverty school had an added benefit for disadvantaged or advantaged students. We found that disadvantaged students were more likely to have a highly qualified teacher if they were in a low-poverty school (see table 4-1). On most indicators of teacher quality in 2000 and 2003, advantaged students fared significantly better when they were in low-poverty schools (0 to 10 percent of students eligible for free lunch) than in high-poverty schools (75 to 100 percent eligible for free lunch). Similarly, disadvantaged students had more qualified teachers in low-poverty schools than in high-poverty schools.

These findings show that disadvantaged students are more likely to have better-qualified teachers if they are in wealthy schools. Significant differences

---

25. These figures combine the percentage of students who had a teacher with a graduate degree and the percentage of students who had a teacher with a BA degree in mathematics.

Table 4-1. *Advantaged and Disadvantaged Students' Teacher Quality in High- and Low-Poverty Schools*[a]
Percent

Teacher quality indicators	Advantaged students[b]		Disadvantaged students[c]	
	Low-poverty schools[d]	High-poverty schools[e]	Low-poverty schools[d]	High-poverty schools[e]
2000				
Certification	95	88	94	84
Graduate major	n.a.	n.a.	21	13
Mathematics major	16	13	42	35
Mathematics education major	n.a.	n.a.	10	13
Inexperienced teacher	n.a.	n.a.	n.a.	n.a.
2003				
Certification	93	83	94	79
Graduate major	n.a.	n.a.	n.a.	n.a.
Mathematics major	28	19	23	20
Mathematics education major	15	11	15	8
Inexperienced teacher	12	19	13	22

Source: Authors' calculations based on NAEP data.
n.a. Not available.
a. Only results significant at the 0.05 level or a higher significance level are shown.
b. Advantaged = No free lunch status.
c. Disadvantaged = Free lunch status.
d. Low-poverty schools = 0 to 10 percent of students are eligible for free lunch.
e. High-poverty schools = 75 to 100 percent of students are eligible for free lunch.

ranged from 15 percent (79 percent of disadvantaged students had a certified teacher in 2003 if they were in a high-poverty school compared with 94 percent of disadvantaged students in low-poverty schools) to only 3 percent (for example, in 2003, 23 percent of disadvantaged students in low-poverty schools had a teacher with a BA in mathematics compared with 20 percent in high-poverty schools).

State by State Data

A second strategy we used to examine gaps in teacher qualification associated with student poverty was to examine changes in state means from 2000 to 2003 for each state, according to eligibility status for free lunch. This enabled us to see how teacher quality has changed for disadvantaged and advantaged students and whether the gaps in teacher quality between advantaged and disadvantaged students have changed. Here it is important to examine the absolute levels of teacher quality as well as the gaps between high- and low-

Table 4-2. *Summary of State-by-State Mean Comparisons
on Teacher Quality Indicators*[a]

Number of states where…	Regular certification	BA degree or higher in mathematics	New teacher
Disadvantaged students were better off in 2003 than in 2000 in this category	7	0	8
Disadvantaged students were worse off in 2003 than in 2000 in this category	7	36	3
There was a teacher quality gap in 2000	15	19	0
Advantaged students were better off than disadvantaged students by greater than 5 percentage points in 2000	3	8	0
Disadvantaged students were better off than advantaged students by greater than 5 percentage points in 2000	0	0	0
There was a teacher quality gap in 2003	16	16	1
Advantaged students were better off than disadvantaged students by greater than 5 percentage points in 2003	5	5	0
The teacher quality gap increased from 2000 to 2003	3	2	2
The increase in the teacher quality gap was 5 percentage points or more	0	0	0
The teacher quality gap decreased from 2000 to 2003	6	10	4
The decrease in the teacher quality gap was 5 percentage points or more	0	4	0

Source: Authors' calculations based on NAEP data.

a. All tests are one-tailed tests. The numbers in the table reflect states with statistically significant differences at the 5 percent level. Only forty states have data in 2000. A teacher quality gap means that advantaged students are better off than disadvantaged students.

poverty students. Findings are presented in table 4-2. Only statistically significant differences are reported.

For the states for which we had data in 2000 and 2003, the teacher quality gap in teacher certification remained the same on average, although in seven states, disadvantaged students became better off in 2003, and in seven states they became worse off (in terms of whether their teachers were certified).[26] So states shifted but the average remained about the same. The

26. Nine states and the District of Columbia did not have NAEP data available in 2000: Alaska, Colorado, Delaware, Florida, New Hampshire, New Jersey, Pennsylvania, South Dakota, and Washington.

inequity in teachers having a BA degree was more pronounced. In thirty-six states disadvantaged students were worse off in 2003 than in 2000, although it was only in five states where they were at more than a 5 percent disadvantage. The teacher quality gap in having a BA in mathematics decreased in 2003 in ten states and increased in only two. Only one state had a teacher quality gap in 2003 in terms of inexperienced teachers.

Are improvements in teacher quality and the narrowing of gaps in teacher quality associated with the implementation of NCLB?

As explained in the analysis section, we used several strategies to answer this second research question. First, we performed a cross-sectional, multi-level analysis to predict the relation between state policy and teacher and teaching indicators in 2000. Second, we modeled change in state policy from 2000 to 2003 and examined whether a change in state policy predicted a gain in teacher quality. Third, we examined whether state policy mitigated the relationship between poverty and teacher quality. The results of each analysis are described below.

Cross-Sectional Findings for National NAEP 2000

Providing assistance to low-performing schools (authority1) dropped out of the analysis because of colinearity. Looking at the direct relations between policy attributes and instruction, only offering resources for professional development (authority2) was associated with instruction—more conceptual emphasis ($\beta = 3.51$, $p = 0.02$, or 35 percent of a standard deviation difference) and procedural teaching ($\beta = 2.37$, $p = 0.05$, or 23 percent of a standard deviation difference). Consistency, specificity, and authority2 were significantly related to measures of teacher quality. Specifically, consistency was associated with an increase in regular certification ($\beta = 0.42$, $p = 0.03$), specificity was marginally related to increased odds of being an inexperienced teacher ($\beta = 2.17$, $p = 0.10$), and authority2 was related to increased self-reported preparedness to teach mathematics ($\beta = 2.20$, $p = 0.05$). Neither of our power measures—ranking low-performing schools or implementing sanctions—was significantly related to teaching or teacher quality.

Our interest here centers on children in poverty, so we included a measure of school poverty, interactions of school poverty, and each of the policy attributes to examine whether the attributes might work differently in high-poverty schools. Examination of results for direct effects shown in table 4-3 indicates that in high-poverty schools, teachers are less likely to use conceptual strategies ($\beta = -0.33$, $p = 0.001$) and have a conceptual emphasis ($\beta = -0.25$, $p = 0.001$), are less likely to be less prepared to teach mathematics ($\beta = -0.28$, $p = 0.001$), and are more likely to be inexperienced (r [odds ratio] =

1.06, $p = 0.01$).[27] Findings in table 4-3 suggest that several of the policy attributes mitigate these negative associations with poverty. In particular, power2 and authority2 are related to several teacher outcomes, and specificity and consistency are marginally related. In high-poverty schools, power2 is associated with marginally more conceptual strategies ($\beta = 0.03$, $p = 0.07$), more self-reported preparedness ($\beta = 0.04$, $p = 0.001$), and the increased likelihood of having a degree in mathematics ($r = 1.01$, $p = 0.001$). Similarly, in high-poverty schools, authority2 is associated with more use of conceptual strategies ($\beta = 0.09$, $p = 0.01$), more conceptual emphasis ($\beta = 0.10$, $p = 0.01$), and marginally more self-reported preparedness ($\beta = 0.05$, $p = 0.07$).

Both consistency (having standards and assessments that are aligned with each other) and specificity (having clear and detailed standards) were marginally related to more conceptual emphasis in high-poverty schools ($\beta = 0.10$, $p = 0.07$ for consistency*free lunch and $\beta = 0.09$, $p = 0.09$ for specificity*free lunch). Specificity interacted with high poverty was marginally significant in predicting more self-reported preparedness ($\beta = 0.09$, $p = 0.08$) and more experienced teachers ($r = 0.96$, $p = 0.08$).

Changes in State Policy Related to Changes in Teacher Quality: 2000 to 2003

There was substantial movement on several policy fronts between 2000 and 2003. During that time period, eleven states adopted measures to assist low-performing schools; nine states started or increased the resources they gave to professional development; and twenty-nine states began ranking schools according to achievement results. Most states had clear and detailed standards as early as 2000, but a handful of states implemented them between 2000 and 2003. Similarly, most states conducted an alignment review in 2000; four states conducted an alignment of their standards and assessments in 2003.

State NAEP

In our second analysis linking policy to teacher quality, we examined how change in state policy (that is, states without the policy in 2000 that adopted it in 2003) was associated with improvements in teacher quality from 2000 to 2003. These results are shown in table 4-4. None of the policy variables except consistency were associated with any changes in our three teacher

---

27. An odds ratio of 1.06 indicates that in high-poverty schools teachers are 6 percent more likely to be inexperienced than are teachers in other schools.

Table 4-3. *Cross-Sectional Relation between State Policies and Teacher and Teaching Quality*[a]

	Conceptual strategies			Conceptual emphasis			Procedural teaching			Self-reported preparedness to teach mathematics topics[b]			Inexperienced teacher[b]			Regular certification[b]			BA degree in mathematics or higher[b]		
	Beta	SE	p value	Beta	SE	p value	Beta	SE	p value	Beta	SE	Decrease in p value	Beta	SE	p value	Beta	SE	p value	Beta	SE	p value
Level 1 (teacher)																					
Intercept	46.21	2.31	0.00	46.29	2.42	0.00	48.65	3.24	0.00	45.59	1.92	0.00	-1.72	0.56	0.01	2.78	0.48	0.00	-0.93	0.40	0.03
Level 2 (school)																					
Free lunch	-0.33	0.08	0.00	-0.25	0.07	0.00	-0.15	0.11	0.17	-0.28	0.06	0.00	1.06	0.02	0.01	0.96	0.03	0.21	1.00	0.03	0.90
*Consistency	0.12	0.11	0.22	0.10	0.05	0.07	0.10	0.13	0.47	0.09	0.07	0.25	0.97	0.03	0.36	0.97	0.02	0.35	1.00	0.02	0.99
*Specificity	0.09	0.07	0.22	0.09	0.05	0.09	-0.005	0.11	0.97	0.09	0.05	0.08	0.96	0.02	0.08	1.04	0.03	0.15	0.97	0.02	0.14
*Authority2	0.09	0.03	0.01	0.10	0.04	0.01	0.05	0.03	0.14	0.05	0.03	0.07	0.99	0.01	0.57	1.00	0.01	0.68	0.98	0.01	0.17
*Power2	0.03	0.02	0.07	-0.01	0.02	0.65	0.03	0.01	0.03	0.04	0.01	0.00	1.00	0.00	0.52	1.00	0.01	0.66	1.01	0.00	0.00
Level 3 (state)																					
Consistency	1.50	1.31	0.26	1.59	1.51	0.30	-1.26	1.73	0.47	1.46	0.89	0.11	0.92	0.29	0.80	0.42	0.38	0.03	1.03	0.33	0.92
Specificity	0.98	1.69	0.56	-1.34	1.72	0.44	-0.45	2.65	0.87	0.60	1.40	0.67	2.17	0.45	0.10	0.81	0.48	0.66	0.91	0.41	0.82
Authority2	1.81	1.25	0.16	3.51	1.38	0.02	2.37	1.16	0.05	2.20	1.10	0.05	0.80	0.31	0.48	2.00	0.51	0.18	1.04	0.23	0.83
Power2	0.23	0.79	0.77	-0.10	0.74	0.90	-0.02	0.64	0.97	0.18	0.77	0.82	0.92	0.22	0.73	0.63	0.39	0.25	1.04	0.15	0.78
Variance components																					
Level 1 variance	62.62			61.23			84.14			59.30			0.58			0.15			0.76		
Level 2 variance	14.19			17.10			12.67			11.34			1.77			27.05			0.99		
df	284			284			284			284			284			284			284		
Chi square	624.07			591.98			492.04			554.02			472.58			-552.32			3,981.37		
p value	0.00			0.00			0.00			0.00			0.00			> 0.5			0.00		
Level 3 variance	8.24			9.84			5.68			4.38			0.52			4.05			0.19		
df	37			37			37			37			37			37			37		
Chi square	126.12			144.98			105.14			82.35			67.41			192.61			73.70		
p value	0.00			0.00			0.00			0.00			0.00			0.00			0.00		

Source: Authors' calculations based on NAEP data.

SE = standard error; df = degrees of freedom.

a. * signifies that there is no level 1 variance because these variables are dichotomous; authority1 and power1 dropped out of the analysis because of colinearity.

b. For dichotomous variables (inexperienced teacher, certification, and BA or higher degree in mathematics), odds ratio are reported.

Table 4-4. *Change in State Policy from 2000 to 2003 Associated with Change in Teacher Quality from 2000 to 2003*

	Inexperienced teacher			Regular certification			Mathematics major or higher		
	Beta	SE	p value	Beta	SE	p value	Beta	SE	p value
Intercept	0.212	0.137	0.132	0.945	0.058	0.00	1.063	0.269	0.00
Consistency	-0.005	0.016	0.757	0.012	0.007	0.083	0.068	0.032	0.040
Specificity	0.049	0.048	0.319	0.009	0.020	0.651	-0.082	0.094	0.389
Authority1	0.044	0.033	0.194	-0.001	0.014	0.933	-0.002	0.644	0.974
Authority2	-0.022	0.017	0.207	-0.007	0.007	0.355	0.027	0.033	0.417
Power1	0.022	0.026	0.414	0.005	0.011	0.647	-0.064	0.051	0.218
Power2	-0.004	0.007	0.519	-0.004	0.003	0.220	-0.016	0.014	0.251
Free lunch	-0.003	0.003	0.405	0.001	0.001	0.525	-0.015	0.006	0.015

Source: Authors' calculations based on NAEP data.

SE = standard error.

quality variables. In states that aligned their standards and assessments (consistency) in 2003 but not in 2000, there was a small increase in the percentage of certified teachers (β = .012, p = 0.08) and teachers with a mathematics major (β = 0.07, p = 0.04).

Does an increase in the percentage of students in poverty predict changes in teacher quality? Since the focus here is on conditions for disadvantaged students, we examined several aspects of how poverty enters into the relation between state policy and teacher quality. First, in the set of models just described, we controlled for free lunch status. A significant coefficient for free lunch would indicate that as the percentage of students in a state who are eligible for free lunch increases (from 2000 to 2003), there was a subsequent increase or decrease in a particular teacher quality variable. As table 4-4 shows, an increase in the percentage of students eligible for free lunch was associated with a small percentage point decrease in the number of teachers with an undergraduate or graduate degree in mathematics (β = –0.015, p = 0.015).

Are the state policy attributes more or less predictive of changes in teacher quality for disadvantaged students? To analyze whether the relationships we found between state policy and teacher quality (reported in table 4-4) were different for advantaged and disadvantaged students, we conducted the analysis on two subsets of our sample—schools in the lowest poverty quartile (advantaged or low-poverty schools) and schools in the highest poverty quartile (disadvantaged or high-poverty schools).

We found that in advantaged schools (results not shown), consistency and power2 were associated with better teacher quality. In states that aligned their standards and assessments in 2003 (consistency), there were increases in the percentages of teachers with certification (β = 0.03, p = 0.09) and with a mathematics degree (β = 0.08, p = 0.03), and an increase in the number of sanctions a state can impose on schools (power2) predicted a 6 percentage point decrease in the percentage of new teachers (β = –0.016, p = 0.07).

In disadvantaged schools (the lowest quartile), changes in policy variables were not as significantly predictive of changes in teacher quality as in advantaged schools, though power2 was marginally significant in predicting changes in teacher degree status. Specifically, an increase in the number of sanctions that the state imposed was associated with a decrease in the percentage of teachers with a BA or higher degree in mathematics (β = –0.038, p = 0.15).

Did the strength of the relationship between poverty and teacher quality change, given changes in state policy? For our final analysis, we examined whether state policy played a role in changing the relation between poverty and teacher quality. Specifically, were disadvantaged students better off (or

Figure 4-1. *The Influence of Power and Poverty on Teacher Certification*

Predicted values of the probability of teacher certification

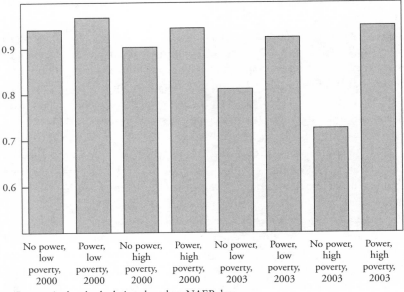

Source: Authors' calculations based on NAEP data.

not as worse off) because of state policy changes? To answer this question, we estimated a set of models that interacted each policy attribute in 2003 with free lunch status (results not shown).

Poor schools were more likely to have teachers without regular certification ($\beta = -0.012$, $p = 0.001$) and without a BA or higher degree in mathematics ($\beta = -0.006$, $p = 0.001$). The policy attributes did not affect the relationship between poverty and inexperienced teachers (which was not significant), but the story is more complicated for degree and major. In states that offered professional development resources in 2003 (authority2), the negative relationship between specificity and having fewer certified teachers increased for children in poverty ($\beta = -0.007$, $p = 0.09$). The act of ranking schools (power1) had the opposite effect. In states that ranked schools, the relationship between power and having more certified teachers increased for disadvantaged students ($\beta = 0.020$, $p = 0.027$). None of the policy variables significantly affected the relationship between poverty and the likelihood of having a teacher with a BA or higher degree in mathematics.

Figures 4-1 and 4-2 illustrate one potentially useful way of interpreting these results. Figure 4-1 shows the relationship of ranking schools (power) and poverty on teacher certification. Note the gap between the second and

Figure 4-2. *The Influence of Specificity and Poverty on Teacher Certification*

Predicted values of the probability of teacher certification

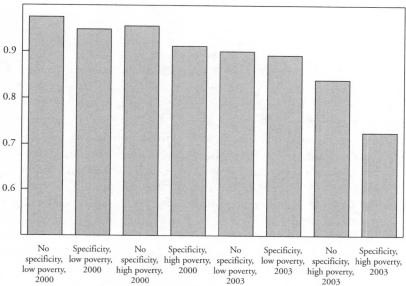

No specificity, low poverty, 2000   Specificity, low poverty, 2000   No specificity, high poverty, 2000   Specificity, high poverty, 2000   No specificity, low poverty, 2003   Specificity, low poverty, 2003   No specificity, high poverty, 2003   Specificity, high poverty, 2003

Source: Authors' calculations based on NAEP data.

fourth bars, "power, low poverty 2000" and "power, high poverty, 2000." Compare this gap with the gap between "power, low poverty, 2003" and "power, high poverty, 2003." As the figure illustrates, the gap between advantaged and disadvantaged students has shifted so that disadvantaged students were more likely to have certified teachers in 2003, if they are in a state with high power, though not by much. If they are in a state with no power, advantaged students are more likely to have a certified teacher (compare "no power, low poverty" with "no power, high poverty"). Also there is a noticeably stark contrast between the percentages of low-income students with certified teachers in states with power (much larger) and without power in 2003. These comparisons suggest that power might play a role in addressing gaps between advantaged and disadvantaged students in term of their teacher's certification.

Figure 4-2 tells a different story. Examining the effects of having clear and detailed standards (specificity) shows that there is no evidence that specificity has helped to close the certification gap; in fact, the gap in states that adopted clear and detailed standards in 2003 has widened (compare the gap between low- and high-poverty states with clear and detailed standards in 2000 with the gap between low- and high-poverty states with clear and detailed standards in 2003). This chart suggests that in states that have adopted clear and detailed standards in 2003 teacher certification has decreased, and this trend is worse for high-poverty schools.

Discussion

Our analyses show that on three key indicators—teacher certification, having a bachelor's degree or higher in mathematics, and teaching experience—disadvantaged students were worse off than advantaged students in 2000, and this did not change much by 2003. But the differences in teacher quality across high- and low-poverty schools were quite small. Thus, in the context of looking at inequalities in opportunities to learning related to teacher quality, the NAEP data suggest that it is more of a problem for all students rather than being a problem for low-income students in particular.

We also saw little change in the gaps in teacher quality from 2000 to 2003 in our state-by-state analysis. The evidence we examined suggests that as of 2003 there have been no great gains in teacher quality overall or in the distribution of teachers so as to lessen the likelihood that disadvantaged students had more less qualified teachers than their advantaged counterparts.

The finding that low-income students had more qualified teachers when they were in wealthy schools than when in poor schools suggests that disadvantaged students do reap some benefits from being in an advantaged school. One of the policy questions this raises is the extent to which the "equitable" distribution of teachers both within and across schools should become more of a focal point of current initiatives on teacher quality. Of course, such a line of thinking raises complex issues of fairness and efficiency that apply to making decisions about who should get the most qualified teachers, given the limited supply. Basing teacher assignment to students on evidence of a teacher's effectiveness with certain groups of students is a potentially useful strategy to consider.[28]

There were several states where the quality of teachers of disadvantaged students decreased on several indicators, which warrants further examination. Since policy initiatives are often a zero-sum game, it is likely that particular policy strategies designed to strengthen one area weaken another. For example, the class size initiative in California, designed to make classes smaller (and thus requires more teachers), could reasonably have the effect of putting less qualified teachers in the classroom. And the chance that the less qualified

28. Gamoran and others (2005).

teachers are distributed nonrandomly to disadvantaged students would be consistent with previously documented local practices.[29]

Are NCLB-related policies associated with improvements in teacher quality? One of the main questions we wish to shed light on is whether state adoption of NCLB-related policies had any effect on the teacher quality gap between disadvantaged and advantaged students. This is a difficult issue to address, given the complex nature of state policy, the simultaneous implementation of multiple policy levers, and the challenge of capturing the effect of change of global state-level policies. Another challenge is that often states implement a particular policy in reaction to a problem (for example, low teacher quality), so associations between policy implementation and teacher quality first reflect this relationship, and only later would cause and effect come into play—but the question of how long it takes a state policy to affect a trend in teacher quality is not clear. Further, in this analysis we examined general NCLB-related policies, not policies directly related to improving teacher quality. In effect we are examining how teacher quality changed, in the context of state movement on NCLB-related policies. Still another factor to consider is how much real change compared with random fluctuation could be expected in teacher quality indicators over a three-year period.

In general we found that for states that are implementing NCLB-related policies if there was any positive movement in teacher quality it was small and that sometimes it was negative. Given the nation's challenges in finding and keeping qualified teachers in the classroom, it is unclear whether the state policy implementation mitigated a decrease in teacher quality that would have been worse or whether state implementation of NCLB-related policies did have a real impact on decreasing teacher quality. In these same estimations, we found that being in a high-poverty school predicted having a teacher with less desirable qualifications. Implementation of certain state policies occasionally was associated with better teacher quality, but implementation did not eliminate this relationship between poverty and teacher quality. Our other findings provide evidence that in states where the percentage of disadvantaged students has increased, teacher quality has decreased. But the relationship between policy attributes and teacher quality for advantaged students is not much different from that of disadvantaged students.

A few findings warrant highlighting because of their similarity to findings from other studies. Specifically, low-income students in states that had aligned standards and assessments (consistency) and provided professional

---

29. Darling-Hammond (2000); Gamoran and others (1995).

development resources (authority) were more likely to have better outcomes on several teacher and teaching quality measures. These findings are consistent with other policy studies that suggest that implementing policies that work through authority may be more likely to foster positive outcomes than those that work mainly through power.[30]

But in our analysis of whether policies changed the strength of the relationship between poverty and teacher quality, we did find that an increase in power mitigated the negative relation between poverty and teacher quality, while specificity was associated with the worsening of the relation between poverty and teacher quality. This set of findings might reflect the complexity of charting changes in state policy, initial associations of state policy with negative conditions where states enact measures to address weaknesses in their system, and the time it takes for policies to have a productive effect, as mentioned earlier. For example, it might be that states especially low on teacher quality were the ones more likely to adopt power policies (which would explain the negative association between power and teacher quality), and the findings might suggest that power does eventually play a positive role, given that over time the implementation of power policies was associated with a decrease in the relation between poverty and low teacher quality. Further, we found that both power2 (number of sanctions a state could impose) and authority2 (offering professional development resources) were related to better teaching and teacher quality in high-poverty schools.

These findings should be considered in light of previous research that has found teacher credentials to have weak links with teaching practice and student achievement, while high-quality professional development has been shown to have strong links. Given the slow movement on improvements in certification and degree requirements (that is, credentials), perhaps the provision of and participation in high-quality professional development should serve as more of a focal point for addressing teacher quality disparities.

Conclusions

NCLB delineated substantial changes in teacher quality that were required to occur on a rapid timetable. We examined the time period from 2000 to 2003 and found no evidence of substantial improvement in teacher quality for disadvantaged (low-income) students. Further, we found that some policies seem to be working in the expected direction, but in no case have the NCLB-

---

30. Desimone (2002); Desimone, Smith, and Phillips (2007).

related policies that states have put into place had a major impact on teacher quality.

Is it difficult for states to meet high-quality teacher requirements, since resources and personnel are being allocated to meet other NCLB requirements? It might be that closing the gap in teacher quality is more difficult in states that are strong in other areas. Given limited resources, school improvement is a zero-sum game. Resources spent on new curricula and tutoring mean that fewer resources are available to devote to teacher quality. This analysis suggests that most states are not on target for making the kind of improvements in teacher quality required by NCLB. Our analysis provides limited evidence that particular state policies may eventually move states in the right direction, but it raises concern that results may not be substantial enough, or fast enough, to satisfy the legislation or our own ideals about equality in teacher quality.

Appendix

Table 4A-1. *National NAEP Sample*

Variable	Mean	SD	Min	Max
Level 1 (teachers)				
Years of experience: 0–2 years	0.17	0.38	0	1
"Counting this year, how many years in total have you taught mathematics?" Recoded as 1 = 2 years or less				
Advanced, regular, or probationary state certificate	0.91	0.29	0	1
"What type of teaching certificate do you have in this state in your main assignment field?" Recoded as 1 = full certification (including advanced professional, regular or standard, probationary)				
Advanced, regular, probationary, temporary, provisional, or emergency state certificate	0.97	0.16	0	1
"What type of teaching certificate do you have in this state in your main assignment field?" Recoded as 1 = full certification (including advanced professional, regular or standard, probationary) or partial certification (including temporary, provisional, or emergency state certificate)				
Conceptual emphasis (standardized)	50.19	9.78	20.25	61.16
"How much emphasis did you or will you give each of the following: (a) developing reasoning and analytical ability to solve unique problems, (b) learning how to communicate ideas in mathematics effectively, and (c) developing an appreciation for the importance of mathematics?" Recoded as 1 = little or no emphasis, 2 = moderate emphasis, 3 = heavy emphasis				

continued on next page

Table 4A-1. *National NAEP Sample—Continued*

Variable	Mean	SD	Min	Max
Level 1 (teachers)—Continued				
Conceptual strategies (standardized)	50.17	9.83	20.41	72.50
"How often do the students in this class do each of the following: (a) write a few sentences about how to solve a mathematics problem, (b) write reports or do mathematics projects, (c) discuss solutions to mathematics problems with other students, (d) work and discuss mathematics problems that reflect real-life situations, (e) solve mathematics problems in small groups or with a partner, and (f) talk to the class about their mathematics work?" Recoded as 1 = never or hardly ever, 2 = once or twice a month, 3 = once or twice a week, 4 = almost every day				
Procedural teaching (standardized)	50.05	9.88	8.60	56.49
"How much emphasis did you or will you give each of the following: (a) learning mathematics facts and concepts and (b) learning skills and procedures needed to solve routine problems?" Recoded as 1 = little or no emphasis, 2 = moderate emphasis, 3 = heavy emphasis				
Teacher preparedness (standardized)	50.76	9.13	–7.93	57.49
"How well prepared are you to teach each of the following topics: (a) number sense, properties, and operations; (b) measurement; (c) geometry and spatial sense; (d) data analysis, statistics, and probability; (e) algebra and functions; (f) estimation; and (g) mathematical problem-solving?" Recoded as 0 = not at all prepared, 1 = not very well prepared, 2 = moderately prepared, 3 = very well prepared				
Math undergraduate or graduate degree	0.40	0.49	0	1
"What were your undergraduate major fields of study?" "What were your graduate major fields of study?" Recoded as 1 = math graduate major or math undergraduate major				
Math undergraduate or graduate degree or any math education degree	0.69	0.46	0	1
"What were your undergraduate major fields of study?" "What were your graduate major fields of study?" Recoded as 1 = math graduate major or math undergraduate major or math education major				
Level 2 (schools)				
Regular school	0.93	0.26	0	1
Magnet school or regular school with a magnet program	0.07	0.26	0	1
Percentage of students eligible for free or reduced-price lunch	43.59	28.52	0	100
"During this school year, about what percentage of students in your school was eligible to receive a free or reduced-price lunch through the National School Lunch Program?" Recoded as a continuous variable using the median values of the categories of response				

continued on next page

Table 4A-1. *National NAEP Sample—Continued*

Variable	Mean	SD	Min	Max
Level 3 (states)				
Consistency = state uses criterion-referenced assessments aligned to state standards in math	0.77	0.43	0	1
Specificity = state has clear and specific standards in math	0.86	0.35	0	1
Authority1 = state provides assistance to low-performing schools	0.60	0.49	0	1
Authority2 = professional development resources	1.28	0.55	0	2
Power1 = state assigns ratings to all schools or identifies low-performing schools	0.60	0.49	0	1
Power2 = number of possible sanctions	0.86	1.08	0	3

Note: Sample size is 895 teachers, 328 schools, and 43 states.

Table 4A-2. *State NAEP (State-Level Fixed Effects) Sample*[a]

Variable	Mean	SD	Min	Max
Percentage of teachers with 0–2 years of experience	0.164	0.038	0.079	0.268
Percentage of teachers with advanced, regular, or probationary state certificate	0.929	0.053	0.747	1
Percentage of teachers with advanced, regular, probationary, temporary, provisional, or emergency state certificate	0.989	0.014	0.915	1
Percentage of teachers with a math undergraduate or graduate degree	0.374	0.139	0.071	0.724
Percentage of teachers with a math undergraduate or graduate degree or any math education degree	0.525	0.156	0.139	0.899
Average schoolwide percentage of students eligible for free lunch	38.744	9.762	17.599	62.091
Consistency = state uses criterion-referenced assessments aligned to state standards in math	0.511	0.503	0	1
Specificity = state has clear and specific standards in math	0.878	0.329	0	1
Authority1 = state provides assistance to low-performing schools	0.667	0.474	0	1
Authority2 = professional development resources	1.078	0.657	0	2
Power1 = state assigns ratings to all schools or identifies low-performing schools	0.822	0.384	0	1
Power2 = number of possible sanctions	1.200	1.537	0	5

Sample size: forty states in 2000 and fifty states in 2003.

a. Variables are defined as in table 4A-1, except that they are aggregated to the state level.

Table 4A-3. *Teacher-Level Interaction Model Sample*[a]

Variable	Observations	Mean	SD	Min	Max
Years of experience: 0–2 years	23,065	0.166	0.372	0	1
Advanced, regular, or probationary state certificate	22,941	0.922	0.268	0	1
Advanced, regular, probationary, temporary, provisional, or emergency state certificate	22,941	0.990	0.100	0	1
Math undergraduate or graduate degree	21,991	0.370	0.483	0	1
Math undergraduate or graduate degree or any math education degree	22,354	0.521	0.500	0	1
Regular school	27,027	0.930	0.256	0	1
Magnet school	27,027	0.070	0.256	0	1
Percentage of students eligible for free or reduced-price lunch	26,506	40.071	26.946	0	100
2003 dummy variable	28,050	2002.028	1.404	2000	2003
Consistency = state uses criterion-referenced assessments aligned to state standards in math	28,050	0.484	0.500	0	1
Specificity = state has clear and specific standards in math	28,050	0.913	0.282	0	1
Authority1 = state provides assistance to low-performing schools	28,050	0.715	0.452	0	1
Authority2 = professional development resources	28,050	1.051	0.627	0	2
Power1 = state assigns ratings to all schools or identifies low-performing schools	28,050	0.883	0.321	0	1

a. Variables are defined similarly to those in table 4A-2.

References

American Federation of Teachers. 2001. *Making Standards Matter 2001: A Fifty-State Report on Efforts to Implement a Standards-Based System.* Washington.

Ballou, Dale. 1996. "Do Public Schools Hire the Best Applicants?" *The Quarterly Journal of Economics* 111, no. 1: 97–133.

Barr, Rebecca, and Robert Dreeben. 1983. *How Schools Work.* University of Chicago Press.

Berends, Mark, and others. 2002. *Challenges of Conflicting School Reforms: Effects of New American Schools in a High-Poverty District.* Santa Monica, Calif.: RAND.

Blank, Rolf, and Doreen Langesen. 2001. *State Indicators of Science and Mathematics Education.* Washington: Council of Chief State School Officers.

Carpenter, Thomas P., and others.1989. "Using Knowledge of Children's Mathematics Thinking in Classroom Teaching: An Experimental Study." *American Educational Research Journal* 26, no. 4: 499–531.

Carroll, John. 1963. "A Model of School Learning." *Teachers College Record* 65, no. 8: 723–33.

Clune, William. 1998. *Toward a Theory of Systemic Reform: The Case of Nine NSF Statewide Systemic Initiatives.* NISE Monograph 16. Madison, Wis.: National Institute for Science Education Research.

Darling-Hammond, Linda. 2000. "Teacher Quality and Student Achievement: A Review of State Policy Evidence." *Education Policy Analysis* Archives 8, no. 1 (http://epaa.asu.edu/epaa/v8n1).

Darling-Hammond, Linda, Barnett Berry, and Amy Thorenson. 2001. "Does Teacher Certification Matter? Evaluating the Evidence." *Educational Evaluation and Policy Analysis* 23, no. 1: 57–77.

Desimone, Laura. 2002. "How Can Comprehensive School Reform Models Be Successfully Implemented?" *Review of Educational Research* 72, no. 3: 433–79.

Desimone, Laura, Thomas M. Smith, and Kristie J. R. Phillips. 2007. "Does Policy Influence Mathematics and Science Teachers' Participation in Professional Development?" *Teachers College Record* 109, no. 5: 1086–122.

Desimone, Laura, and others. 2005a. "Beyond Accountability and Average Math Scores: Relating Multiple State Education Policy Attributes to Changes in Student Achievement in Procedural Knowledge, Conceptual Understanding and Problem Solving in Mathematics." *Educational Measurement: Issues and Practice* 24, no. 4: 5–18.

Desimone, Laura, and others. 2005b. "The Distribution of Teaching Quality in Mathematics: Assessing Barriers to the Reform of United States Mathematics Instruction from an International Perspective." *American Educational Research Journal* 42, no. 3: 501–35.

Education Week. 2001. *Quality Counts 2001*: "A Better Balance," vol. 20, no. 17 (http://www.edweek.org/rc/articles/2004/10/15/qc-archive.html).

———. 2002. *Quality Counts 2002*: "Building Blocks for Success," vol. 21, no. 17.

———. 2003. *Quality Counts 2003*: "If I Can't Learn from You," vol. 22, no. 17.

———. 2004. *Quality Counts 2004*: "Count Me In: Special Education in an Era of Standards," vol. 23, no. 17.

Ferguson, Ronald, and Helen Ladd. 1996. "How and Why Money Matters: An Analysis of Alabama Schools." In *Holding Schools Accountable: Performance-Based Reform in Education*, edited by Helen Ladd, pp. 265–98. Brookings.

Finn, Chester, Jr., and Michael Petrilli. 2002. *The State of State Standards.* Washington: Thomas B. Fordham Foundation.

Fuhrman, Susan, ed. 2001. *From the Capitol to the Classroom: Standards-based Reform in the States.* One Hundredth Yearbook of the National Society for the Study of Education, Part II. University of Chicago Press.

Gamoran, Adam. 1986. "Instructional and Institutional Effects of Ability Groups." *Sociology of Education* 59, no. 4: 185–98.

Gamoran, Adam, and Robert Mare. 1989. "Secondary School Tracking and Educational Inequality: Compensation, Reinforcement or Neutrality?" *American Journal of Sociology* 94, no. 5: 1146–183.

Gamoran, Adam, and others. 1995. "An Organizational Analysis of the Effects of Ability Grouping." *American Educational Research Journal* 32, no. 4: 687–715.

Gamoran, Adam, and others. 2005. *National Center for Research on State and Local Education Policy.* Proposal to IES. Proposal to Institute for Education Sciences. Madison: University of Wisconsin, Wisconsin Center for Education Research.

Goldhaber, Dan, and Dominic Brewer. 2000. "Does Teacher Certification Matter? High School Teacher Certification Status and Student Achievement." *Educational Evaluation and Policy Analysis* 22, no. 2: 129–45.

Hallinan, Maureen. 1987. "Conceptualization of School Organization and Schooling." In *Social Organizations of Schools*, edited by Maureen Hallinan, pp. 125–60. New York: Plenum.

Hiebert, James, and others. 1996. "Problem Solving as a Basis for Reform in Curriculum and Instruction: The Case of Mathematics." *Educational Researcher* 25, no. 4: 12–21.

Ingersoll, Richard. 2002. *Out of Field Teaching, Educational Inequality, and the Organization of Schools: An Exploratory Analysis*. Seattle: University of Washington, Center for Study of Teaching and Policy.

Monk, David, and Jennifer King. 1994. "Multi-Level Teacher Resource Effects on Pupil Performance in Secondary Mathematics and Science: The Role of Teacher Subject Matter Preparation." In *Contemporary Policy Issues: Choices and Consequences in Education*, edited by Ronald Ehrenberg, pp. 29–58. Ithaca, N.Y.: ILR Press.

Murnane, Richard, and Barbara Phillips. 1981. "Learning by Doing, Vintage, and Selection: Three Pieces of the Puzzle Relating Teaching Experience and Teaching Performance." *Economics of Education Review* 1, no. 4: 691–93.

[NCES] National Center for Education Statistics. 1999. *The NAEP 1996 Technical Report*. NCES 1999–452. Washington: U.S. Department of Education, Office of Educational Research and Improvement.

———. 2001. *The Nation's Report Card: Mathematics 2000*, by James S. Braswell and others. NCES 2001–517. Washington: U.S. Department of Education, Office of Educational Research and Improvement.

———. 2003. *The Condition of Education 2003*, by John Wirt and others. NCES IES Publication 2003-067. Washington: U.S. Department of Education, Institute of Education Sciences.

Oakes, Jeannie. 1985. *Keeping Track: How Schools Structure Inequality*. Yale University Press.

Porter, Andrew. 1994. "National Standards and School Improvement in the 1990s: Issues and Promise." *American Journal of Education* 102, no. 4: 421–49.

———. 1995. "The Uses and Misuses of Opportunity-to-Learn Standards." *Educational Researcher* 24, no. 1: 21–27.

———. 2005. "Prospects for School Reform and Closing the Achievement Gap." In *Measurement and Research in the Accountability Era*, edited by Carol Dwyer, pp. 59–95. Mahwah, N.J.: Lawrence Erlbaum Associates.

Porter, Andrew, and others. 1988. "Content Determinants in Elementary School Mathematics." In *Perspectives on Research on Effective Mathematics Teaching*, edited by Douglas Grouws and Thomas Cooney, pp. 96–113. Hillsdale, N.J.: Lawrence Erlbaum Associates. (Also Research Series 179, East Lansing: Michigan State University, Institute for Research on Teaching.)

Porter, Andrew, and others. 1993. *Reform Up Close: An Analysis of High School Mathematics and Science Classrooms*. University of Wisconsin-Madison.

Sanders, William, and June Rivers. 1996. *Cumulative and Residual Effects of Teachers on Future Student Academic Achievement*. Knoxville: University of Tennessee, Value-Added Research and Assessment Center.

Schmidt, William, Curtis McKnight, and Senta Raizen. 1997. "A Splintered Vision: An Investigation of U.S. Science and Mathematics. Executive Summary." East Lansing:

Michigan State University, U.S. National Research Center for the Third International Mathematics and Science Study (http://ustimss.msu.edu/splintrd.pdf).

Schmidt, William, and others. 2001. *Why Schools Matter: A Cross-National Comparison of Curriculum and Learning.* San Francisco: Jossey-Bass.

Schwille, John, and others. 1988. "State Policy and the Control of Curriculum Decisions." *Educational Policy* 2, no. 1: 29–50.

Stevens, Floraline. 1993. "Applying an Opportunity-to-Learn Conceptual Framework to the Investigation of the Effects of Teaching Practices via Secondary Analyses of Multiple-Case Study Summary Data." *Journal of Negro Education* 62, no. 3: 232–48.

U.S. Department of Education. 2004. *No Child Left Behind, A Toolkit for Teachers.* Rev. ed. Washington.

5

Grade Retention in the Age of Standards-Based Reform

ROBERT M. HAUSER
CARL B. FREDERICK
MEGAN ANDREW

Signed into law in January 2002, the No Child Left Behind Act (NCLB) codifies a long-standing shift away from an emphasis on school resources in education policy to an emphasis on standards-based reform. The shift stems in part from a large body of research suggesting that inputs of school resources do not explain student achievement and, also, from sustained concern about the relative quality of education in the United States compared with other developed nations.[1]

Most states began to move toward standards-based reform in the 1990s, well before the passage of NCLB. For example, several years before NCLB was instituted by the Bush administration, President Clinton declared his intention "to end social promotion."[2] This declaration led several state and local education agencies to institute new and, in many cases, test-based criteria for promotion from one elementary school grade to the next.

This research has been supported in part by the Russell Sage Foundation, by the Vilas Estate Trust at the University of Wisconsin–Madison, and by a center grant for population research from the National Institute of Child Health and Human Development to the Center for Demography and Ecology at the University of Wisconsin–Madison.

1. Jencks and others (1972); Hanushek (1986, 1996); U.S. Department of Education (1983).

2. Clinton (1998); Jacques Steinberg, "Clinton Urges Tough Love for Students Who Are Failing." *New York Times*, October 1, 1999, p. 18.

State and federal movement toward standards-based reform and standardized testing is troubling. The past history of large-scale assessment provides many instances in which the availability of tests of educational progress has led to their use in decisions about students, whether or not the tests or their mode of administration are well suited for high-stakes decisions.[3] Because of the conjunction of standards-based reform and the use of test-based decisions about individual students as instruments of reform, we think it is reasonable to investigate whether retention in grade increased in American schools from the late 1990s through the early years of the present decade. If this is the case, there are likely to be very serious, long-term effects on the educational attainment and subsequent life course of students who are held back.[4]

Under past, current, and foreseeable educational regimes, students who are held back typically fail to catch up academically. Because they become overage for grade, they are more likely to drop out and less likely to attend or complete college.[5] Moreover, it is well established that minority and poor students are more likely to be held back in grade than majority and middle-class students, so students from deprived backgrounds are the most likely to suffer from an increase in grade retention.

In this paper, we assemble evidence about trends and differentials in grade retention using data from the Census Bureau's October Current Population Survey and from state education agencies. Using descriptive statistics and multivariate models, we evaluate whether or not grade retention has increased under recent standards-based reforms, focusing in particular upon low-income students. Generally, we find a steady increase in grade retention, continuing an upward trend in grade retention rates since the 1970s. State and census data suggest that national increases in retention have generally been concentrated in the early grades and, in the case of the state data, have occurred in spurts. This increase was steeper for children in the lowest quarter of the income distribution, compared with that of higher-income groups, from about 1998 until just before the NCLB Act was signed in 2002. However, retention rates temporarily spiked in 2003 for children in the entire bottom half of the income distribution, implying that NCLB has had fleeting but deleterious effects on retention rates for the poorest children. Overall, in our multivariate models students in the lowest-income quarter are 41 percent more likely to be retained than are students in the highest quarter. In contrast, students in the second quarter are 14 percent more likely to be retained.

3. National Research Council (1999).
4. Hauser, Pager, and Simmons (2004); Hauser, Simmons, and Pager (2004).
5. Andrew (2006).

The small overall increases in retention rates mask the substantial increases in the total number of children retained and the additional resources required to educate these students for an additional year. Furthermore, this increase has occurred to a large extent among low-income children, the very group NCLB is intended to help. In its first years of implementation, NCLB does not appear to have had direct and severe effects on national grade retention rates, but neither has it reduced the upward trend. We begin with a brief review of the literature.

Research on Grade Retention

Unfortunately, no national data collection mechanism or repository for promotion or retention statistics exists, and most data on retention are based on indirect measures or limited samples. Similarly, no national educational information system monitors the extent to which tests are used to make decisions about promotion or retention. National trends in grade retention rates are best approximated by a proxy measure, the share of children who are below the modal grade for their age.

In consequence, there is a mix of uncertainty, approximation, contradiction, and speculation about the prevalence of grade retention in American schools.[6] Reliable and recent estimates based on data from Current Population Surveys suggest, "At least 15% of pupils are retained between ages 6 to 8 and ages 15 to 17, and a large share of retention occurs either before or after those ages."[7] These estimates also suggest that the prevalence of retention increases substantially over the course of students' educational careers, growing by about 10 percentage points by ages nine through eleven and by about another 5 percentage points by ages twelve through fourteen.

A number of correlates of grade retention have been identified. Research has established stark gender differences in grade retention: boys are more likely to be retained than are girls at every level of the K–12 educational system.[8] Racial and ethnic differences in retention rates are also prominent. Using census data, the National Research Council (NRC) reported that the shares of students below modal grade for age were relatively similar among racial and ethnic groups at ages six through eight, but are 5 to 10 percentage points higher for Blacks and Hispanics than those for Whites just three years

6. For example, compare Karweit (1999) and Eide and Showalter (2001).
7. Hauser, Pager, and Simmons (2004, p. 98).
8. Byrd and Weitzman (1994); National Research Council (1999); Dawson (1998).

later (at ages nine through eleven).[9] By ages fifteen through seventeen, the rate of being below modal grade for age ranges from 40 to 50 percent among Blacks and Hispanics, but it is much lower among Whites at 25 to 35 percent. Within the same age group, the rate of children below the modal grade for age in the lowest fifth of the income distribution is 20 percentage points higher than that for children in the middle 60 percent of the income distribution and more than 35 percentage points higher than that for children in the highest-income group. However, these income-based differentials appear to have decreased since the mid-1990s.[10]

Beyond gender and race and ethnic differentials, a higher incidence of retention is associated with a disadvantaged socioeconomic background, living in a single-parent home, living in a central city or in the southern Census region, having been born to a teenage mother, having parents with low measured IQ and education, and having parents with a health or behavioral problem.[11]

Despite the intended benefits of grade retention, research suggesting it has positive effects on student outcomes is sparse, and methodological and analytical problems render these results suspect. For example, Karl Alexander, Doris Entwisle, and Susan Dauber argued that grade retention in the early primary grades halted the downward slide of low-achieving students and prepared them to succeed in later grades.[12] The positive effects appeared for students who were retained once and only after the first grade in a cohort of 1,000 Baltimore students. Over time, even among this select group of students, the apparently positive effects of grade retention diminished, so retained students reaped no long-term positive benefits. Critics of Alexander, Entwisle, and Dauber's work have argued that the supposedly positive effects of grade retention actually reflect regression to the mean and represent no real benefit in the first place.[13] Moreover, the data collected by these authors showed significant detrimental effects of grade retention on a much larger number of students retained in the first grade. Finally, their analyses controlled some student characteristics subsequent to the retention decision.[14]

In a second example, Brian Jacob and Lars Lefgren also found positive effects of grade retention using a regression discontinuity design with data

9. National Research Council (1999).

10. Hauser (2004, p. 290).

11. Corman (2003); Hauser, Pager, and Simmons (2004); National Research Council (1999); Hauser (2004).

12. Alexander, Entwisle, and Dauber (2003).

13. Shepard, Smith, and Marion (1996); Alexander (1998); Hauser (2005).

14. Hauser (2005).

from students in the Chicago Public Schools.[15] Several aspects of the authors' research give reason for pause despite the sophisticated research design. In their study, retention substantially increased the achievement of third graders in reading and math, but the effect on reading became insignificant two years after retention, and the effect on math achievement was barely significant at the $p = 0.05$ level and fell by half a year after retention. This suggests that Jacob and Lefgren's findings may reflect regression to the mean, as in other research that has found a nominally positive effect of retention. Moreover, these results speak only to the effects of retention among a narrowly defined population of students given a specific set of circumstances: largely minority and low socioeconomic status, testing at about the twentieth percentile of the national distribution in a single urban school district with strong incentives for test performance, and where a variety of programs are in place to enhance student achievement. For example, these programs included after-school tutoring for retained students beginning a third of the way through the study. Thus results may not reflect the effects of retention so much as extra tutoring, which can be implemented without retaining a student, and, all else aside, may not generalize to the larger population.

In contrast to the work by Alexander and others and by Jacob and Lefgren, most research suggests that grade retention is associated with negative student outcomes. Meta-analyses of retention effects have been particularly helpful in isolating the extent to which retention may help or harm students, and they generally show that grade retention is harmful to students. Prominent among these meta-analyses are those of C. Thomas Holmes and Shane Jimerson.[16]

Holmes assessed sixty-three studies spanning almost ninety years from 1900 through the 1980s. When promoted and retained students were compared one to three years later, the retained students' average levels of academic achievement were at least 0.4 standard deviation below those of promoted students. In these comparisons, promoted and retained students were the same age, but the promoted students had completed one more grade than the retained students. Promoted and retained students were also compared when the retained students were a year older than the promoted students but had completed equal numbers of additional grades. Here, the findings were less consistent but still negative. When the data were weighted by the number of estimated effects, retention initially had a positive effect on academic

---

15. Jacob and Lefgren (2004).
16. Holmes (1989); Jimerson (2001).

achievement after one more grade in school, but this effect faded away completely after three or more grades. When the data were weighted by the number of independent studies, rather than by the estimated number of effects on achievement, the average effects were negligible in every year after retention. Of the sixty-three studies Holmes reviewed, fifty-four yielded overall negative effects of retention, and only nine yielded overall positive effects. Holmes concluded, "On average, retained children are worse off than their promoted counterparts on both personal adjustment and academic outcomes."[17]

Jimerson updated Holmes's classic meta-analysis by examining twenty studies of the association between retention and academic achievement and socioemotional adjustment spanning the period from 1990 to 1999.[18] Jimerson combined studies comparing same-grade and same-age outcomes and, unlike Holmes, did not break out same-grade and same-age results. However, Jimerson's results were consistent with Holmes's, suggesting that the associations between grade retention and student outcomes and characteristics have been quite stable over time. On average, retained students scored 0.39 standard deviation lower on various academic achievement measures than students who were not retained. They also scored 0.22 standard deviation lower on socioemotional outcomes than similar students who were not retained.

Since the publication of Jimerson's meta-analysis, evidence against retention as the primary method of remediation continues to emerge. Linda Pagani and others found negative effects of retention on academic achievement among children in Quebec using an autoregressive model of academic achievement.[19] In another regression discontinuity design using the same data as Jacob and Lefgren, Jenny Nagaoka and Melissa Roderick found no difference between third grade retainees' test scores and those of their regularly promoted peers two years after being retained.[20] Guanglei Hong and Stephen Raudenbush used data from the Early Childhood Longitudinal Survey, Kindergarten Cohort (ECLS-K), with multilevel propensity score stratification and found that retaining children in kindergarten led to lower academic achievement in the next school year.[21] In a national sample, Russell Rumberger and Katherine Larson found that previously retained eighth grade students were far less likely to earn a high school diploma. Similarly, Elaine Allensworth found that low-achieving eighth graders in Chicago who

17. Holmes (1989, p. 27).
18. Jimerson (2001).
19. Pagani and others (2001).
20. Jacob and Lefgren (2004); Nagaoka and Roderick (2004).
21. Hong and Raudenbush (2005).

failed to pass through to the ninth grade were more likely to drop out of school.[22] Megan Andrew found that the long-term effects of grade retention reach beyond high school completion for a national sample of students, affecting the likelihood of entry into a postsecondary institution and completing a baccalaureate degree.[23]

Grade retention is a common and prominent means to remedy academic failure in the U.S. educational system. Yet the practice does not appear to bestow many of the intended benefits upon students who are retained in grade and incurs considerable costs. One cost-benefit analysis suggests grade retention costs school systems upward of $3.5 billion a year, assuming a conservative 1 percent retention rate annually, which is less than half the retention rate we have estimated.[24] Finances aside, better solutions are available. The NRC report on high-stakes testing concludes, "Neither social promotion nor retention alone is an effective treatment, and schools can use a number of possible strategies to reduce the need for these either-or choices—for example, by coupling early identification of such students with effective remedial education."[25]

Given the weight of the evidence that grade retention has deleterious effects on retained students and society in general, it is logical to ask: in the current political climate, with its emphasis on standards-based reform, is grade retention increasing? The brief history of NCLB makes it difficult to discern its effects, either nationally or at the state level. However, because many states had already moved toward standards-based reform in the 1990s, we can get some traction on this question by looking at trends in retention during the years preceding the passage of NCLB as well as those immediately following.

Analytic Strategy

We begin with data from October Current Population Surveys to assess trends in grade retention since 1996 for all students and by race, gender, and socioeconomic status. We then turn to data collected from the state educational agencies, comparing differences and similarities in the two sources of data. We ask three basic questions:

---

22. Rumberger and Larson (1998); Allensworth (2004).
23. Andrew (2006).
24. Eide and Goldhaber (2005, p. 198).
25. National Research Council (1999, p. 278).

—Given the diffusion of standards-based reform within education and the subsequent use of tests in retention decisions, have grade retention rates increased during the past decade?

—Are there different trends in grade retention in subpopulation groups, especially those defined by socioeconomic status, or at specific grade levels?

—Are there regional and state variations in grade retention trends across time and, particularly, in the past decade? Do these data corroborate general trends observed in the census data?

Data and Methods

In our first analyses, we use data from October School Enrollment Supplements to the Current Population Survey. Since 1994 the survey has collected data on children's grade of enrollment in the previous year as well as the current year. This allows us to construct a direct measure of the probability that children are retained in grade. We limited our sample to people aged five to twenty in each survey from 1996 through 2004.[26] Additionally, we eliminated those who were enrolled below kindergarten in the year before the survey, those who were enrolled above twelfth grade in the current year of the survey, twelfth grade repeaters, and observations that were missing one or both of the enrollment variables.[27] This yielded an unweighted sample of 230,696 cases. Finally, we eliminated 2,177 cases (1.0 percent) reporting a grade progression other than single retention, normal promotion, or double promotion (skipping one grade) for a final analytic sample of 228,519 cases.

For the logistic regressions, we have further restricted the age range to ages five through seventeen to include data on parents' education and occupation.[28] Cases with missing data are dealt with in two different ways, depending on the reason data were missing. If an observation was missing income and head of household's education, it was dropped from the sample. For observations with missing data on occupation and spouse's education because a household head was not in the labor force or was not married, we used a dummy variable adjustment procedure which has been shown to be unbiased

---

26. We excluded data from the first two available years because of data quality issues.

27. We must omit students who were enrolled in the twelfth grade in the previous year because our other exclusions eliminate all twelfth graders who were *not* retained. This would leave us with no variation with which to estimate our models.

28. Above age seventeen, youths are less likely to live with their parents, thus breaking the link between school enrollment and social and economic characteristics of householders.

where data are missing because they could not exist.[29] Eliminating ineligible observations as well as those with missing data yielded a final analytic sample of 154,112 cases for the logistic regression analyses.

In addition to the year of the survey and the previous year's grade, we include both demographic and social background covariates. The demographic variables include gender, race, region, urban or rural residence, and the number of children living in the household. (It is important to note that children living in the same household are not necessarily siblings because the Current Population Survey [CPS] is a household survey rather than a family survey.) There are four categories of race and ethnicity: non-Hispanic Black, non-Hispanic White, Hispanic (any race), and Other. Region is also divided into four categories: Northeast, South, Midwest, and West. The urban residence dummy variable pertains to students who live in major central cities.

The social background covariates include the natural log of household income, the household head's education and occupational status, the spouse's education and occupational status, and a dummy variable indicating whether the household head (and spouse) own their home. Again, the household head and spouse are usually, but not necessarily, the child's parents. We divide the educational attainment measures into two variables to tease out piecewise linear effects of parental education before and after the transition from high school to college.

We also collected data on grade retention rates from state educational agencies. We build on earlier retention data through the mid-1990s provided by the states to the National Research Council's Committee on Appropriate Test Use.[30] We contacted states' educational offices and requested whatever grade retention trend data were available, particularly since the 1990s, and we compiled these data together with the existing data from the National Research Council. Not every state collects these data, nor did every state respond to our request. However, we are able to provide descriptive data on grade retention rates since the 1990s for fourteen states across all regions of the United States.

Incidence of Retention: CPS

We begin with a discussion of analyses employing CPS data. Overall, 2.73 percent of the CPS sample reported being retained in the year preceding the survey, and 0.34 percent reported experiencing a double promotion or skip-

---

29. Allison (2002).
30. National Research Council (1999, pp. 138–46).

Figure 5-1. *Percentage of Students Retained, by Race and Year*

Percent

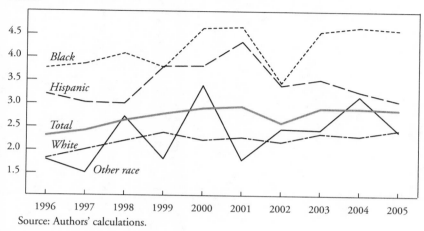

Source: Authors' calculations.

ping a grade.[31] Figure 5-1 plots the trend in overall retention rates by year and race. Focusing on the trend line of the total retention rate, the absolute change is not very large; the largest difference between annual rates is 0.63 percentage point. However, there is a clear increasing trend from the beginning of this time period until the retention rate appears to level off near 3 percent per year from 2003 on.

How big is a difference of less than 1 percentage point at this level of retention? Assume that the probabilities of being retained are independent and constant across grade levels. During the twelve years from kindergarten through eleventh grade, 75.5 percent of students are expected to reach their senior year of high school on time if subject to a 2.31 percent retention rate at each grade level. This figure drops to 69.9 percent never retained if 2.94 percent of students are retained in each grade.

The assumptions made in these simulated examples are surely violated. However, these illustrative estimates are not much higher than previous estimates of the proportion of children who have ever been retained.[32] Moreover, analyses of data from the National Education Longitudinal Study of 1988 (NELS 88) show that children are rarely retained twice.[33] Table 5-1 shows the number of children retained in each grade level in each year.

31. For analytic purposes, the double-promotions are combined with normal progressions.
32. National Research Council (1999).
33. Andrew (2006); see also Shepard and Smith (1989, p. 8).

Table 5-1. *Percentage of Students Retained, by Previous Year's Grade and Year of Survey*

Previous year's grade	1996	1997	1998	1999	2000	2001	2002	2003	2004	2005
Kindergarten	4.91	3.63	3.72	3.69	4.84	5.12	4.29	4.68	5.77	5.45
First	5.62	6.63	7.13	4.52	6.99	6.71	6.87	9.12	9.09	9.76
Second	1.67	2.17	2.75	2.22	2.79	2.45	2.32	1.99	2.33	2.26
Third	1.57	1.78	2.24	3.38	2.11	1.71	1.67	2.49	2.05	1.81
Fourth	1.61	1.72	1.16	1.75	1.64	2.21	1.93	1.86	1.37	1.14
Fifth	1.38	1.04	1.16	1.31	2.11	1.49	1.69	1.55	1.33	1.60
Sixth	1.37	1.36	1.95	1.93	2.55	1.88	1.85	1.25	2.09	1.51
Seventh	1.76	1.73	2.18	3.05	3.07	2.28	1.90	2.94	1.44	2.98
Eighth	1.02	1.51	1.79	2.75	1.94	1.86	1.73	2.01	3.03	1.63
Ninth	3.13	2.93	2.21	4.04	2.67	4.11	2.29	3.45	2.66	2.69
Tenth	1.95	2.20	2.39	2.23	2.09	2.29	2.73	2.01	1.79	1.80
Eleventh	1.30	1.79	2.55	2.46	1.97	3.32	1.70	1.54	1.97	1.71
Proportion of the synthetic cohort that enters twelfth grade "on time"	75.77	74.85	72.75	71.29	70.17	69.69	72.97	69.99	69.93	70.33

Source: Authors' calculations.

Figure 5-2. *Percentage of Students Retained, by Race and Grade*

Percent

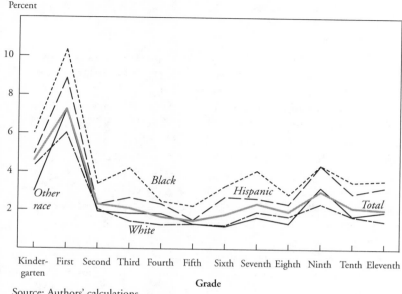

Source: Authors' calculations.

Again, assuming that the chance of being retained is independent across grade levels, we can construct period retention rates for the synthetic cohort of students who progress through school at the observed rates of retention in each year. These estimates are displayed in the bottom row of table 5-1. As in the calculation based on annual retention rates, the predicted proportion of students who enter twelfth grade on time declines steadily from 75.8 percent in 1996 to 70.3 percent in 2005.

The overall proportion of students retained varies across grade levels, as shown in figure 5-2. In kindergarten 4.6 percent of students are retained, and in first grade more than 7 percent of students are retained. This proportion decreases by two-thirds in second grade and hovers between 1.5 and 2 percent until eighth grade, excepting a jump to 2.3 percent in seventh grade. Ninth graders report the highest probability of retention outside of the first two years of schooling at just over 3 percent, but this is still less than half the probability of first graders. In tenth and eleventh grades, the proportion retained falls back down to around 2 percent. First grade retention stands out as considerably higher than retention in other grades. Though no research has assessed why this is the case, differences in academic preparation in the home before school entry are probably the cause. These differences may not be as evident in kindergarten, which is not universal and has a considerably different, less academic curriculum, hence the jump in first grade retention.

Retention and Race

Figure 5-1 also displays the change in retention probabilities over time, disaggregated by race. Black students are at the highest risk of being retained, followed closely by Hispanics. White students and those of other races have the lowest rates of retention over time. The gap between Black and White students is fairly constant until 2000 when Black retentions begin to increase relative to those of Whites. Likewise, the gap between Hispanics and Whites is fairly constant but with a slight increase from 1999 to 2001.

Blacks and Hispanics also experience more retentions at specific grade levels than Whites and students of other races, as shown in figure 5-2. The gaps are most severe in kindergarten and first grade. After that the percentages seem to converge through the elementary and middle grades until they slightly diverge once more in high school. Overall, retention rates for minority children are more variable, particularly for children in the Other category. This variability is largely a function of the smaller sample of minority children in the CPS. Blacks and Hispanics each make up 13 percent of the sample, while children of other races make up only 6.4 percent. The remaining two-thirds of the sample are non-Hispanic Whites.

Retention and Gender

Figure 5-3 disaggregates the yearly trends in retention by gender. The aggregate trend line is included in figure 5-3 for reference (as it is in figures 5-4 through 5-6). This confirms findings of previous studies that boys experience more retentions than girls, which appear in every year. The gap in the percentage of retentions between boys and girls is widest during the middle of this period, especially in 1999 and 2000; before and after that period, the trends for boys and girls are remarkably parallel.

Figure 5-4 shows the retention rates by gender and grade. While boys are consistently retained with greater frequency than are girls across all grades, the gap begins to widen in the sixth grade—perhaps a consequence of puberty—and is most severe in the ninth grade. This gap closes by the eleventh grade.

Retention and Income

In figures 5-5 and 5-6 the trends are disaggregated by quarters of the income distribution. There are no surprises here: children who come from the most prosperous families are least likely to be retained. The biggest gap between

Figure 5-3. *Percentage of Students Retained, by Gender and Year*

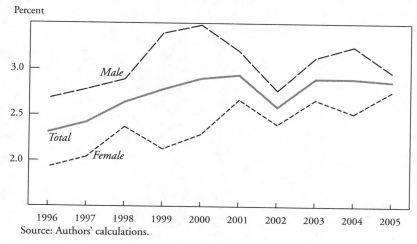

Percent

Source: Authors' calculations.

Figure 5-4. *Percentage of Students Retained, by Gender and Grade*

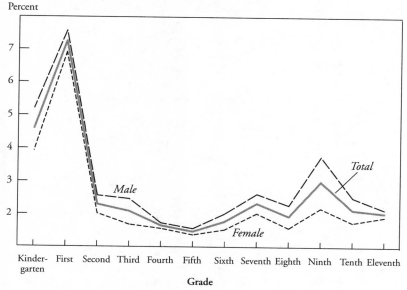

Percent

Grade

Source: Authors' calculations.

Figure 5-5. *Percentage of Students Retained, by Income Quartile and Year*

Percent

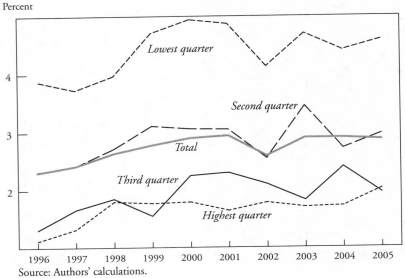

Source: Authors' calculations.

Figure 5-6. *Percentage of Students Retained, by Income Quartile and Grade*

Percent

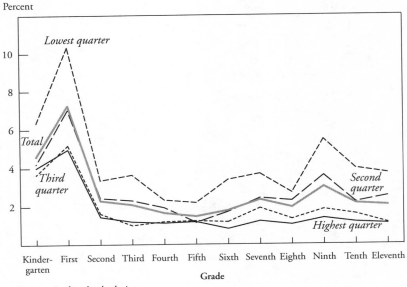

Source: Authors' calculations.

adjacent categories over time is that between the lowest and second quarters. The smallest such gap is between the third and fourth quarters, possibly indicating a threshold effect of family income. Again figure 5-6 shows a now-familiar pattern: the biggest differences in retention rates by income occur during kindergarten and first grade; rates converge during the middle grades and then diverge again during high school.

Multivariate Analysis

Next we turn to our multivariate analysis. In this portion of the analysis, we employ two basic models: a standard logistic regression and a logistic regression model with proportionality constraints. These constraints can provide a clearer picture of which students' characteristics have similar—or different—effects on grade retention. In combination, these multivariate models test the descriptive patterns discussed above. We begin with the standard logistic regression. This model estimates retention in the year before the survey as a function of the grade in which a student was enrolled during the previous year, the year of the survey, and demographic and social background variables:

$$(1) \qquad \text{logit}(P(Y_i = 1)) = \alpha_j X_{ij} + \alpha_k W_{ik} + \sum_h \beta_h Z_{ih},$$

where Y_i indicates whether student i reports being retained; α_j is the intercept for year j, indexed by the dummy variable, X_{ij}; α_k is the intercept for grade k, indexed by the dummy variable, W_{ik}; and β_h is the coefficient of demographic and social background covariate Z_{ih}. This model divides the effects of the various groups of variables into two classes. The αs are additive intercepts that adjust for the mean levels of retention in each grade level and year, and the βs are the effects of individual characteristics, holding the grade- and year-specific retention levels constant. In both this and the following model, the social background and demographic characteristics are expressed as deviations from their means to facilitate interpretation.

Estimates from this model are listed in the first set of columns (two left columns) of table 5-2, under Simple Logit. The intercepts for year of survey follow the trend presented in figure 5-1. The intercept for 1997 is not reliably different from the omitted category (1996), but the differences with 1996 are significant in each subsequent year. The intercept for each grade is significantly different from that of the omitted category (kindergarten), and the effect of previous year's grade also follows the trend shown in figure 5-2. Average first graders are more likely to be retained than are kindergartners. The rest of the grade levels have lower intercepts. With the other covariates

Table 5-2. *Results from Logits Predicting Retention in the Year before the Survey*

Variable	Simple logit		LRPC	
	β	SE	β	SE
Previous year's grade				
First	0.4038***	0.0576	0.4122***	0.0599
Second	−0.8351***	0.0794	−0.8201***	0.0824
Third	−0.9403***	0.0820	−1.0759***	0.0933
Fourth	−1.0689***	0.0856	−1.0706***	0.0893
Fifth	−1.1415***	0.0878	−1.1409***	0.0910
Sixth	−1.2232***	0.0911	−1.2784***	0.0980
Seventh	−0.7735***	0.0780	−0.8332***	0.0837
Eighth	−1.0566***	0.0865	−1.0837***	0.0903
Ninth	−0.5613***	0.0742	−0.6352***	0.0797
Tenth	−0.7239***	0.0809	−0.7681***	0.0842
Eleventh	−0.8451***	0.0882	−0.8689***	0.0898
Year of survey				
1997	0.0563	0.0825	0.1245	0.0901
1998	0.2481**	0.0799	0.3008***	0.0873
1999	0.2364**	0.0807	0.2531**	0.0888
2000	0.2793***	0.0808	0.3319***	0.0879
2001	0.2768***	0.0780	0.3169***	0.0851
2002	0.1808*	0.0797	0.2271**	0.0866
2003	0.2374**	0.0802	0.2887***	0.0868
2004	0.3366***	0.0795	0.3613***	0.0863
2005	0.1924*	0.0819	0.2496**	0.0882
Demographic characteristics				
Black	0.2688***	0.0595	0.2569***	0.0698
Hispanic	0.0328	0.0581	0.0623	0.0602
Other race	−0.0107	0.0762	−0.0063	0.0788
Male	0.2318***	0.0350	0.2400***	0.0496
Midwest	−0.2707***	0.0551	−0.3097***	0.0712
South	0.2381***	0.0496	0.2245***	0.0610
West	−0.2750***	0.0549	−0.3018***	0.0708
Major central city	0.3183***	0.0658	0.3329***	0.0827
Number of children in household	0.0714***	0.0137	0.0704***	0.0171
Social background characteristics				
Household head's occupation	−0.0009	0.0012	−0.0015	0.0013
Household head's K–12 education	−0.0082	0.0109	−0.0123	0.0108
Household head's postsecondary education	−0.0455***	0.0123	−0.0480***	0.0142

continued on next page

Table 5-2. *Results from Logits Predicting Retention in the Year before the Survey—Continued*

Variable	Simple logit		LRPC	
	β	SE	β	SE
Social background characteristics—continued				
Spouse's occupation	−0.0046***	0.0014	−0.0043**	0.0016
Spouse's K–12 education	−0.0023	0.0122	0.0051	0.0122
Spouse's postsecondary education	0.0089	0.0049	0.0087	0.0052
Lowest income quartile	0.3427***	0.0666	0.3609***	0.0865
Second income quartile	0.1307	0.0581	0.1553*	0.0645
Third income quartile	−0.0720	0.0546	−0.0749	0.0581
Home ownership	−0.1600***	0.0439	−0.1613***	0.0501
Lambda j				
First grade	—	—	−0.0644	0.1191
Second grade	—	—	−0.0873	0.1613
Third grade	—	—	0.6338**	0.2212
Fourth grade	—	—	0.0265	0.1795
Fifth grade	—	—	−0.0045	0.1846
Sixth grade	—	—	0.3379	0.2095
Seventh grade	—	—	0.3716*	0.1891
Eighth grade	—	—	0.1921	0.1928
Ninth grade	—	—	0.4832*	0.1946
Tenth grade	—	—	0.3597	0.1948
Eleventh grade	—	—	0.1870	0.1973
Lambda k				
1997	—	—	−0.3270*	0.1439
1998	—	—	−0.2556	0.1425
1999	—	—	−0.0484	0.1577
2000	—	—	−0.2572	0.1457
2001	—	—	−0.1738	0.1449
2002	—	—	−0.2255	0.1470
2003	—	—	−0.2845*	0.1446
2004	—	—	−0.0527	0.1608
2005	—	—	−0.3557*	0.1479
Missing household head's occupation	0.081	0.0659	0.0690	0.0662
Missing spouse's occupation	0.1357***	0.0401	0.1463**	0.0465
Constant	−3.4203***	0.0756	−3.4418***	0.0818
Observations	154,112		154,112	
Log-likelihood	−15682.027		−15656.454	

Source: Authors' calculations.

*p < 0.05; **p < 0.01; ***p < 0.001.   — Not applicable; SE = standard error; LRPC: see p. 140.

held constant the intercepts for students in ninth, tenth, and seventh grades in order of magnitude are the next higher intercepts relative to kindergarten.

The effects of race and ethnicity are in the expected directions. The Black-White difference is significant at the $p = 0.001$ level, but the other differences are not statistically significant. The exponentiated coefficient indicates that Black students are 31 percent more likely to be retained during this period than are White students.[34] The difference between boys and girls is also significant. Boys are 26 percent more likely to be retained than are girls. Additional children living in the household also increase one's chances of experiencing retention, all else being equal; each additional child increases the odds of retention by 7 percent.

The differences between places of residence are all significant. Relative to children in the Northeast, southerners are 27 percent more likely to be retained. Both midwesterners and westerners are 24 percent less likely to be retained compared with their northeastern counterparts. Residing in a major central city increases the odds of being retained by 37 percent relative to students in smaller cities and in suburban and rural areas.

Only five of the social background variables significantly affect the likelihood that a student was retained in the past year. Each year of father's postsecondary education reduces the likelihood of retention by 4.4 percent. Students whose parents own their home are 15 percent less likely to be retained. An increase of ten points in the spouse's occupational status score decreases the odds of retention by almost 5 percent. Income is also negatively associated with retention, and, again, we see evidence of the threshold effect between students in the lowest and second quarters of the income distribution that we saw in the bivariate relationships. Students in the lowest quarter of family income are 41 percent more likely to be retained than are students in the highest quarter. Students in the second quarter are 14 percent more likely to be retained, but students in that and in the third highest quarter do not have significantly different odds of retention compared with students in the highest quarter of family income.

We now turn to the second model, the logistic regression model with proportionality constraints on the effects of the covariates (LRPC). We find this model useful because it allows us to estimate important differences and similarities in the effect of students' characteristics across grade and time in a single equation. Alternatively, one could run separate, fully interacted models by

---

34. Thirty-one percent comes from the odds ratio implied by the coefficients in table 5-2 (exp(0.27) = 1.31).

year and grade of retention that would allow the slopes of all covariates to vary freely. However, this strategy is cumbersome and produces an overwhelming number of coefficients to interpret. Moreover, the effects of the covariates may not vary substantially. If this is the case, the fully interactive models will not provide any more information than does the LRPC model.[35] By estimating a single equation model, we assume that changes in the association between retention and demographic and social background characteristics behave similarly across time, excepting a proportional or scalar difference. In this way, we provide a more parsimonious characterization of differentials in grade retention. The LRPC model (equation 2) is similar to the model in equation 1 except it constrains grade level and year interactions for each demographic and social background covariate:[36]

$$(2) \qquad \text{logit}(P(Y_i = 1)) = \alpha_j X_{ij} + \alpha_k W_{ik} + \sum_h \beta_h Z_{ih} + \lambda_j \left(\sum_h \beta_h Z_{ih} \right)$$

$$+ \lambda_k \left(\sum_h \beta_h Z_{ih} \right),$$

In this model α_j, α_k, β_h, X_{ij}, W_{ik}, and Z_{ih} are defined as above.[37] The coefficients λ_j and λ_k scale the effects of the social background and demographic covariates by the same proportion for each grade level, j, and year, k. These estimates are listed in the second set of columns of table 5-2, under LRPC. According to standard model fit statistics, the LRPC model better describes the data. Compared with the simple logistic regression, the LRPC model reduces Akaike's Information Criterion (AIC) by 13.15 and is the preferred model according to the likelihood ratio test.[38] There appear to be real, sys-

35. In supplementary analyses, we compared the LRPC model presented here with a model including all possible interactions between student characteristics, grade of retention, and year. The LRPC model presented here is preferred by the Akaike Information Criterion (AIC) (a difference of 278) and the Bayesian Information Criterion (BIC) (a difference of 3,848) but not by the likelihood ratio test (a difference of 440 with 359 df). The last finding is not surprising, given the exceptionally large size of the sample; see Raftery (1995); Weakliem (1999).

36. Hauser and Andrew (2006).

37. As with all logistic regression models, this model is identified by fixing the variance of the error to a constant ($\pi \gamma / \sqrt{3}$). Thus true differences across groups are empirically indistinguishable from heterogeneity in the conditional variance by groups. Scaling effects, as with all coefficients in this and similar models, should be interpreted with this caveat in mind; see Allison (1999) and Mare (2006).

38. Because of the large sample size, the LRPC actually increases BIC by 176. The AIC and the BIC are similar to a likelihood ratio test but provide a more conservative estimate of model fit for nested and non–nested models; see Burnham and Anderson (1998) and Raftery (1995).

tematic differences in the effects of the covariates across grades and years, but the evidence in favor of the LRPC model is not unequivocal.

The interpretation of the LRPC coefficients may be counterintuitive. As mentioned above, each λ is a scalar that proportionally increases or decreases the magnitude of the demographic and social background coefficients. Because we treat grade level and year as nominal categories, the β coefficients are the effects for the omitted category: kindergarteners in 1996. The effects for other grades and other years are obtained by factoring the linear predictor out of equation 2. This yields a scalar multiplier of $1 + \lambda_j + \lambda_k$ for each regression coefficient. Thus negative signs do not imply a change in the direction of the effect unless $\lambda_j + \lambda_k < -1$, which is never the case in these estimates.

An example may be helpful. For the sake of simplicity, consider a slightly revised model from the one estimated here, a model with only a proportionality constraint for each year. Assume we are specifically interested in the scalar for 1997, λ_{1997}. Recalling that the total scaling effect in a model must be equivalent to the sum of the specified scalars plus one, if λ_{1997} were equal to -0.34, the magnitude of the β coefficient of each variable Z_{ih} in 1997 would be two-thirds the size of the corresponding coefficient in 1996: $1 + (-0.34) = 0.66$. That is, the proportionality constraints imply that slopes of the demographic and social background characteristics change similarly across grade level and across time.

The composite scalars are listed in table 5-3. Because they combine additively, the trends are easily summarized in figures 5-7 (year) and 5-8 (grade). All else equal, the magnitudes of the coefficients on social background characteristics are generally not reliably different from kindergarten levels, but there are three statistically significant positive spikes: at third, seventh, and ninth grades. These grades are indicated in figure 5-8. The increased effects of social background at the key promotional gates, third and ninth grades, indirectly suggest that retention decisions are being made with high-stakes tests in mind, either as a result of poor test scores or in anticipation thereof. The seventh grade scalar is only marginally different from that for kindergarten ($p = 0.049$).

As above, the trend line in the scalar values over time must be interpreted with caution because only three years, 1997, 2003, and 2005, are statistically distinguishable at the 5 percent level from the omitted category, 1996, as indicated in figure 5-7. Holding grade level constant, there is a large drop in the scalar between 1996 and 1997. Further analysis with additional years of data will be necessary to learn whether the 2004 peak is an aberration or may signal a longer upward turn in the effects of demographic

Table 5-3. *Combined Scalar for Each Grade Level in Each Year*

Grade	1996	1997	1998	1999	2000	2001	2002	2003	2004	2005
Kindergarten	1.000	0.673	0.744	0.952	0.743	0.826	0.774	0.716	0.947	0.644
First	0.936	0.609	0.680	0.887	0.678	0.762	0.710	0.651	0.883	0.580
Second	0.913	0.586	0.657	0.864	0.655	0.739	0.687	0.628	0.860	0.557
Third	1.634	1.307	1.378	1.585	1.377	1.460	1.408	1.349	1.581	1.278
Fourth	1.026	0.700	0.771	0.978	0.769	0.853	0.801	0.742	0.974	0.671
Fifth	0.996	0.669	0.740	0.947	0.738	0.822	0.770	0.711	0.943	0.640
Sixth	1.338	1.011	1.082	1.289	1.081	1.164	1.112	1.053	1.285	0.982
Seventh	1.372	1.045	1.116	1.323	1.114	1.198	1.146	1.087	1.319	1.016
Eighth	1.192	0.865	0.936	1.144	0.935	1.018	0.967	0.908	1.139	0.836
Ninth	1.483	1.156	1.228	1.435	1.226	1.309	1.258	1.199	1.431	1.127
Tenth	1.360	1.033	1.104	1.311	1.102	1.186	1.134	1.075	1.307	1.004
Eleventh	1.187	0.860	0.931	1.139	0.930	1.013	0.961	0.903	1.134	0.831

Source: Authors' calculations.

Figure 5-7. *Changes in Scalar Value, by Year*

Scalar

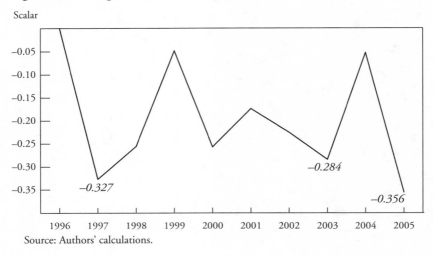

Source: Authors' calculations.

Figure 5-8. *Changes in Scalar Value, by Grade Level*

Scalar

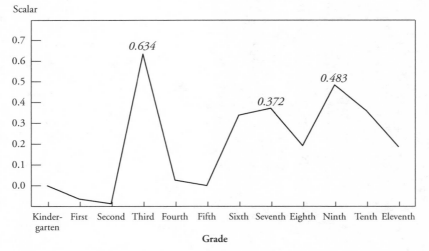

Source: Authors' calculations.

and social background characteristics on retention rates. Excepting the spike in 2004, the LRPC model indicates that a reduction in ascriptive barriers to promotion, in which the influence of social background is generally decreasing after 2001, is concurrent with, but not necessarily a direct result of, NCLB.

We use the predicted differences between students from households in the lowest income quarter and those in the highest to illustrate the substantive interpretation of the composite scalars in table 5-3. The baseline coefficient for children in the lowest income quarter from table 5-2 is 0.34. This means that low-income kindergartners in 1996 were 41 percent more likely than were high-income kindergartners in 1996 to be retained the following year.[39] The implied coefficient for kindergartners in 1997 is 0.34 × 0.673 = 0.23. Therefore, low-income kindergartners the next year were only 26 percent more likely to be retained. Similarly, the implied coefficient for third graders in 2001 is 0.34 × 1.46 = 0.50, which indicates an increase in relative retention rates of 65 percent between low- and high-income students.

It is important to emphasize that the increased effects of social background variables do not imply that retention decisions are made directly on the basis of race, gender, or socioeconomic standing. Instead, they probably reflect the growing importance of well-documented racial and socioeconomic test-score gaps, given the increased use of testing under the banner of standards-based reform. These findings are consistent with a retention system based increasingly on test scores, but since the CPS data do not include any measure of academic ability or performance, we lack direct evidence of that. Large-scale assessments are not widely used in kindergarten and in first or second grades, so other mechanisms must account for trends at those grade levels. One possibility is that the anticipation of later, test-based retention accounts for increased retention in the primary grades.[40]

Incidence of Retention: State Reports

Generally, grade retention rates in the CPS data have increased very modestly since the mid-1990s amid the shift to a more rigorous standards-based regime. Do state-level reports of retention data corroborate this picture of grade retention trends? To answer this question, we collected data from state educational agencies and combined them with existing data on grade reten-

39. (exp(0.34) = 1.41).
40. Jacob (2005).

tion rates by state.[41] Perhaps not surprisingly, state retention rate data confirm many of the broader trends observed in the CPS data. Overall growth in state retention rates is marginal, though some slight upward growth is observed over time in some grades in some states. Sudden spikes are observed in retention rates for some states, but retention rates generally return to previous levels in the next school year. Absolute levels of grade retention by region reflect noted disparities in the literature: southern states have considerably higher rates of retention than other states. Data on New York are limited, but it appears that, at least in the case of ninth grade retention, rates for New York are comparable to those in the South and higher than in neighboring states in the Northeast and in the Midwest.

Some notable patterns are apparent in the state data, and particular states present interesting case studies. For example, when growth in retention did occur from the early 1990s through the present, this growth was often concentrated in kindergarten and the early primary grades. Tennessee and Texas both evince this pattern. On the basis of trend data for Tennessee for the 1980s through the 2003–04 school year, we see that kindergarten retention steadily grows over time with a 1 percentage point jump between the 2000–01 and 2001–02 school years. The state maintained a similar rate of retention in the next year. Texas shows a similar pattern to that of Tennessee with about a 1 percentage point increase in kindergarten retention between the 1998–99 and 2003–04 school years. Texas also saw nearly a 1 percentage point increase in the retention rate in second grade in the same time span, with 40 percent of the increase occurring between the 2000–01 and 2001–02 school years. In approximately the same time span, Texas saw about a 1.5 percentage point increase in grade retention in the third grade as well. Connecticut similarly exhibits a 1 percentage point increase in kindergarten grade retention in the same time period. In the available data, grade retention rates at higher grades show an overall decline or stability in these states.

In contrast, retention rates in Kentucky in the primary grades remain relatively stable across time for the data available, but grade retention increases in the secondary grades. Growth in retention rates for the secondary grades is characterized by unusual spikes in this state. For example, grade retention in the ninth grade alone jumps a comparatively large 2 percentage points in the 1998–99 school year. In the following school year (1999–2000), the same cohort of students was subject to a 1.2 percentage point increase in retention.

---

41. We have not attempted to reconcile state-to-state differences in the definition of retention. These data are available upon request for some states by year and grade.

Alabama follows a similar trend line. In the available data, grade retention decreases in the primary grades but increases after about the 2000–01 school year for all secondary grades. In the ninth, tenth, and twelfth grades, this increase was steady and retention rates did not return to the previous levels in subsequent years. In the four-year span from the close of the 2000–01 school year to the 2004–05 school year, retention increased 1.5 percentage points in the ninth grade alone in Alabama.

Another common pattern in the state data was a sharp spike in retention rates in one year, followed by a return to the previous level in the next school year. This pattern was observed in Wisconsin. Overall, Wisconsin exhibited a low and relatively stable retention rate that is characteristic of other midwestern states but is in stark contrast to many southern states. Despite the relative stability of the retention rate in the state of Wisconsin, there is an unusual spike in eighth grade retention in the 2000–01 school year when the retention rate unexpectedly doubles and jumps 1 percentage point. Yet the eighth grade retention rate returned to normal within the next year or so. The same pattern occurs in Maine in multiple grades. Between the 2000–01 and 2001–02 school years, grade retention jumps about 2.25 percentage points in kindergarten before returning to the previous level of retention in the following year. Grade retention jumps 2 percentage points in the third grade in the 1999–2000 school year and similarly returns to the previous level in the next year. At the same time, overall retention rates in Maine show little movement. North Carolina also shows similar spikes in grade retention rates in the third, fifth, and eighth grades—key gateway grades—in the 2001–02 school year.

Ohio represents a striking example of the spike pattern observed in other states. Trend data on grade retention rates for Ohio show that in the 1999–2000 school year, *all* primary grades (K–8) exhibit increases in grade retention rates on the order of 2.5 to 3.7 percentage points, but retention rates returned to previous levels in the next school year. Yet, at least for kindergarteners, retention rates jump right back up again in the 2001–02 school year. Twelfth grade retention jumped a seemingly improbable 8 percentage points between 2003–04 and 2004–05—from 3 to 11 percent—and this is likely attributable to the introduction of a more demanding high school exit examination in 2004–05 in that state.

Despite several temporary spikes, retention rates have not been highly responsive to the introduction and expansion since the 1990s of standards-based reforms associated with high-stakes testing and concerns over social promotion. Some states, such as New Mexico, show growth in overall retention rates since the introduction of NCLB in January 2002 or since the

1990s under states' individual accountability initiatives, but this trend is not uniform. Instead, if retention rates do increase over time in states, this increase is concentrated in kindergarten and the early primary grades or key transition grades such as the ninth grade. Alternatively, if increases in grade retention rates are apparent and appear to be concurrent with the accountability and standards movements, these increases are usually reversed in the next year or soon thereafter. Thus the story in grade retention rates over time, if any, appears to be that states do exhibit short-term increases in grade retention rates associated with standards-based reform but reverse the increases in the next year. Displaying retention trend data by grade does illustrate an important point. Though states' overall retention rates often showed little to no growth—even decreases in grade retention from the early 1990s on—this often masks other important trends, such as increased kindergarten retention.

Conclusion

Comparing data from the October Current Population Survey and the state education agencies yields two consistent findings. First, there has not been an abrupt and sustained increase in the levels of retention in the decade just before and after passage of NCLB. The CPS data indicate increasing levels of retention since 1996, but this follows a longer trend beginning in the 1970s.[42] It may be the case that the move to standards-based reform since the 1990s is the source of this upswing in retention since 1996, since a large number of states implemented such reforms well before the 2002 signing of NCLB. However, without more detailed data regarding when individual states implemented a standards-based agenda, we are unable to definitively respond to this possibility. We also observed a decline in differential retention rates by social background and demographic characteristics through 2005, excepting an abrupt increase in 2004. It may be the case that state-implemented accountability regimes, which were not uniformly tied to federal funding and strict student achievement guidelines, may not have had as severe implications for students' progress through school as NCLB. Thus it is possible that a significant portion of states' accountability regimes, implemented well before NCLB, weakened the link between sociodemographic characteristics and retention. Obviously, this remains conjectural given the available data.

42. Frederick and Hauser (2005).

Some significant spikes in retention are observed in the data, particularly in the state data and in the CPS data near the time NCLB was passed. Again, it is difficult without more information to explain these sudden increases and subsequent corresponding declines in grade retention rates. Immediately available information suggests that, at least in the case of Ohio, these spikes may be tied to the use of tests to make promotion decisions. This spike pattern also mimics other trends observed in the accountability literature in the case of student test scores. For example, Daniel Koretz observes a sharp decline in student test scores with the introduction of new accountability tests, which are typically followed by a subsequent sharp increase in test scores within a few years.[43] It may be the case that tests are in fact being used to make promotion decisions but that as test scores return to previous levels, because of coaching (as Koretz posits) or some other mechanism, the retention rate returns to previous levels. The trends observed by Koretz and seen in the states' data jointly suggest this may be the case.[44] However, this is by no means a definitive conclusion, and it remains to be tested in future research. Some spikes in state retention rates also occurred just before the passage of the NCLB Act, offering slight evidence in support of our conjecture that many states' accountability regimes may not have been as stringent in their consequences for students before it was certain that federal legislation would mandate strict achievement guidelines and sanctions. Anticipating the passage of NCLB, some states may have begun assessing stronger penalties at the student level.

Second, both sources of data suggest retention very early in a student's career—in kindergarten and first grade—may have been somewhat more responsive to the increasing popularity of accountability regimes. This trend is troubling. Even Alexander, Entwisle, and Dauber, who offer a qualified endorsement of grade retention, conclude that students who are retained in the first grade experience serious negative consequences, both academically and emotionally.[45] As state testing regimes mature under NCLB and more data become available, it will be possible to see whether these trends continue. However, we note that testing in the lower grades is not mandated by NCLB, so any link between NCLB and increased retention in kindergarten or first grade must be an anticipatory effort to stave off possible academic problems later in a student's educational career, rather than a direct conse-

43. Koretz (2002).
44. Koretz (2002).
45. Alexander, Entwisle, and Dauber (2003).

quence of the federal law. Indeed, evidence from the Chicago public schools suggests this is an underlying source of the observed increase in grade retention in the early primary grades. Jacob finds that grade retention increased 3.6 percentage points in the first and second grades, 64 percent of which was attributable to the introduction of high-stakes tests in the third grade.[46]

Recommendations

Accumulated observational evidence strongly supports the finding that retention in grade has no lasting, positive effects on students' academic achievement or socioemotional development and that, on the contrary, it has negative long-term effects, most notably increasing the cost of K–12 schooling and the likelihood of dropping out of high school.

LOCAL, STATE, AND NATIONAL DATA SYSTEMS FOR GRADE RETENTION INFORMATION.   In this paper, as in other efforts to monitor trends and differentials in retention, we have had to rely on a short time series of demographic data and on incomplete administrative reports from individual states, which are of doubtful comparability. Neither of these data sources includes any measure of academic achievement or any direct measure of the use of large-scale assessments or other tests in decisions about retention. Given the existing and likely growing importance of retention as a characteristic of schooling in the age of accountability, along with clear differentials in the likelihood of retention by race and ethnicity and socioeconomic status, local, state, and national data systems should be created to monitor the extent, correlates, and consequences of grade retention. For example, districts and states should be required to track and monitor retention rates for major population groups, just as they now monitor test score performance under NCLB. Indeed, one could argue that valid interpretation of differences in test scores across time and across population groups cannot be made without information on retention. Just as school absences and accommodations affect aggregate academic achievement, so also do absences of age-appropriate students from tested populations. Information about retention should be included in the Common Core of Data and in the National Assessment of Educational Progress.

MANDATORY SUPPLEMENTARY SERVICES FOR STUDENTS AT RISK OF GRADE RETENTION.   A more immediate need is to make NCLB supple-

46. Jacob (2005).

mentary services mandatory, either as a concomitant service to or a substitute for retention, and to provide them earlier. Extant NCLB provisions include supplemental services for students attending schools that fail to make adequate yearly progress in a consecutive number of years, but these services are voluntary and receive secondary emphasis compared with other facets of NCLB, such as testing and measuring student achievement. Research on the supplementary service provision of NCLB is scarce but generally suggests considerable problems with delivery, arguably due to the voluntary nature of these services and their secondary importance in the act. The take-up rate of these services among eligible students is low—just 11 percent for tutoring services.[47] Moreover, students receiving tutoring services face high student-to-teacher ratios and do not necessarily attend regularly. However, when services are mandatory and delivery problems are addressed, students can and do benefit. Jacob and Lefgren's work on grade retention in the Chicago public schools suggests that the positive effects associated with grade retention are largely the result of mandatory tutoring services for at-risk students.[48] Increased supplementary services are especially important because of the likelihood that they will be received by poor students, who, as we have shown, are disproportionately affected by grade retention.

LARGE-SCALE, NATIONAL RANDOMIZED EXPERIMENT ON GRADE RETENTION. If there is real doubt about the effects of grade retention—a position that can be argued persuasively because so much of the available evidence is purely observational—then there should be a large-scale, national experiment on grade retention with random assignment of poorly performing individual students to retention, promotion, or promotion with remediation.[49] Education researchers have traditionally rejected the idea of such an experiment on the grounds that it would be harmful to the retained students, but if we really do not know whether or not retention causes the deleterious outcomes identified in the literature, an ethical argument against random assignment cannot be made. Moreover, we would argue that it is surely more harmful in the long run to subject poorly performing students to a harmful educational practice—whether it be promotion or retention—than it is to determine which policy is more beneficial to students.

47. See Farkas and Durham, chapter 7 in this volume.
48. Jacob and Lefgren (2004).
49. Alan B. Krueger, "But Does It Work?" *New York Times*, November 7, 1999, pp. A4, A46; Burtless (2002).

RESOURCES AND INCENTIVES TO IMPLEMENT AND FOLLOW GUIDELINES FOR APPROPRIATE USE OF HIGH-STAKES TESTS. Finally, the history of testing practice confirms that when tests are given, educators will use them to make decisions about individual students, whether or not they are well designed for that purpose. The massive growth of testing under accountability-based reforms and especially under NCLB implies an obligation to use tests wisely and fairly for the purposes for which they were designed. Otherwise, as our findings suggest, the equity goals of NCLB may well be undermined by negative, unintended consequences of inappropriate test use. There is no lack of guidelines for the appropriate use of high-stakes tests, but there are few resources or incentives to educate and guide test users or to enforce appropriate use.[50] Given the role of the federal government in mandating increased testing under NCLB, we think that appropriate regulations and enforcement mechanisms for test use should be included in the forthcoming reauthorization of NCLB.[51]

Given the tentative conclusions that can be made with the present data, more research is clearly needed. We will continue to exploit the CPS data to monitor grade retention trends. We also hope to obtain more detailed data on state accountability regimes. We want to combine this information with CPS data to more closely track the relationship between grade retention and testing. With these more detailed data, we will be able to address fully the questions of whether and how much accountability regimes, particularly after the passage of NCLB, have affected student promotion decisions. For the time being, we conclude that grade retention rates have not been dramatically responsive to the increasing popularity of accountability regimes, both before and immediately after the passage of NCLB. However, for particular groups, such as first graders, accountability regimes characterized by high-stakes testing appear to have marked effects. Time will tell if this remains the case.

References

Alexander, Karl L. 1998. "Letter to the Editor." *Psychology in the Schools* 35, no. 4: 402–04.
Alexander, Karl L., Doris R. Entwisle, and Susan L. Dauber. 2003. *On the Success of Failure: A Reassessment of the Effects of Retention in the Primary Grades.* Cambridge University Press.
Allensworth, Elaine. 2004. "Ending Social Promotion: Dropout Rates in Chicago after Implementation of the Eighth-Grade Promotion Gate." Chicago: Consortium for Chicago School Research.

50. American Educational Research Association (1998); National Research Council (1999).
51. See, for example, U.S. Department of Education, Office for Civil Rights (2000).

Allison, Paul D. 1999. "Comparing Logit and Probit Coefficients across Groups." *Sociological Methods Research* 28, no. 2: 186–208.

Allison, Paul D. 2002. *Missing Data*. Thousand Oaks, Calif: Sage Publications.

American Educational Research Association, American Psychological Association, and National Council on Measurement in Education. 1998. *Standards for Educational and Psychological Testing (Draft Standards)*. Washington: American Psychological Association.

Andrew, Megan. 2006. "Retained and Re-Tracked? Evidence of the Effects and Mechanisms of Primary Grade Retention for Educational Attainment." CDE Working Paper 2006-05. University of Wisconsin–Madison, Center for Demography and Ecology.

Burnham, Kenneth P., and David R. Anderson. 1998. *Model Selection and Inference: A Practical Information-Theoretic Approach*. New York: Springer.

Burtless, Gary. 2002. "Randomized Field Trials for Policy Evaluation: Why Not in Education?" In *Evidence Matters: Randomized Trials in Education Research*, edited by Frederick Mosteller and Robert Boruch, pp. 179–97. Brookings.

Byrd, Robert S., and Michael L. Weitzman. 1994. "Predictors of Early Grade Retention among Children in the United States." *Pediatrics* 93, no. 3: 481–87.

Clinton, William J. 1998. "Memorandum to the Secretary of Education." Washington: White House Press Release.

Corman, Hope. 2003. "The Effects of State Policies, Individual Characteristics, Family Characteristics, and Neighbourhood Characteristics on Grade Repetition in the United States." *Economics of Education Review* 22, no. 4: 409–20.

Dawson, Peg. 1998. "A Primer on Student Grade Retention: What the Research Says." *NASP Communiqué* 26, no. 8: 28–30.

Eide, Eric R., and Dan D. Goldhaber. 2005. "Grade Retention: What Are the Costs and Benefits?" *Journal of Education Finance* 31, no. 2: 20, 195–214.

Eide, Eric R., and Mark H. Showalter. 2001. "The Effect of Grade Retention on Educational and Labor Market Outcomes." *Economics of Education Review* 20, no. 6: 563–76.

Frederick, Carl B., and Robert M. Hauser. 2005. "Have We Put an End to Social Promotion? Changes in Grade Retention Rates among Children Aged 6 to 17 from 1972 to 2003." Paper presented at the American Sociological Association conference Comparative Perspectives, Competing Explanations. Philadelphia, August 13–16.

Hanushek, Eric A. 1986. "The Economics of Schooling: Production and Efficiency in Public Schools." *Journal of Economic Literature* 24, no. 3: 1141–177.

———. 1996. "A More Complete Picture of School Resource Policies." *Review of Educational Research* 66, no. 3: 397–409.

Hauser, Robert M. 2004. "Progress in Schooling." In *Social Inequality*, edited by Kathryn M. Neckerman, pp. 271–318. New York: Russell Sage Foundation.

———. 2005. "K. L. Alexander, D. R. Entwisle, S. L. Dauber, on the Success of Failure, A Reassessment of the Effects of Retention in the Primary School Grades, 2nd Edition." *Journal of School Psychology* 43, no. 1: 87–94.

Hauser, Robert M., and Megan Andrew. 2006. "Another Look at the Stratification of Educational Transitions: The Logistic Response Model with Partial Proportionality Constraints." In *Sociological Methodology 2006*, edited by Ross M. Stolzenberg, pp. 1–26. Washington: American Sociological Association and Blackwell Publishers.

Hauser, Robert M., Devah I. Pager, and Solon J. Simmons. 2004. "Race-Ethnicity, Social Background, and Grade Retention." In *Can Unlike Students Learn Together? Grade*

Retention, Tracking, and Grouping, edited by Herbert J. Walberg, Arthur J. Reynolds, and Margaret C. Wang, pp. 97–114. Greenwich, Conn.: Information Age Publishing.

Hauser, Robert M., Solon J. Simmons, and Devah I. Pager. 2004. "High School Dropout, Race-Ethnicity, and Social Background from the 1970s to the 1990s." In *Dropouts in America: Confronting the Graduation Rate Crisis*, edited by Gary Orfield, pp. 85–106. Cambridge, Mass.: Harvard Educational Publishing Group.

Holmes, C. Thomas. 1989. "Grade Level Retention Effects: A Meta-Analysis of Research Studies." In *Flunking Grades: Research and Policies on Retention*, edited by Lorrie A. Shepard and Mary Lee Smith, pp. 16–33. London: Falmer Press.

Hong, Guanglei, and Stephen W. Raudenbush. 2005. "Effects of Kindergarten Retention Policy on Children's Cognitive Growth in Reading and Mathematics." *Educational Evaluation and Policy Analysis* 27, no. 3: 205–24.

Jacob, Brian. 2005. "Accountability, Incentives and Behavior: Evidence from School Reform in Chicago." *Journal of Public Economics* 89, nos. 5-6: 761–96.

Jacob, Brian A., and Lars Lefgren. 2004. "Remedial Education and Student Achievement: A Regression-Discontinuity Analysis." *Review of Economics and Statistics* 86, no. 1: 226–44.

Jencks, Christopher, and others. 1972. *Inequality: A Reassessment of the Effect of Family and Schooling in America*. New York: Basic Books.

Jimerson, Shane R. 2001. "Meta-Analysis of Grade Retention Research: Implications for Practice in the 21st Century." *School Psychology Review* 30, no. 3: 420–37.

Karweit, Nancy L. 1999. "Crespar Report." Baltimore, Md.: Center for the Education of Students Placed at Risk, Center for Social Organization of Schools.

Koretz, Daniel M. 2002. "Limitations in the Use of Achievement Tests as Measures of Educators' Productivity." *Journal of Human Resources* 37, no. 4: 753–77.

Mare, Robert D. 2006. "Statistical Models of Educational Stratification: Hauser and Andrew's Models for School Transitions." In *Sociological Methodology 2006*, edited by Ross M. Stolzenberg, pp. 27–37. Washington: American Sociological Association and Blackwell Publishers.

Nagaoka, Jenny, and Melissa Roderick. 2004. *Ending Social Promotion: The Effects of Retention*. Chicago: Consortium for Chicago School Research.

National Research Council, Committee on Appropriate Test Use. 1999. *High Stakes: Testing for Tracking, Promotion, and Graduation*, edited by Jay P. Heubert and Robert M. Hauser. Washington: National Academy Press.

Pagani, Linda, and others. 2001. "Effects of Grade Retention on Academic Performance and Behavioral Development." *Development and Psychopathology* 13, no. 2: 297–315.

Raftery, Adrian E. 1995. "Bayesian Model Selection in Social Research." In *Sociological Methodology 1995*, edited by Peter V. Marsden, pp. 111–63. Cambridge, Mass.: Basil Blackwell.

Rumberger, Russell W., and Katherine A. Larson. 1998. "Student Mobility and the Increased Risk of High School Dropout." *American Journal of Education* 107, no. 1: 1–35.

Shepard, Lorrie A. 1998. "On the Success of Failure: A Rejoinder to Alexander." *Psychology in the Schools* 35, no. 4: 404–07.

Shepard, Lorrie A., and Mary Lee Smith. 1989. *Flunking Grades: Research and Policies on Retention*. London: Falmer Press.

Shepard, Lorrie A., Mary Lee Smith, and Scott F. Marion. 1996. "Failed Evidence on Grade Retention." *Psychology in the Schools* 33, no. 3: 251–61.

U.S. Department of Education, National Commission on Excellence in Education. 1983. *A Nation at Risk: The Imperative for Educational Reform.* Washington: U.S. Department of Education.

U.S. Department of Education, Office for Civil Rights. 2000. *The Use of Tests When Making High-Stakes Decisions for Students: A Resource Guide for Educators and Policymakers.* Washington: U.S. Department of Education.

Weakliem, David. 1999. "A Critique of the Bayesian Information Criterion in Model Selection." *Sociological Methods and Research* 27, no. 3: 359–97.

6

Do High School Exit Exams Influence Educational Attainment or Labor Market Performance?

THOMAS S. DEE
BRIAN A. JACOB

The federal government has recently taken a central role in promulgating standards-based education reform through the No Child Left Behind (NCLB) Act of 2001. In particular, NCLB has introduced explicit requirements for student testing, as well as consequences for schools that fail to make "adequate yearly progress" toward specific achievement goals. The implementation of this landmark legislation continues to unfold at the state level as the 2013–14 deadline for raising all students to academic proficiency approaches.[1] A question of particular interest about these ongoing standards-based reforms is whether they will be able to close the achievement gaps that contribute to the persistence of poverty and economic inequality.

While NCLB focuses exclusively on *schools* as a unit of accountability, many states have responded to the legislation by implementing programs to hold *students* accountable. Of course, this is not a new phenomenon. The so-called first wave of education reform began approximately thirty years ago as several states began to introduce standardized tests that students were required to pass to graduate. Around the same time, states began to introduce

We would like to thank Wei Ha and J. D. LaRock for excellent research assistance. All remaining errors are our own.

1. Lynn Olson, "Room to Maneuver," *Education Week* 25, no. 15, December 15, 2005, pp. S1–S5.

requirements that students pass an explicit number of core academic courses to graduate.

NCLB appears to have accelerated this trend. By 2000 eighteen states had passed a high school exit exam, most of which were implemented in the 1980s. Since the passage of NCLB, two states (Arkansas and Massachusetts) have implemented exit exams, and three states (Louisiana, Tennessee, and Virginia) have made existing exams substantially more rigorous. Seven other states plan to introduce such requirements within the next seven years.[2] Nearly all states now have explicit requirements for how many core academic courses high school graduates must complete.

Despite their widespread acceptance, these student-focused reforms have been the subject of little rigorous empirical scrutiny. The literature that is available provides contradictory evidence on the fundamental consequences of these state initiatives. In this study, we present new empirical evidence on how these state reforms—in particular, exit exams—influenced educational attainment and early labor market experiences. This study makes three broad contributions to the extant literature. One involves the analysis of more recent datasets (that is, data from the 2000 Census and the Common Core of Data [CCD] from the National Center for Education Statistics [NCES]) and state policy changes. A second contribution is the use of research designs that are robust to potential confounding factors and that allow us to synthesize our findings with the prior literature. Third, we directly examine how the effects of these policies may have varied by race, gender, and ethnicity and assess what these findings suggest about the effects of first-wave reforms on children in poverty.

We find evidence that these student-focused standards-based reforms have exacerbated inequality. Our analysis of data of the 2000 Census indicates that exit exams led to particularly large increases in the dropout rates of Black students. Similarly, our analysis of Minnesota's recent exit exam, based on the NCES' Common Core of Data, indicates that this state's graduation requirement increased the dropout rates in school districts with relatively large concentrations of minority students as well as in urban and high-poverty school districts while reducing the dropout rates in suburban and low-poverty school districts.

At the same time, we find some evidence that these policies may have benefited certain groups. For example, our analysis of data from the 2000 Census indicates that exit exams improved some longer-term outcomes (for example, college matriculation, labor-market outcomes) for Hispanic females

2. Sullivan and others (2005).

and Blacks. Similarly, the positive effects of exit exams in Minnesota's suburban and more affluent school districts suggest the potentially beneficial incentive effects of these types of policies.

This study is organized as follows. The second section provides background on the first-wave reforms and discusses the prior literature. The third section presents new evaluation results based on data from the 2000 Census. The fourth section presents complementary evidence based on dropout data from the Common Core of Data. The chapter concludes with a discussion of what these results suggest about the effects of ongoing standards-based reforms.

"First-Wave" Education Reforms

In the 1970s, there was a growing perception that the quality of public schools was in decline and that the high school diploma, in particular, was no longer a meaningful credential that vouched for a student's skills and motivation.[3] These concerns were often voiced most prominently by local business leaders concerned with the quality of the entering workforce. Nearly every state responded to these concerns by instituting testing programs designed to assess students' basic skills.[4]

Conceptual Framework

The intent of most of these new testing programs was to identify low-performing students and provide them with sources of remediation. However, a number of states also began to require that students pass a performance threshold to graduate.[5] These exit exams (EEs), particularly in their earliest incarnations, typically required that students demonstrate math and reading skills at only an eighth or ninth grade level. Furthermore, students often began taking these exams as early as eighth or ninth grade and were typically given multiple retesting opportunities so that they could graduate. Nonetheless, the failure rates on these exams often proved politically unacceptable, and states would sometimes lower their cut scores or adjust their exemptions in response.[6]

In addition to these test-based standards, states also began introducing a particular type of "process" standard during this period that required high

3. See, for example, Popham (1981).
4. Pipho (1978).
5. States typically delayed the enactment of these exit exams to provide students with adequate notice, to allow for the development of the tests and curricular changes, and in response to court challenges (see table A6-1).
6. See, for example, Catterall (1989).

school graduates to complete an explicit number of courses, particularly in core academic areas. These reforms accelerated after *A Nation at Risk* decried "cafeteria-style" curricula and recommended that the adoption of a "New Basics" curriculum that included four years of English and three years of social studies, science, and mathematics.[7] Only a few states adopted the "New Basics" requirements, but virtually every state introduced or increased its course graduation requirements (CGRs) over the last three decades.

The public discourse that accompanied the adoption of these policies focused on encouraging the academic effort of students and reinvigorating the high school diploma as a meaningful education credential. However, these reforms could conceivably influence student outcomes in several distinct and sometimes contradictory ways. For example, the most obvious potential consequence of exit exams is to elicit increased academic effort from students. The potential education benefits of exit exams could also extend beyond the marginal student from whom they might encourage additional effort. In particular, one study discusses how the higher and external standards implied by exit exams might limit the "nerd harassment" and peer pressure that encourages high-ability students to shirk educational effort.[8]

However, the introduction of exit exams could also have unintended, pejorative consequences for the effort and achievement of particular students. For example, the existence of a testing requirement could reduce the academic engagement of very low-performing students who see little chance of passing the exam. It has also been suggested that standards like exit exams could reduce performance among high-achieving students by prominently signaling relatively low public expectations.[9] In fact, the authors of *A Nation at Risk* voiced this concern, suggesting that minimum competency tests would become maximum standards and lower the expectations for high-ability students.

Another conjectured benefit of exit exams is that their high-stakes consequences will promote student achievement by improving the performance of schools and teachers. For example, the literature on "effective schools" has identified several characteristics associated with successful schools. These critical traits include clearly defined objectives, a common mission, continuous monitoring of student performance, and appropriate remediation for under-

7. National Commission on Excellence in Education (1983).
8. Bishop (1999).
9. See, for example, Phillips and Chin (2001).

achieving students.[10] This literature suggests that the introduction of exit exams could make schools more effective by establishing clear objectives and providing student-specific assessments. Exit exams may also encourage (and facilitate) the targeting of remediation efforts to the neediest students in a manner that reduces minority achievement gaps.

However, exit exams could also harm the performances of the school and teachers. For example, high-stakes exit exams could lead teachers to focus their instruction on a limited set of skills or use more didactic teaching methods (both of which might be described as "teaching to the test") that are less effective at fostering intellectual engagement and higher-order critical skills.[11] Indeed, there is strong evidence that high-stakes educational accountability policies lead to strategic placement of low-achieving students into special education or bilingual programs to avoid testing.[12] Of course, provisions of NCLB that require nearly all students to take the exams are intended to mitigate this concern. However, there is even evidence that accountability may lead teachers and administrators to manipulate student exam scores to falsely improve student performance.[13]

As noted above, one of the key motivations for the first-wave education reforms was to ensure that a high school diploma was a signal that a student had mastered important skills. This suggests that the other potentially important consequences of exit exams involve their effects on employer perceptions. More specifically, exit exams may have changed the signal (of achievement and hard work) that a high school diploma provides by changing the composition of workers with different education levels. Proponents generally argue that stricter graduation requirements will increase the benefit of a high school diploma because employers will know that high school graduates have mastered certain skills. What is less often realized, however, is that the introduction of stricter graduation requirements may also enhance the signal conveyed by *not* completing high school. Consider the simplest case in which the new standards have no incentive effects and merely reduce the fraction of those able to obtain a diploma. In this case, the average ability level of the graduates will increase because the lowest-achieving students who received diplomas under the old standard no longer receive diplomas under the new standard. However, the average ability level among dropouts will also increase because the students who were pushed into the dropout group under

10. Purkey and Smith (1983); Purkey and Smith (1985); Stringfield and Teddlie (1988).
11. Murnane and Levy (2001); Airasian (1987); Koretz and Barron (1998); Jacob (2005).
12. Jacob (2005); Figlio and Getzler (2002); Cullen and Reback (2006).
13. Jacob and Levitt (2003).

the new standard are higher achieving than those who were already in the dropout group under the old standard. The sorting induced by the new requirements will therefore improve the labor market outcomes for both dropouts and graduates.[14]

Prior Literature

The prior discussion indicates that the likely effects of the first-wave standards on student outcomes should be viewed as an open, empirical question. However, despite the prominence of standards-based reforms, these long-standing state-level experiments have actually been the subject of relatively little empirical scrutiny. The evidence that does exist is generally mixed and unsatisfactory. This is largely due to two issues: the lack of consistent and reliable data on outcomes such as achievement or educational attainment and the difficulty of differentiating between effects due to the exit exams and effects due to other related policies or conditions in the state at the time. In this subsection, we review several recent studies, highlighting the two difficulties described above.[15]

Several studies conducted cross-sectional analyses of educational attainment and labor market performance using nationally representative datasets such as High School and Beyond (HS&B) and the National Educational Longitudinal Survey of 1988 (NELS:88). One cross-sectional analysis of NELS:88 found that exit exams only increased dropout probabilities for low-ability students.[16] Another study found similar results with the NELS:88: namely, course graduation requirements reduced the probability of seniors graduating from high school, and state exit exams increased dropout rates for students with below-average grades but increased the number of GEDs (general equivalency diplomas) and the average time spent in high school.[17] A third study presented evidence that course graduation requirements, but not state exit exams, increased dropout rates.[18] That analysis is based both on data that have one observation for each state in each year as well as data that have observations on individuals from HS&B and NELS:88, although the exit exam effect is based exclusively on cross-sectional comparisons and does not separately examine lower-achieving students. However, a more recent study, which used a later wave of data from NELS:88, found that high school

---

14. Betts and Costrell (2001).
15. For a survey of earlier research, see Jacob (2001).
16. Jacob (2001).
17. Bishop and Mane (2001).
18. Lillard and DeCicca (2001).

examination requirements were not associated with increased chances of leaving school without a diploma or a GED, even among low socioeconomic status and low-achieving students.[19]

A significant limitation of these studies is that they had a limited ability to control for state-specific factors that may be correlated with student outcomes as well as with the adoption of exit exams or course graduation requirements. For example, one might be concerned that states adopted stricter graduation requirements in response to a decline in student performance, in which case the effects of exit exams or course graduation requirements would likely be biased toward finding negative policy effects. Although the studies cited above attempted to control for state-specific factors such as employment rates, per pupil expenditures, and other things that might influence student outcomes, one might still be concerned about the type of trend described above or some other unobservable state factor. Moreover, analyses based on NELS:88 cannot provide information on cohorts other than on those expected to graduate in 1992.

Another recent study used data from the 1990 Census Public Use Microdata Sample (PUMS) to address several of these concerns.[20] The PUMS used in the study was a 5 percent sample from the Census that includes a variety of information on individuals including age, race, gender, "state of birth" (which serves as a proxy for the state in which one attended secondary school), highest grade completed, employment, and earnings. Using age and state of birth, this study determined whether individuals would have been subject to course graduation requirements or exit exams as adolescents. It then employed a difference-in-difference strategy that involved comparing the outcomes of individuals within the same state who experienced different policies because of their age and the timing of when the policies were introduced. By controlling for fixed effects for state of birth, this approach controls for any time-invariant state characteristics that might be correlated with policy adoption and student outcomes. This study concluded that exit exams reduced the probability of completing high school, but only for Black males. However, the study also found that exit exams created passive labor market rewards for Black males in the form of increased employment in their twenties, an outcome consistent with the hypothesis that these testing regimes changed the signals associated with dropping out and graduating.[21]

---

19. Warren and Edwards (2005).

20. Dee (2003).

21. Dee (2003) considers part-time as well as full-time employment and in some specifications includes controls for whether the respondent was enrolled in school (presumably college)

Finally, several recent studies have utilized state-level data on enrollment and completion rates to examine this issue. Some found that exit exams increased dropout rates, while others found no effects on completion rates.[22] Two other studies suggested that this recent work had several serious methodological shortcomings: for example, information about exit exams is often inaccurate, the state-level measures of completion rates have important flaws, and many of these studies fail to account for unobserved heterogeneity across states.[23]

One of these recent studies addressed these issues of measurement and specification.[24] More specifically, the authors utilized state-level panel data on high school completion rates from 1975 to 2002 and examined three dependent variables:

—A status dropout measure that treats high school diplomas and GEDs as equivalent: this measure is derived from data from the Current Population Survey (CPS) on sixteen- to nineteen-year-olds who are not enrolled in school and do not have a diploma or GED

—A measure of high school completion that uses data from the Common Core of Data: this measure is defined as the ratio of the number of high school completers (which is available for each state and year over many years) to the number of ninth graders enrolled three academic years earlier, after adjusting for interstate migration

—The percent of sixteen- to nineteen-year-olds in a state who take the GED

They found that exit exams were associated with lower completion rates and higher rates of people taking the GED exam and that these relationships were stronger in states with more difficult exams, higher poverty levels, and more racial and ethnic minorities.

The authors noted that state-level high school dropout rates from the CPS have substantial limitations, but they chose to report results on this measure

---

at the time of the interview. At the time of the interview, all respondents would have been at least twenty years of age. Moreover, the author found that exit exams had no impact on the likelihood that Black males would enroll in college. Together, these facts suggested that the employment effects were not driven by the fact that high school dropouts were more likely to be employed than enrolled students. While these results are consistent with a scenario in which the implementation of an exit exam changes the composition of dropouts and graduates, the findings are also consistent with a scenario in which the implementation of the exam changed the actual skills acquired by students (dropouts as well as graduates). However, Dee also found that exit exams were associated with reductions in students taking core academic courses.

22. Amrein and Berliner (2002); Carnoy and Loeb (2002); Greene and Winters (2004); Warren and Jenkins (2005); Marchant and Paulson (2005).

23. Warren, Jenkins, and Kulick (2005); Warren (2005).

24. Warren, Jenkins, and Kulick (2005).

so that they could compare their results with prior research. The authors' preferred measure was their estimated high school completion rate. A related analysis suggested that this measure was not biased by interstate migration, grade retention, or changes in the size of incoming high school cohorts.[25] However, the authors noted that this measure is modestly biased by international migration and student retention in the eighth grade. From the perspective of evaluating the effects of exit exams, the first study had two more substantive shortcomings. One was that the aggregate state-year completion rates made it more difficult to examine the important question of how the effects of exit exams may have varied by race, gender, and ethnicity. Second, this study did not address the issue of whether exit exams have had their conjectured effects on subsequent labor market outcomes.

Another study applied a distinctly novel research design to the dropout question.[26] The author examined the impact of the exit exam in Texas utilizing a regression discontinuity design in which he compared students who barely pass and barely fail the test. He found two particularly interesting results. First, there was no evidence of a discouragement effect. That is, students who barely failed the exam in tenth or eleventh grade were no more likely to drop out than were students who barely passed the exam in these grades. Second, the exam did ultimately reduce the likelihood of graduation. Students who barely failed the final exam had significantly lower chances of holding either a diploma or a GED and were less likely to attend postsecondary schooling compared with those who barely passed. The author estimated that roughly 1 percent of Texas students do not graduate because they cannot pass the test, which implies a relative effect of roughly 5 percent (relative to the mean dropout rate).[27]

The most recent studies of high school exit exams provide mixed evidence on the basic question of whether they increased the likelihood of dropping out of high school. This study contributes to this literature in several distinct ways:

—We use the most recently available data, which allow us to assess whether the more recent (and generally more rigorous) exit exams uniquely influenced educational attainment.

—Unlike several of the prior studies, we also focus on the important question of whether these reforms had unique effects by race, gender, or ethnicity.

25. Warren (2005).
26. Martorell (2004).
27. The relative effect is calculated by dividing the absolute effect (1 percentage point) by the average dropout rate (20 percent), which yields 1 ÷ 20 = 0.05 or 5 percent.

—Our study examines the effects of exit exams on subsequent labor market outcomes, not just on educational attainment.

Evidence from the 2000 Census

In this section, we present new evidence on the impact of exit exams and course graduation requirements using data from the 2000 Census Public Use Microdata Sample (2000 PUMS). The PUMS data offer several other advantages relative to the CPS and CCD data used in the analyses described above. First, the large number of respondents in the PUMS allows one to precisely identify very small policy effects, and a better ability to detect race-specific responses to educational policies. Second, the background information on race and gender allows one to examine the impact of educational policies across important demographic subpopulations. Third, the self-reported data on educational attainment avoid some of the problems associated with the imputed high school completion measures in prior research.[28] Also, because PUMS respondents report educational attainment as of 1999, for most birth cohorts the data will allow an individual who takes longer than four years to finish high school to be counted as completing. Finally, the PUMS provides information on other interesting and important outcomes such as college attendance, employment, and earnings.

However, the PUMS has several important limitations. First, because of interstate mobility, state of birth is an imperfect proxy for the state in which a child attended secondary school. This measurement error will tend to attenuate the effects of the state-level education policy variables such as exit exams and course graduation requirements. Second, respondents may systematically misreport educational attainment or employment. On the one hand, if this misreporting is (conditionally) random with respect to relevant characteristics, it will simply increase the residual variation in our models and thus decrease the precision of our estimates. On the other hand, if an individual's tendency to misreport his or her educational attainment is correlated with the existence of an exit exam and course graduation requirements, the misreporting may introduce bias into our estimates. A third and related problem is that the PUMS questionnaire does not distinguish between conventional high school graduates and GED completers. In light of the possibility that exit exams encourage students to drop out but also attain a GED, this Census coding convention implies that our results will

---

28. See, for example, Warren, Jenkins, and Kulick (2005).

understate the true policy-induced reductions in the likelihood of graduating from high school.

Data

The 2000 PUMS consists of approximately 14 million respondents (5 percent of the population) who completed the long-form questionnaire to the decennial Census (U.S. Bureau of the Census 2003).[29] The PUMS includes a host of information on respondents, including age, race, gender, state of birth, current state of residence, educational attainment, and labor market performance. One particularly useful feature of the PUMS is that, because it contains individuals from multiple birth cohorts within each state, one can exploit within-state variation in exit exams and course graduation requirements instead of the cross-state variation to estimate the effects of these policies.

Our extract from the PUMS data consists of the 2,925,005 White (non-Hispanic), Hispanic, and Black respondents who were aged eighteen between 1980 and 1998 and who were born in one of forty-nine states.[30] Two of the outcome variables defined for each respondent identify educational attainment, a binary indicator for high school graduation and another for college entrance.[31] We limited the sample to those who were at least eighteen by 1998 because of the biases that could be generated by state-specific trends in the "incomplete spells" of high school completion and college entrance among cohorts that were younger at the time of the Census interview.[32] The other dependent variables reflect the labor market experiences of each PUMS respondent. One is a binary indicator for employment participation, which is defined for all respondents.[33] The other is the natural log of average weekly wages, which is defined only for 2,429,250 respondents. This wage variable

---

29. U.S. Census Bureau (2000).

30. See Ruggles and others (2004). Respondents born in Nebraska were omitted since that state does not use Carnegie units in defining its graduation standards. The inclusion of Nebraska does not change the results for exit exams. We identified the year in which each respondent was eighteen by their age on enumeration day (April 1, 2000). Respondents from the District of Columbia or those born abroad were also excluded.

31. College entrants are those whose highest reported educational attainment was "Some college, no degree" or higher. It should be noted that this sample, of course, includes students who attended private schools. However, their inclusion is arguably appropriate since it is possible that students may switch schools to avoid the consequences of stricter standards.

32. Angrist and Evans (1999).

33. Those who report that they are not in the labor force are defined as unemployed to avoid omitting discouraged workers. However, the exclusion of these respondents does not substantively alter the subsequent results.

is the ratio of pretax wage and salary income reported for the previous calendar year to the corresponding number of weeks worked.

Using the respondents' birth years and states of birth, we determine whether each individual was subject to an exit exam and course graduation requirements. Specifically, we assign to each respondent the policies regarding exit exams and course graduation requirement that applied to the high school graduating class in his or her state of birth when the respondent was eighteen years old. For example, a twenty-seven-year-old respondent born in Virginia would have been eighteen years old in 1991 and thus was assigned the policies in place for the graduating class of 1991 in Virginia. Table 6A-1 presents data on exit exams by state and year. Here, "year" refers to a graduating class rather than a calendar year. For example, when we say that "Virginia had an exit exam in 2000," we mean that the high school graduating class of 2000 in Virginia was subject to the exam.

Similar to at least one other recent study, this study distinguishes between more and less difficult exit exams based on the difficulty of the material included in the exam.[34] Specifically, if any component of a state exit exam assessed material that was first presented during the high school years (that is, in ninth grader or later), the exit exam is referred to as a more difficult exam. Information on the grade level of the material assessed in an exit exam was gathered from a variety of sources, including official reports published by state departments of education as well as newspaper accounts of the exit exam.[35] Note that this definition has several shortcomings. Because districts may introduce material at different grade levels, it is difficult to determine whether this measure is comparable across states. In addition, states can alter the difficulty of an exam by adjusting the required passing score, so that it is possible that an exam containing "less difficult" material may actually be more difficult to pass relative to an exam covering more difficult material.

The second dummy identifies whether the state had high, academically focused course graduation requirements (CGRs) in effect for that graduating class. "High" CGRs are defined here as a required high school curriculum that includes at least 3 Carnegie units in English, 2 in social studies, 1 in sci-

34. Warren, Jenkins, and Kulick (2005).
35. It is worth noting that our investigation revealed several potential mistakes in the classification adopted by Warren, Jenkins, and Kulick (2005). For example, the authors indicated that the Florida exam became "more difficult" in 1993, whereas our research indicates that this did not occur until the introduction of the Florida Comprehensive Assessment Test (FCAT) in 1996. Similarly, they indicated that Louisiana's exit exam was "more difficult" since its inception in 1991, while our research indicates that it did not reach this level of difficulty until the introduction of a new exam in 2003.

ence, and 1 in mathematics.[36] "Very high" CGRs are defined here as a curriculum that requires the following: 4 Carnegie units in English, 3 in social studies, 2 in math, and 2 in science.

Table 6-1 presents summary statistics for our sample. Roughly 87 percent of respondents graduated from high school, and 57 percent attended at least some college. About 14 percent of the sample is Black, and 3 percent is Hispanic.[37] More than 75 percent of respondents were employed at the time of the survey. Approximately 32 percent of state-year observations have an exit exam, but only 5 percent have a more difficult exit exam. Rigorous course graduation requirements are more common, with 75 percent of state-year observations requiring at least 3 units of English, 2 units of social studies, and 1 unit of math and science and 25 percent requiring 4, 3, 2, and 2 or more (respectively).

Empirical Strategy

The goal of our analysis is to estimate the causal impact of exit exams and course graduation requirements on educational attainment and labor market outcomes. Our primary concern is that unobserved factors may be correlated with both the introduction of these policies and our outcome measures, which could lead our estimates to understate or overstate the true "causal" impact of the educational policies. Since these reforms were state policies that were enacted in particular years, we are most concerned about unobserved state- or time-specific factors, perhaps including things such as economic conditions or other educational policies. To mitigate this concern, we estimate what are often referred to as state-year panel data models. By focusing exclusively on changes that take place *within* states over time, this approach removes the possible biases due to unobserved time-invariant state-level determinants of educational attainment and labor market performance. We are effectively comparing the differences among cohorts in the "treatment" states before and after the introduction of new standards to the contemporaneous cross-cohort changes in the "control" states.

The basic specification used for regression models based on these data is:

$$(1) \qquad Y_{ist} = \beta X_{ist} + \gamma Z_{st} + \mu_s + \alpha_t + \varepsilon_{ist},$$

36. Some studies represent state CGR policies by the total number of Carnegie units required. However, this measure may more accurately reflect the focus of reform efforts (for example, a major emphasis of *A Nation at Risk* was to increase the number of courses that students take in core academic areas).

37. The proportion of Hispanics is lower than the national average since we exclude all respondents who were foreign-born.

where Y_{ist} is the dependent variable for respondent i in state of birth s and birth cohort t, and the matrix $\mathbf{X}$ includes observed, individual-level traits. In most models, the individual covariates simply include binary indicators for race and gender. In the models for labor market outcomes, we also estimate models that control for measures of educational attainment (that is, separate dummy variables for high school graduates, those with some college, and those with bachelor degrees) and a dummy variable for whether the respondent attended school within the last year.[38] We discuss the estimates from the reduced form as well as the more complete models in the next section. The terms μ_s and α_t represent fixed effects specific to each state of birth and year of birth. The term ε_{ist} is a mean-zero random error. We report Huber-White heteroscedastic-consistent standard errors, which allow for arbitrary correlation of errors within each state of birth.[39] For specifications with dichotomous outcome variables, we estimate probit models; for other specifications, we estimate OLS (ordinary least squares) models.

The matrix $\mathbf{Z}$ includes determinants that were specific to the birth cohorts within each state. These determinants include the two independent variables of interest: dummy variables that reflect the state EE and CGRs policies in place for each birth cohort at age eighteen. These and other state-year controls were matched to the respondents by their state of birth and year of birth. As noted earlier, the measurement error introduced by relying on state of birth will lead to attenuation bias in these state-level variables, suggesting that the reported estimates can be interpreted as lower bounds on the true effects.[40]

As suggested earlier, the identification strategy embedded in this model makes a potentially important contribution to our understanding of the consequences of exit exams and course graduation requirements because it removes the possible biases due to unobserved time-invariant state-level determinants of educational attainment and labor market performance. The inclusion of state fixed effects means that we are effectively comparing the differences among cohorts in the "treatment" states before and after the introduction of new standards to the contemporaneous cross-cohort changes in the "control" states.

We present some evidence on the empirical relevance of relying on within-state versus cross-state comparisons by comparing the results of models that

38. The school attendance variable is meant to control for the fact that those respondents still in school over the last year would have had limited labor market experiences. This specification is similar to those used by Bishop and Mane (2001).

39. Bertrand, Duflo, and Mullainathan (2004).

40. We found that the results were similar in models that matched respondents to the state-year variables by their state of residence five years before the Census.

Table 6-1. *Descriptive Statistics for the PUMS Analysis*

Source (definition)	Full sample				Less difficult exit exam		More difficult exit exam	
	Min	Max	Mean	SD	Mean	SD	Mean	SD
Dependent variables								
High school graduate — 2000 PUMS (completed high school—may or may not have obtained further education)	0	1	0.873	0.333	0.859	0.348	0.826	0.379
Attended college — 2000 PUMS (enrolled in college—may or may not have obtained further education)	0	1	0.573	0.495	0.568	0.495	0.508	0.500
Employed — 2000 PUMS (those not in the labor force are included as unemployed)	0	1	0.755	0.430	0.740	0.439	0.676	0.468
Average weekly earnings[a] — 2000 PUMS (total annual salary income divided by number of weeks worked)	0.077	325,000	615	1,178	617	1,205	380	807
Ln(average weekly earnings) — 2000 PUMS	-2.565	12.692	6.080	0.802	6.082	0.795	5.624	0.745
Main independent variables								
Less difficult exit exam (EE) — Various sources (in effect for the high school graduating class in the respondent's state of birth in the year that the respondent was seventeen years old; covers material below ninth grade level)	0	1	0.317	0.465	1.000	0.000	0.000	0.000
More difficult EE — Various sources (covers material at ninth grade level or higher)	0	1	0.053	0.224	0.000	0.000	1.000	0.000
Moderately rigorous course graduation requirements (CGRs) — Various sources (at least 3 Carnegie units in English, 2 in social studies, 1 in math, 1 in science)	0	1	0.746	0.436	0.444	0.497	0.516	0.500
Very rigorous CGRs — Various sources (at least 4 in English, 3 in social studies, 2 in math, 2 in science)	0	1	0.234	0.423	0.456	0.498	0.484	0.500
Individual covariates								
Female — 2000 PUMS	0	1	0.506	0.500	0.509	0.500	0.501	0.500
Black — 2000 PUMS	0	1	0.135	0.342	0.212	0.409	0.168	0.374

Variable	Source	Min	Max	Mean	SD	Mean	SD	Mean	SD
Hispanic	2000 PUMS	0	1	0.033	0.178	0.027	0.161	0.068	0.252
Enrolled in school	2000 PUMS	0	1	0.152	0.359	0.152	0.359	0.327	0.469
High school graduate (completed high school but did not obtain any further education)	2000 PUMS	0	1	0.300	0.458	0.291	0.454	0.318	0.466
Some college (completed high school and enrolled in college or obtained an AA degree)	2000 PUMS	0	1	0.354	0.478	0.337	0.473	0.415	0.493
BA (obtained a BA degree or higher)	2000 PUMS	0	1	0.219	0.414	0.231	0.422	0.093	0.290
State-level time-varying covariates									
Poverty rate	*Statistical Abstract of the United States* (in respondent's state of birth when the respondent was seventeen years old)	0.024	0.180	0.139	0.036	0.150	0.036	0.148	0.030
Unemployment rate	*Statistical Abstract of the United States* (in respondent's state of birth when the respondent was seventeen years old)	0.029	0.272	0.068	0.021	0.064	0.015	0.058	0.009
Ln(number of eighteen-year-olds in the state)	Census (in respondent's state of birth when the respondent was eighteen years old)	8.814	13.050	11.647	0.832	11.754	0.702	12.148	0.401
Average in-state tuition at lowest-level state college (dollars)	State of Washington Higher Education Coordinating Board (in respondent's state of birth when the respondent was seventeen years old)	0.000	2,698	727	362	802	352	813	336
K–12 student-teacher ratio	*Digest of Educational Statistics* (in respondent's state of birth when the respondent was seventeen years old)	1.900	27.400	17.965	2.496	17.082	1.727	16.133	1.182
Average K–12 teacher salary (2000 dollars)	*Digest of Educational Statistics* (in respondent's state of birth when the respondent was seventeen years old)	11,448	50,647	27,242	8,757	28,305	8,020	34,309	5,320
State issued school report cards for K–12	Various sources (policy in respondent's state of birth when the respondent was twelve years old)	0	1	0.015	0.121	0.019	0.137	0.035	0.184
Number of executions	Various sources	0	37	0.845	3.219	0.859	0.348	0.826	0.379

Source: 2000 PUMS.

Min = minimum value; Max = maximum value; SD = standard deviation.

a. There are a very small number of cases where the average weekly wage is less than $10 and, as in the case of the minimum, less than $1. These are clearly data entry errors, but because there are so few such cases, they were kept in the data.

do and do not include the state fixed effects. As a further ad hoc check on the validity of this specification, in some models we include an additional predictor variable—namely, the number of state executions that took place in a respondent's state of birth when the respondent was eighteen years of age as a predictor.[41] Insofar as one believes that state executions should not have had a large and statistically significant effect on educational attainment, for example, the finding of such effects would suggest the presence of specification error. One virtue of using state executions for this type of "falsification exercise" is that there was considerable variation over this period both within states and across states in the number of state executions.

In the preferred specifications, which include state fixed effects, the possible sources of omitted variable biases are the unobserved determinants of Y that are also related to the timing of new standards within states. The matrix Z addresses this concern by including other regression controls that vary by state and year. For example, new state standards were sometimes part of omnibus education bills that included other policy changes such as increased spending. To control for the possible effects of school spending, some models include, as an independent state-level variable, per pupil expenditures in K–12 public schools when the respondents were sixteen- to seventeen-years-old. For example, respondents who were eighteen in 1980 were matched to the school expenditures in their state during the 1978–79 school year. Another state-year control in most models is the state unemployment rate when the respondent was seventeen years old. This variable is expected to have a positive effect on educational attainment since it reduces the opportunity costs associated with remaining in school.[42]

A recent study presented evidence that the natural variation in the size of the population of a particular birth cohort could also influence educational attainment.[43] At the college level, this could occur if temporary increases in cohort size were not fully matched by an increased supply of enrollment space at local colleges and universities. At the secondary level, increased cohort size may reduce the benefits of remaining in school by lowering school quality.[44] Therefore, we also include a measure of cohort size based on the natural log of the U.S. Census Bureau's estimate of eighteen-year-olds in the respondent's state of birth at age eighteen. We also include a measure of

---

41. See, for example, Dee (2003).

42. Duncan (1965).

43. Card and Lemieux (2001).

44. Card and Lemieux (2001) found that cohort size was associated with significant increases in pupil-teacher ratios.

the real costs of postsecondary tuition based on the in-state rate at "lower-level" state colleges and universities when the respondent was seventeen-years-old.[45] As a control for within-state changes in socioeconomic conditions, we also matched each respondent to the poverty rate in their state when they were seventeen years old. Finally, we include one additional measure of a related policy concerning educational accountability in the state at the time the respondent was eighteen years of age: a binary variable indicating whether the state issued report cards for individual schools.

Results

Table 6-2 shows the marginal effects evaluated at the mean derived from probit models predicting the likelihood of graduating from high school. Column 1 presents what might be described as the baseline specification, which includes individual demographics (that is, indicators for Black and female) along with state and year fixed effects. There is no significant relationship between the likelihood of dropping out and the existence of either an exit exam or course graduation requirements. In column 2, we see that adding controls for time-varying state variables does not change the results. The standard errors on the EE and CGRs variables imply that our analysis has the power to detect effects of roughly +/− 0.4 percentage point, which translates into roughly 3 percent if one uses an average dropout rate of 12.7 percent as a baseline.

The specification shown in column 3 includes separate indicators for more and less difficult exit exams and course graduation requirements but does not find effects that are significant at conventional levels. It is also possible that the impact of exit exams and course graduation requirements evolves over time, as students, parents, and teachers become more familiar with the new requirements. In results not shown here, we test for an interaction between the existence of a less difficult exit exam and the number of years it has been required, but we do not find any significant results.[46]

Column 4 serves as a specification check. In this specification, we include the number of state-year executions in the model as a predictor. Since we do not think that the number of executions could have any causal impact on the contemporaneous high school completion rate, if this variable is a significant

45. See Card and Lemieux (2001) and Kane (1994). Complete data on community college tuition were not available for several states. For these states (New Hampshire, South Dakota, California, and South Carolina), we used state college tuition.
46. The more difficult exit exams have not been in place long enough to obtain reliable estimates on the time trend for these exams.

Table 6-2. *Probit Estimates of the Effect of High School Graduation Requirements on High School Completion*[a]

Independent variable	(1)	(2)	(3)	(4)	(5)
Any exit exam	−0.001	−0.002	. . .	. . .	. . .
	(0.003)	(0.002)			
Less difficult exit exam	. . .	. . .	−0.002	−0.002	−0.005**
			(0.002)	(0.002)	(0.001)
More difficult exit exam	. . .	. . .	−0.005	−0.006*	−0.007**
			(0.003)	(0.003)	(0.003)
Any course graduation requirements	−0.001	−0.002	. . .	. . .	. . .
	(0.003)	(0.002)			
Moderately difficult course graduation requirements	. . .	. . .	−0.002	−0.002	−0.002
			(.002)	(.002)	(.002)
Very difficult course graduation requirements	. . .	. . .	0.001	0.001	0.000
			(0.002)	(0.002)	(0.002)
Number of years following introduction of exit exams	. . .	. . .	. . .	. . .	. . .
Number of state executions when the individual was 18	. . .	. . .	. . .	0.0003**	0.0001
				(0.0001)	(0.0002)
Mean of the dependent variable	0.873	0.873	0.873	0.873	0.873
State-year controls	no	yes	yes	yes	yes
Division-specific cubic time trends	no	no	no	no	yes
Number of observations	2,925,005	2,925,005	2,925,005	2,925,005	2,925,005

Source: 2000 PUMS.

*Significant at the 10 percent level; **significant at the 5 percent level.

. . . Not applicable.

a. The dependent variable is "high school completion." The unit of observation is the individual. The marginal effect evaluated at the mean is shown in each cell. Standard errors shown in parentheses are adjusted to account for clustering of errors within the state of birth.

The sample includes individuals aged twenty to thirty-eight on census day. Residents from Nebraska and the District of Columbia are excluded. Only individuals indicating race as White, Black, or Hispanic are included.

More difficult exit exams are those in which the tested material is at the ninth grade level or higher. *Rigorous course graduation requirements* are defined as those which require students to earn at least 3 Carnegie units in English, 2 in social studies, 1 in math, and 1 in science. *Very rigorous course graduation requirements* are defined as those which require at least 4 units in English, 3 in social studies, 2 in math, and 2 in science.

All models include individual demographic controls (binary indicators for female and Black) and fixed effects for state of birth and year of birth. State-year controls include the unemployment rate, the natural log of the number of eighteen-year-olds, the poverty rate, the average teacher salary, the average student-teacher ratio, and an indicator for whether the state issued report cards for K–12 schools.

predictor, then we might be concerned that we have omitted an important time-varying state characteristic that influences educational outcomes and might bias our estimates. Indeed, we find that the number of state executions is positively associated with the high school graduation rate, which raises concerns about our previous specification.

In an effort to more completely account for time-varying state characteristics that might confound our analysis, in column 5 we include a series of division-specific time trends. Specifically, we interact linear, squared, and cubed terms for the number of years since 1979 with nine indicators for each of the different census divisions (that is, New England, Middle Atlantic, East North Central, West North Central, South Atlantic, East South Central, West South Central, Mountain, and Pacific) for a total of 27 additional covariates (that is, three-year variables × nine census divisions). These covariates control for any factors that may have been changing over time in different parts of the country, including such things such as economic conditions we do not pick up with the unemployment rate, social norms or public policies that pertain to educational attainment, or other factors. In column 5, we see that once we control for these time trends, the coefficient on state executions drops dramatically and is no longer significant.

Turning to the estimates of the education policy variables in column 5, we see that both more and less difficult exams are negatively associated with the likelihood that a student completes high school. Specifically, the easier exit exams are associated with a 0.5 percentage point reduction in the likelihood of completion which, given a baseline dropout rate of 12.7 percent, translates into a 4 percent increase in the probability of dropping out. More difficult exit exams are associated with a 0.7 percentage point or 5.5 percent increase in the probability of dropping out. In contrast, neither the moderate nor the very rigorous CGRs appear to be associated with changes in high school completion.

Table 6-3 shows the results for high school completion separately by race and gender. The specification includes division-specific time trends and thus is comparable with column 5 in table 6-2, with the exception that the models are estimated separately by race and gender, which allows all of the coefficients to vary across groups (that is, a completely unrestricted model).[47] As discussed above, one would expect more rigorous graduation requirements to have a larger negative impact on lower-achieving students, for which we use

---

47. The one difference between the model in column 5 of table 6-2 and the models in table 6-3 is that the former includes an indicator for state executions while the latter do not.

Table 6-3. *Probit Estimates of the Effect of High School Graduation Requirements on High School Completion, by Race and Gender*[a]

Independent variable	All (1)	White male (2)	Black male (3)	Hispanic male (4)	White female (5)	Black female (6)	Hispanic female (7)
Less difficult exit exam	−0.005**	−0.005**	−0.013**	0.032	−0.0002	−0.006	0.0003
	(0.001)	(0.002)	(0.005)	(0.021)	(0.0017)	(0.004)	(0.0188)
More difficult exit exam	−0.006**	−0.006*	−0.018**	0.023	−0.002	−0.021**	0.032
	(0.003)	(0.003)	(0.008)	(0.032)	(0.003)	(0.008)	(0.019)
Moderately difficult course graduation requirements	−0.002	0.0003	−0.003	0.007	−0.003*	−0.003	0.005
	(0.002)	(0.0020)	(0.005)	(0.016)	(0.002)	(0.005)	(0.014)
Very difficult course graduation requirements	−0.0002	0.005**	−0.007	0.008	−0.004*	−0.001	0.008
	(0.0025)	(0.003)	(0.006)	(0.016)	(0.002)	(0.006)	(0.018)
Mean of the dependent variable	0.873	0.878	0.752	0.701	0.908	0.817	0.755
Number of observations	2,925,005	1,212,102	184,909	47,044	1,221,388	210,997	48,543

Source: 2000 PUMS.

*Significant at the 10 percent level; **significant at the 5 percent level.

a. The dependent variable is "high school completion." The unit of observation is the individual. The marginal effect evaluated at the mean is shown in each cell. Standard errors shown in parentheses are adjusted to account for clustering of errors within state of birth.

The sample includes individuals aged twenty to thirty-eight on census day. Residents from Nebraska and the District of Columbia are excluded. Only individuals indicating race as White, Black, or Hispanic are included.

More difficult exit exams are those in which the tested material is at the ninth grade level or higher. *Rigorous course graduation requirements* are defined as those which require students to earn at least 3 Carnegie units in English, 2 in social studies, 1 in math, and 1 in science. *Very rigorous course graduation requirements* are defined as those which require at least 4 units in English, 3 in social studies, 2 in math, and 2 in science.

All models include individual demographic controls (binary indicators for female and Black); fixed effects for state of birth and year of birth; a cubic division-specific time trend; and the following state-year controls: the unemployment rate, the natural log of the number of eighteen-year-olds, the poverty rate, the average teacher salary, the average student-teacher ratio, and an indicator for whether the state issued report cards for K–12 schools.

race and ethnicity as a proxy. Consistent with this hypothesis, we find that exit exams reduce the likelihood of high school completion for Black students by twice as much as they do for White students. More and less difficult exit exams are associated with a 1.3 and 1.8 percentage point reduction, respectively, in the likelihood of high school completion among Black males, which translates into relative dropout effects of roughly 5.2 and 7.3 percent, respectively. Among Black females, easier exit exams do not appear to have significant effects, but more difficult exams are associated with a 2.1 percentage point (11 percent) reduction in the likelihood of completing high school. Interestingly, exit exams do not appear to affect high school completion rates for White females, though they sharply reduce the completion rates among White males. Overall, the existence of course graduation requirements is not associated with changes in high school completion rates, although they do seem to reduce the probability of high school completion for White females.

The results for Hispanics are somewhat more puzzling. Our point estimates suggest that exit exams *increase* the likelihood of high school completion among Hispanics. While the estimates are not significant at conventional levels, the point estimates are large in magnitude and thus may warrant further exploration in subsequent research. We tested the extent to which the somewhat anomalous Hispanic results are due to particular states. It appears that the positive effect of exit exams for Hispanic males is due largely to New York State. If one eliminates New York, the point estimates for more and less rigorous exit exams are both quite close to zero and are not close to statistical significance.[48] The results for Hispanic females do not appear to be due to any single state. One possible explanation for the difference in estimated effects among Black and Hispanic students is that Hispanic students may have been eligible for language-related exemptions and testing accommodations, although this seems less likely given the fact that our sample is limited to native-born Hispanics.[49] It is also possible that schools with predominantly Hispanic populations were more effective in responding to the policies.

As discussed above, the expected effect of exit exams and course graduation requirements on college attendance is unclear. On the one hand, if some of the students who were prevented from graduating from high school because of the requirements would have attended college, we would expect the policies to reduce attendance. On the other hand, if the requirements led other students to be better prepared for college (or to believe that they were

---

48. The point estimates (and standard errors) for more and less rigorous exit exams are 0.007 (0.015) and –0.002 (0.026), respectively (data not shown).
49. Sullivan and others (2005, chapter 6).

better prepared for college), then one would expect the policies to increase postsecondary enrollment. In practice, it seems likely that one would expect to find a negative relationship at the very bottom of the ability distribution but perhaps find a somewhat positive relationship at somewhat higher points on the ability distribution. In general, however, it seems unlikely that we would expect to find any effect among moderate- or high-ability students, for whom the requirements were probably not a binding constraint. In results not shown here, we find that exit exams do not have a significant influence on college attendance. One notable exception is for Hispanic females who faced a more difficult exit exam. These students were considerably more likely to enroll in college than were their counterparts who did not face a difficult exit exam.

The evidence presented thus far is largely consistent with the concerns sometimes raised by critics of standards-based reforms—namely, higher requirements may reduce educational attainment among disadvantaged groups. Moreover, the findings shown in tables 6-2 and 6-3 are consistent with our earlier work.[50] As noted earlier, however, a full evaluation of these policies should consider the impact of more rigorous graduation standards on labor market performance. An examination of the labor market effects is also interesting insofar as business leaders frequently express concern with the quality of their workforce, and they were often instrumental in the adoption of the exit exams and course graduation requirements. Indeed, higher standards may benefit students by inducing greater effort in high school, which is later rewarded in the labor market. They may also influence the relative returns of a high school degree by changing the signal associated with the diploma, although, as discussed above, it is not clear whether this will improve the earnings of high school graduates relative to dropouts, since student sorting alone would suggest that higher standards would raise the ability level of both graduates and dropouts.

Table 6-4 presents results for reduced-form models predicting employment. The covariates are identical to those in the earlier models. Models that control for educational attainment and whether the respondent is currently in school yield comparable results. Overall, the results seem to suggest that neither exit exams nor course graduation requirements had any substantial impact on employment. There is some evidence that exit exams may be associated with slight reductions in employment for Blacks and increases for White females, although these results are quite small in magnitude and only

50. Jacob (2001); Dee (2003).

Table 6-4. *Probit Estimates of the Effect of High School Graduation Requirements on Employment, by Race and Gender*[a]

Independent variable	All (1)	White male (2)	Black male (3)	Hispanic male (4)	White female (5)	Black female (6)	Hispanic female (7)
Less difficult exit exam	0.0005	-0.001	-0.009*	-0.019	0.009*	-0.001	0.006
	(0.0024)	(0.003)	(0.005)	(0.020)	(0.005)	(0.005)	(0.010)
More difficult exit exam	0.003	-0.002	0.004	-0.028	0.009*	-0.009	0.031*
	(0.004)	(0.004)	(0.009)	(0.030)	(0.005)	(0.007)	(0.018)
Moderately difficult course graduation requirements	-0.0002	0.0005	-0.001	-0.023	0.003	-0.010	0.043**
	(0.0017)	(0.0025)	(0.006)	(0.017)	(0.004)	(0.006)	(0.012)
Very difficult course graduation requirements	-0.002	0.002	-0.0002	-0.006	-0.004	-0.008	0.050**
	(0.002)	(0.003)	(0.0063)	(0.020)	(0.004)	(0.007)	(0.017)
Mean of the dependent variable[b]	0.755	0.840	0.600	0.713	0.721	0.643	0.627
Number of observations	2,925,005	1,212,102	184,909	47,053	1,221,388	211,007	48,453

Source: 2000 PUMS.

*Significant at the 10 percent level; **significant at the 5 percent level.

a. The dependent variable is "employed." The unit of observation is the individual. The marginal effect evaluated at the mean is shown in each cell. Standard errors shown in parentheses are adjusted to account for clustering of errors within state of birth.

The sample includes individuals aged twenty to thirty-eight on census day. Residents from Nebraska and the District of Columbia are excluded. Only individuals indicating race as White, Black, or Hispanic are included.

More difficult exit exams are those in which the tested material is at the ninth grade level or higher. *Rigorous course graduation requirements* are defined as those which require students to earn at least 3 Carnegie units in English, 2 in social studies, 1 in math, and 1 in science. *Very rigorous course graduation requirements* are defined as those which require at least 4 units in English, 3 in social studies, 2 in math, and 2 in science.

All models include individual demographic controls (binary indicators for female and Black); fixed effects for state of birth and year of birth; a cubic division-specific time trend; and the following state-year controls: the unemployment rate, the natural log of the number of eighteen-year-olds, the poverty rate, the average teacher salary, the average student-teacher ratio, and an indicator for whether the state issued report cards for K–12 schools.

b. In some cases, the sample sizes differ slightly from those shown in table 6-3 because the Probit estimation procedure drops observation cells with no variation in the outcome, and the results from this procedure can differ across outcomes.

marginally significant. Once again, there is a somewhat puzzling improvement for native-born Hispanic females. Employment rates increase by 0.9 percentage point (1.2 percent given a baseline of 72.1 percent) for these students when they face exit exams and course graduation requirements.

Table 6-5 presents results for earnings. Note that only respondents who reported earnings greater than zero are included in these specifications. While the estimates are quite noisy, a few tentative patterns emerge. The introduction of course graduation requirements is not significantly related to earnings. However, exit exams (particularly the more difficult ones) tended to reduce the subsequent earnings of White and Hispanic students while increasing those of Black students. The wage gains of Black students are somewhat surprising in light of their reduced educational attainment and the evidence of wage losses among non-Black students. This heterogeneous pattern of results cannot be easily reconciled as a signaling phenomenon and instead suggests that there were unique incentive effects of exit exams by race and ethnicity, at least at the center of the wage distribution.

To summarize, our results indicate that exit exams led to statistically significant reductions in high school completion, which were concentrated among Black students and White males. In terms of labor market outcomes, our results indicate that exit exams may have increased the subsequent earnings of Black students while reducing those of White students. Finally, our results highlight a surprising and puzzling positive effect of stricter graduation requirements, particularly exit exams, on the outcomes of native-born Hispanic females. For example, our estimates indicate that exit exams improved the college matriculation and employment of native-born Hispanic females.

Evidence from the Common Core of Data (CCD)

The evaluation results based on the 2000 Census indicate that exit exams, particularly the most difficult ones, reduced the probability of completing high school among White males and Black students. However, there are a number of reasons to be concerned that these estimates may understate the true effects of exit exams on the probability of completing high school. For example, the use of state of birth to match PUMS respondents to their state exit exam requirement could introduce measurement error. To the extent this measurement error promotes attenuation bias, the true effect of exit exams on educational attainment would be understated.

A second issue that would also lead our results to understate the true effect of exit exams on the probability of completing high school is that the PUMS

Table 6-5. *OLS Estimates of the Effect of High School Graduation Requirements on Earnings, by Race and Gender*[a]

Independent variable	All (1)	White male (2)	Black male (3)	Hispanic male (4)	White female (5)	Black female (6)	Hispanic female (7)
Less difficult exit exam	-0.005	-0.014*	0.012	-0.040	-0.009	0.005	-0.004
	(0.005)	(0.008)	(0.008)	(0.034)	(0.006)	(0.007)	(0.021)
More difficult exit exam	-0.012	-0.027*	0.022*	-0.071*	-0.022**	0.028*	-0.005
	(0.009)	(0.016)	(0.011)	(0.039)	(0.011)	(0.015)	(0.038)
Moderately difficult course graduation requirements	-0.001	-0.006	-0.002	-0.011	0.004	0.007	0.001
	(0.005)	(0.007)	(0.009)	(0.023)	(0.006)	(0.008)	(0.028)
Very difficult course graduation requirements	0.003	0.003	-0.012	0.011	0.004	-0.004	0.021
	(0.007)	(0.009)	(0.010)	(0.041)	(0.007)	(0.009)	(0.032)
Mean of the dependent variable	6.080	6.289	6.023	6.057	5.910	5.847	5.804
Number of observations	2,429,250	1,073,357	139,183	39,109	974,508	166,250	36,843
R-squared	0.1945	0.2063	0.1185	0.1361	0.1188	0.1063	0.0992

Source: 2000 PUMS.

*Significant at the 10 percent level; **significant at the 5 percent level.

a. The dependent variable is "ln(average weekly wages)." The unit of observation is the individual. Standard errors shown in parentheses are adjusted to account for clustering of errors within state of birth.

The sample includes individuals aged twenty to thirty-eight on census day. Residents from Nebraska and the District of Columbia are excluded. Only individuals indicating race as White, Black, or Hispanic and who reported earnings greater than zero are included.

More difficult exit exams are those in which the tested material is at the ninth grade level or higher. *Rigorous course graduation requirements* are defined as those which require students to earn at least 3 Carnegie units in English, 2 in social studies, 1 in math, and 1 in science. *Very rigorous course graduation requirements* are defined as those which require at least 4 units in English, 3 in social studies, 2 in math, and 2 in science.

All models include individual demographic controls (binary indicators for female and Black); fixed effects for state of birth and year of birth; a cubic division-specific time trend; and the following state-year controls: the unemployment rate, the natural log of the number of eighteen-year-olds, the poverty rate, the average teacher salary, the average student-teacher ratio, and an indicator for whether the state issued report cards for K–12 schools.

survey did not distinguish high school completers from GED completers.[51] A third issue is that, because the PUMS data provide "status" data on educational attainment (that is, the total share meeting a definition at a given point in time), they do not identify precisely when exit exams may have increased the probability of dropping out. In other words, this evidence does not identify whether most students dropped out after failing their initial attempts (that is, early in high school) or persisted with retests through twelfth grade. The design of improved remediation for the dropout risk ostensibly created by exit exams could benefit from evidence of such grade-by-grade risks. A fourth and more general concern is that the empirical evidence based on an alternative identification strategy would provide useful evidence on the robustness of the Census results.

This section addresses several of these concerns by presenting different evidence on whether (and when) exit exams increased the probability of dropping out of high school. This analysis is based on unique, *district-level* dropout data that the National Center for Education Statistics began collecting in the early 1990s through the Common Core of Data.[52] Generally, the NCES has only reported these data from states that used dropout definitions that conformed to their standard, which is described below.[53] Fortunately, over the last fifteen years, the number of states that have chosen to conform to their definition has increased. However, because of the limited overlap between states that have consistently reported these dropout data and states that introduced exit exams during this period, we focus on the experiences within one particular state, Minnesota.

Graduation Requirements in Minnesota

In the early 1990s, the Minnesota legislature and the state board of education expressed their intention to develop "results-oriented" high school graduation requirements for the state's public school students. As in many other states, the motivation for these requirements came from business and community leaders concerned that students did not have the basic skills necessary for productive employment and responsible citizenship. The subsequent

51. There is evidence that exit exams increased rates of GED completion (for example, Warren, Jenkins, and Kulick 2005).

52. Prior analyses based on NCES data have relied on state-level reports of the number of high school diplomas granted and measures of the relevant enrollment base, often with attempted adjustments for the effects of grade retention and migration; see, for example, Greene and Winters (2004), Warren, Jenkins, and Kulick (2005).

53. In more recent years, the CCD also reports dropout data from states that use a similar definition of a dropout except for their calendar conventions.

graduation rules required that students pass "Basic Skills Tests" (BSTs) in math, reading, and writing to graduate. Passing scores on the math and reading tests were first required of the graduating class of 2000 (that is, of graduates who were ninth graders during the 1996–97 school year). The requirement that public high school graduates achieve a passing score on the writing test was delayed until the graduating class of 2001.[54]

Another prominent component of Minnesota's new high school graduation requirements was that students demonstrate higher-order understanding through complex and highly controversial performance-based assessments known as the "Profile of Learning." These standards became effective somewhat later (beginning with students entering ninth grade during the 1998–99 school year). While there is some evidence that the unpopular Profile influenced classroom practice, its implementation was highly uneven.[55] After several years of legislative wrangling, the state effectively transferred control over these standards to local school districts.[56] Then, shortly after our study period (in 2003), the Profile was abolished entirely. Unsurprisingly, we found that the Profile had no distinct effects on dropout rates separate from those of the BSTs requirement. Nonetheless, a caveat about our reduced-form results is appropriate because the timing of these policy changes overlapped considerably.[57]

For all the reasons discussed earlier, whether Minnesota's BSTs requirement actually increased or decreased dropout rates is clearly an open empirical question. When Minnesota's 80,000 eighth graders first took the BSTs in the spring of 1996, the pass rates seemed surprisingly low to many observers; only 63 percent passed the reading test, and 76 percent passed the math test. And these initial passing rates were substantially lower among minority and low-income students.[58]

However, the ultimate effect of the BST requirements on dropout rates could be attenuated by a number of factors. For example, relative to other

54. Beginning with the class of 2001, the cut score required to pass the BST also increased from 70 percent of questions answered correctly to 75 (see Allie Shah, "More 12th Graders Fail Skills Tests; New Writing Test, Stricter Scoring Affect Results," *Minneapolis Star Tribune*, June 1, 2001, page 1A).

55. Avery, Beach, and Coler (2003).

56. See Avery, Beach, and Coler (2003) for details.

57. However, it should be noted that the grade-specific heterogeneity in our BST results is clearly consistent with exit exam effects but less plausibly related to the Profile.

58. Maureen M. Smith and Duchesne Paul Drew, "Skills-Test Failure Rate High for Minority, Poor Students," *Minneapolis Star Tribune*, May 25, 1996, page 1A. It is interesting that the gaps in pass rates among White and minority students are larger in Minnesota than in other states (Gayler and others 2004, p. 37).

states with exit exams, Minnesota provided an unusually high number of retest opportunities (eleven). Like most other states with exit exams, the state also required school districts to develop individualized remediation plans for each student who failed a BST in eighth or ninth grade.[59] The state also provided flexibility and testing accommodations for students with disabilities and for those who were English language learners (ELL). For example, students with an individualized education program (IEP) could have their BSTs cut scores lowered by their local IEP team. And ELL students who had been enrolled for fewer than three years in a school where the primary instructional language was English were exempted from the graduation requirements.[60]

The BSTs in math and in reading were administered in eighth through twelfth grades while the writing test was first taken in tenth grade. The first cohort required to pass the BSTs in math and reading took these exams for the first time as eighth graders in the spring of 1996. The cohort required to pass the BST in writing took this test for the first time as tenth graders in the spring of 1999. The implementation of the BST requirements attracted relatively little public notice, especially relative to the more controversial Profile of Learning standards. One exception occurred in 2000 when scoring errors led to some students being mistakenly told they failed the test, including about fifty seniors who were denied diplomas.[61] There were also two incidents of teachers being accused of stealing copies of the high-stakes exams.[62] It is interesting that during the summer of 2005, which is after our study period, the Minnesota legislature enacted legislation to replace the BSTs with tests that were geared to higher-level grade content and that were aligned to state content standards.[63]

Common Core of Data

The National Center for Education Statistics (NCES) collaborates annually with state education agencies to organize a variety of data on all public schools and school districts (such as staffing, enrollments, and finances) into the Common Core of Data. The data items collected by the CCD are based on consistent definitions that have been developed by the NCES and state

59. Gayler and others (2004, table 10).
60. The state also translated the math BST into Hmong, Somali, Spanish, and Vietnamese (Sullivan and others 2005, p. 172).
61. Brian Bakst, "Diplomas Denied to Fewer Seniors because of Test Error than Estimated," Associated Press State and Local Wire, August 15, 2000.
62. Associated Press State and Local Wire, "Cass Lake-Bena Teacher Accused of Stealing Copy of State Test," April 2, 2001.
63. Sullivan and others (2005, table 3).

representatives over several decades. Beginning in the early 1990s, the CCD included district-level and grade-level data on dropouts from a growing number of states (including Minnesota) whose reporting practices conformed to the NCES definitions.

The CCD uses an "event" dropout definition. More specifically, a student is designated as a dropout for a particular school year if the student was enrolled at some time during the school year and met several explicit criteria as of October 1 in the next school year. These criteria are that the student in question was not enrolled, had not graduated or completed an approved educational program (for example, the GED), had not transferred, and was not absent because of death or a school-recognized illness or because of suspension. The CCD reports dropout rates that are based on these dropout data and specific to each district and grade. These rates were constructed by dividing the number of NCES-defined event dropouts for each district and grade by its corresponding enrollment base for that school year.[64]

The grade-specific dropout rates in the CCD are not perfect measures. Most notably, it would be preferable to separate GED completers from conventional graduates. Furthermore, a problem with any event measure is that it will not reflect subsequent reenrollment by a student who drops out except through a change in the enrollment base. However, as noted earlier, these data also have several unique benefits. For example, relative to the PUMS data, individuals attending public schools can be matched without measurement error to their high school graduation requirements. Furthermore, because these dropout rates accommodate both grade retention and student mobility, they are not subject to the concerns that have been the focus of studies using state-year high school completion rates based on adjusted enrollment data.[65]

Another unique feature of these grade-specific dropout rates is that they facilitate a somewhat unusual empirical strategy for identifying the effects of Minnesota's high school graduation requirements on educational attainment. That strategy, which is described below, relies on the fact that within each district and year, we observe the dropout rates in grades, some of which are constrained by Minnesota's exit exam policies and some of which are not. The unit of observation for this analysis is the dropout rate for each unique dis-

---

64. States do not report this enrollment base directly. Instead, the NCES constructs these variables from grade-specific enrollments from schools within the district.

65. See, for example, Warren (2005). The NCES gives states autonomy in verifying a student's transfer status (for example, transcript requests or withdrawal notices with signed parental assurances about reenrollment) but discourages reliance on unsubstantiated reports.

trict-grade-year observation over the nine school years from 1994–95 to 2001–02. We applied several edits to the pooled CCD files to create a dataset suitable for this analysis. For example, we deleted school districts that were regional service agencies or state or federal agencies providing services to special-needs populations as well as districts without students. We also deleted districts that did not serve students in a grade from ninth through twelfth.

We also deleted a small number of observations where the dropout rate was either negative or greater than 100. However, the results presented here are similar when these observations are included with imputed dropout rates of 0 or 100 percent. We also applied an imputation to correct a coding convention used for the Minnesota data for the 1994–95 and 1996–97 school years. Specifically, in most years, roughly a quarter of the district-grade observations for Minnesota had no dropouts. However, for the 1994–95 and 1996–97 school years, only one district-grade observation had a dropout rate of zero. Instead, districts in these years with positive enrollments were coded as missing or not applicable for dropout rates that should have been zero. We have imputed zero to these observations but checked that the results are similar without this imputation and when data from these two school years are omitted.

As noted earlier, an issue of particular interest is whether exit exams have unique effects among high-poverty students or those who are racial or ethnic minorities. To address these issues, we matched the Minnesota school districts to 1995 data on the percentage of children in poverty within the district and to 1993–94 data aggregated from the school-level CCD files on the racial and ethnic composition of the district's students. The grade-level dropout data in the CCD are actually defined by race, ethnicity, and gender during this period. However, we use district-level data on minority composition because the relevant enrollment bases for the CCD's race and ethnicity-specific dropout data were not collected. Specifically, the school-level CCD only started collecting grade-specific enrollments by race, ethnicity, and gender in the 1998–99 school year. Our final, analytical sample omits the observations that could not be matched to these poverty and demographic data. An examination of these observations indicated that they largely consisted of administrative school districts that had been incorrectly flagged in the CCD and school districts, largely charter schools, which had been created during the sample period.[66] The final dataset consists of an unbalanced panel of 10,502 grade-level dropout rates for the approximately 350 districts observed in each of nine academic years.

---

66. Our results are quite similar in specifications that include these observations.

Specifications

Our approach to evaluating the effects of Minnesota's BST requirements on dropout rates exploits the variation generated by the fact that the exit exam was first required of the graduating class of 2000. State exit exams were often first tied to a specific graduating class while the cohort was in eighth or ninth grade to avoid the perceived unfairness and possible court challenges associated with subjecting those already in high school to a requirement they could not have anticipated. This sort of phased introduction creates potentially useful variation in policy exposure both across grades and within grades over time. For example, the first high school cohort subject to the new exit exam requirements was in ninth grade during the 1996–97 school year. However, the cohorts in tenth through twelfth grades during that year did not have to pass the BSTs but did share the determinants of dropout rates common to their district and year. In the subsequent school year, the grades constrained by the BST requirements expanded to include both ninth and tenth graders and by the 1999–2000 school year the students in all four grades. The figures in bold in table 6-6 identify the grade-year observations subject to the BST requirements during the school years for which we have CCD dropout data.

The variation in BST exposure (X_{gdt}) across grades and within grades over time implies that the effect of this policy (β) on dropout rates (y_{gdt}) can be identified conditional on fixed effects unique to each grade (μ_g), district (α_d), and year (λ_t):

(2) $$y_{gdt} = \beta X_{gdt} + \mu_g + \alpha_d + \lambda_t + \varepsilon_{gdt}$$

Furthermore, because the policy change of interest varies by grade and year in all observed districts, equation 2 can be extended to condition on fixed effects unique to each district-grade combination (μ_{gd}) and to each district-year combination (α_{dt}):

(3) $$y_{gdt} = \beta X_{gdt} + \mu_{gd} + \alpha_{dt} + \varepsilon_{gdt}$$

The standard errors reported for these specifications are clustered at the grade-district level. Clustering at this cross-sectional level leads to the more conservative (that is, larger) standard errors and is consistent with concerns about the possible influence of serial correlation.[67]

---

67. See Bertrand, Duflo, and Mullainathan (2004). Specifically, we found that these standard errors were larger than those that were uncorrected and those calculated using the conven-

Table 6-6. *Mean Dropout Rates in Minnesota School Districts, by Grade and School Year*[a]

School year	Grade 9	Grade 10	Grade 11	Grade 12
1993–94	1.15	2.41	3.37	3.44
1994–95	1.14	2.71	3.26	4.07
1995–96	1.27	2.70	3.78	4.21
1996–97	1.29	2.71	3.73	3.89
1997–98	1.16	2.58	3.92	4.48
1998–99	0.90	2.29	3.00	3.68
1999–2000	0.91	1.95	3.18	3.94
2000–01	0.80	1.94	2.67	3.97
2001–02	0.73	1.75	2.99	4.06

Source: The annual Common Core of Data (CCD) universe surveys from 1993–94 to 2001–02.

a. The unit of observation is the grade (9–12) within a school district in a given school year (N = 10,502). The bold numbers identify grade-year combinations, which were required to pass Minnesota's Basic Skills Tests (BSTs).

The conditional means in table 6-6 illustrate how the dropout rates in Minnesota's public high schools varied across grades and over time while the BST requirements were implemented. Casual difference-in-differences comparisons based on these means can illustrate the basic logic of this identification strategy. For example, the dropout rate for tenth graders fell by 0.13 percentage point (that is, 5 percent) in the 1997–98 school year, which was when tenth graders were first subject to the BST requirements. Over that same time period, but in the higher grades not subject to the requirements (eleventh and twelfth grades), the dropout rates *increased* by at least 0.18 percentage point. These simple comparisons suggest that the BST requirements reduced the tenth grade dropout rate in Minnesota.

OLS estimates based on equations 2 and 3 generalize such basic comparisons.[68] However, they also provide a framework for identifying whether the effects of BST requirements varied by grade. For example, as noted earlier, if these exit exams had a strong discouragement effect, we might expect to find

tional White procedure. We also found basically similar results in weighted least squares (WLS) specifications when the enrollment base was the weight. However, the WLS estimates did indicate that the twelfth grade dropout rate is larger than that based on ordinary least squares (OLS). We suspect that this reflects the heterogeneous effects of Minnesota's exit exam by district traits (for example, larger dropout effects in larger urban districts), an issue we examine directly in our analysis.

68. We report OLS estimates based on a linear probability model. Because a large share of observations have no dropouts, procedures like a grouped logit are not feasible. However, after making a small imputation to observations with no dropouts (see Greene 2005, p. 689), we did

that they led to particularly large increases in the ninth and tenth grade dropout rates. Alternatively, these exit exams could increase the dropout rate more substantially among twelfth graders if students remain in school and persist in attempting to pass the BSTs despite earlier failures. We examine this issue by evaluating the reduced-form effects associated with interactions between a BST dummy variable and grade-specific dummy variables.

The basic panel-data research design outlined here (that is, exploiting the policy variation within grades over time) has not to our knowledge been utilized elsewhere. Therefore, this approach may provide a useful complement to more conventional panel-data evaluations like that presented in section 3. However, like any empirical evaluation, this approach also turns on implicit, maintained assumptions that may not, in fact, be valid.

In particular, this approach implicitly assumes that the common shocks to dropout rates in a particular year have a similar effect across all four grades. However, violations of this assumption could reasonably occur and perhaps bias these results. For example, suppose that during the economic expansion of the late 1990s the dropout rates of twelfth graders (who were generally not subject to exit exams) grew relative to the contemporaneous dropout rates for the earlier grades (which often were subject to exit exams). This pattern would occur if twelfth graders were particularly likely to leave high school as Minnesota's unemployment rate fell during the late 1990s. Similarly, the later increases in Minnesota's unemployment rate (during 1999, 2000, and 2001) could have led to particularly large reductions in the dropout rate of twelfth graders, just as twelfth graders were also being required to pass the BSTs. Under this particular scenario, our reduced-form estimates would have a negative bias because of unrelated year effects unique to a particular grade.

Although it is not possible to address these important concerns definitively, we can examine their empirical relevance through selective adjustments to the groups of grades included in our evaluations. For example, the assumption that there are common grade-year shocks is more likely to be valid when comparing only near grades (for example, just eleventh and twelfth grades). We discuss evidence on whether these sample restrictions influence our results. As an additional approach, we also examine specifications that allow us to condition on grade-year fixed effects by using contemporaneous dropout data from the neighboring states (North Dakota and

find that a grouped logit specification generated results similar to those reported here. Another problem with a grouped logit in this context is that, because the dropout rates tend to be low, and the number of students aggregated in each observation tends to be fairly large, this specification generates suspiciously small standard errors (Greene 2005, p. 689).

Iowa), which were well represented in the CCD dropout data during this period and did not introduce exit exams.[69] The point estimates from these specifications were basically similar to those described below (that is, negative effects in earlier grades and a positive effect in the twelfth grade). However, these point estimates were also more imprecise and their values were somewhat sensitive to which of the two control states was included. More disturbingly, we found that the dropout rates in Minnesota had preform trends that differed significantly from Iowa and North Dakota, which suggests that the identifying assumptions for these specifications were not valid.

Results

Table 6-7 presents the basic evaluation results based on the full sample of district-grade-year observations. The initial specifications (columns 1 and 2) condition only on district, year, and grade fixed effects. However, the subsequent models (columns 3 through 8) introduce district-grade and district-year fixed effects. These results indicate that overall the introduction of the BSTs requirement was associated with small and statistically insignificant reductions in the dropout rates. However, these estimates consistently indicate that the assumption of a common BSTs effect across grades obscures heterogeneous effects across grades. More specifically, these estimates indicate that the introduction of an exit exam *reduced* the dropout rate in both tenth and eleventh grades by about 0.3 to 0.4 percentage point (9 to 16 percent) but *increased* the dropout rate in the twelfth grade by a similar amount (approximately 8 percent). These findings suggest that Minnesota's exit exam policy improved student and school performance in the earlier high school grades and did not discourage students from remaining in school. However, these results also indicate that the existence of the BSTs requirement constrained students who could not pass the exams after repeated attempts. A recent study based on longitudinal data from Texas similarly found that exit exams increased the dropout rate through their effect on students sitting for their "last chance" exam.[70]

It is interesting to note that the results in table 6-7 are quite similar across specifications that condition on the fixed effects interactions. And these interactions have considerable explanatory power, increasing the R^2 by approximately 50 percent. In results not shown here, we find comparable results in specifications based only on the dropout rates from more similar

69. This approach would be analogous to a difference-in-difference-in-differences strategy (see, for example, Gruber 1994).
70. Martorell (2004).

Table 6-7. *Estimated Effects of Minnesota's Basic Skills Test on Dropout Rates*[a]

Independent variable	(1)	(2)	(3)	(4)	(5)	(6)	(7)	(8)
BSTs	-0.136	...	-0.164	...	-0.088	...	-0.115	...
	(0.134)		(0.129)		(0.135)		(0.134)	
BSTs × grade 9	...	-0.140	...	-0.197	...	-0.119	...	-0.179
		(0.155)		(0.158)		(0.157)		(0.165)
BSTs × grade 10	...	-0.419**	...	-0.432**	...	-0.358**	...	-0.364**
		(0.172)		(0.156)		(0.172)		(0.151)
BSTs × grade 11	...	-0.356*	...	-0.372**	...	-0.284	...	-0.299*
		(0.202)		(0.165)		(0.211)		(0.175)
BSTs × grade 12	...	0.332*	...	0.306*	...	0.361*	...	0.331**
		(0.177)		(0.152)		(0.187)		(0.166)
Statistics								
R^2	0.5252	0.5262	0.6827	0.6836	0.6305	0.6314	0.7824	0.7833
District effects	yes	yes	no	no	no	no	no	no
Year effects	yes	yes	yes	yes	no	no	no	no
Grade effects	yes	yes	no	no	yes	yes	no	no
District-grade effects	no	no	yes	yes	no	no	yes	yes
District-year effects	no	no	no	no	yes	yes	yes	yes

Source: The annual Common Core of Data (CCD) universe surveys from 1993–94 to 2001–02.
*Significant at the 10 percent level; **significant at the 5 percent level.
. . . Not applicable.
BSTs = Basic Skills Tests.
a. The unit of observation is the grade (9–12) within a school district in a given school year (N = 10,502). Standard errors, adjusted for clustering at the grade-district level, are reported in parentheses.

(that is, closer) grades. These results suggest that year effects unique to particular grades are not a source of confounding biases in these evaluations.

The remaining results, which are based on the data from all four grades, examine how the grade-specific effects of the BSTs requirement varied by a variety of observable district traits. The results in the first panel of table 6-8 are based on dividing the observed school districts into quartiles based on their prereform position in the distribution of the percentage of students who were Black or Hispanic. It should be noted that there are relatively few minority students in Minnesota (roughly 5 percent of students were Black and 2 percent were Hispanic), even in the districts in the top quartile of this distribution. Therefore, these estimates should be understood as identifying the effect for the average student in these districts rather than the effect for a minority student per se.[71] Nonetheless, the results in table 6-8 suggest that the dropout effects of the BSTs requirement differed noticeably across these districts. For example, in the districts with higher concentrations of minorities, the BSTs led to particularly large increases in the twelfth grade dropout rate (0.69 to 0.92 percentage point). However, these results also indicate that the BSTs led to relatively large reductions in the tenth and eleventh grade dropout rates.[72] Also of interest is that the BSTs requirement had small and statistically insignificant effects in the districts with the lowest concentration of minority students.

The results in the next panel are based on dividing districts into quartiles based on their 1995 position in the state distribution of the percentage of children in poverty. The results for high-poverty districts tend to be statistically imprecise. However, the point estimate for the twelfth grade dropout effect is approximately twice as large as that for the full sample. These results indicate that the reductions in tenth and eleventh grade dropout rates were concentrated in the lower-poverty districts. In fact, in the lowest-poverty districts, the BSTs requirement was also associated with reductions in the twelfth grade dropout rate.

The next specification attempts to refine these comparisons by focusing on the observations from districts in the top halves of the state distributions

71. Because the PUMS analysis suggested that the effects of exit exams differed for Black and Hispanic students, we also considered more disaggregated measures of minority students. However, the results based on these data were quite similar. Among other things, this could reflect that the Hispanics observed in the CCD files include both native-born and foreign-born students.

72. The distinct effects of exit exams in high-minority districts were similar in models that excluded the Minneapolis and St. Paul districts.

Table 6-8. *Estimated Effects of Minnesota's Exit Exam on Dropout Rates, by District Traits*[a]

Districts in sample	Estimated effect of BSTs by grade				Sample size
	Grade 9	Grade 10	Grade 11	Grade 12	
Full sample	−0.179	−0.364**	−0.299*	0.331**	10,502
	(0.165)	(0.151)	(0.175)	(0.166)	
Percentage of minority students					
Top quartile	−0.054	−0.618**	−0.194	0.924**	2,623
	(0.291)	(0.266)	(0.262)	(0.277)	
Third quartile	−0.250	−0.272	−0.171	0.689**	2,627
	(0.283)	(0.273)	(0.306)	(0.296)	
Second quartile	−0.499	−0.542*	−0.700*	−0.329	2,624
	(0.354)	(0.321)	(0.412)	(0.338)	
Bottom quartile	0.103	−0.015	−0.114	0.066	2,628
	(0.383)	(0.334)	(0.392)	(0.390)	
Percentage of children in poverty					
Top quartile	0.044	−0.182	0.115	0.699	2,596
	(0.408)	(0.357)	(0.413)	(0.434)	
Third quartile	0.207	0.163	0.100	0.625**	2,626
	(0.280)	(0.251)	(0.277)	(0.272)	
Second quartile	−0.472*	−0.750**	−0.195	0.496*	2,640
	(0.251)	(0.242)	(0.238)	(0.298)	
Bottom quartile	−0.489	−0.677**	−1.192**	−0.478*	2,640
	(0.357)	(0.326)	(0.417)	(0.289)	
Above median in percentage of minority students and children in poverty	0.216	0.179	0.405	1.285**	2,132
	(0.332)	(0.303)	(0.339)	(0.313)	
Urban	0.445	−0.365	−0.314	3.13**	316
	(0.577)	(0.757)	(0.928)	(1.07)	
Suburban	−0.413	−0.840**	−0.669**	−0.131	2,351
	(0.294)	(0.272)	(0.263)	(0.239)	
Rural	−0.129	−0.205	−0.177	0.357*	7,835
	(0.211)	(0.189)	(0.230)	(0.212)	

Source: The annual Common Core of Data (CCD) universe surveys from 1993–94 to 2001–02.
*Significant at the 10 percent level; **significant at the 5 percent level.
BSTs = Basic Skills Tests.
a. The unit of observation is the grade (9–12) within a school district in a given school year (N = 10,502). All models condition on district-year and district-grade fixed effects. Standard errors, adjusted for clustering at the grade-district level, are reported in parentheses.

of percentage of minority students and percentage of children in poverty. These results suggest that the BSTs led to increased dropout rates across all four grades with a particularly large and statistically significant effect on the twelfth grade dropout rate. The final set of results in table 6-8 examines the unique effects associated with a district's urbanicity. A striking result is that the BSTs requirement led to a particularly large increase in the twelfth grade dropout rate in urban districts (over 3 percentage points) and to a lesser extent an increase in rural districts. In contrast, the beneficial effects of the BSTs requirements (reductions in tenth and eleventh grade dropout rates) were largely concentrated in suburban school districts.

In sum, the evidence from Minnesota's experience with exit exams is consistent with several of the claims made by both proponents and critics of these policies. For example, these results indicate that the BST requirement was actually associated with reductions in the dropout rates for earlier high school grades. This result is consistent with the hypothesis that Minnesota's exit exam improved student effort and school performance.

Mapping these results into an implied change in the high school graduation rate is not straightforward, in part because these data are based on event dropouts who may later reenroll. However, assuming that event dropouts do not return to school and using the prereform dropout rates as a base, the full sample results (reductions in the dropout rate in ninth through eleventh grades and an increase in twelfth grade) imply that the overall high school graduation rate increased by approximately one-half of a percentage point (an increase of approximately 0.5 percent given an implied graduate rate of 89.2 percent).

However, critics of exit exams would not be surprised to find that these improvements were concentrated in lower-poverty and suburban districts. In contrast, the increased dropout rates were found in urban districts and those with higher shares of minority students and children in poverty. In fact, calculations based on these point estimates indicate that the implied changes in the high school graduation rates for these districts were consistently negative. For example, in urban districts during the 1993–95 period, the implied high school graduation rate was 75.1 percent. The results in table 6-8 imply that this rate fell to 72.7 percent as a result of the BSTs requirement, a decrease of approximately 2.4 percentage points (3.2 percent).

Conclusions

The notion that high school graduates should meet high academic standards has a universal appeal. The increasing importance of cognitive skills for economic success in recent years adds a sense of urgency to standards-based reforms in high school. However, some doubt whether binding standards can effectively improve student or school performance. There are also concerns about whether standards-based reforms may exacerbate economic inequality by harming the students most at risk of academic failure. This study attempts this broader debate by presenting new evidence on the educational and economic consequences of the earliest, standards-based reform—mandatory exit exams for high school students.

Our results, based on data from the 2000 Census, indicate that exit exams led to particularly large increases in the dropout rates of Black students. Similarly, our analysis of Minnesota's recent exit exam, based on the NCES' Common Core of Data, indicates that this graduation requirement increased the dropout rates in school districts with relatively large concentrations of minority students as well as in urban and high-poverty school districts. Furthermore, Minnesota's exit exam also reduced the dropout rates in suburban and low-poverty school districts. Taken at face value, these findings imply that these standards-based reforms have exacerbated both poverty and inequality.

However, a number of factors suggest that the implications for poverty are not quite so straightforward. For example, our analysis of data from the 2000 Census provided some evidence that exit exams improved longer-term outcomes (for example, college matriculation, labor-market outcomes) for Hispanic females and Blacks. These changes could reflect both the signaling and the incentive effects of exit exams. The possible incentive effects of standards-based reform were also suggested by our evidence that exit exams reduced the early high school dropout rates in some of Minnesota's school districts.

These ambiguities suggest a number of possibly fruitful directions for further research. For example, as states continue to both introduce exit exams and simultaneously develop richer, longitudinal data on student achievement, it should become possible to identify how the incentive effects of exit exams may have changed the distribution of cognitive achievement. Second, the evidence that exit exams reduced the dropout rates in some districts (for example, in low-poverty districts) suggests it would be useful to learn more about the mediating factors that may have facilitated these improvements. Third, it would be useful to develop further evidence on whether exit exams generally encourage students to drop out during twelfth grade and to identify the implications of this pattern for both targeted remediation and reform.

Table 6A-1. *High School Exit Exams*[a]

State	1979	1980	1981	1982	1983	1984	1985	1986	1987	1988	1989	1990	1991	1992	1993	1994	1995	1996	1997	1998	1999	2000	2001	2002	2003	2004	2005
Alabama	0	0	0	0	0	0	1	1	1	1	1	1	1	1	1	1	1	1	1	1	1	2	2	2	2	2	2
Arkansas	0	0	0	0	0	0	0	0	0	0	0	0	0	0	0	0	0	0	0	0	0	0	0	0	0	1	1
Delaware	0	0	1	1	1	1	1	1	1	1	1	1	1	0	0	0	0	0	0	0	0	0	0	0	0	0	0
Florida	0	0	0	1	1	1	1	1	1	1	1	1	1	1	1	1	2	2	2	2	2	2	2	2	2	2	2
Georgia	0	0	0	0	0	1	1	1	1	1	1	1	1	1	1	1	2	2	2	2	2	2	2	2	2	2	2
Hawaii	0	0	0	1	1	1	1	1	1	1	1	1	1	1	1	1	1	1	1	1	1	0	0	0	0	0	0
Indiana	0	0	0	0	0	0	0	0	0	0	0	0	0	0	0	0	0	0	0	0	0	0	2	2	2	2	2
Louisiana	0	0	0	0	0	0	0	0	0	0	0	0	0	0	0	0	0	0	0	0	0	1	1	2	2	2	2
Maryland	0	0	0	1	1	1	1	1	1	1	1	1	1	1	1	1	1	1	1	1	1	1	1	1	1	1	1
Massachusetts	0	0	0	0	0	0	0	0	0	0	0	0	0	0	0	0	0	0	0	0	0	0	0	2	2	2	2
Minnesota	0	0	0	0	0	0	0	0	0	0	0	0	0	0	0	0	0	0	0	0	0	1	1	1	1	1	1
Mississippi	0	0	0	0	0	1	1	1	1	1	1	1	1	1	1	1	1	1	1	1	1	1	1	1	1	1	1
Nevada	0	0	0	0	1	1	1	1	1	1	1	1	1	1	1	1	1	1	1	1	2	2	2	2	2	2	2
New Jersey	0	0	0	0	0	0	1	1	1	1	1	1	1	1	1	2	2	2	2	2	2	2	2	2	2	2	2
New Mexico	0	0	0	0	0	0	0	0	0	1	1	1	1	1	1	1	1	1	1	1	1	1	1	1	1	1	1
New York	1	1	1	1	1	1	1	1	1	1	1	1	1	1	1	1	1	1	1	1	1	2	2	2	2	2	2
North Carolina	0	1	1	1	1	1	1	1	1	1	1	1	1	1	1	1	1	1	1	1	1	1	1	1	1	1	1
Ohio	0	0	0	0	0	0	0	0	0	0	0	0	0	0	2	2	2	2	2	2	2	2	2	2	2	2	2
South Carolina	0	0	0	0	0	0	0	0	0	0	1	1	1	1	1	1	1	1	1	1	1	1	1	1	1	1	1
Tennessee	0	0	0	0	1	1	1	1	1	1	1	1	1	2	2	2	2	2	2	2	2	2	2	2	1	2	2
Texas	0	0	0	0	0	0	0	1	1	1	1	1	2	2	2	2	2	2	2	2	2	2	2	2	2	2	2
Virginia	0	0	1	1	1	1	1	1	1	1	0	0	0	0	0	0	1	1	1	1	1	1	1	1	1	2	2

Source: Data are drawn from a variety of sources, including a comprehensive Lexis-Nexis search of news articles from the relevant states from roughly 1978 to 2005 and from a variety of academic articles.

a. The coding is as follows:

0 = state did not have a high school exit exam for the graduating class in that year

1 = state had a high school exit exam for the graduating class in that year that tested material below the ninth grade level

2 = state had a high school exit exam for the graduating class in that year that tested material on the ninth grade level or above

References

Airasian, Peter W. 1987. "State Mandated Testing and Educational Reform." *American Journal of Education* 95, no. 3: 393–412.

Amrein, Audrey L., and David C. Berliner. 2002. "High-Stakes Testing, Uncertainty, and Student Learning." *Education Policy Analysis Archives* 10, no. 18 (March 28). (http://epaa.asu.edu/epaa/v10n18/ [January 15, 2007]).

Angrist, Joshua D., and William N. Evans. 1999. "Schooling and Labor Market Consequences of the 1970 State Abortion Reforms." In *Research in Labor Economics*, edited by Solomon W. Polachek, pp. 75–113. Stamford, Conn.: JAI Press.

Avery, Patricia G., Richard Beach, and Jodiann Coler. 2003. "The Impact of Minnesota's 'Profile of Learning' on Teaching and Learning in English and Social Studies Classrooms." *Education Policy Analysis Archives* 11, no. 7 (February 16). (http://epaa.asu.edu/epaa/ v11n7/ [December 23, 2005]).

Bertrand, Marianne, Esther Duflo, and Sendil Mullainathan. 2004. "How Much Should We Trust Differences-in-Differences Estimates?" *Quarterly Journal of Economics* 119, no. 1: 249–76.

Betts, Julian R., and Robert M. Costrell. 2001. "Incentives and Equity under Standards-Based Reform." In *Brookings Papers on Education Policy 2001*, edited by Diane Ravitch, pp. 9–55. Brookings.

Bishop, John H. 1999. "Nerd Harassment, Incentives, School Priorities, and Learning." In *Earning and Learning: How Schools Matter*, edited by Susan E. Mayer and Paul E. Peterson, pp. 231–79. Brookings.

Bishop, John H., and Ferran Mane. 2001. "The Impacts of Minimum Competency Exam Graduation Requirements on High School Graduation, College Attendance and Early Labor Market Success." *Labour Economics* 8, no. 2: 203–22.

Card, David, and Thomas Lemieux. 2001. "Dropout and Enrollment Trends in the Postwar Period: What Went Wrong in the 1970s?" In *An Economic Analysis of Risky Behavior among Youths*, edited by Jonathan Gruber, pp. 439–82. University of Chicago Press.

Carnoy, Martin, and Susanna Loeb. 2002. "Does External Accountability Affect Student Outcomes? A Cross-State Analysis." *Educational Evaluation and Policy Analysis* 24, no. 4: 305–31.

Catterall, James S. 1989. "Standards and School Dropouts: A National Study of Tests Required for High School Graduation." *American Journal of Education* 98, no. 1 (November):1–34.

Cullen, Julie, and Randall Reback. 2006. "Tinkering Towards Accolades: School Gaming under a Performance Accountability System." Working Paper. University of California–San Diego, Economics Department.

Dee, Thomas S. 2003. "The 'First Wave' of Accountability." In *No Child Left Behind? The Politics and Practice of Accountability*, edited by Paul E. Petersen and Martin R. West, pp. 1–20. Brookings.

Duncan, Beverly. 1965. "Dropouts and the Unemployed." *Journal of Political Economy* 73, no. 2 (April): 121–34.

Figlio, David N., and Lawrence S. Getzler. 2002. "Accountability, Ability, and Disability: Gaming the System." NBER Working Paper 9307. Cambridge, Mass.: National Bureau of Economic Research.

Gayler, Keith, and others. 2004. "State High School Exit Exams: A Maturing Reform." Washington: Center on Education Policy.

Greene, Jay P., and Marcus A. Winters. 2004. "Pushed Out or Pulled Up? Exit Exams and Dropout Rates in Public High Schools." Education Working Paper 5. New York: Manhattan Institute.

Greene, William H. 2005. *Econometric Analysis*, 5th ed. Upper Saddle River, N.J.: Prentice Hall.

Gruber, Jonathan. 1994. "The Incidence of Mandated Maternity Benefits." *American Economic Review* 84, no. 3: 622–41.

Jacob, Brian A. 2001. "Getting Tough? The Impact of High School Graduation Exams." *Educational Evaluation and Policy Analysis* 23, no. 2: 99–122.

————. 2005. "Accountability, Incentives, and Behavior: Evidence from School Reform in Chicago." *Journal of Public Economics* 89, nos. 5–6: 761–96.

Jacob, Brian A., and Steven Levitt. 2003. "Rotten Apples: An Investigation of the Prevalence and Predictors of Teacher Cheating." *Quarterly Journal of Economics* 118, no. 3: 843–77.

Kane, Thomas. 1994. "College Entry by Blacks since 1970: The Role of College Costs, Family Background, and the Returns to Education." *Journal of Political Economy* 102, no. 5 (October): 878–911.

Koretz, Daniel M., and Sheila M. Barron. 1998. "The Validity of Gains in Scores on the Kentucky Instructional Results Information System (KIRIS)." MR1014. Santa Monica, Calif.: RAND.

Lillard, Dean R., and Philip P. DeCicca. 2001. "Higher Standards, More Dropouts? Evidence Within and Across Time." *Economics of Education Review* 20, no. 5 (October): 459–73.

Marchant, Gregory J., and Sharon E. Paulson. 2005. "The Relationship of High School Graduation Exams to Graduation Rates and SAT Scores." *Education Policy Analysis Archives* 13, no. 6. (http://epaa.asu.edu/epaa/v13n6/ [January 16, 2007]).

Martorell, Francisco. 2004. "Do High School Graduation Exams Matter? A Regression Discontinuity Approach." Working Paper. University of California–Berkeley.

Murnane, Richard J., and Frank Levy. 2001. "Will Standards-Based Reforms Improve the Education of Students of Color?" *National Tax Journal* 54, no. 2 (June): 401–15.

National Commission on Excellence in Education. 1983. *A Nation at Risk: The Imperative for Educational Reform*. Washington: U.S. Government Printing Office.

Phillips, Meredith, and Tiffani Chin. 2001. Comment on "Incentives and Equity under Standards-Based Reform." In *Brookings Papers on Education Policy 2001*, edited by Diane Ravitch, pp. 61–66. Brookings.

Pipho, Chris. 1978. "Minimum Competency Testing in 1978: A Look at State Standards." *Phi Delta Kappan* 59, no. 9 (May): 585–88.

Popham, W. James. 1981. "The Case for Minimum Competency Testing." *Phi Delta Kappan* 63, no. 2: 89–91.

Purkey, Stuart C., and Marshall S. Smith. 1983. "School Reform: The District Policy Implications of the Effective Schools Literature." *Elementary School Journal* 85, no. 3: 353–89.

————. 1985. "Effective Schools: A Review." *Elementary School Journal* 83, no. 4: 427–52.

Ruggles, Steven, and others. 2004. Integrated Public Use Microdata Series, Version 3.0. Minneapolis: University of Minnesota, Minnesota Population Center (www.ipums.umn.edu).

Stringfield, Samuel, and Charles Teddlie. 1988. "A Time to Summarize: The Louisiana School Effectiveness Study." *Educational Leadership* 46: 43–49.

Sullivan, Patricia, and others. 2005. "State High School Exit Exams: States Try Harder but Gaps Persist." Washington: Center on Education Policy.

U.S. Census Bureau. 2005. *2000 Census of Population and Housing, Public Use Microdata Sample, United States: Technical Documentation 2003*. PUMS/15-US (RV). Washington: U.S. Department of Commerce, Economics and Statistics Administration.

Warren, John Robert. 2005. "State-Level High School Completion Rates: Concepts, Measures, and Trends." *Education Policy Analysis Archives* 13, no. 51: 1–35 (http://epaa.asu.edu/epaa/vol13.html).

Warren, John Robert, and Krista N. Jenkins. 2005. "High Stakes Graduation Tests and High School Dropout in Texas and Florida, 1979–2001." *Sociology of Education* 78, no. 2: 122–43.

Warren, John Robert, and Melanie R. Edwards. 2005. "High School Exit Examinations and High School Completion: Evidence from the Early 1990s." *Educational Evaluation and Policy Analysis* 27, no. 1: 53–74.

Warren, John Robert, Krista N. Jenkins, and Rachael B. Kulick. 2005. "High School Exit Examinations and State-Level Completion and GED Rates, 1975–2002." Working Paper. University of Minnesota, Department of Sociology.

PART III

Looking Forward:
Standards, Sanctions,
and the Future of NCLB

7

The Role of Tutoring in Standards-Based Reform

GEORGE FARKAS
RACHEL E. DURHAM

There always have been, and likely always will be, children who have difficulty making adequate progress in school. This can be due to a variety of
risk factors, some of which are social and economic. Thus, although the incidence of such learning difficulties is higher among the poor, the condition is
far from unknown among middle- and upper-class students. Before looking at
the services offered to poor children who are falling behind, it is useful to ask:
What is the most effective, widely available treatment to help these students?
In particular, how do well-educated and affluent parents typically respond
when they discover that their child is experiencing learning difficulties?

When the problem first occurs, many middle- and upper-class parents try
to assist the child themselves. If this is not successful, they often hire a tutor
to work with their child one-to-one. There is a large and growing industry in
providing such tutoring, including, at the high end, tutors who earn $100 an
hour and more. If such tutoring is unsuccessful, and the school cannot help,
a final resort is to move the child to a private school that specializes in
instruction for learning disabled students. These schools typically have small
class sizes, highly structured curricula, and very high levels of tuition.

We are grateful for comments on previous drafts by Adam Gamoran and several anonymous reviewers. Of course, any errors are our own.

Central to these efforts is small group or one-to-one instruction from a trained teacher or tutor, utilizing a highly structured curriculum. Such tutoring has also been used in programs aimed at low-income children who have fallen behind in their school performance. Research suggests that one-to-one tutoring is the most effective form of remediation.[1] Large-scale tutoring programs, carefully implemented by researchers, typically produce student achievement effect sizes that range from 0.25 to 0.50.[2]

Another feature of these strategies used by middle- and upper-class parents is that they go outside the child's public school to find an answer to their child's learning difficulties. That is, parents use the private market for educational services to help children who are not succeeding in public schools. Thus it is not surprising that when congressional advocates of school vouchers for private-sector schooling were unable to insert a voucher provision into the No Child Left Behind (NCLB) Act of 2001, they compromised instead on a provision to increase after-school tutoring, defined as *supplemental educational services* (SES), to at-risk, low-income students. The hope of these voucher advocates was to spark the creation of an industry of outside providers who would help low-income, at-risk students to succeed, even within failing public schools.

The result is that, under NCLB, if a Title I school fails to make adequate yearly progress (AYP)—the minimum proficiency target that schools must reach every year on state achievement tests—for three years, all low-income students in that school must be offered free SES (tutoring).[3] The providers of this tutoring must be on the approved list for the state in which the school is located. Providers on this list may include any of the following: nonprofit groups, for-profit companies, local community programs, colleges or universities, national organizations, faith-based groups, private and charter schools, and public schools and districts that have shown AYP. Districts must spend up to an amount equal to 20 percent of their Title I, Part A allocation on SES and transportation related to student transfers to other public schools.[4] Funds remaining after meeting parent demand for tutoring and transportation services may be spent for other district purposes.

---

1. Wasik and Slavin (1993).

2. Invernizzi (2002).

3. Title I schools are those that enroll a high percentage of students from low-income households.

4. For NCLB regulations, see the website of the U.S. Department of Education. For a discussion of the federal Title I program, the principal mechanism for federal funding in support of low-income K–12 students, see Farkas and Hall (2000).

This represents a significant addition to public policy for at-risk, low-income students. Tutoring, either one-to-one or small group, has always been a feature of the Title I program. But such tutoring occurs during the school day, typically as a pullout from regular classes, and is provided by regular school district personnel as a part of regular school operations and under full control of the district. By contrast, SES tutoring is intended to come from outside providers, after school, on the weekends, or during the summer. Thus the possibility exists to shift as much as 20 percent of the Title I program budget (currently totaling about $12 billion) to a new industry of for-profit and nonprofit organizations, which are focused on supplementary tutoring when school is not in session. In view of failed efforts to insert school voucher provisions into the law, supplementary educational services represent the furthest advance of privatization efforts within public schooling.

In this paper we assess the consequences of these policies. We address the following questions. First, how extensively have supplemental educational services been implemented? Second, what have been the characteristics and costs of the services provided? Third, what have we learned about program effectiveness? Fourth, how have program regulations shaped the structure of the market for SES? Finally, what can be done to make the program more effective?

How Extensively Have Supplemental Educational Services Been Implemented?

Program implementation was greatly retarded by the NCLB provision that supplementary services are available to low-income students only after their school fails to achieve AYP for three consecutive years. As a consequence, wide-scale implementation of the program was delayed. However, since this slow beginning, program enrollment has trended upward. During the 2002–03 school year, fewer than 100,000 students participated nationwide.[5] During the 2003–04 school year, this number increased to 218,031, which was 11 percent of those eligible. This participation rate increased to 19 percent during 2004-05; it has been highest for elementary school students and much lower for older students.[6] Further increases likely occurred subsequently. Should this level of participation be regarded as positive, since nationwide implementation of *any* program is an enormous undertaking,

5. Peterson (2005).
6. Stullich, Eisner, and McCrary (forthcoming); Zimmer and others (2007).

Table 7-1. *Top Fifteen Most Frequently Approved Providers of SES*

Provider name	Number of states provider has been approved in
PLATO Learning, Inc. (formerly Lightspan, Inc.)	43
Failure Free Reading	40
Newton Learning, a division of Edison Schools, Inc.	36
Huntington Learning Centers, Inc.	36
Brainfuse Online Instruction	31
Education Station, a Sylvan Partnership	31
The Princeton Review, Inc.	30
Club Z! In-Home Tutoring Services	28
Sylvan Learning Systems, Inc.	25
I CAN Learn Education Systems by JRL Enterprises, Inc.	25
Kumon Math and Reading Centers	25
Babbage Net School	24
Cambridge Educational Services, Inc.	20
EdSolutions, Inc.	20
Lindamood-Bell Learning Processes	19

Source: tutorforkids.org (Washington: SESQ Center, American Institutes for Research) (www.tutorsforkids.org, [September, 19, 2005]).

SES = supplemental educational services.

and SES implementation is clearly progressing? Or should it be regarded as unsatisfactory, since a program reaching only about 20 percent of eligible students is unlikely to have a major impact in raising the overall performance of the group? We return to this issue below and at the conclusion of the paper.

Providers of Services

The availability of SES funding has already created a large and heterogeneous industry of providers. By 2005 more than 2,000 organizations were involved. To enter, each had to successfully complete the steps needed to become approved in at least one state. Large organizations sought approval in all or most states. Table 7-1 shows the top fifteen most frequently approved providers as of the fall 2005.

It is evident that these large providers, aiming for national coverage, are almost exclusively for-profit companies. Familiar names such as Sylvan, Edison Schools, The Princeton Review, and PLATO Learning are represented. But what about the distribution of the full range of providers who qualified to offer services? This is shown in table 7-2, for May 2004. Six percent are faith based, 9 percent provide their services online, and 55 percent are pri-

Table 7-2. *Types of SES Providers, Nationwide, May 2004*[a]

Type of provider	Percentage of providers
Faith based (private)	6
Online (private)	9
Other private	55
School districts and public schools	25
Colleges and universities	2
Other or unknown	4
Total	100

Source: U.S. Department of Education (2005), exhibit 8.
SES = supplemental educational services.
a. N = 1,890; percentages do not add to 100 because of rounding.

vate, falling into other than these two categories. Fully 25 percent are public school districts, offering services to their own students. (Districts are permitted to do this if they have made AYP.) Only 2 percent are colleges and universities. The remaining 3 percent are unknown.

This shows that the two principal types of providers are, on the one hand, a heterogeneous group of providers who are neither faith based nor online, and on the other hand, school districts themselves. The importance of the latter, and the competition they provide to the former, are issues we shall return to below.

An update of these numbers for the 2004–05 school year suggests that nationwide, about half of state-certified SES providers were private, for-profit companies.[7] Next most common were private nonprofits, constituting about 18 percent of certified providers. Following these two are school districts, constituting 14 percent of certified providers. This apparent decline of school districts as a share of providers (from 25 percent the previous year) is likely due to the general increase in other providers, combined with the fact that districts not making AYP are prohibited from being SES providers. However, we should keep in mind that districts may constitute a smaller share of providers, while still having a large enrollment of SES students in a particular area.

More detail regarding the situation at the local level is provided by the results of systematic case studies undertaken across nine school districts in six states during 2003–04, the second year that the supplemental services provi-

7. Center on Education Policy (2005), p. 125.

Table 7-3. *SES Students and Providers in Nine Case Study School Districts, 2003–04*

District	Number of schools required to offer SES	Number of students eligible for SES	Percentage of students served	Number of providers
1. Large central city 80 percent minority	24	12,918	14	14
2. Large central city 56 percent minority	1	356	86	5
3. Midsized central city 99 percent minority	20	9,781	11	6
4. Large central city 91 percent minority	42	40,000	9	10
5. Urban fringe of large city 23 percent minority	3	650	14	12
6. Midsized central city 70 percent minority	4	1,199	28	12
7. Midsized central city 71 percent minority	10	5,264	7	6
8. Large central city 77 percent minority	5	3,659	13	5
9. Large central city 90 percent minority	104	190,000	10	27

Source: U.S. Department of Education (2005), exhibits 3 and 5.
SES = supplemental educational services.

sions of NCLB had been in effect.[8] Information on students and providers across these districts is summarized in table 7-3.

Recipients of Services

The nine school districts vary from large to midsized. Most were in central cities and had high percentages of minority enrollment. Given the requirement that a school had to fail to make AYP for three years in a row, it is not surprising that during 2003–04, school districts varied dramatically in the number of schools required to offer SES. District 2 had only one such school, whereas district 9 had fully 104 schools in this category. The median district had 10 schools in this category.

The number of students eligible for SES varied accordingly. The high was 190,000 students in the 104 schools in district 9; the low was 356 students

8. U.S. Department of Education (2005).

in the one school in district 2. The median was 5,264 students in the ten schools in district 7. Since the program was just getting under way in many localities, it is not surprising that relatively small percentages of eligible students were served. Across the nine sites, the median was 13 percent of eligible students served. As for the number of service providers per site, this ranged from five to twenty-seven, with a median of ten. Thus a relatively modest number of providers were offering tutoring in each site.

As for the recipients of services, as mandated by the legislation, they have been low-income students in grades K–12 of Title I schools that failed to make AYP for three consecutive years. Reports from the field suggest that, at least during the early years of the program, only a small percentage of eligible students were enrolled, and that among these, student attendance at after-school tutoring sessions was often a problem.[9] Thus we may suppose that those students who were least engaged in school, and perhaps those whose families suffered from the greatest risk factors, were more likely to be absent. The most likely recipients were the more engaged of those low-income students in failing Title I schools.

Reports for the 2004–05 school year suggest that the percentage of eligible students receiving SES increased from the previous year, but only modestly. One study put this at less than 20 percent nationally.[10] Should this relatively low participation rate be attributed to a deficiency in the supply of services, with too little tutoring being offered? Or is it due to weak demand, with few eligible parents and students desiring to be tutored?

Both supply and demand appear to be involved. On the supply side, the creation of a set of suppliers who have invested in the capability to provide services nationwide was delayed by the limited availability of SES funding in the program's first few years. This was primarily due to the requirement that a school fail to achieve AYP for three years before SES funds became available to its students. A second reason for the delay was due to the need to put state certification procedures in place and the time needed for providers to respond to these. Further, school district administrators needed to become familiar with the SES program and its requirements. Finally, some districts deliberately restricted SES implementation by outside providers, seeking instead to become large providers themselves, so that they could retain the maximum amount of federal funding within their own budgets. However, most of these issues have been resolved, and increasing numbers of schools

9. There is some evidence that attendance was better when tutoring was located within the school building or when SES providers offered incentives for attendance.

10. Center on Education Policy (2005), p. 125.

are reaching the end of their three-year grace period on attaining AYP. As discussed below, many providers have found it possible to achieve high profit rates through SES delivery. As a consequence, more than 2,000 providers, including a number of large, multistate operators, have been state-certified in a relatively short period of time. This is not surprising, given the existence of a large and experienced educational services sector and the well-known ability of American entrepreneurs to respond to profit-making opportunities. Thus it seems unlikely that in the years ahead there would be an absence of willing SES providers constituting a significant impediment to the growth of program participation rates.

The demand side is likely to pose a greater obstacle to long-term increases in program participation. It is central to SES regulations that tutoring is offered as an after-school program. In more than ten years of implementing tutoring programs, the first author of this paper has found that it is much easier to achieve successful implementation as a pullout program during school hours than after school. By 3:00 p.m., most students feel that they have already had enough of school. Even when an after-school recreation program is provided, students tend to scatter and are difficult to find when the tutor is ready for them. And this is particularly the case for the most at-risk students, who also tend to be those whose parents have the fewest resources and are the most disorganized.[11] Thus lack of sustained interest in after-school tutoring on the demand side—from at-risk students—is likely to put a limit on the participation rates that can be achieved by SES programs, even after start-up difficulties have been overcome.

Characteristics and Costs of the Services Provided

What are the details of the tutoring services provided and the costs of these services? These issues were investigated across the nine case study districts in a study sponsored by the U.S. Department of Education.[12] Results showed that tutoring shared the same characteristics across all nine sites. It was usually provided several times a week (but not every day), in the student's own school, at the end of the school day. Tutoring sessions usually lasted an hour. Tutors were typically certified teachers, often from the same school. Contact hours varied widely, as did instructional strategies. Instruction was usually in small groups, ranging from three to fifteen students. The district itself was a provider in

---

11. Dynarski and others (2003); Vandell and others (2005).
12. U.S. Department of Education (2005).

three of the sites—its services were similar to those of other providers. In one of these districts (district 1), the district's program provided a modest share of the total tutoring. But in the other two districts (districts 2 and 9) the district program was by far the largest provider. This raises an issue we shall return to later—the interests of at least some districts in running these programs themselves and not allowing outside providers much, if any, share.

At each school, providers needed a minimum number of students to make it financially viable to offer a program. Competition among providers was sometimes intense. Also, in almost every district, there was at least one provider who withdrew from a school because program interest was too low.

Seventy-five percent of the providers operated their program at the school site; the remaining 25 percent operated offsite. Just under half of the providers offered students transportation to and from tutoring or transportation from the school to the student's home after tutoring ended.

Tutoring was usually offered for one to two hours per day, two or three times a week, after the school day ended. The total number of tutoring hours each child received was determined by the amount each district had allocated as their Title I per pupil cost relative to the amount charged by the child's tutoring provider. Each tutoring provider was able to work with the child until the per pupil allocation was exhausted. Thus low-cost providers were able to offer far more contact hours than high-cost providers. As a consequence, the number of tutoring hours children received varied widely.[13] For example, even within the same district, a provider who charged $14 per hour was able to offer a total of 100 hours for each student, while one who charged $50 per hour offered only 28 hours. The authors reported that, overall, the average number of hours was sixty but that this varied widely, since few providers were "average." If students received two to three hours of tutoring per week, they typically exhausted their Title I funding allocation by the end of ten to twenty weeks. Consequently, most students stayed in tutoring for only one marking period or one semester, and providers who began early in the school year had to recruit a new set of students partway through the year.

More information on these issues is provided in table 7-4, which shows detailed characteristics of the tutoring offered in district 1 of the case study, the district with the largest number of providers for which such detail was available.

Of the fourteen providers in this site, six were national or multistate, six were local, one was the district itself, and one was faith based. (Here and else-

13. U.S. Department of Education (2005), p. 44.

Table 7-4. *Detailed Characteristics of SES Service Providers in Case Study School District 1*

Type of provider	Cost per contact hour (dollars)	Number of contact hours per student	Number of students served	Tutoring format
Private				
National	22	44	14	Small group
	32	30	1	Individualized
	12	100	295	Small group
	20	35	14	Small group
	30	34	841	Small group
Multistate	40	25	85	Individualized
Local	15	54	3	Small group
	40	25	21	Small group
	250 per month	42	28	Individualized
	11	57	123	Small group
	5	150	9	Small group
Foundation	22	45	30	Small group
School district	15	32 or 64	290	Small group
Faith based	26	18	23	Individualized

Source: U.S. Department of Education (2005), exhibit A-1.
SES = supplemental educational services.

where, faith-based or online providers are identified as such.) Of these fourteen providers, only four offered individualized tutoring, which served a total of only 137 students, less than 8 percent of the total. Thus the great majority of students were tutored in small groups.

By far the largest provider was a national organization that tutored approximately half the total number of eligible students at a cost of $30 per contact hour. It provided approximately thirty-four hours of tutoring per student. By contrast, the next largest provider, also a national organization, charged $12 per contact hour and provided 100 hours per student. Most of the other providers fell between these extremes.

It should be noted that providing these services can be very profitable. For example, if the provider that charged $30 per contact hour (which is on a *per student* basis) did so in groups of five students, the provider would be taking in $150 per hour of the tutor's time, while perhaps paying the tutor only $30 per hour or less. Even with administrative and other costs, this structure (or one with even larger tutoring group sizes) can generate very high rates of profit, particularly after start-up costs have been recaptured.

Table 7-5. *Detailed Characteristics of SES Service Providers in Case Study School Districts 4 and 9*

Type of provider	Cost per contact hour (dollars)	Number of contact hours per student	Number of students served	Tutoring format
District 4				
Private				
National	15	68	291	Small group
	35	30	91	Small group
	30	40	110	Small group
	30	40	922	Small group
Local	31	39	51	Small group
	18	66	479	Small group
	20	60	79	Small group
	40	30	186	Small group
	17	70	436	Small group
School district	12	86	155	Small group
District 9				
Private				
National	40	30	104	Individualized
Local	40	30	1,300	Small group and individualized
	40	30	528	Individualized
School district	40	30	9,000	Small group
Faith based	40	30	900	Small group and individualized

Source: U.S. Department of Education (2005), exhibit A-1.
SES = supplemental educational services.

Further information is shown in table 7-5, where detailed characteristics of service providers are displayed for the two districts in the study with very large numbers of eligible students—districts 4 and 9. Once again, the great majority of students were tutored in a group rather than in a one-to-one setting. Beyond this, however, the two districts have very different provider profiles. District 4 had a relatively heterogeneous group of providers, with the largest being a national organization, the two next in size were local organizations, and the district itself was only the fifth-largest provider. In this case the district itself had the lowest cost and the highest number of contact hours per student.

By contrast, in District 9, the district was itself the largest provider, being reported as serving fully 9,000 students. Only five of the reported twenty-seven providers (see table 7-3) were interviewed, and all charged $40 per hour and offered thirty contact hours per student. This is an example of a very large school district that itself dominates the provision of after-school tutoring and charges as much as the other providers.

What about instructional approaches and curricula? The authors of the systematic case studies interviewed approximately three providers in each of the nine districts they studied. The results are summarized in table 7-6. Most providers used student-to-teacher ratios of four to one or five to one, or higher. The great majority also used certified teachers to provide assistance with reading, mathematics, or homework.

However, underneath this apparent uniformity, the researchers found very eclectic content and approaches to instruction. Most providers focused on reading instruction; a smaller number taught mathematics. Some provided scripted lessons; others just helped with homework. Some lessons were organized around reading out loud; others involved phonics-based instruction. Provider curricula are required to be aligned with state standards, but this was rarely checked by local districts. Instead, they assumed that this had been part of the state's approval process. Some providers increased this alignment by having their tutors help students practice for state assessments. In cases where tutors were also classroom teachers, this sometimes provided a good integration with classroom work.

We made a number of efforts to collect more information about the curriculum and instruction underlying particular SES programs, although gaining specific information about content was quite difficult. Resources ostensibly designed to assist parents in choosing an appropriate provider for their children were invariably lacking in specifics on program content and curriculum. However, we were able to visit a local office of Sylvan Learning, which was the sixth and ninth most frequently approved provider in table 7-1.

We observed afternoon sessions beginning at 3:00 p.m., 4:00 p.m., and 5:00 p.m. Certified teachers worked with students in groups of one, two, or three students. Direct instruction was accompanied by seatwork. The program director said that all teachers were certified, and that 3-to-1 was the largest student-to-teacher ratio used. Most were elementary school students, although some were older, and instructional groups were of mixed age levels. The curriculum was relatively structured, with a good mix of phonics and more holistic approaches to reading. (Sylvan operates a franchise system, in which local franchise operators are required to use materials provided by the company.) Standardized assessments and record-keeping were being used.

Table 7-6. *Instructional Characteristics, across Sampled SES Service Providers in All Case Study Districts*[a]

District	Student-to-tutor ratio	Content and grades	Staffing
1			
A	12:1	Math, reading	Certified teachers
B	6:1	Reading	Certified teachers
C	1:1	Homework help	No requirements
2			
A	Up to 10:1	Math, K–4	Certified teachers
B	4:1	Reading, K–5	Certified teachers
C	5:1–10:1	Reading, K–4	n.a.
3			
A	15:1	Test prep and reading, K–8	Certified teachers
B	3:1	Math, reading, K–12	Certified teachers
C	8:1	Math, reading, K–12	Certified teachers
4			
A	10:1	Reading, math, 1–12	Certified teachers
B	15:1	Reading, math, 2–6	Certified teachers
C	6:1	Reading, math, 1–6	Certified teachers
5			
A	10:2	Reading, math, K–8	Certified teachers
B	15:1	Reading, math, K–8	Certified teachers
C	8:1–10:1	Reading, math, K–8	Certified teachers
6			
A	4:1	Homework, reading, math, 1–8	Certified teachers
B	4:1	Reading, math, 1–8	College graduates
C	*	Math, reading, 1–8	High school students, college graduates
7			
A	5:1	Math, reading, K–8	Certified teachers, counselors
B	5:1	Math, reading, K–8	Retirees, parents, certified teachers
C	5:1	Math, reading, K–8	Certified teachers
8			
A	6:1	Math, 1–6	Certified teachers
B	10:1	Math, language arts, 6–12	Certified teachers, college graduates
C	10:1	Reading, math, 1–6	College graduates
9			
A	5:1	Reading, math, 1–12	Certified teachers
B	1:1	Math, language arts, 1–12	Certified or in-training teachers
C	1:1	Math, language arts, K–12	Certified teachers, college graduates
D	1:1–4:1	Math, language arts, K–12	Certified teachers, college graduates
E	1:1	Math, language arts, K–12	Certified teachers, college graduates

Source: U.S. Department of Education (2005), exhibit A-2.

n.a. Not available; SES = supplemental educational services.

* = Students work independently. Tutors are available if students need assistance.

a. The letters represent the separate SES service providers that were sampled in each district.

Overall, we saw a relatively high-quality program, with a relatively low student-to-teacher ratio and good time-on-task by the students observed.

With regard to others among the most frequently approved providers (table 7-1), we sought out literature describing their programs, and, where possible, undertook telephone interviews with representatives. We also sampled web-based materials that compared some of the programs. We learned the following.

PLATO Learning, the program approved by the most states, is based on instructional software that the student uses while sitting at a computer workstation. A teacher-tutor is available in the room to supervise and assist a group of students. The student-teacher ratio is unclear. From the company's literature, the software appears to include research-based instructional techniques, but how well students actually apply themselves to the software and the gains they are able to achieve are unknown.

Failure Free Reading is the program approved by the second largest number of states. It too is an instructional software program, and as with PLATO Learning, student-teacher ratios and student engagement with, and success in using the software are unknown. (It should be noted that this and the other providers point to many studies that have found large effects for their programs, but such studies generally have research designs that are too weak to provide reliable results.)

Newton Learning, a division of Edison Schools, is the program approved by the third largest number of states. This program provides scripted lessons for local teachers and other school staff to use with groups of students after school. The program is managed by a local site director hired by Newton; teachers and staff are hired locally. As with other similar programs, teacher-student ratios are unknown.

Huntington Learning Centers, Inc., is approved by the fourth largest number of states. It is similar to Newton Learning; Education Station, A Sylvan Partnership (the sixth most approved program); The Princeton Review, Inc. (the seventh most approved); Sylvan Learning (the ninth most approved); and Kumon Math and Reading Centers (the eleventh most approved) in that all of these programs provide small group and seatwork-based instruction using their own curricular materials. A web-based comparison aimed at parents showed that Huntington charges $48 per day, Sylvan charges $40 to $48 per day, and Kumon charges $22 per day.[14] It appears that Kumon may use lower-cost (uncertified) teachers.

14. My Learning Partners (www.mylearningpartners.net [January 15, 2006]).

Brainfuse Online Instruction is approved by the fifth largest number of states. This is an online tutoring service, where students seated at computer workstations are connected to live tutors (who have at least a BA). We were not able to learn the details of how this program has been implemented in the schools. However, it is interesting that Babbage Net School (the program approved by the twelfth largest number of states) is an online, self-paced program. The percentage of time students spend interacting with a live tutor compared with the time they spend with completely automatic self-paced tutoring is unknown in web-based providers.

Club Z! In Home Tutoring Services was approved by the eighth largest number of states. This company began by offering in-home, one-to-one tutoring, which largely consisted of a tutor assisting with the student's assigned homework. However, the company's brochure suggests that it is moving toward a small group, school-based program like that of other SES providers.

To summarize, the largest SES providers have adopted one of two models. In the most common model, the company uses proprietary curricular materials and employs local teachers to supervise and instruct students in small groups. These materials are typically of good quality, comparable with others that are widely used in classrooms. Quality issues include high student-to-teacher ratios, low student attendance, and lack of engagement with learning.

In the second tutoring model, companies have developed computer software and online tutoring services. In this model the students sit at computer workstations, with the groups of students being supervised by one or more adults from the school or the company. Once again, student learning depends crucially on attendance and engagement with the material.

Program Effectiveness

Although these programs make many claims, the effectiveness of few if any of them has been documented by studies utilizing adequate research designs. It is to this issue of program evaluation that we now turn.

Prior Research on After-School Programs

There have been relatively few independent, professional evaluations of the effectiveness of after-school programs, and even fewer utilizing an adequate research design. However, the studies by Dynarski and others evaluating the

21st Century Community Learning Centers program stand out within this literature as having excellent designs.[15]

The legislation authorizing this program of federal funding for after-school programs was passed in 1994. After a slow start, the program grew rapidly, increasing from $40 million in 1998 to $1 billion in 2002. By 2004 the program provided funding to 2,250 school districts to support programs based in 7,000 public schools.

Dynarski and others conducted separate studies of elementary and middle school programs. The authors report that the typical program was open for three hours after school, four or five days per week, and had about forty-five students on an average day. The program usually provided a snack, followed by homework time, and was overseen by a mix of certified teachers and paraprofessionals. Homework assistance involved setting aside time for students to do their homework. After this, students could choose from a mix of activities, including gym, board games, computer lab, and arts and crafts. Most centers also provided some form of teaching or tutoring.

The evaluation design for the study of elementary school programs involved random assignment of students to treatment and control groups within each program. The middle school study design was based on a matched comparison group of program nonparticipants in host or other schools.

Both first- and second-year reports from this evaluation are now available, and the findings are consistent with one another.[16] As a result of the program, elementary, but not middle school students, reported feeling safer during after-school hours. Elementary school parents were more likely to attend school events than were middle school parents. Elementary school students averaged about sixty days of program attendance, while middle school attendance was much lower, averaging about thirty-one days.

The program had little positive impact on academic achievement. For neither elementary nor middle school students did the program increase completion of homework assignments. (There was even some evidence of *decreased* homework completion among elementary school students.) For elementary school students, there was no effect on reading test scores or grades. For middle school students there was no effect on grades in English, mathematics, or science, although there was a positive effect on grades in social studies. There were few impacts on social development outcomes, such as helping other students after school.

---

15. Dynarski and others (2003, 2004).
16. Dynarski and others (2003, 2004).

Following up on this research, Vandell and others hypothesized that Dynarski's study may have failed to find positive effects because it sampled the broad range of available programs. Instead, Vandell and others chose to focus their study on high-quality after-school programs and a target population of students from low-income families, especially single-parent households.[17]

Instead of a random assignment or matched comparison group design, Vandell and others used a cluster analysis to divide their study sample into four groups: high program and high activity, high program and low activity, low supervision, and supervised at home. This allowed for the fact that students treated these after-school programs as only a subset of their available after-school options. The first group was active not only in the program but also in other after-school activities. The second group was active in the program only. The third group was relatively uninvolved in supervised after-school activities, and the final group spent much of their after-school time at home. The authors used teacher judgments to measure student academic performance, work habits, and other behaviors.

Vandell's study estimated program effects by regressing change in the dependent variable against dummy variables for the three participation groups (high program and high activity, high program and low activity, and supervised at home), plus control variables, including the pretest score on the variable. Thus their method compares all three groups to the low supervision group. (There is, of course, a possibility of selection bias in this methodology, since the low supervision group may be particularly low performing as a consequence of attitudes and behaviors that are not controlled in the analysis.)

In this methodology, the most direct test of program effects derives from the comparison of outcomes for the high program and low activity group and the unsupervised group. Among elementary school students, all effects are positive and statistically significant. Among middle school students, none are statistically significant. We conclude that high-quality after-school programs may have positive effects for at-risk elementary school students who participate strongly in them, at least by comparison with outcomes for the low supervised group. However, there appear to be no significant effects for middle school students.

How can we reconcile the findings of Vandell's study with those of Dynarski's? They both found no effects of after-school programs for middle school students, so this finding is well supported. As for elementary school programs, Dynarksi's random assignment study of the full population of

17. Vandell and others (2005).

these programs, with its finding of little positive effect, must be preferred. However, the finding of Vandell and others, that high-quality elementary school programs have positive effects, at least when at-risk students who participate in them are compared with unsupervised students, suggests that further research on these programs may be warranted.

These prior studies of after-school programs provide a useful background for measuring the likely effects of the programs implemented under the SES provisions of NCLB. However, there is a second background of program implementation and evaluation against which to judge the likely effects of SES. This is the larger Title I program, of which SES is merely the latest extension.

SES as a Component of Title I

From its inception in 1966 up through 2000, annual federal expenditures on Title I of the Elementary and Secondary Education Act (of which NCLB was the 2001 reauthorization) grew at a modest rate, rising to $7.9 billion in 2000. However, by 2004, Title I expenditures had grown to $12.3 billion, an increase of approximately 50 percent in only four years.[18] Thus one major change under NCLB has been an unprecedented rate of increase in the funds available for compensatory services to low-income students in low-performing schools.

Unfortunately, prior evaluations of Title I have found that the program has had little or no effect in narrowing achievement gaps for low-income students.[19] In a wide-ranging review, Farkas and Hall pointed out a number of reasons for this.[20] First, the program has never had a coherent curriculum. Instead, it has always been merely a funding stream for local district administrators to use as they liked. Second, teachers rarely had specific training in the most effective curricula for use with students having learning difficulties. Third, add-on Title I services typically consisted of group instruction, with as many as five to eight students in the group, which many researchers believe to be an ineffective strategy for students who are already behind, who bring a variety of performance levels and learning problems to the group and often have weak school engagement. (Although it is widely believed that small group instruction is less effective than one-to-one instruction, a belief that we share, the published scientific evidence on this issue is small to nonexistent. We return to this issue below.)

18. Sunderman, Kim, and Orfield (2005), p. 11, table 1.3.
19. Carter (1983); Puma and others (1997).
20. Farkas and Hall (2000).

As Farkas and Hall previously discussed, these problems persisted through the 1970s and 1980s, leading to a call for more effective interventions using one-to-one tutoring and more highly structured curricula, including the use of phonics instruction for reading in the early elementary grades.[21] Evidence shows that each of these interventions is effective with low-income students who have fallen behind. However, they observed that even as these new approaches were being tried in some districts during the 1990s, the reauthorization of Title I in 1994 introduced a fourth set of problems, related to the significant increase in the use of schoolwide Title I programs. A schoolwide program is one in which Title I funds can be applied to any school expenditure, instead of having to be targeted to add-on services for the lowest performers. Consequently there is the temptation to spend Title I money on general expenses, such as computers and other things. This temptation is difficult for school administrators to resist, particularly when their costs keep rising but local taxpayers resist school tax increases. It seems likely that, since reauthorization of Title I in 1994, this fungibility has reduced the share of Title I dollars spent on add-on services to the most at-risk students.

In sum, we must assess the effectiveness and costs of added-on SES after-school tutoring services against a background in which "regular" Title I services have typically been ineffective because they involved group tutoring rather than one-to-one tutoring, used ineffective curricula and teachers untrained in special techniques for children with learning difficulties, and often redirected program funds to other purposes than to add-on services.

Without a properly designed evaluation specifically targeted on SES programs, we cannot be sure how effective these programs are in closing the achievement gaps experienced by low-income children. However, the situation does not look promising. The two studies by Dynarski and others found no effect of after-school programs on school achievement or engagement for either elementary or middle school students. The study by Vandell and others examined only high-quality programs and found no effects for middle school students. They did find effects for elementary school students, but largely among the subset of students who participated very strongly in these programs, and this effect was measured by comparing these strongly active students with unsupervised students.

Very recently, Zimmer and others released a study that used student fixed-effects regression analysis on data from seven large urban school districts to

<hr>

21. Borman and others (2005); Farkas (1998); Farkas and Hall (2000); Snow, Burns, and Griffin (1998); Wasik and Slavin (1993).

estimate the effects of SES participation on math and reading achievement during the 2004–05 school year.[22] They report that, overall, SES participation had significant positive effects on both math and reading, with effect sizes of 0.09 standard deviation (above the district mean) for mathematics, and 0.08 standard deviation for reading. Such significant positive effects are, of course, encouraging, but effect sizes below 0.1 standard deviation are not large enough to go very far toward closing achievement gaps. Further, when one examines the calculations underlying this result in detail, one finds that, across the seven districts, one district appears anomalous, with unusually large effects, whereas the other six districts have effects generally smaller than the 0.09 and 0.08 reported for the group as a whole. Indeed, the median effect size across the seven districts is 0.04 standard deviation for math, and 0.06 standard deviation for reading. Thus these findings are consistent with other results, suggesting that *if* SES as currently implemented increases student achievement, the effects are quite modest in size.

Title I itself has long been ineffective. Efforts to improve it were focused on one-to-one instruction and highly structured curricula. Now, at least in the SES programs evaluated by the U.S. Department of Education, instead of one-to-one tutoring, the education field seems to have taken a step backwards by using group instruction.[23] Further, the median instructional group size being observed in SES programs today is six to one (recall table 7-6), which is probably too large to be effective.

Summary of SES Program Effectiveness

SES programs have attendance problems, sessions that meet only two or three times per week, and a lack of clarity regarding curricula. In many cases, program charges seem to be unconscionably high. (For example, a teacher is paid $30 per hour and works with a group of six students; her time is billed to the district as 6 × $30 = $180 per hour, and the program operators net $150 per hour. Even after their other program costs are added in, contractors seem to be obtaining an unusually high profit rate.) This leads to a limited number of sessions for many students. In the experience of the first author in implementing one-to-one tutoring across more than forty school districts over fifteen years, even when delivered one-to-one, a minimum of fifty or sixty highly structured tutoring sessions are required to see good effects.[24] Thus it seems unlikely that students receiving this many, or even a smaller

22. Zimmer and others (2007).
23. U.S. Department of Education (2005).
24. Farkas (1998).

number, of sessions in *groups as large as six or more students* will make substantial progress.

Program Regulations and Market Structure

Many advocates of the SES provisions in NCLB were seeking a "private-sector solution" to the public schools' inability to raise the performance of low-income students. Unable to pass legislation for school vouchers, they settled on a compromise designed to encourage for-profit firms and nonprofit organizations to provide after-school tutoring on a large scale. They saw this legislation as empowering parents to choose the provider of tutoring that they wanted for their child. It was also designed to stimulate the creation of an industry of SES providers and to accustom the schools to dealing with them. The resulting competition among providers was expected to result in better services for children, at a lower unit price than previously.

Implementation of SES was delayed by the legislative provision that schools had to fail to make adequate yearly progress for three years before their students were entitled to supplemental services. However, by 2005, a large-scale SES industry was in operation. It involved approximately 2,000 providers that had been certified by at least one state, including a group of industry leaders that had been certified by half or more of the states. Although less than 20 percent of eligible students are being served nationwide, this rate is increasing.

Although relatively new (at least in its present form), the SES industry is vibrant. However, struggles over program regulations and market structure continue to hamper SES implementation. Prominent among these struggles is the regulation that districts identified as in need of improvement cannot themselves be providers of SES. Very large districts (those in major cities) are particularly likely to fall into this category. Indeed, during the 2004–05 school year, 52 percent of very large districts were ineligible to offer supplemental services. By contrast, the figure for large districts was 23 percent; for medium districts, 14 percent; and for small districts, 7 percent.[25] Thus the very large districts stand to lose large amounts of Title I dollars to outside SES providers.

The Chicago School District has battled the U.S. Department of Education for a waiver of NCLB regulations to allow the district to operate its own after-school program with Title I funds. The district also made it difficult for

25. Center on Education Policy (2005).

outside organizations to provide SES services. Amid much publicity, Secretary of Education Margaret Spellings granted this waiver on September 1, 2005.[26] In return, the Chicago School District agreed to facilitate access to students, parents, and schools by outside SES providers. Newspapers such as the *New York Times* have reported that other large districts, including New York, Boston, and Los Angeles, have also made it difficult for outside providers to enroll their students. One feature of program implementation in at least some districts has been the struggle between the local district and outside providers over who will spend the bulk of SES funds.

Some privatization advocates have argued that designating school districts as financial intermediaries between SES providers and the parents of eligible students is a flaw in the legislation—that these districts have a conflict of interest, since they can keep for internal use any Title I funds that are not spent on SES.[27] The conflict is evident, and there is certainly truth to this claim. Yet one wonders how much difference it makes whether after-school programs are managed by outside providers or the district itself. After all, many providers merely hire the school's own teachers to tutor groups of three to twelve students in the school's own building. Why should they be able to make a profit on a service that the school itself is perfectly capable of offering?

This question goes to the heart of the issues raised by the effort to create an industry of private for-profit and nonprofit SES providers—will competition in this industry spark a significant improvement in after-school tutoring programs? On the pro side of this argument, competition among providers of most goods and services has always been good for consumers. But to see real gains, consumers (that is, the parents of students eligible for SES) need to be empowered and provided with information so that they can make meaningful choices among alternative suppliers. Time will be necessary for consumers and suppliers to become accustomed to competition in the marketplace.

On the con side of the argument, SES providers have thus far shown little sign of meaningful innovation. They are merely taking off-the-shelf curricula or instructional software and using the school's own teachers to deliver it to relatively large groups of students during after-school hours. Thus we may be wasting large sums of money by offering these providers management fees for large-group instruction that has produced no Title I gains when delivered during school hours. Historically, only two innovations have reliably pro-

---

26. Sam Dillon, "Education Law Is Loosened for Failing Public Schools," *New York Times*, September 2, 2005, p. 12.

27. Peterson (2005).

duced gains—highly structured curricula and one-to-one tutoring. On the one hand, both can be offered after school without the need of an outside provider, and the profits going to outside providers could be better used to reduce instructional group size. On the other hand, perhaps competition among providers for these management fees is necessary, since local school districts may not be able to be trusted to effectively manage after-school programs themselves.

Recommendations for Improvement

It is not easy to successfully implement compensatory education programs in low-income schools. Evidence for this includes massive Title I ineffectiveness during the 1970s, 1980s, and 1990s.[28] It was because this ineffectiveness was recognized that different groups undertook extensive efforts in the 1990s to create and implement more effective service delivery models.[29] These efforts typically involved a highly structured curriculum, delivered by highly trained instructors, operating as one-to-one tutors in a pullout program during the school day. Such efforts were used because it was widely believed that the failure of Title I was due to inadequate curricula and staff training, combined with medium to large group instruction. Yet supplemental educational services as they are currently delivered involve eclectic curricula delivered in groups with high student-to-teacher ratios— ratios of six to one and higher are very common (table 7-6). Thus SES seems to be returning to earlier, less effective teacher training and teacher-to-student instructional ratios. Further, SES programs are now delivered after school rather than as a pullout program during the school day. After school, it is difficult to guarantee regular student attendance, and both students and teachers may have difficulty concentrating on their work. This is one reason that after-school programs are often ineffective.[30] Therefore, current implementation of SES appears to combine a weakness of prior Title I programs (group instead of one-to-one instruction) with a new weakness that Title I did not previously have—after-school instead of during-school operations.

Our experience with supplementary tutoring services suggests that moving to in-school, rather than after-school, service delivery may be quite

28. Arroyo and Zigler (1993); Farkas and Hall (2000); Puma and others (1997).
29. See, for example, Borman and others (2005); Farkas (1998); Pinnell and others (1994); Wasik and Slavin (1993).
30. Dynarski and others (2003, 2004).

important in increasing instructional effects.[31] But in view of existing legislation as well as current educational policy trends, this seems unlikely to occur.
A move toward one-to-one tutoring, or at least smaller group instruction,
may be more achievable in this policy environment. However, the competitive forces brought into play by the SES legislation and regulations appear to
be too weak to force such improvements. This is because school districts
stand between parents and providers, relatively few providers are available at
many local sites, parents are often uninformed about what makes instruction
effective for their children, and students are typically unenthusiastic about
after-school tutoring. One solution would be to assign tutoring vouchers to
parents and attempt to achieve the full force of market competition to
improve SES delivery. However, this type of policy seems unlikely to be
passed by Congress. Under these circumstances it seems best to simply mandate lower student-to-teacher ratios:

*Recommendation: Three-to-one ratios of student to teacher should be required
of all providers.* The weakness of competitive forces in local markets for SES
should also be addressed.[32] Particularly important is the lack of information
made available to parents regarding the details of the programs offered by
alternative providers. For example, parents often have little idea that their
child's after-school program may consist of little more than sitting in a group
of twelve students while the teacher talks, or, alternatively, sitting at a computer by themselves with relatively little engagement.

*Recommendation: Parents should be offered information about the implemen-
tation details of competing SES programs, including the opportunity to observe the
programs in action.* Another problem is that student participation in SES programs is low, and among participants, daily attendance is low. Program participation is rising as states, districts, parents, and providers become more experienced with program regulations, while attendance is likely to be more of a
problem, particularly for middle and high school students. Since SES is based
on student and parental choice, participation and attendance levels cannot be
mandated. However, efforts must be made to keep them as high as possible.

*Recommendation: Incentives should be provided to districts, providers, stu-
dents, and parents to keep program participation and attendance at high levels.*
Curricula seem generally to be of high quality, and most providers are using
either certified teachers or other acceptably qualified personnel. Thus, if
lower student-teacher ratios and higher participation and attendance could

31. Farkas (1998).
32. For a similar point, see Burch, Steinberg, and Donovan (2007).

be achieved and if, further, a competitive market existed within which parents could make informed choices among real alternatives, SES programs would likely be operating as successfully as possible.

Recommendations for Research

The absence of positive Title I effects for small- and medium-sized group instruction during the 1970s, 1980s, and 1990s convinced many researchers and practitioners that one-to-one instruction with its intensity, privacy, and custom-tailoring was likely to be the best way to achieve positive outcomes for students who had already fallen behind their classmates. Indeed, this notion was fundamental to the creation of a program—Reading Recovery—that is widely used today in Title I programs throughout the country.[33] In a much-cited review of five one-to-one tutoring programs, Wasik and Slavin found that all five were effective in raising student achievement.[34] After publication of this study, researchers and practitioners focused on a number of other issues related to one-to-one instruction—particularly, should the ideal program be phonics or whole language–based (or perhaps a combination of the two), and should efforts focus on measuring the relative effectiveness of teachers compared with that of paraprofessional tutors?

But have any studies been published explicitly comparing the relative effectiveness of one-to-one with the effectiveness of small group tutoring? In perhaps the most complete formal meta-analysis of studies on the effectiveness of one-to-one tutoring, Elbaum and others reported on two unpublished dissertations that they say found one-to-one and small group instruction to be equally effective.[35] However, we examined these studies and found them to be so flawed as to provide no evidence of support of the efficacy of small group tutoring. At the same time, a study by Rashotte, MacPhee, and Torgesen *does* appear to demonstrate that under carefully controlled conditions, small group instruction can be effective.[36] To what, then, should we attribute the apparent ineffectiveness of SES as currently implemented?

First, there is the well-documented failure of Title I to achieve any positive effects using small group interventions during the 1970s, 1980s, and 1990s.

33. For evidence in support of Reading Recovery, see Pinnell and others (1994). For a dissenting view, see Rasinski (1995). We agree with those who criticize this program for its continued inattention to true phonics-based instruction, but this point is controversial.

34. Wasik and Slavin (1993).

35. Elbaum and others (2000).

36. Rashotte, MacPhee, and Torgesen (2001).

Second, the first author has had wide experience observing and implementing tutoring programs in hundreds of schools across more than forty school districts. He found that achieving positive effects is not easy and is sometimes not attained even with one-to-one tutoring. Thus it stands to reason that if a less intense method—small group tutoring—is used, success will be even more difficult to attain. Finally, there is the large number of published studies of effective one-to-one tutoring programs, combined with the fewer number of published studies of successful small group tutoring. It is well known that authors and journals are relatively uninterested in publishing null findings—there is little interest in programs that do not work. This may account for the paucity of studies on small group instruction.

But might it be possible to create an effective tutoring program with, say, a two-to-one ratio of students to teachers? This would halve the cost of one-to-one instruction. Or perhaps an effective program could even be achieved with a three-to-one ratio? More generally, if program effectiveness declines with increases in group size, what are the shape and rapidity of that decline? Clearly, it would be desirable to have a reliable answer to this question.

Recommendation: The optimal tutoring group size question should be addressed by a study in which curriculum and teacher skills are held constant and students in after-school programs are randomly assigned to tutoring groups of varying size. To effectively spend approximately two billion dollars on SES each year, scientific evidence is needed on the benefits and costs of varying tutoring group sizes. Meanwhile, SES has not been implemented in a controlled environment. Given the chaotic and heterogeneous conditions under which SES programs have been implemented, it is desirable to study the effects of alternative implementation conditions on SES program effectiveness. If billions of dollars are going to be spent on supplemental educational services, we should be willing to invest at least 1 percent of this cost in finding out what works best in delivering these services.

Recommendation: A study is needed in which various implementation conditions—after-school versus during-school instruction, training and monitoring of tutors, instructional curricula—are systematically varied, along with tutoring group size, to find the most cost-effective combinations. And then there are the more general difficulties associated with SES implementation in low-income communities. Can enough qualified tutors be found in these communities to successfully lower the tutor-to-student instructional ratio? Can schools that are already overstressed and underperforming be expected to successfully implement SES? Can low-income, low-resource parents, who often have difficulty coping with the daily stresses of their lives, become sophisticated consumers of SES programs offered to their children? The first author's experience in implementing a highly structured paraprofessional tutoring program across multiple low-income school districts suggests that sufficient numbers of skilled tutors, many from outside the district, can be recruited, trained, and managed in their delivery of one-to-one tutoring services, but that doing so requires extraordinary efforts led by an outside organization that is experienced and focused on this goal.[37] As discussed earlier, the market forces created by existing SES legislation do not seem to be calling such organizations into existence. But this is an empirical matter, regarding which we need more evidence.

Recommendation: The studies of tutor-to-student ratios and of program implementation conditions recommended above should be conducted across districts and schools that vary sharply in their poverty rate, size, and other characteristics. Evidence is needed on how to deliver effective SES in schools serving even the poorest students and their families.

References

Arroyo, Carmen G., and Edward Zigler. 1993. "America's Title I/Chapter I Programs: Why the Promise Has Not Been Met." In *From Head Start and Beyond: A National Plan for Extended Childhood Intervention*, edited by E. Zigler and S. Styfco, chapter 3. Yale University Press.

Borman, Geoffrey D., and others. 2005. "The National Randomized Field Trial of Success for All: Second-Year Outcomes." *American Educational Research Journal* 42, no. 4: 673–96.

Burch, Patricia, Matthew Steinberg, and Joseph Donovan. 2007. "Supplemental Educational Services and NCLB: Policy Assumptions, Market Practices, and Emerging Issues." *Educational Evaluation and Policy Analysis* 29, no. 2: 115–33.

Carter, Launor F. 1983. *A Study of Compensatory and Elementary Education: The Sustaining Effects Study.* Washington: U.S. Department of Education, Office of Program Evaluation.

Center on Education Policy. 2005. *From the Capital to the Classroom: Year 3 of the No Child Left Behind Act.* Washington.

Dynarski, Mark, and others. 2003. "When Schools Stay Open Late: The National Evaluation of the 21st Century Community Learning Centers Program." Washington: U.S. Department of Education.

Dynarski, Mark, and others. 2004. *When Schools Stay Open Late: The National Evaluation of the 21st Century Community Learning Centers Program: New Findings.* Washington: U.S. Department of Education, Institute of Education Sciences, National Center for Education Evaluation and Regional Assistance.

37. Farkas (1998).

Elbaum, Batya, and others. 2000. "How Effective Are One-to-One Tutoring Programs in Reading for Elementary Students At Risk for Reading Failure? A Meta-Analysis of the Intervention Research." *Journal of Educational Psychology* 92, no. 4: 605–19.

Farkas, George. 1998. "Reading One-to-One: An Intensive Program Serving a Great Many Students While Still Achieving Large Effects." In *Social Programs That Work*, edited by J. Crane, pp. 75–109. New York: Russell Sage.

Farkas, George, and L. Shane Hall. 2000. "Can Title I Attain Its Goal?" *Brookings Papers on Education Policy 2000*, edited by Diane Ravitch, pp. 59–103. Brookings.

Invernizzi, Marcia. 2002. "The Complex World of One-on-One Tutoring." In *Handbook of Early Literacy Research*, edited by Susan B. Neuman and David K. Dickinson, pp. 459–70. New York: Guildford Press.

Peterson, Paul. 2005. "Making Up the Rules as You Play the Game." *Education Next* 5, no. 4: 42–49.

Pinnell, Gay Su, and others. 1994. "Comparing Instructional Models for the Literacy Education of High-Risk First Graders." *Reading Research Quarterly* 29, no. 1: 8–39.

Puma, Michael J., and others. 1997. *Prospects: Final Report on Student Outcomes*. Washington: U.S. Department of Education, Planning and Evaluation Service.

Rashotte, Carol A., Kay MacPhee, and Joseph K. Torgesen. 2001. "The Effectiveness of a Group Reading Instruction Program with Poor Readers in Multiple Grades." *Learning Disability Quarterly* 24 (Spring): 119–34.

Rasinski, Timothy V. 1995. "Commentary: On the Effects of Reading Recovery: A Response to Pinnell, Lyons, Deford, Bryk, and Seltzer." *Reading Research Quarterly* 30: 264–70.

Snow, Catherine E., M. Susan Burns, and Peg Griffin, eds. 1998. *Preventing Reading Difficulties in Young Children*. Washington: National Academy Press.

Stullich, Stephanie, Elizabeth Eisner, and Joseph McCrary. Forthcoming. *National Assessment of Title I Report to Congress*, vol. I: *Implementation of Title I*. Washington: U.S. Department of Education, Institute of Education Sciences, National Center for Education Evaluation and Regional Assistance.

Sunderman, Gail L., James S. Kim, and Gary Orfield. 2005. *NCLB Meets School Realities*. Thousand Oaks, Calif.: Corwin Press.

U.S. Department of Education. 2005. *Case Studies of Supplemental Services under the No Child Left Behind Act: Findings from 2003–04*. Washington: DOE, Office of Planning, Evaluation and Policy Development, Policy and Program Studies Service.

Vandell, Deborah L., and others. 2005. "The Study of Promising After-School Programs: Examination of Intermediate Outcomes in Year 2." Madison: Wisconsin Center for Education Research.

Wasik, Barbara, and Robert Slavin. 1993. "Preventing Early Reading Failure with One-to-One Tutoring: A Review of Five Programs." *Reading Research Quarterly* 28, no. 2: 178–200.

Zimmer, Ron, and others. 2007. *State and Local Implementation of the* No Child Left Behind Act: *Volume I—Title I School Choice, Supplemental Educational Services, and Student Achievement*. Prepared for the U.S. Department of Education, Office of Planning, Evaluation and Policy Development, Policy and Program Studies Services. Santa Monica: Calif.: RAND.

8

NCLB School Choice and Children in Poverty

PAUL T. HILL

Critics of No Child Left Behind (NCLB) complain that it imposes unrealistic performance expectations on public schools and then forces school districts to find alternative placements for children in schools that fall short.[1] Behind these provisions, critics claim, is a political strategy that will brand public schools as failures, thereby opening the door for charter schools and other forms of school choice, including vouchers.

Defenders claim that NCLB only creates logical consequences for performance based on long-established principles of standards-based reform policies that had already been enacted in forty-nine of the fifty states. These policies set standards for student achievement in every grade, create tests aligned with the standards, and pledge that the state will ensure that every student has access to a school that can help him or her meet the standards. No Child Left Behind uses the states' own tests and performance standards, but it puts teeth in the requirement that had become a dead letter in most states—to do something for children in consistently low-performing schools.

This chapter takes a critical view of both the critics' and the defenders' claims and asks three main questions:

1. See Farkas and Durham on NCLB tutoring in chapter 7 of this volume.

—What are the goals of the choice provisions of No Child Left Behind? What does the law guarantee and what does it leave undefined?

—What risks and potential benefits do the choice provisions create for poor and disadvantaged children in city school districts?

—What can state and local implementers do to increase the likelihood that the choice provisions of NCLB lead to positive outcomes for poor children?

How Clear Are the Goals and Consequences of the Choice Provisions?

As usual, those who celebrate and those who criticize NCLB's choice policy have valid concerns, but both exaggerate.

NCLB's approach to labeling schools makes many public schools look bad. This must have been obvious from the beginning to anyone on the legislative committees or in the House-Senate conference that negotiated the final form of the bill. Using their own standards, many states had labeled large numbers of schools as low performing. Moreover, No Child Left Behind's language requiring options for children in schools labeled failing was plain for everyone to see.

Whether the performance standards were meant to be unfair is another question. The adequate yearly progress (AYP) provision—a rough measure of whether students in a school are meeting targets based on the same school's (but not necessarily the same children's) performance level the year before — shows all the marks of a hastily crafted legislative vehicle. AYP's effects surely had not been modeled carefully or vetted by experts on the properties of test scores. As a result, the requirement that every subgroup in a school must show AYP had the perverse effect of putting schools serving diverse populations at a disadvantage.[2] It also led to labeling some schools as failures even if their average student scores were quite high.

These results probably were not intended by the Bush administration or its Democratic congressional allies, including Senator Edward Kennedy (D-Mass.) and Representative George Miller (D-Calif.). AYP has produced results no one will defend. Nor is there any reason to think opponents who hoped to discredit No Child Left Behind engineered the AYP language. It is more likely that they were assembled quickly by politicians and staff lawyers who hoped to reach agreement so they could move on to other things.

2. Kane and Staiger (2002).

It is also difficult to say exactly how much choice NCLB was intended to create or to estimate how much, for whom, and in what forms will choice ultimately emerge as a result.

Some members of the bipartisan coalition that enacted NCLB clearly intended it to create major new opportunities for charter school operators and others who would like to run publicly funded schools of choice. But not all coalition members favored or expected that result. NCLB gives parents whose children are in low-performing schools the option of choosing a higher-performing school, but it also allows districts to offer other options such as tutoring. Moreover, NCLB implies but does not expressly establish a positive obligation for districts to create new schools if there are no seats in higher-performing schools available. In addition, NCLB does not give parents a private right of legal action against districts that fail to create any of the promised options.

The NCLB choice provision is a legislative compromise whose meaning will become clear only through the pulling and hauling of bureaucratic rule-making, enforcement, and intergovernmental politics.

To date, the choice provisions have proven weak.[3] Because politicians on both sides of the aisle wanted to avoid imposing national standards, they allowed states to use their own tests and set their own expectations about how much a child should learn in a year. Nothing in No Child Left Behind prevents states from recalibrating their learning expectations in order to avoid placing a "failed" label on large numbers of schools. As an NEA newsletter reports, some have done so.

> For the second year in a row, [in 2005–06] many states amended their Title I accountability plans and implemented changes making it statistically easier to make AYP. These changes were done with the approval of the Department of Education. Examples include:
> —Use of confidence intervals giving a wider range of schools passing grades;

---

3. Numbers from two cities illustrate the potential for expansion of choice driven by No Child Left Behind. In Baltimore during the 2003–04 school year, 27,000 students, one-third of the district's total enrollment, were eligible to transfer to higher-performing schools, but only 301 seats in such schools were available. In Chicago, 270,757 students were eligible to transfer but only 1,097 seats were available at thirty-eight schools. Both cities are under pressure to create many new options, and Chicago has pledged to transform dozens of existing schools and start 100 new schools via chartering and contracting out.

—A larger minimum "N" size for certain subgroups such as students with disabilities and ELL students (which means fewer schools have to "count" these students' scores in determining AYP);

—Overall increases in the minimum "N" size for all schools and subgroups; and

—A reduction in the state's minimum percent of students who have to be proficient from originally set levels.[4]

Many districts tried to avoid implementing the choice and tutoring provisions at all, or they have informed parents too late for them to be able to exercise choices.[5] As William Howell documents, in Fall 2003 in Worcester, Massachusetts, almost 4,700 students in the public schools were entitled to transfer to higher-performing schools, but only one student actually transferred. In 2003–04, only 5.6 percent of eligible students nationwide requested transfer to higher-performing schools and only 1.7 percent actually transferred.[6]

Some states might be able to avoid labeling any of their schools as failing for a long time, maybe indefinitely. For them the NCLB choice provisions are moot. However, some states are serious about their standards and are not likely to change them just to evade a federal requirement—these include Massachusetts, Texas, and Florida. Other states have only one or two districts likely to have many schools consistently low performing enough to bring the NCLB choice provisions into effect. Illinois is an example: since only Chicago is likely to need to provide options, the rest of the state is not concerned enough to cause the legislature to alter its standards or tests.

There are, in addition, localities that seem prepared to seize on the NCLB choice provisions as an opportunity. The state of Louisiana and the cities of New York and Chicago, for example, have initiated major efforts to develop new schools, citing NCLB requirements as at least partial justification. More than one local superintendent has confided to this author that pressure from the U.S. Department of Education could strengthen the hands of local leaders who want to create new schooling options but need help overcoming union and other resistance. These superintendents are following a practice

4. National Education Association, Great Public Schools for Every Child: Issues in Education, "More Schools Are Failing NCLB Law's 'Adequate Yearly Progress' Requirements: Emerging Trends under the Law's Annual Rating System" (www.nea.org/esea/ayptrends0106.html [February 14, 2006]).

5. Howell (2006, pp. 255–64).

6. Brown (2004).

common under Title I and federal programs for handicapped children, treating a federal requirement as a transfer of political capital that allows local leaders to take desired actions but place the blame on "the feds."

From this perspective the accommodating stance on NCLB enforcement taken by Education Secretary Margaret Spellings has witheld hoped-for political support from state and local leaders who had intended to use the NCLB choice provisions more aggressively. For example, the U.S. Department of Education's decision not to back Maryland State Superintendent Nancy Grasmick's efforts to take over failing Baltimore schools undercut other state and local leaders who wished to claim their hands were forced by a federal requirement.[7]

Like previous federal K–12 initiatives, NCLB is essentially an intervention into local politics. Whether states and localities create new options or find ways of evading the requirements depends a lot more on what state and local officials want to do than on the text of the law.[8]

The choice provisions of NCLB are not yet irrelevant, but they are less potent than opponents would make them out to be. To this point the federal government has not forced any locality to create new options, and it has not created a monitoring or enforcement regime that could put school districts under any duress.[9]

If NCLB survives until 2014, when all students are supposed to be able to meet AYP, pressure for new options is likely to grow. Some localities have chosen to create new options, whether because of superintendent initiative (Sacramento, California), determined city leadership (Chicago), or state takeover (Philadelphia and Oakland, California). Even if the federal government never seriously enforces the options requirement, increasing numbers of districts might try to create alternatives for children in consistently low-performing schools.

Risks and Benefits for Poor Children

If NCLB's choice provisions develop some teeth and require districts to offer new choices for children in the lowest-performing schools, might those children end up worse off? The existing set of low-performing urban schools are not necessarily the worst imaginable. All of them have teachers with some rele-

---

7. *Education Week* (2006).
8. Hill (1979).
9. A compliance instruction issued to the state of California in summer 2006 might, however, signal the beginning of more aggressive federal action on behalf of options.

vant training, instructional materials and equipment, and the benefits of established curricula and testing routines. No matter how disappointing their performance might be, some alternatives could be worse. Chicago and many other districts have recognized this and have refused to create an illusion of options by allowing children to transfer among existing low-performing schools.

Creating effective new schools is also not easy. Thus the most obvious risk posed by the NCLB options requirements is that children might end up in schools where they could learn even less than in their schools of origin. The following subsections summarize what is known about the possible consequences of the NCLB choice provisions for disadvantaged children's test scores and other school outcomes.

Research on Test Scores Tells Us Little about Risks and Benefits

For more than thirty years, scholars have been studying, and engaging in controversy about the benefits of school choice. The controversy has passed through three phases. In the 1970s and 1980s, researchers argued about James Coleman's findings that Catholic schools were particularly effective in raising test scores for disadvantaged students, especially African Americans.[10] In the 1990s, arguments focused on consequences of the test score in programs intended to increase the numbers of disadvantaged students in private (especially Catholic) schools by offering vouchers and scholarships. The third and current phase focuses on the effectiveness of new public schools of choice created under state charter laws.

Researchers have tried to estimate the benefits and risks of choice directly, by comparing patterns of test scores among students attending schools of choice with control groups of similar students attending regular public schools. The earlier studies, typified by those done by Coleman, compared private school students with demographically similar students in public schools. Later studies led by Paul Peterson and various colleagues compared students receiving vouchers and attending private schools with control groups of students who had applied for vouchers (in some cases publicly funded and in other cases supported by wealthy individuals) but lost out in lotteries.[11]

Though many of these studies were carefully done, none have produced overwhelmingly strong or unassailable results. In some cases, subtle differ-

10. Coleman and Hoffer (1987); Coleman, Hoffer, and Kilgore (1982); Bryk, Lee, and Holland (1993).
11. Greene, Peterson, and Du (1998); Witte (2000); Metcalf and others (2003). See also Howell and others (2001); Rouse (1998); Witte (1998); Howell and others (2003).

ences in definitions (for example, of students' racial characteristics) can determine whether a finding is positive or null.[12] Though choice advocates and opponents have made claims about the significance of particular findings (for example, that voucher-redeeming African American fourth graders in New York City outscored similar students in public schools), examples are selected from a much larger set of mixed results. Moreover, when positive results appear, they do not fit any definite pattern or theory: in one city, voucher-using African American boys might test better than controls in some grade-subject combination, but the same pattern does not appear elsewhere. Though the vast majority of achievement differences reported by Peterson and colleagues favor students using vouchers, mathematics outcomes for middle school African American boys were negative in Washington, D.C.[13]

As in other scientific fields, measurement and analytical methods are improving. In Washington, D.C., ongoing studies of the voucher program include a great deal more sensitive measurement of children's learning experiences than was possible in earlier studies. Thus future results, even if mixed, might be more interpretable. For now, however, we have little more than the commonsense surmise that was possible before the voucher experiments began: a low-income student using a voucher to attend a private school might benefit, depending on the attributes of the student, his or her match to the school, the school's quality, and many other factors. Though there is little evidence that attending a school of choice will harm a student, the research results do not exclude that possibility in some cases.

Though there is no scientific consensus about the benefits of choice, policy has evolved as if the positive findings were definitive following this logic: if Catholic schools are more effective for disadvantaged students, then increase the number of students who can attend them, via vouchers funded by government and private parties. Further, if there is a limited number of places available in existing private schools, create public programs that will encourage creation of new schools that have some of the attributes of private schools—independence, control of hiring and programmatic decisions, and admission by choice.

Although the arguments about the effectiveness of Catholic and other private schools are far from resolved, today's controversy about charter schools is the one most relevant to NCLB choice. NCLB identifies charter schools as a possible alternative for students attending schools that consistently fail to

12. See, for example, Krueger and Zhu (2003).
13. Wolf, Howell, and Peterson (2000, table 17).

meet AYP. The law as now drawn does not require any district to create new charter schools. Nevertheless, there are definite pressures toward chartering. A district that created new charter schools as options for children in schools labeled failing would not face any federal charges of noncompliance; moreover, local groups favoring charter schools can buttress their case for new charter schools by citing NCLB.

But, politics aside, is there any evidence that new charter schools are likely to perform better than the district schools for which they are an alternative? To date there are no studies of charter schools expressly formed in response to No Child Left Behind. There is a growing body of research on student outcomes in charter schools, but it is fair to ask whether available studies are relevant to the NCLB case. Charter schools started in response to NCLB would by definition admit students whose prior educational experience was substandard, and many would need to operate in neighborhoods where district-run public schools experienced difficulty recruiting and keeping teachers. Thus charter schools started under NCLB would face serious challenges, and anyone evaluating them would have to take careful account of their students' prior academic difficulties. NCLB charter schools might, on the other hand, benefit from "floor effects" if their students' growth had been retarded by exceptionally poor instruction, so that even a mediocre charter school might unlock hidden student potential.

Many available studies of charter schools take no account of students' prior experiences.[14] Nearly half of the charter school studies done to date used simple one-year snapshots of test scores and make mean-to-mean comparisons of students in charter and district-run schools without controlling carefully for student characteristics. However, some very high-quality studies have been published in the past two years. These studies followed students' score trajectories over several years and controlled in detail for student characteristics.[15] Available studies of charter schools in Texas, North Carolina, Florida, and the city of San Diego observed actual student gain scores before and after attending charter schools.[16] Dale Ballou has studied Idaho charter schools using computer adaptive tests administered to charter and control

14. For an extensive review of studies to date and analysis of how states and localities can obtain more valid results on charter schools, see Charter School Consensus Panel (2006).

15. Because these states are just starting to build their longitudinal student databases, these studies are still unable to analyze the trends of test scores of all students attending charter schools. No one can tell whether results would be different if scores for all charter students were available.

16. Texas: Hanushek, Kain, and Rivkin (2002); North Carolina: Bifulco and Ladd (2006); Florida: Sass (2006); San Diego: Betts, Rice, and Zau (2006).

students at least twice each year.[17] Caroline Hoxby and Jonah Rockoff studied three inner-city Chicago charter schools that were oversubscribed and had kept track of admissions lottery losers.[18] Although the latter study did not calculate gains before and after students entered charter schools, it focused on neighborhoods very much like those in which NCLB charters are likely to arise and controlled student characteristics by randomization.

All these studies reported mixed results, with charter school students apparently benefiting in some subjects at some grade levels and doing worse than comparison groups in others. All studies with longitudinal data showed that charter school test scores were lower in the first year of operation than in later years and that charter school students eventually caught and in some cases outpaced the comparison groups. The authors characterized their net findings differently: Eric Hanushek, John Kain, and Steven Rivkin; Tim Sass; and Hoxby concluded that the results were net positive about charter school performance; Julian Betts, Lorien Rice, and Andrew Zau found no consistent differences; and Robert Bifulco and Helen Ladd concluded that students in North Carolina charter schools, especially African Americans in inner cities, had net negative outcomes.

Most of these authors were careful to point out the special circumstances of schools in their sample, and they warned against extrapolation to charter schools elsewhere. Ballou, Bettie Teasley, and Tim Zeidner's findings illustrated the probable site-specific character of most results to date. They showed that scores rose for students who switched into charter schools and fell for students who switched out of charter schools (both findings positive about charter effectiveness) but that scores for students who stayed in charter schools declined over time. Because their outcome data are different from those in other studies and come from a state where chartering is new and the population of charter schools is rapidly changing, it is not clear what their results imply outside Idaho.

Aside from the results of these few studies, the research on charter schools can tell us little about the effects of NCLB choice on student achievement. Because data on charter school performance are not always readily available, researchers have used what they could get. The Charter School Consensus Panel found that twelve studies made aggregate comparisons of charter and public schools while not specifying which grade levels were analyzed.[19]

17. Ballou, Teasley, and Zeidner (2006).
18. Hoxby and Rockoff (2004).
19. Charter School Consensus Panel (2006).

Although twenty-six studies examined charter performance in particular states, none started with data that could be considered representative of all the charter schools or students in the area studied.

Forty-one states have charter schools, but the available research covers schools in only thirteen states, with five studies on California, four on Texas, and three on Florida. Only nine studies compare achievement across two or more states. Of these, four are meta-analyses that try to discern trends from studies done in single states, using disparate samples and methods. Because of the low quality of many studies (twelve make uncontrolled mean-to-mean comparisons), it is hard to know how to aggregate the results: does one well-done study outweigh ten weak ones that draw the opposite conclusion?

Many of the scholars who have studied charter schools are skilled and imaginative, so why is the body of research available so weak? One answer is that charter schools are relatively new and evidence on their performance is just emerging. Another is that significant funding for charter school research is just becoming available. To this point researchers have had to take advantage of whatever data they could get and learn what they could even if the results were imperfect.

A big step toward more meaningful results will be a shift in emphasis from making general statements about all charter schools to explaining causes of variation in outcomes. For now, however, we have very little that can be used to project the consequences of NCLB's choice requirements.

Other Risks and Benefits of Choice

There are other possible risks and benefits besides those measured by test scores alone. On the risk side, if NCLB leads to the creation of new school options, some children might be left behind in schools that others—both students and teachers—have fled. These "remainder schools" might be worse for the students who remain than they were before the options were created.

There is a further social risk: as families re-sort themselves into options, more advantaged students might be separated from less advantaged ones. This separation could worsen racial and class segregation and have negative school quality effects for the poorest children.

The potential benefits of choice are mirror images of the risks. Students who choose might get into better schools or, in a subtler possibility, might get into schools that are better matched to their personal learning needs than are the schools they previously attended. The results might be evident in test scores or other measures such as student attendance, persistence in school, graduation, and college attendance.

A second potential benefit is that local public school districts, fearing the loss of students and money, might compete with the alternatives by improving the most threatened schools or by creating new schools that would keep choosers within the district. This could create a better supply of schools that might benefit all students including those whose parents had not bothered to exercise choice.

A third possible benefit is that re-sorting students according to instructional tastes or parents' views of individual student needs might create more integrated student bodies (for example, in schools emphasizing arts, languages, science, public service, and so on) than now exist in big city school systems, or at least student bodies that are neutral with respect to race and income mixing.

How great are these risks and how likely the benefits? In 2003 the National Working Commission on School Choice examined evidence about the links between choice and such outcomes as student learning, harm to children left behind as others opt out of public schools, positive changes in school supply, and increased segregation. In every case it was clear that the links between choice and these outcomes were complex and contingent, not deterministic.[20] School choice does not cause any important outcomes directly. Instead, choice sets off a chain of events that might or might not lead to a particular outcome. Thus, whether an individual child whose parents exercise choice learns more depends on many factors—the quality of schools available, whether parents can learn enough about the options to find a school that matches the child's needs, whether the child gets admitted to the school his or her parents choose and can gain physical access to it, and whether once admitted that child makes the level of effort the school requires.

The commission concluded that the links between choice and other outcomes are similarly complex. In general, student learning, segregation, and consequences for children left behind in public schools depend not on choice itself but on how it is designed, the specific conditions under which it is introduced, and what actions educators, families, and government subsequently take.

Links between choice and segregation are mediated, and the results impossible to predict a priori. For example, segregation effects depend in part on the preexisting racial mix of the public school student body. In Washington, D.C., where existing schools are dismal and virtually all students are

20. National Working Commission on Choice in K–12 Education (2003).

African American, choice has a good chance of encouraging better schools, at no risk of generating greater segregation. In a city with racially integrated schools—if such a city exists—choice could easily upset delicate racial balances.

The commission identified a number of factors that intervene between choice and most outcomes.

FUNDING. Choice can benefit children only if they can transfer to good schools, and good schools require reasonable amounts of money to operate. If a child whose parents choose brings very little money with him or her, three bad things happen: few good existing schools offer to accept students; even fewer good new schools will start up; and schools that do accept students will have strong incentives to favor advantaged children and avoid more challenging poor and minority children.

PARENT INFORMATION. Poor parents who have never been able to choose are not in the habit of looking for information about schools and lack experience using it. When offered choices, parents naturally think of prominent private schools, but these seldom have many vacancies and are often poorly equipped to serve children with weak basic skills. Parents need to be informed about how to exercise choice about all the options that are available. More important, they need rich information about what different schools offer and how effective these schools are with children who have different interests and learning styles. Such information is not readily available now. After a few years, private information providers (such as California's EdSource) might fill the need. When choice programs are new, however, poor parents might not know how to get the information they need to make good choices.

ADMISSIONS RULES. Choice can help disadvantaged children only if they can get into the schools their parents choose. This requires fair admissions rules and processes. Schools in a competitive environment have strong incentives to guarantee good results by handpicking the students easiest to educate. Unless something is done to counteract those incentives, choice can enable some schools to become bastions of privilege. Policies that require schools to accept applications from everyone who applies and, if they get more applications than seats available, select students by lottery are generally necessary. This implies rules and organization that do not just emerge automatically.

SCHOOL FREEDOM TO USE RESOURCES IN NEW WAYS. Choice could raise the quality of all schools if public schools were able to respond to competition by improving their teaching staffs and instructional programs. However, public school collective bargaining agreements are hardwired to keep low-performing schools in existence while making it extremely difficult for them to improve. Because of the placement rights of senior teachers, schools in challenging neighborhoods are staffed with shifting casts of inexperienced teachers and, due to the low salaries of new teachers, low real per pupil spending. Such schools have no capacity to respond to competition, and choice might make them even less attractive to capable teachers and thoughtful families. Choice will be blamed politically for these schools' further declines, even though the underlying process is one that was set up by the school board and teachers union.

It is easy to see the importance of these factors for producing good outcomes of any school choice program, including ones created in response to No Child Left Behind. However, the majority of state charter school laws and all voucher initiatives provide much less money for students who would attend schools of choice than for those same students had they remained in public schools.[21] In a locality where charter schools would have to hire teachers, rent and heat facilities, and buy equipment in the same marketplace as district-run schools, they could not hope to compete for the best of anything. The rhetorical excesses of some choice supporters ("we can do a better job for half the money public schools get") were definitely not sound guides to the development of quality schools.

Nor have the political architects of choice policy thought much about parent information, admissions rules, arrangements for fair lotteries, or ways of allowing public school districts to compete for students. Those who rely on the adage "the market will provide" might be right in the long run, but in the short run things can be very messy. If the poorest parents cannot learn about choices or if schools find backdoor ways of excluding the most disadvantaged, poor children cannot benefit. If district-run schools get worse in the face of competition but never close (as happened in New Zealand where schools were allowed to stay open even after they had lost many students and their best teachers), the students who remain will be worse off. Critics of choice programs are unlikely to note that teacher job protection, not the introduction of choice, was the root cause.[22]

21. See, for example, Osberg (2006).
22. Fiske and Ladd (2000).

Can the Risks Be Managed?

In theory, the risks defined above could be managed by smart policymakers and implementers who wanted to make choice work and had the freedom of action to implement choice creatively. But in reality, how hard would that be? There is a growing body of work on policy and resources discussed above. Some studies focus on factors that seem logically related to positive outcomes for children who use choice programs to change schools, such as how to make sure equal funding is available for the education of students whether they attend district-run schools or schools of choice and how to inform parents about all their options. Others focus on factors logically related to negative outcomes, such as increased segregation or harm to the quality instruction for children remaining in traditional public schools.

One institution, the National Center for the Study of Privatization in Education, has published a series of such studies in the past two years.[23] In addition, the Center on Reinventing Public Education's Doing School Choice Right initiative has also launched a series of studies in search of answers on such questions as the following:

—What information do poor and minority families want about schools of choice and what sources do they trust?

—How can school districts fund schools of choice with a policy that monies follow the child from school to school?

—How can school districts faced with competition maintain the quality of instruction for children remaining in their schools?[24]

In combination, the studies done in the past two years tell us quite a lot about the possible risks and benefits of NCLB choice and the actions necessary to avoid harm and gain benefits.

INFORMING POOR PARENTS. This is the area in which the most has been learned in the past few years. In a study of interdistrict transfers in Minnesota published by National Center for the Study of Privatization in Education, Randall Reback found that parents were much more interested in test scores of schools they might choose than in the composition of student bodies in the receiving schools.[25] Courtney Bell found that high- and low-income parents do not necessarily seek different attributes in schools.[26] However, low-

23. Bell (2005); Reback (2005); Chakrabarti (2005); Burian-Fitzgerald (2005); Booker and others (2005); Walsh (2005); Booker, Zimmer, and Buddin (2006).
24. See CRPE, "Doing School Choice Right" (www.crpe.org/dscr/index.shtml).
25. Reback (2005).
26. Bell (2005).

income parents generally consider a more limited set of schools, even in situations where their actual choice sets have been dramatically expanded by public programs. The tendency for these parents is to consider a very limited set of schools defined by the neighborhoods and social circles in which they normally move. This can lead poor parents to act as if their only real choices are among low-performing schools. Thus, if the only schools that poor parents consider are low performing, then they will consider low-performing schools. The key is to expand parents' choice sets so that they know about and consider schools outside their immediate geographic and social milieus.

Paul Teske with Jody Fitzpatrick and Gabriel Kaplan has just published the results of a new study of parent information use for the Doing School Choice Right project mentioned above. They found that the experience of choice in itself led poor parents to start asking about differences among schools and to look for information to inform their choices.[27] As they report, poor parents were usually motivated to consider choices because they were unhappy with the schools their children attended. They wanted to choose a school that did not have the same problems as the one their child was attending, that is, a school that was safe, not chaotic, not harsh or rejecting. They often had ideas about the specific needs of an individual child and wanted information that would help them judge whether a particular school was a good match. The sources they developed and the information they sought resembled those used by middle-class parents:

—They trusted recommendations made by other parents, and they wanted to see schools for themselves.

—They did use many of the published sources, but they wanted to talk with people who have made choices and been in the schools themselves.

—They wanted to know about schools' average achievement levels but did not always assume that their child would learn best in the school with the highest scores.

—They were especially interested in a school that had a serene environment and positive social climate and a focus on learning, especially whether the school helps or ignores children who are struggling.

District leaders who want low-income families to know they have choices and to weigh the pros and cons of different schools must consider those parents' particular needs. Informing parents requires thought and organization. Descriptions of school programs and data on performance must be available and accessible to the trusted community leaders whom parents will seek out

27. Teske, Fitzpatrick, and Kaplan (2007).

for advice. Outreach to community opinion leaders can help ensure that parents become informed.

FUNDING SCHOOLS OF CHOICE. In the United States it is difficult to say exactly how much money is spent on the education of a particular student or in a specific school. States provide money for education in myriad ways, by paying salaries of teachers and administrators, funding construction, paying for equipment and professional development, and funding (through categorical programs) special services for designated groups of students. Districts distribute these funds among schools, central office services, and other district operations but seldom keep track of exactly how much goes where. As Marguerite Roza, Lawrence Miller, and Claudine Swartz have shown, actual per pupil spending can vary by a factor of four among the schools in one district.[28] These variations, moreover, are not caused by categorical programs but by district-level decisions, for example, assigning extra teachers to particular schools, ignoring unusually high average teacher salaries paid in schools in the most advantaged neighborhoods, and distributing central office services unevenly.

Today, money does not follow students, and districts do not track differences in spending on one child versus another. Districts can report their average per pupil expenditure, but this is computed simply by summing up all expenditures and dividing by the number of students served. In reality the money is distributed among tens of thousands of different budgets, and nobody knows for sure how much is spent on a particular school, service, or student.

If, as the National Working Commission on School Choice concluded, the quality of schools of choice and the willingness of schools to take their fair share of challenging students depend on equitable amounts of money following students wherever they enroll, school districts' management of funds poses a major challenge. Districts are not set up to distribute funds along with pupils. To accommodate the needs of choice programs, districts would have to develop new accounting and distribution systems, and dismantle old ones.[29]

A new set of studies led by Marguerite Roza is trying to determine whether districts can legally distribute their funds on a per student basis and how their accounting systems must be changed. These studies have just

28. Roza, Miller, and Swartz (2005); see also Roza and Hill (2004).
29. See, for example, Roza and Hawley-Miles (2005).

begun, but it is clear that there are few serious legal barriers to the kind of funding system required by choice. Most state funding programs allocate to districts according to particular formulas, but they do not necessarily expect the same formulas to control use of funds within the districts. Districts have mirrored state formulas as a way to avoid disputes. However, districts could reprogram many state funds toward per pupil allocation.

Districts would need to adopt accounting systems that track funds on a per pupil basis all the way down to the school level. Thus every school's income would consist of the sum of amounts brought by students. Districts also need to account for schools' total actual expenditures, including teacher salaries and benefits, and to provide school balance sheets that show real dollar income and real dollar expenditures. To the degree possible, districts should allocate the funds for purchase of central office services to schools, with transparent charges for services actually used by the school.

Teacher collective bargaining agreements and job tenure of central office staff—not state law—are the greatest barriers to full implementation of pupil-based funding. Competition due to choice can justify district leaders' efforts to overcome these barriers. These are local political issues, not legal or technical barriers.

AVOIDING SEGREGATION. Whether choice worsens student segregation by race or income depends on the preexisting degree of segregation, on whether parents of different groups choose different schools, and on whether school admissions are fair or biased. The existing research does not allow projections of the effects of NCLB choice provisions, but it does suggest that worse segregation is far from inevitable.

Rajashri Chakrabarti found that lotteries in Milwaukee could be unbiased if they were administered independently and if people were allowed to increase their own odds of winning by offering extra money.[30] Parents rich and poor cared more about outcomes than inputs and were willing to countenance sorting by ability but not by income.

Patrick Walsh found that *cream skimming*—when advantaged families use choice to cluster in particular schools—was a much less powerful force than generally understood. This is particularly true in central cities, where the families exercising choice are mainly African American.[31] The schools these students leave and move into through choice are racially and socially homo-

---

30. Chakrabarti (2005).
31. Walsh (2005).

geneous. As Walsh comments, estimates of creaming effects are often exaggerated because analysts assume that public schools in the absence of choice are more heterogeneous than they are.

Walsh also estimated the peer effects of creaming in an urban environment to be extremely small. As he concluded, for cream skimming to lower math scores by a decile, the peer effect would have to be larger than could be created by magically changing college-educated parents into high school dropouts.

Reback's study mentioned above found that parents' choices alone were not likely to create large racial disparities in city schools. Families did, however, make choices that stratified children by ability. (It is not clear whether such "ability grouping" was caused by the efforts of choosing parents to get away from less able students or whether it was a more benign result of matching students with schools organized to meet their needs.)

Reback was less positive about whether schools will make unbiased choices. As he found, schools could limit poor children's opportunities by hiding vacancies and otherwise keeping options off the market until more attractive options came along. He therefore urged that admissions processes be controlled by public agencies, not by individual schools.

AVOIDING HARM TO STUDENTS AND SCHOOLS LEFT BEHIND BY CHOICE. Districts losing large numbers of students also lose money provided by the state and federal governments, and they can be forced to reassign teachers, reduce course offerings or other services, and close schools. Deliberately created choice programs can cost districts students. Unfortunately, for anyone hoping to understand the effects of choice, districts also lose students in many other ways, and many (though not all) districts with large numbers of low-performing schools are suffering secular declines in school enrollments.

The difficulty of isolating the effects of choice can be seen from an analysis of Seattle's prospective losses to charter schools. Amy Anderson showed that Seattle lost a total of about 3,500 students because of factors other than graduation in 2003–04.[32] The district did not know how many of those students moved out of the district, enrolled in private schools, or just quit going to school. At the time of her analysis, a new state law (since repealed) would have permitted the creation of about 500 new charter school seats in the city every year. As Anderson suggested, it was impossible a priori to know whether the new charter school seats would cause the district to lose 500

32. Anderson (2004).

more students each year, or no students (if charter schools were filled with students who would have left the district anyway), or some number in between.

This estimating difficulty is extreme in districts like Seattle (and Baltimore; Washington, D.C.; Philadelphia; Detroit; Cleveland; Dayton and Cincinnati; St. Louis; Milwaukee; Salt Lake City; San Diego; San Francisco; Fresno, California; Portland; and Minneapolis) that have steadily lost student population for many years. Seattle, for example, has suffered a net annual loss of more than 1,500 students each year for thirty-five years, and Dayton has fewer than 17,000 students, from a student population of more than 60,000 in the early 1960s. In general, only those districts that have become major immigrant destinations are growing or maintaining steady enrollment. (These include Miami, Los Angeles, New York, and Houston.) For the majority of other districts, choice might be less a cause than a consequence of their protracted decline.

For such cities with a declining student population, new choice programs do not cause any fundamentally new problems. However, as a study by Michael DeArmond, Christine Campbell, and Kacey Guin revealed, choice could galvanize attention to a problem that had long been ignored.[33] Unlike the steady loss of students to private schools and suburban districts, losses to choice hurt: they are attributed directly to the district's failures, and they require districts to transfer funds to someone else.

As DeArmond, Campbell, and Guin found in Dayton and Milwaukee, the introduction of new voucher and charter programs created a sense of emergency that could strengthen the hands of school and district leaders. Choice enables district leaders to declare an emergency and force teachers, parents, and administrators to recognize that the district and its schools are in a competitive environment. In such a situation, district leaders must give families and good teachers reasons to stick with their schools. District leaders can then be empowered to cut central office costs and put a greater share of total funds into schools so that the schools can increase the focus on instruction. District leaders can take other measures such as

—accounting for funds explicitly on a per student basis;

—looking hard at the productivity of centrally managed programs including professional development;

—Reducing fixed costs, such as funds allocated for unused buildings and inefficient transportation systems;

33. DeArmond, Campbell, and Guin (2006).

—abandoning schools that large numbers of families are eager to escape so that other schools can have the funds they need to make themselves competitive.

This research is still under way. But its results to date suggest that choice seldom introduces wholly new problems for city districts, and in some cases it does not detectably add to the loss of students. Moreover, choice does not lead inevitably to the collapse of school districts or the decline of quality of instruction available to students. The results depend much more on the district response to competition than on the presence of a publicly funded choice program.

Conclusion: Practical Problems Are Serious But Manageable

Whether NCLB's choice provisions will help or harm students who are currently in low-performing schools depends on how practical issues are resolved: student-based funding, information and outreach to poor parents, fair admissions, and school freedom to use resources adaptively. None of these issues defy human solution. After all, public program implementation in many fields, not just education, must address such issues. But government administrators who implement choice reluctantly or without careful thought are unlikely to solve the hardest problems.

Practical solutions to these problems require analysis and experimentation with ways of allowing public funds to follow students to schools of choice, informing parents, assessing school performance, and maintaining a level playing field between district-run schools and schools of choice. Many superintendents, school boards, and teachers union leaders are reluctant to undertake such experiments because they would put pressure on the district-run public schools. Thus needed experimentation with school choice is prevented not because it is undesirable but because school boards and unions, whose interests are tied to traditional public schools, have the power to prevent it.

It is, however, possible to extract lessons from the new research about how states and localities might approach the choice provisions and how researchers might assess their consequences.

Perhaps the most important conclusion is that districts can do sensible things to avoid harm and increase the likelihood of benefits to children whose parents have choices. These include providing enough funding for pupils who transfer to encourage formation of quality choice options. This might involve seeking state permission to allocate funds in legal but unusual ways and cutting back on central office operations in proportion to the loss of students. Constructive actions also include investing in rich information for parents, making sure community leaders whom poor parents trust are extremely well informed, and encouraging all schools to be open to extended parent visits. Current district approaches to NCLB choice involve many actions that are not sensible; for example, such approaches as telling parents at the last minute that they have choices and creating stressful procedures for parents who want to choose new schools fall short.

District leaders can also prevent harm to students left behind when others exercise their option by refocusing district spending on instruction, merging very weak schools into stronger ones, and eliminating unproductive fixed costs.

Community institutions, such as the mayor's office, can also reduce the likelihood of segregation by overseeing fair admissions processes and lotteries.

Even if done all at once these are surely incomplete prescriptions. The confusing research on charter school outcomes suggests that there is a great deal more to be known about what makes a new school work well and how schools of choice can make full use of their advantages of student matching and family commitment.

Those who support NCLB choice need to undertake serious work on how choice can be made to work well for students and quickly. Prochoice foundations have preferred to support limited studies of choice experiments, such as those in Milwaukee, Cleveland, and New York designed to measure any learning differences between similar groups of students in private and public schools. But to date there has been too little fine-grained analysis about what sorts of schools work (and do not work) for what students. Scholars and foundations have resisted getting into this grubby work, but they can no longer avoid it.[34]

The work required is ordinary research and development: identifying barriers to implementing choice, reviewing the experience of people who have tried to overcome the barriers, inventing and testing new solutions, and disseminating the results. The results of such studies would complicate the choice debate. They would almost certainly show that the good schools do not come easy or cheap. They would also show that gaining all the benefits of choice requires serious investment, thoughtful design, skillful execution, and constant attention.

The results would be disillusioning in the good sense, showing that choice itself is not a magic bullet, but that introducing market-like elements into public education can stimulate and reward intelligent problem solving. Taking on the nuts and bolts of choice implies the abandonment of generaliza-

34. An excellent example of the work needed is Betts and Loveless (2006).

tions about the market. But public officials and foundations willing to take on the hard questions of how choice works, for whom, and under what conditions can make the NCLB choice provisions less risky and more likely to produce benefits.

References

Anderson, Amy Burke. 2004. *Charter Schools in Washington State: A Financial Drain or Gain?* Seattle, Wash.: Center on Reinventing Public Education.

Ballou, Dale, Bettie Teasley, and Tim Zeidner. 2006. "Charter School Outcomes in Idaho." Paper presented at the National Conference on Charter School Research. Vanderbilt University, Nashville, Tennessee, September 29.

Bell, Courtney. 2005. "All Choices Created Equal? How Good Parents Select Failing Schools." Occasional Paper 106. Columbia University, National Center for the Study of Privatization in Education.

Betts, Julian R., and Tom Loveless, eds. 2005. *Getting Choice Right.* Brookings.

Betts, Julian R., Lorien A. Rice, and Andrew C. Zau. 2006. *Does School Choice Work? Effects on Student Integration and Achievement.* San Francisco: Public Policy Institute of California.

Bifulco, Robert, and Helen F. Ladd. 2006. "The Impacts of Charter Schools on Student Achievement: Evidence from North Carolina." *Education Finance and Policy* 1, no. 1 (Winter): 50–90.

Booker, Ken, Ron Zimmer, and Richard Buddin. 2006. "The Effect of Charter Schools on School Peer Composition." Occasional Paper 110. Columbia University, National Center for the Study of Privatization in Education.

Booker, Ken, Scott Gilpatric, Timothy Gronberg, and Dennis Jansen. 2005. "The Effect of Charter Schools on Traditional Public Schools." Occasional Paper 104. Columbia University, National Center for the Study of Privatization in Education.

Brown, Cynthia. 2004. *Choosing Better Schools, a Report on Student Transfers under the No Child Left Behind Act.* Washington: Citizens Commission on Civil Rights.

Bryk, Anthony S., Valerie Lee, and Patrick Holland. 1993. *Catholic Schools and the Common Good.* Harvard University Press.

Burian-Fitzgerald, Marisa. 2005. "Average Teacher Salaries and Returns to Experience in Charter Schools." Occasional Paper 101. Columbia University, National Center for the Study of Privatization in Education.

Chakrabarti, Rajashri. 2005. "Do Vouchers Lead to Sorting Even under Random Private School Selection? Evidence from Milwaukee Voucher Program." Occasional Paper 100. Columbia University, National Center for the Study of Privatization in Education.

Charter School Consensus Panel. 2006. *Key Issues in Studying Charter Schools and Achievement: A Review and Suggestions for National Guidelines.* Seattle, Wash.: National Charter School Research Center.

Coleman, James S., and Thomas Hoffer. 1987. *Public and Private High Schools.* New York: Basic Books.

Coleman, James, Thomas Hoffer, and Sally Kilgore. 1982. *High School Achievement: Public, Catholic, and Private Schools Compared.* New York: Basic Books.

DeArmond, Michael, Christine Campbell, and Kacey Guin. 2006. *No Longer the Only Game in Town: Helping Traditional Public Schools Compete*. Seattle, Wash.: Center on Reinventing Public Education.

Education Week. 2006. "Maryland Lawmakers Override Veto; Baltimore Schools Stay in Local Control," vol. 25, no. 32: 1.

Fiske, Edward B., and Helen F. Ladd. 2000. *When Schools Compete: A Cautionary Tale*. Brookings.

Greene, Jay P., Paul E. Peterson, and Jiangtao Du. 1998. "School Choice in Milwaukee: A Randomized Experiment." In *Learning from School Choice*, edited by Paul E. Peterson and Brian Hassel, pp. 335–57. Brookings.

Hanushek, Eric A., John F. Kain, and Steven G. Rivkin. 2002. "The Impact of Charter Schools on Academic Achievement." Stanford, Calif.: Hoover Institution.

Hill, Paul T. 1979. *Enforcement and Informal Pressure in the Implementation of Federal Education Programs*. Santa Monica, Calif.: RAND.

Howell, William G. 2006. "School Choice in No Child Left Behind." In *Choice and Competition in American Education*, edited by Paul E. Peterson, pp. 255–64 (chapter 22). New York: Rowman and Littlefield.

Howell, William G., Patrick J. Wolf, David E. Campbell, and Paul E. Peterson. 2003. "School Vouchers: Results in Randomized Field Trials." In *The Economics of School Choice*, edited by Caroline M. Hoxby, pp. 107–44. University of Chicago Press.

Howell, William G., Patrick J. Wolf, Paul E. Peterson, and David E. Campbell. 2001. "Effects of School Vouchers on Student Test Scores." In *Charters, Vouchers, and Public Education*, edited by Paul E. Peterson and David E. Campbell, pp. 136–59. Brookings.

Hoxby, Caroline M., and Jonah E. Rockoff. 2004. "The Impact of Charter Schools on Student Achievement." Harvard University, Taubman Center for State and Local Government, Kennedy School of Government (www.economics.harvard.edu/faculty/hoxby/papers/hoxbyrockoff.pdf).

Kane, Thomas J., and Douglas O. Staiger. 2002. "Volatility in School Test Scores: Implications for Test-Based Accountability Systems." In *Brookings Papers on Education Policy, 2002*, edited by Diane Ravitch, pp. 235–83. Brookings.

Krueger, Alan B., and Pei Zhu. 2003. "Another Look at the New York City School Voucher Experiment." Working Paper 9418. Cambridge, Mass.: National Bureau of Economic Research (January).

Metcalf, Kim K., and others. 2003. *Evaluation of the Cleveland Scholarship and Tutoring Program: 1998–2001*. Bloomington, Ind.: Center for Evaluation.

National Working Commission on Choice in K–12 Education. 2003. *School Choice: Doing It the Right Way Makes a Difference*. Brookings.

Osberg, Eric. 2006. "Charter School Funding." In *Charter Schools against the Odds*, edited by Paul T. Hill. Palo Alto, Calif.: Education Next Press.

Reback, Randall. 2005. "Supply and Demand in a Public School Choice Program." Occasional Paper 99. Columbia University, National Center for the Study of Privatization in Education.

Rouse, Cecilia E. 1998. "Private School Vouchers and Student Achievement: An Evaluation of the Milwaukee Parental Choice Program." *Quarterly Journal of Economics* 113, no. 2 (May): 553–602.

Roza, Marguerite, and Karen Hawley-Miles. 2005. *Understanding Student-Based Budgeting as a Means to Greater School Resource Equity.* Seattle, Wash.: Center on Reinventing Public Education.

Roza, Marguerite, and Paul T. Hill. 2004. "How Within-District Spending Inequities Help Some Schools to Fail." In *Brookings Papers on Education Policy 2004*, edited by Diane Ravitch, pp. 201–27. Brookings.

Roza, Marguerite, Lawrence Miller, and Claudine Swartz. 2005. *Peeling Back the Layers of Spending: An Examination of District Expenditures in Denver Public Schools.* Seattle, Wash.: Center on Reinventing Public Education.

Sass, Tim R. 2006. "Charter Schools and Student Achievement in Florida." *Education Finance and Policy* 1, no. 1 (Winter): 91–122.

Teske, Paul, Jody Fitzpatrick, and Gabriel Kaplan. 2007. *Opening Doors: How Low Income Parents Search for the Right School.* Seattle, Wash.: Center on Reinventing Public Education.

Walsh, Patrick. 2005. "Is There Any Cream to Skim? Sorting Within-School, and the Scope for Cream-Skimming." Occasional Paper 109. Columbia University, National Center for the Study of Privatization in Education.

Witte, John F. 1998. "The Milwaukee Voucher Experiment." *Educational Evaluation and Policy Analysis* 20, no. 4: 229–51.

———. 2000. *The Market Approach to Education: An Analysis of America's First Voucher Program.* Princeton University Press.

Wolf, Patrick J., William G. Howell, and Paul E. Peterson. 2000. "School Choice in Washington, D.C.: An Evaluation after One Year." Paper prepared for the Conference on Vouchers, Charters, and Public Education. Program on Education Policy and Governance, Harvard University, March.

9

The Peculiar Politics of No Child Left Behind

TOM LOVELESS

The modern era is considered one of the most politically polarized in history. On Capitol Hill, Democrats and Republicans frequently engage in highly charged ideological battles. A notable divergence from the strident partisanship occurred in 2001 as a left-right coalition formed that successfully steered the No Child Left Behind Act (NCLB) through Congress. When President Bush signed the bill into law in January 2002, Senator Edward M. Kennedy stood by his side. Four years later, NCLB faces stiff resistance from state and local authorities. Ironically, given the bipartisan support for the law, the rebellion against NCLB also seems to come from both Democrats and Republicans—from the political left and the right. On the one hand, some states and local school districts feel they are getting a raw deal because the federal government is not doing enough, especially in terms of funding, to help local educators meet the requirements of the act. The state of Connecticut, for example, is suing the Department of Education for more NCLB money to cover student assessment. The state of Utah, on the other hand, has a more fundamental objection, that NCLB trespasses on state sovereignty over educational matters. Only scaling back the law's ambitious reach, not more money, will satisfy this complaint.

The author thanks Katharyn Field-Mateer for research assistance.

Most of what we know about anti-NCLB sentiment comes from press coverage. Scant research has methodically examined the politics of NCLB or marshaled empirical evidence to investigate support and opposition to the act at the state level. This study analyzes national polling data to assess public opinion on NCLB and examines the political activities of states and localities to evaluate political resistance to the act.

The political opposition strikes at the heart of NCLB. The goal of making schools more equitable, in particular, improving the education of children from poor families, brought together the bipartisan coalition supporting NCLB. Before NCLB, the Elementary and Secondary Education Act (ESEA) operated as a typical federal program pursuing redistributive objectives; it allocated additional resources to low-income schools to purchase supplies, personnel, curricula, and other educational materials that schools in impoverished communities could not otherwise afford. Educators used these additional resources to improve the education of poor children. Reauthorizations of ESEA through 1994 left this arrangement intact. The theory was simple: more money produces better education, and high-poverty schools need more money.

The theory of NCLB is different. Resources are viewed as incentives. In exchange for federal monies, local educators agree to produce certain outcomes. If they do not produce the promised outcomes, federal funding is cut off. With the exception of the portions of NCLB that deal with teacher quality, the law takes an agnostic position on how educators should convert resources into student achievement. The sanctions of NCLB—parental choice, supplemental services, reconstitution of schools—are components of the new incentive structure and do not produce new revenue streams. Schools that do not make adequate yearly progress with Black, Hispanic, or poor children face the threat of these sanctions. Putting a new incentive structure into place creates winners and losers, and we can expect those interests to play out in the politics surrounding the implementation of NCLB.

This paper is organized into five sections. The first section reviews national polling data on NCLB. Opponents to NCLB have argued that the more people know about the law, the more likely they are to oppose it. Is this true? More generally, as the accountability provisions of NCLB are now being enforced, is public support for the law waning? The second section turns to state politics. What does the research literature say about how states have responded to NCLB?

The third section explains empirical methods that were used to analyze state reactions. I devised a scale to reflect the magnitude of state rebellion against the act. On one end of the scale are states that have taken legislative or legal action against NCLB. On the other end of the scale are states that either have taken no action against the act or have defeated legislative efforts to circumvent NCLB. Using this scale, I test several factors that may influence a state's response to NCLB, among them political culture, student achievement, demographic characteristics, and resource constraints. The fourth section describes the findings of the analysis.

The fifth section of the paper concludes by assessing whether state and local opposition to the implementation of NCLB has weakened the foundation of political support for NCLB. What obstacles must NCLB overcome to survive? The left-right coalition that originally supported No Child Let Behind rallied around the belief that NCLB would help children in poverty. Has that changed? Has opposition to NCLB undermined the view that the law represents a legitimate means of improving the education of poor and minority students?

National Polls on NCLB

Two national polls on NCLB, one conducted by Phi Delta Kappan and Gallup and the other by the Educational Testing Service, provide data spanning the years since the law's inception.[1] They also include questions that assessed how well informed respondents were about NCLB. In 2003 the authors of the Kappan poll concluded that the more people knew about NCLB, the less likely they were to support the act, a point that was reiterated in the release of 2005 Kappan poll results.[2] How strong is the evidence supporting this conclusion?

The argument is based on two simultaneous trends. The first is that the public is becoming more familiar with NCLB. In table 9-1, the ETS-Hart poll shows that the percentage of respondents who had heard a great deal or a fair amount about NCLB grew from 31 percent in 2001 to 61 percent in 2005.[3] The second trend is that, although more people consistently favor NCLB than oppose it, the gap between support and opposition is narrowing. In the ETS-Hart poll, the lead of supporters over opponents shrank from 12 percent in 2001 to 4 percent in 2005. The Phi Delta Kappan poll reports a similar trend (table 9-2). In 2003, 69 percent confessed that they did not

---

1. ETS (2005), the poll was conducted by Peter D. Hart Research Associates and The Winston Group; Rose and Gallup (2005).

2. Rose and Gallup (2005).

3. The question in 2001 asked about "the President's plan."

Table 9-1. *ETS-Hart Polls on No Child Left Behind*
Percent

Awareness of NCLB	2001	2002	2003	2004	2005
Heard a great deal or a fair amount	31	39	n.a.	54	61
Opinion of NCLB					
Positive	30	n.a.	36	39	41
Negative	18	n.a.	28	38	37

Source: ETS-Hart poll 2001–05. Data provided by Peter D. Hart Research Associates, Inc. on behalf of ETS.
n.a. Not available.

Table 9-2. *Phi Delta Kappan–Gallup Polls on No Child Left Behind*
Percent

Opinion of NCLB	2003	2004	2005
Don't know enough to say	69	55	45
Positive	18	24	28
Negative	13	20	27

Source: Phi Delta Kappan/Gallup Poll 2003–2005.

know enough about NCLB to express an opinion, a figure that declined to 45 percent in 2005. At the same time, the margin of support for NCLB narrowed. In 2003, 18 percent of respondents expressed positive sentiments, and 13 percent expressed negative sentiments. In 2005 respondents with a favorable view had increased 10 percentage points to 28 percent, and negative sentiments had increased by 14 percentage points to 27 percent, leaving favorable and unfavorable opinions in a statistical dead heat.

Of course, arguing that these simultaneous trends are related is speculative. It could be, as the Kappan pollsters assumed, that after people learn more about NCLB, they do not like what they learn. But the causal relationship could operate in the opposite direction. People may form a negative opinion first—perhaps from something they have read or from personal experience with NCLB sanctions—and then seek more information. At the same time that public awareness of NCLB was growing, the law's penalties for low-performing schools began to be applied. Implementation of the law's consequences, rather than more knowledge, may be fueling the opposition to NCLB. In some communities, after local schools are singled out for needing improvement or teachers complain to parents about the testing requirements

Table 9-3. *Public Opinion of No Child Left Behind: Unaided Versus Aided Group*[a]
Percent

Opinion of NCLB	Unaided group	Aided group
Positive	45	41
Negative	38	37
Don't know enough	11	19

Source: ETS-Hart poll 2005. Data provided by Peter D. Hart Research Associates, Inc. on behalf of ETS.

a. Omitted from the table are responses of "neutral" and "not sure."

of NCLB, sympathetic citizens may then seek to get to the bottom of NCLB's punitive provisions.

The 2005 ETS-Hart poll tested the "more knowledge, more opposition" theory. Respondents were divided into two groups. The first group was simply asked its opinion of NCLB. The second group was provided some basic information about the law and then asked its opinion. This aided group was told that the federal government provides funding to local school districts and that NCLB requires states to set educational standards and to test students annually to see if the standards are being met. Did having this information affect the aided group's opinions?

Table 9-3 displays the data. The aided group did indeed express a slightly less positive view of NCLB than did the unaided group. But that is not the headline result of this little experiment. The intriguing outcome is that the aided group appeared less sure of its opinion than the group without any information. The number of people in the aided group who said that they did not have enough information to form an opinion (19 percent) was substantially larger than that of the unaided group (11 percent). In this case, learning about NCLB provoked uncertainty—and a need for more information, not less. The public seems to know a few essential facts of the act— maybe only that it involves education and is a Bush administration policy. Gaining information beyond that stirs more questions than it resolves. The data from this split sample offer limited support for the conclusion that gaining more knowledge about NCLB increases opposition. Stronger support is given to the notion that as people learn about NCLB, they realize that they need to know more to form a truly informed opinion.

What else do the polls tell us about the public's view of NCLB? The most recent polls show support for and opposition to NCLB evenly balanced among the general public, with the gap between the two sides tightening since

Table 9-4. *Demographic Breakdown of Public Opinion on*
No Child Left Behind[a]

Characteristic	Favorable	Unfavorable	Percent difference
Democrat	34	52	−18
Independent	45	34	+11
Republican	57	27	+30
Urban	44	40	+4
Suburban	44	39	+5
Rural	48	34	+14
White	46	40	+6
Black	44	34	+10
Hispanic	46	32	+14
Less than $25,000	43	32	+11
$25,000–$49,999	51	34	+17
$50,000–$74,999	47	36	+11
More than $75,000	42	49	−7

Source: ETS-Hart poll 2005. Data provided by Peter D. Hart Research Associates, Inc. on behalf of ETS.

a. Omitted from the table are responses of "neutral" and "not sure."

the law was passed. Sentiments vary by demographic group (table 9-4).[4] Partisanship is evident as Democrats decisively oppose NCLB and Republicans are strongly in favor. Independents break out in favor of the act, 45 percent to 34 percent opposed. Rural residents give NCLB a heartier endorsement than do urban or suburban residents. Blacks and Hispanics are more likely than are Whites to favor NCLB, and people making $75,000 or more per year are more likely to oppose NCLB than are people making less. The race and income data are interesting in that they cut against typical party affiliations. Blacks and Hispanics, who generally vote Democratic, line up in support of NCLB, one of the Bush administration's most prominent domestic programs. Respondents with incomes greater than $75,000, who often lean toward Republican policies, constitute the income group most skeptical of NCLB.

The partisan split on NCLB is surprising for two reasons. First, the bipartisanship of the coalition that pushed the law through Congress is not mirrored in public opinion. Second, as just noted, key constituents of the Democratic and Republican parties diverge from their parties' position on the law.

4. Data provided by Peter Hart Research Associates on behalf of ETS.

Are there parts of the law that the public supports and other parts that it opposes? Indeed there are, and that allows opponents and supporters of NCLB to single out different pieces of polling data to claim that their respective arguments enjoy popular support. Backing for NCLB appears strongest when general views on accountability are solicited, but opposition grows as specific details of the law are provided. For example, strong support exists for regularly testing students and holding students and educators accountable for results, the bedrock principles of NCLB. When a 2004 poll by Americans for Better Education asked whether the federal government should be able to hold states and local schools accountable "to make sure student performance is improving," 71 percent said that it should, and 25 percent said it should not.[5] But support for the idea begins to wane when the question is worded differently, especially if the meaning of accountability is fleshed out. In the Kappan poll in 2005, for example, 68 percent say a single test cannot provide a fair picture of student achievement. Fully 80 percent want subjects other than reading and math to be assessed. And support for standards-based assessment declines when tests are described as "high-stakes" tests. A Results for America poll in 2004 found 68 percent support for NCLB and 22 percent opposed, but when prompted about the "high-stakes" testing of NCLB, 51 percent supported this part of the act, and 45 percent opposed it.[6]

This observation, that Americans believe in test-based accountability and yet are leery of "high-stakes" testing, is important to note. Most people embrace accountability, but only an accountability devoid of unpleasant consequences. Actions that sound punitive or unfair are frowned upon. Should federal funds be withheld from schools classified as "failing"? Nearly three-quarters of Americans say no. What about shutting down failing schools? Only 31 percent support such a move. By a margin of 68 percent to 28 percent, respondents do not believe that special education students should be held to the same standards as other students. And 62 percent (compared with 34 percent) think that the test scores of special education students should not be a factor in deciding if a school "is in need of improvement." The public believes that counting special education scores in accountability systems is unfair to both schools and to the students themselves.[7]

Before moving on to state politics, allow me to summarize the major findings of national polls on NCLB. The American public initially favored NCLB by a comfortable margin, but polls from 2001 to 2005 show oppo-

5. Americans for Better Education (2004).
6. Results for America (2004).
7. Kappan poll of 2005; see Rose and Gallup (2005).

nents steadily gaining on the law's supporters. In 2005 sentiments were
evenly divided. The argument that opposition has grown because people have
become more informed about NCLB is only weakly supported by evidence.
Support for NCLB differs among several groups. Republicans favor NCLB
more than Democrats, rural residents more than urban or suburban dwellers,
African Americans and Hispanics more than Whites, and middle- and low-
income workers more than those making more than $75,000 per year. The
public favors the core idea of NCLB—testing students and holding schools
accountable for student learning—but does not want accountability to
include negative consequences. Those are the public opinions that frame the
national politics of NCLB. The paper now examines the politics of NCLB at
the state level.

Influences on the Politics of NCLB at the State Level

What factors might shape how a state responds to NCLB? Political cultures
are prominent in producing variation in state approaches to public policy.[8]
Patterns of governance are anchored in regional histories, and they persist.
Several northeastern states were pioneers in creating common schools in the
nineteenth century while many southern states lagged behind and did not
offer publicly financed common schools until Reconstruction. Patterns were
established that make education politics look out of step with how contemporary regional politics are usually characterized. When Horace Mann was
appointed the first secretary to the Massachusetts state board of education in
1837, schools in the state already had been operating for nearly 200 years.
Today education governance in the Northeast, on the one hand, is noted for
a deeply ingrained belief in local control, reflecting the bottom-up origins of
the school system and contradicting an otherwise liberal bent toward an
activist state government. In the South, on the other hand, a generally conservative political culture restrains the power of state government—except in
education. Southern states continue to direct most educational matters from
the statehouse, a reminder that the region's school systems have their origins
in the Reconstruction period.

   Federalism traditionally refers to how power is shared between the states
and Washington, D.C. Under NCLB, the federal government establishes an
overall policy framework—goals and general procedures—but states are
allowed latitude in implementation, an arrangement James Cibulka calls

---

8. Elazar (1966).

"regulatory federalism."[9] As noted above, Utah considers NCLB intrusive for dictating policy on what traditionally has been exclusively state terrain. Tensions develop in the sharing of power by the federal and state governments, of course, but similar tensions arise within states. The major responsibilities that have been reserved for state education officials under NCLB—creating and administering tests, determining levels of student proficiency, defining highly qualified teachers—impinge on local prerogatives. Indeed, Lance Fusarelli observed that NCLB reinforces a trend toward gubernatorial control of school reform. It not only takes the questions of whether and how schools should be held accountable out of the hands of local school districts but also out of the hands of state legislatures.[10] In short, NCLB concentrates power in the executive branch of state government; it grants state education officials the authority to force reluctant local districts to test students and to hold schools accountable, and it does so without the approval of state legislatures.

As noted above, empirical research on the states' reactions to NCLB is sparse, reflecting the brief period of time since the law was enacted. Resource constraints played a role in the first few years of implementation, especially in light of tight state budgets in the 2001–04 period.[11] A ranking by the Education Commission of the States (ECS) in 2003 found that only ten states were "on track" to meet the highly qualified teacher requirements of NCLB. Analyzing the ECS rankings, Lisa Dotterweich and Ramona McNeal found that states with greater minority diversity were more likely to have implemented NCLB's teacher quality provisions.[12] Paul Manna discovered a weak effect of a state's percentage of disadvantaged students increasing the likelihood of implementing NCLB's accountability provisions.[13]

Overall, most analysts have been impressed with NCLB's implementation, especially when compared with NCLB's predecessor, the Improving America's Schools Act of 1994 (IASA). William Wanker and Kathy Christie observed that only seventeen states fully complied with IASA.[14] The procedures that states must follow under NCLB are more specific and the Department of Education has enforced the act more diligently than what was the

9. Cibulka (1996); see also Sunderman (2003).

10. Fusarelli states, "Though legitimate, many of the objections and political posturing about states' rights and unfunded federal mandates appear to be little more than negotiating tactics to force compromise on NCLB." Fusarelli (2005), p. 131.

11. Sunderman and Kim (2007).

12. Dotterweich and McNeal (2004).

13. Manna (2004).

14. Wanker and Christie (2005).

case under IASA.[15] Solid progress has been made in adopting standards and in implementing assessment and accountability systems.[16]

Despite the success, press accounts of state resistance to NCLB are numerous.[17] William Mathis, Kevin Fleming, and Wendy Lecker employed multivariate models to analyze state resistance to NCLB.[18] Testing several variables, they found no relationship between a state's level of "objection to the 'federal imposition'" of NCLB and the following: National Assessment of Educational Progress (NAEP) scores, percentage of schools not making adequate yearly progress (AYP), indicators of economic disadvantage, percentage of rural students, or political partisanship. Also, states that had ordered evaluations of the fiscal impact of NCLB on state resources—and had calculated an onerous financial burden—were not found to be unduly rebellious. Instead, the researchers concluded that the rebellion against NCLB was driven largely by individual state political environments.

The literature identifies several phenomena that should be scrutinized to analyze the politics of NCLB, including political cultures, resources, student achievement, and demographic profiles of the fifty states. Although Mathis, Fleming, and Lecker found that most of these constructs bear no relationship to the rebellion against NCLB, perhaps an examination of contemporary data with a different analytical approach will arrive at a different conclusion.

How the Analysis of State Politics Was Conducted

This portion of the study investigates what is driving political opposition to NCLB in the states. I created a six-level scale to reflect states' reactions to NCLB. On one end of the scale (level six) are Connecticut, which filed suit against the federal government over funding the expanded student assessment required by the act, and Utah, which passed a law prohibiting local districts from implementing portions of NCLB that are "unfunded" or in conflict with state law (see appendix 9A-1 for the states' rankings, appendix 9A-3 for a list of NCLB activities by state, and appendix 9A-4 for a list of sources). Slightly less resistant are nine states (level five) that allow local opt outs in law or prohibit spending state money on implementing NCLB—or in which local districts sued or took other legal action on NCLB. These states are Col-

---

15. McDermott and Jensen (2005).

16. *Education Week* (2006).

17. A list of state resistance can be found in appendix 9A-3 and sources of information in appendix 9A-4.

18. Mathis, Fleming, and Lecker (2005).

orado, Illinois, Louisiana, Maine, Michigan, New Jersey, Pennsylvania, Texas, and Vermont. The remaining categories include states in which legislation to allow districts to opt out of NCLB may have passed one legislative house but was not passed into law (level four); states in which resolutions critical of NCLB are pending, have been introduced, or in some cases passed (level three); states in which anti-NCLB legislation was defeated (level two); and at the opposite end, states in which no measurable action was taken against NCLB (level one). This six-level scale of political resistance to NCLB serves as the dependent variable in the analyses below.

The scale differs from the study by Mathis, Fleming, and Lecker in how level-two states are coded. In their study, states that considered but did not pass anti-NCLB legislation were coded as somewhat opposed to the law. Enough opposition was present in these states to spawn a legislative proposal. In the current study, these same states were treated as somewhat supportive of NCLB, the reasoning being that by voting down an anti-NCLB resolution, legislators expressed support for the act.

Explanatory variables measure four clusters of influence on states' reactions to NCLB: political culture, student achievement, demographic characteristics, and resources. Appendix 9A-2 describes all of the variables, provides summary statistics, and lists data sources. Briefly, the explanatory variables are the following.

POLITICAL CULTURE. Party of governor, state legislature, and attorney general; presidential vote in 2000 and 2004; and region (if southern state). Despite the initial nonpartisan congressional support for NCLB, polls show a partisan split on NCLB among the electorate. State politicians are expected to follow the preferences of local voters rather than those of politicians in Washington, D.C. Democratic states are expected to oppose NCLB, the chief domestic accomplishment of a Republican president and Congress. Southern states, having implemented testing and accountability systems before NCLB, are expected to appear sympathetic to the law.

DEMOGRAPHIC. Race and ethnicity, students in poverty, and measures of Black and Hispanic segregation. Critics of NCLB have charged that the law will unfairly penalize schools serving students in poverty and minority students because of the demographic profiles of many low-performing schools.

STUDENT ACHIEVEMENT. NAEP scores in 2005 for eighth grade math, NAEP scores for racial and ethnic groups and for students in poverty, score gaps on NAEP between demographic groups, and percentages of schools making adequate yearly progress. States with better achievement profiles (higher NAEP scores and more schools making AYP) are expected to be more compliant in responding to NCLB than are states with lower achievement. States with larger achievement gaps between White and non-White students—and between poor and nonpoor students—are expected to resist NCLB. They have the most to lose by changing from an entitlement program (which ESEA was), in which they can argue for more resources to tackle achievement gaps, to an incentive-based program (NCLB), in which states are penalized if they do not close such gaps.

RESOURCES. Funding, including the percentage of K–12 spending from the federal government, and measures of teacher quality, including the percentage of highly qualified teachers in high-poverty schools. Greater compliance is expected from states that are more dependent on federal funding and greater resistance from states that face tougher hurdles in staffing schools with highly qualified teachers.

The study is limited, as are all studies that attempt to statistically model state behavior by a dependent variable with only fifty observations. This is especially problematic with multivariate logistic regressions that produce numerous empty cells or cells with reduced counts. Therefore, in interpreting the data, I rely on evaluating bivariate relationships instead of interpreting parameter estimates from multivariate models. Although the relationships uncovered are merely correlational, I speculate as to some of the causal mechanisms that may connect political influences with states' behaviors.

Means and standard errors of resistance to NCLB are reported for high and low levels of the explanatory variables (that is, dummies were created). For nondichotomous variables, cut points defining high and low levels were determined by examining quartile means to see where threshold effects occurred. Then one-way ANOVAs were run, producing F statistics that were tested for significance. For example, the mean resistance levels for each quartile (Q) of the Black-White NAEP gaps were (Q1) 2.7, (Q2) 3.0, (Q3) 2.6, and (Q4) 3.9. Resistance in quartile 4 clearly stands out, which encompasses states with gaps greater than 36.5 points. Quartile 4 states were coded as the high level of this variable (dummy of 1), the other quartiles as the low level (dummy of 0), and then resistance levels were analyzed with a one-way ANOVA.

The paper now turns to an analysis of what is driving political opposition to NCLB in the states.

Table 9-5. *Analysis of State Resistance Ratings, by Political Influences*[a]

Variable cluster	Low group	High group	Definition of high group
Political culture			
South	3.33	2.50*	Southern state
	(1.49)	(1.40)	
Blue	2.76	3.65*	Voted for the Democratic
	(1.43)	(1.62)	candidate in the last two
			presidential elections
Student achievement			
Percentage of schools making	2.60	3.60**	Greater than 77.5 percent
AYP in 2004	(1.41)	(1.44)	of schools
Percentage of schools making	2.42	3.39**	Greater than 59.5 percent
AYP in 2005	(1.24)	(1.52)	of schools
Mean 2005 NAEP scores of	2.35	3.70***	Mean NAEP score is
Black students	(1.26)	(1.42)	between 248.5 and
			260.5
Mean 2005 NAEP scores of	2.67	3.50**	Mean NAEP score is
all students	(1.27)	(1.61)	between 274 and 284
Demographic characteristics			
Percentage of students who	3.45	2.00***	Greater than 21.1 percent
are Black	(1.41)	(1.28)	of students
Percentage of students who	2.89	3.75*	Greater than 13.6 percent
are Hispanic	(1.45)	(1.54)	of students
Gap between White and Black	2.73	3.90**	Gap is greater than 36.5
students on 2005 NAEP	(1.31)	(1.73)	points
Resources			
Federal funding	3.59	2.52**	More than 8.3 percent of
	(1.53)	(1.27)	K–12 revenue

Source: See appendix 9A-4.

AYP = adequate yearly progress.

a. Figures are means, and standard deviations are in parentheses. A higher mean denotes greater resistance. F-test, ***$p < 0.01$; **$p < 0.05$; *$p < 0.10$.

Analysis of Resistance from the States

State and local objections to NCLB have been widely covered by the press. Table 9-5 presents data on state resistance to NCLB and four clusters of state-level variables: political culture, student achievement, demographic characteristics, and resources.

Political Culture

As revealed in table 9-5, geography matters in how states respond to NCLB. Southern states are the most compliant toward NCLB, and states outside the

South offer the most resistance. This is consistent with the historical tendency of southern states to centralize education policy at the state level and for states in the Northeast to devolve powers of governance to local school districts. Under NCLB, state officials gain the authority to sanction educators according to students' test scores, power that in many states was held exclusively, if at all, by local schools and school districts. Southern states are comfortable with NCLB's allocation of authority, having implemented state testing programs and accountability systems long before NCLB. States in which local control of educational governance is strongest, in contrast, have reacted the most negatively toward NCLB.

Also note that blue states, those that voted Democratic in both the 2000 and 2004 presidential elections, are more resistant to NCLB. Red states are more supportive. The pattern revealed here is consistent with the tendency of red states' movement toward less tax effort, fewer state government expenditures, and less reliance on a professional bureaucracy to implement policies. This politically conservative philosophy mirrors the theory underlying NCLB and amplifies how much NCLB is a break from the past. And it is even true for southern states, despite state centralization in education. States located outside the South, and, in particular, states that voted Democratic in the past two elections, are more hostile toward NCLB's underlying theory.

Student Achievement

Some findings on the relationship of student achievement and states' resistance to NCLB are counterintuitive. For example, states that are most at risk of experiencing NCLB sanctions are not complaining. The vast majority of NCLB's sanctions target schools failing to make adequate yearly progress (AYP). States with more than 77.5 percent of their schools making AYP in 2004 are more likely to oppose NCLB than are states with lower rates of success. The same pattern holds true for 2005, although the effect is evident for states with more than 59.5 percent of schools making AYP. States that have a significant number of low-performing schools—as defined by AYP formulas—are more supportive of NCLB than those with fewer low-performing schools.

A similar puzzling finding arises from examining state NAEP scores. It is not the states registering low NAEP scores that oppose NCLB. On the NAEP eighth grade mathematics test given in 2005, states that scored at both ends of the continuum—either in the top or bottom dozen states on the test—were complacent toward NCLB. Resistant states showed up in the middle of the distribution, with scale scores between 274 and 284 (the mean of state NAEP scores was 279 with a standard deviation [SD] of 7). So the highest-scoring states, which might spurn federal reform efforts as unnecessary, and the lowest-scoring states, which might have the most to lose from any federal regulation based on student achievement, did not exhibit resistance to NCLB.

The complacency of high-achieving states toward NCLB can be plausibly explained by the fact that they have little to lose from sanctions based on test scores. But why do low-achieving states—and those with large numbers of schools failing to make AYP—hold a sanguine view of NCLB? Lessons learned from the politics of other education policies may be helpful in proposing reasonable but nonetheless speculative answers to that question. Very often, public opinion polls conducted in communities with low student achievement report broad support for strong reforms—and the opposite occurs in areas with high-performing schools. Vouchers, for example, receive their greatest support in urban areas and the least support in suburbs.[19] As noted above, NCLB offers state officials powerful interventions to use with persistently failing schools. These interventions were not available under most state laws before NCLB and, because of the nature of state politics, were impossible to get through most state legislatures. The federal law provides political cover to education officials in states in which NCLB-like accountability is politically untenable—first, by forcing reluctant states to create accountability systems, and second, by requiring that states sanction low-achieving schools. State officials who impose unpleasant and unpopular consequences on low-performing schools can say, "Sorry, the feds made us do it."

Demographic Characteristics

States with larger Black populations (more than 21.1 percent of students) are more supportive of NCLB. The ESEA's legacy as a federal instrument for educational equity may be in evidence here, as well as Blacks more fervent support for NCLB than that of Whites. Blacks want schools fixed—now—and they embrace policy interventions that reflect such urgency. In addition, states with large gaps in Black-White test scores are more likely to oppose NCLB. States with Black-White gaps of at least 37 points on the 2005 NAEP (again, eighth grade math, mean of 32.5, SD of 7) are more resistant toward NCLB than are states with narrower gaps.

A negative reaction based on achievement gaps is a rational response to the accountability provisions of NCLB. States with large achievement gaps, even liberal states outside the South, have the most to lose under NCLB's

19. Moe (2001).

regime of incentives that target equity. By requiring the disaggregation of test score data, NCLB forced many states to recognize the severity of achievement deficits for poor and minority students. In an interview, Secretary of Education Margaret Spellings suggested that Connecticut should be working to reduce achievement gaps rather than suing the federal government:

> In Connecticut, my understanding . . . is that they want to measure every other year and not provide annual assessment as is required in the statute. . . . I think it's regrettable, frankly, when the achievement gap between African-American and Anglo kids in Connecticut is quite large. And I think it's unfortunate for those families and those students that they are trying to find a loophole to get out of the law as opposed to attending to the needs of those kids.[20]

The recent action of the NAACP, joining the Bush administration in defending NCLB against the lawsuit by the state of Connecticut, underscores the sympathy many Black leaders feel toward NCLB.[21]

It is interesting to note that the effect runs in the opposite direction for Hispanics. States with a larger percentage of Hispanic students (more than 13.6 percent) are more likely to oppose NCLB than are states with smaller Hispanic populations. The finding for Hispanics also runs contrary to national polling data. Recall that for Hispanics, the advantage of favorable over unfavorable opinions on NCLB (14 points, see table 9-4) exceeds that of Whites (6 points) and Blacks (10 points).

Like the effect of larger Black-White test score gaps, a larger Hispanic population within a state may be influencing the attitudes of political elites toward NCLB. The issue of testing, and in what language tests are to be administered, has raised the concern of activist groups. The National Associa-

---

20. The *NewsHour with Jim Lehrer*, April 7, 2005. In an editorial for the *Washington Post*, Spellings wrote, "Annual assessments are nonnegotiable, because what gets measured gets done. This is at the heart of accountability. The data must also be reported by student group— African Americans, Hispanics, those with special needs, etc.—so that those who need the most help aren't hidden behind state or district-wide averages. Some states have asked for waivers from the law. Some have sought to exempt whole grades or student groups from annual assessments. Others have sought to keep some students' test scores under wraps. That is simply unacceptable. It undermines the very purpose of the law. Perhaps not coincidentally, some of these same states have the largest achievement gaps in the nation, with minority students lagging dozens of points—whole years, really—behind their white peers." See Margaret Spellings, "Our High Schools Need Help," *Washington Post*, April 2, 2005, p. A21.

21. Avi Salzman, "NAACP Is Bush Ally in School Suit Versus State," *New York Times*, February 1, 2006, p. 3.

tion for Bilingual Education (NABE) joined a group of sixty-five organizations that signed a letter opposing NCLB in October 2004. The 2005 annual conference of NABE included several speakers who were critical of the act and urged bilingual educators to oppose it.[22] That said, the Hispanic community is split on the issue. La Raza is part of the Achievement Alliance, a group supportive of NCLB that also includes the Education Trust, the Business Roundtable, the Citizens' Commission on Civil Rights, and the National Center for Educational Accountability.[23]

A large Hispanic student population may give education officials pause regarding test scores under NCLB. Despite ambitious literacy programs nationwide, reading scores on NAEP have been flat for the past decade. Because of large numbers of Hispanic students who are English language learners, Hispanic reading scores are low. And the proportion of Hispanic students is growing steadily. *Education Week* quoted Marshall S. Smith, deputy secretary of education in the Clinton administration, "had the proportion of all groups remained constant over the decade, the average national gain would have been greater than 10 points" in eighth grade reading.[24]

Resources

States for which federal funds make up less than 8.3 percent of K–12 revenue are more likely to object to NCLB than are states with a greater reliance on federal funding. Greater dependency on federal revenue may inhibit states from publicly challenging NCLB, a case of states not wanting to bite the hand that feeds them. Conversely, states that are more reliant on local revenues to shoulder the burden of financing K–12 education may feel that the federal government should not tell them how to run their schools. Bear in mind, however, that because the federal Title I program targets high-poverty schools, states receiving more federal money also tend to have more students in poverty, along with other characteristics that the current study has discovered are correlated with support for NCLB, including lower NAEP scores, fewer schools making AYP, and being located in the South. Out of the top twenty recipients most dependent on federal funding in 2002 (states ranked by share of K–12 revenue from federal sources), eleven are southern states.[25]

22. Zehr (2005).
23. Scoon (2005).
24. *Education Week* (2006), p. 10.
25. U.S. Department of Education, *Digest of Education Statistics 2004*, table 154 (nces.ed.gov/programs/digest/d04/tables/dt04_154.asp).

There is another reason to doubt that federal revenue is as influential as suggested here. In 2002, state governments provided 49.2 percent of K–12 revenue, and local governments 40.5 percent. The federal share was only 7.9 percent. Historically, the federal share has never exceeded 10 percent, peaking at 9.8 percent in 1980, President Carter's last year in office and the first year of the U.S. Department of Education.

Summary and Conclusion

I conclude by tying together the two analytical sections of the paper—the examination of national polling data and state resistance to NCLB—and discussing implications for the future of NCLB and efforts to improve educational quality for poor and minority children.

The two analyses paint a clear picture of who tends to support and oppose NCLB, whether the supporters and opponents are individuals or entire states. Individual supporters tend to be Republican, residents of rural areas, Black or Hispanic, and middle- and low-income workers. Opponents are more likely to be Democratic, residents of suburban or urban areas, White, and upper-income professionals. States that tend to support NCLB are red states in presidential elections, score in the very bottom or very top quartiles of NAEP, serve student populations that are more than 21.1 percent Black or less than 13.6 percent Hispanic, exhibit narrower than average Black-White test score gaps, receive more than 8.3 percent of K–12 revenue from the federal government, and are located in the South. States that are opposed tend to be blue states in presidential elections, fall in the middle quartiles of NAEP scores, have relatively small Black or relatively large Hispanic populations, exhibit larger than average Black-White test score gaps, receive less than 8.3 percent of K–12 revenue from federal sources, and are located in the eastern, midwestern, or western regions of the country.

Many of these characteristics overlap, of course. The characteristics that are seemingly contradictory call for closer scrutiny, primarily because in them may be found clues to the fate of NCLB. The left-right coalition that formed to pass NCLB was itself a political contradiction. The future of NCLB, and its reauthorization in 2007, hinge on holding that coalition together. The crosscutting political influences unearthed in the foregoing analysis expose fault lines that opponents could exploit to seriously weaken NCLB—or on which supporters could focus their energies to shore up and boost support.

Consider equity. From the beginning, the authors of NCLB framed the legislation as a civil rights issue. Support from groups such as the Education Trust and politicians such as Representative George Miller and Senator Edward M. Kennedy reinforced that theme. Blacks, Hispanics, and blue-collar workers continue to support NCLB, but states with large Hispanic populations tend to be critical of the law. By hammering away at NCLB's goal of raising the achievement of poor and minority youngsters, supporters of NCLB may force politicians in several states to reconcile their opposition to NCLB with the favorable opinions of minority constituents. Opponents of NCLB, however, can make hay out of the fact that schools receiving sanctions under NCLB serve predominantly poor and minority populations. Sanctioning schools—the hard edge of accountability—is not popular with the public. Emphasizing who receives NCLB's penalties may dampen enthusiasm for the idea that NCLB promotes equity. True, the claim "the more people hear about NCLB, the more they oppose it" is an exaggeration, but people who hear about school sanctions emphatically dislike them.

How AYP is calculated will surely enter the debate. The U.S. Department of Education recently announced a pilot program that will allow ten states to experiment with growth models, which calculate AYP on the basis of students' year-to-year progress instead of on the percentage of students meeting proficiency targets. Shifting to a growth model makes it easier for schools in the bottom of the achievement distribution to meet AYP. Some schools are currently boosting test scores but not raising enough students to proficiency to satisfy AYP requirements. These schools tend to serve large poor and minority populations. Shifting to growth models will remove them from lists of schools "in need of improvement."

Politically, installing growth models in NCLB would blunt the argument that schools with poor, minority populations disproportionately experience sanctions. Supporters can highlight numerous high-poverty schools that are making significant academic progress under the law. But adopting growth models is not without risks. Commenting on the pilot program, the Citizens' Commission on Civil Rights issued a statement that said, "We fear that too many school board members and educators will view the growth-model approach as an invitation to water down expectations for student achievement in order to reduce the numbers of schools identified for improvement."[26] The fear is that low-scoring students may make significant

26. Olson and Hoff (2005).

progress but still leave school without the skills necessary to succeed as an adult. This concern must be addressed, but when NCLB comes up for reauthorization, look for modification of AYP requirements to emerge as a potential area of compromise in the arguments over equity.

Funding will also receive attention during reauthorization. In 2001 the ink was barely dry on NCLB when several Democrats who had supported the legislation in Congress, including Senator Kennedy, accused the Bush administration of reneging on a deal to fully fund the act. The Bush administration may be open to significantly increasing NCLB funding. Sweetening the pot never hurts in cooling opposition in Congress. Additional funding would also receive applause from liberal voters. And the conservative base of support that NCLB enjoys might view additional funding favorably if it were tied to incentives for pursuing the law's objectives. However, if NCLB's supporters stray too far from the core belief that properly crafted incentives, not more dollars, offer the best chance of improving schools, they risk alienating NCLB's political base.

Southern states are NCLB's strongest supporters. In one of the interesting twists of education politics, they also favor centralized governance of education. Big government, in this case, does not mean expensive government. Southern states feature constrained budgets, somewhat regressive tax structures, and an aversion to publicly financed social programs. States in the Northeast, on the other hand, typically lean toward liberal politics but place educational governance in the hands of local school districts. NCLB enhances the power of state governments to change schools. Northeastern states may temper their opposition to NCLB if they are able to use this new authority to advance values and interests "of the commonwealth."

The peculiar politics of NCLB first surfaced when the law passed Congress in 2001. NCLB consists of conservative ideas—testing, accountability, and incentives—wrapped in liberal clothing—a big federal program that seeks, as its primary objective, the equalization not only of educational opportunity but also of educational outcomes. A left-right coalition successfully guided NCLB through Congress. Now, NCLB faces conservative and liberal opponents. The politics of NCLB, with reauthorization on the horizon, highlights both the law's greatest promise and its greatest perils.

Appendix 9A-1. Scale of Resistance to NCLB by State

Level 6: Filed suit as a state or established statewide circumvention of NCLB's power

Utah   Connecticut

Level 5: Allows local opt outs in law, prohibits spending state money on implementing NCLB; local districts sued or took other legal action

Colorado   New Jersey
Illinois   Pennsylvania
Louisiana   Texas
Maine   Vermont
Michigan

Level 4: Opt out legislation is pending: legislation was considered and passed in one house but has not been passed into law

Hawaii   Ohio
Indiana   Oregon
Minnesota   Wisconsin
Nevada
New Mexico

Level 3: Legislation introduced and passed but no opt out

California   South Carolina
Idaho   South Dakota
Iowa   Tennessee
Kansas   Virginia
Kentucky   Washington
Nebraska   West Virginia
Oklahoma   Wyoming
Rhode Island

Level 2: Legislation defeated

Arizona   New Hampshire
Florida   North Dakota
Maryland

Level 1: Neutral or supportive

Alabama   Missouri
Alaska   Montana
Arkansas   North Carolina
Georgia   New York
Massachusetts   Delaware
Mississippi

Appendix 9A-2. Variables Measuring Political Influences[a]

Variable	Mean (SD)	Description	Source
Resource constraints			
Highly qualified teachers	87.08 (13.48)	Percentage of classes taught by highly qualified teachers	"Room to Maneuver," *Education Week* (2005) (www.edweek.org/media/ nclb_1214qualified.pdf)
Highly qualified teachers in high-poverty schools	84.0 (15.20)	Percentage of classes in high-poverty schools taught by highly qualified teachers	"Room to Maneuver," *Education Week* (2005) (www.edweek.org/media/ nclb_1214qualified.pdf)
Percent federal	8.66 (2.90)	Percentage of state K–12 spending coming from federal government	*Digest of Education Statistics*, NCES (2004), table 154 (nces.ed.gov/programs/digest/ d04/tables/dt04_154.asp)
Percent state	51.0 (11.35)	Percentage of state K–12 spending coming from state government	*Digest of Education Statistics*, NCES (2004), table 154
Percent local	37.63 (11.99)	Percentage of state K–12 spending coming from local government	*Digest of Education Statistics*, NCES (2004), table 154
Per pupil expenditures	$7,980.82 (233.34)	Average annual state expenditure per pupil (dollars)	State facts (www.schoolmatters.com/)
Achievement			
2005 NAEP state score	278.56 (7.18)	Mean score on NAEP eighth grade math	Author's calculations using main NAEP Data Explorer (nces.ed.gov/ nationsreportcard/nde/)
2005 White	286.28 (5.99)	Mean NAEP score for White students	Author's calculations using main NAEP Data Explorer
2005 Black	254.25 (7.25)	Mean NAEP score for Black students	Author's calculations using main NAEP Data Explorer
2005 Hispanic	261.89 (5.67)	Mean NAEP score for Hispanic students	Author's calculations using main NAEP Data Explorer
2005 Nonpoor	287.4 (5.63)	Mean NAEP score for nonpoor students	Author's calculations using main NAEP Data Explorer
2005 Poor	263.38 (6.83)	Mean NAEP score for poor students	Author's calculations using main NAEP Data Explorer
Black-White gap	32.5 (7.07)	Gap between Black and White students on 2005 NAEP	Author's calculations using main NAEP Data Explorer
Hispanic-White gap	25.9 (5.3)	Gap between Hispanic and White students on 2005 NAEP	Author's calculations using main NAEP Data Explorer
Poor-Nonpoor gap	23.82 (4.73)	Gap between poor and nonpoor students on 2005 NAEP	Author's calculations using main NAEP Data Explorer

Variable	Mean (SD)	Description	Source
Achievement—Continued			
NAEP-state test gap	24.54 (19.22)	Gap between percentages of students proficient on NAEP and on state tests in 2003 (eighth grade math)	Author's calculations from data provided by U.S. Department of Education, Title I Mathematics Steering Committee
AYP2005	73.15 (16.74)	Percentage of schools making AYP in 2005	"Room to Maneuver," *Education Week* (2005) (www.edweek.org/media/ nclb_1214.pdf)
AYP2004	76.06 (14.02)	Percentage of schools making AYP in 2004	"Room to Maneuver," *Education Week* (2005) (www.edweek.org/media/ nclb_1214.pdf)
Demographic			
White	67.83 (17.83)	Percentage of students who are White	NAEP, "State Profiles" (nces.ed.gov/ nationsreportcard/states/)
Black	14.51 (13.35)	Percentage of students who are Black	NAEP, "State Profiles"
Hispanic	10.91 (12.28)	Percentage of students who are Hispanic	NAEP, "State Profiles"
Poor	37.42 (10.39)	Percentage of students who are eligible for free or reduced-price lunch	NAEP, "State Profiles"
Black segregation	0.40 (0.49)	1 if rated a "most segregated state for Black students"; 0 otherwise (percentage of Blacks in 90 to 100 percent minority schools)	Orfield and Lee (2004), (% Blacks in 90–100% minority schools), p. 27
Hispanic segregation	0.40 (0.49)	1 if rated a "most segregated state for Hispanic students"; 0 otherwise (percentage of Hispanics in 90 to 100 percent minority schools)	Orfield and Lee (2004), p. 28
Politics and political culture			
Blue	0.34 (0.48)	1 if voting for the Democratic candidate in the 2000 and 2004 presidential elections; 0 otherwise	"Election Results, " *CNN.com* (2005) (www.cnn.com/ELECTION/ 2004/pages/results/president/)
Blue Senate	0.46 (0.50)	1 if majority party in the state Senate is Democratic; 0 otherwise	"2005 Partisan Composition of State Legislatures," National Conference of State Legislatures (www.ncsl.org/ncsldb/elect98/ partcomp.cfm?yearsel=2005)
Blue House	0.48 (0.50)	1 if majority party in the state House is Democratic; 0 otherwise	National Conference of State Legislatures (www.ncsl.org/ncsldb/ elect98/ partcomp.cfm?yearsel=2005)
Blue governor	0.44 (0.50)	1 if governor is a Democrat; 0 otherwise	"State Officials," Project Vote Smart (www.vote-smart.org/index.htm)

Variable	Mean (SD)	Description	Source
Politics and political culture—Continued			
Blue attorney general	0.54 (0.50)	1 if attorney general is a Democrat; 0 otherwise	Project Vote Smart (www.vote-smart.org/index.htm)
Most traditionalist	0.25 (0.44)	1 if greater than 7.33 on Sharkansky scale (upper quartile of Sharkansky's scale)	Sharkansky (1969), p. 72
Most moralist	0.25 (0.44)	1 if less than 3 on Sharkansky scale (bottom quartile of Sharkansky's scale)	Sharkansky (1969), p. 72
Individualist	0.31 (0.07)	1 if an individualist state on the Elazar scale	Gray, Hanson, and Jacob (1999), p. 24 (adapted from Elazar [1984], p. 136)
Centralization	3.59 (0.66)	Rating on Wirt's school centralism scale	Wirt (1980)
South	0.27 (0.06)	1 if a southern state; 0 otherwise (Alabama, Arkansas, Florida, Georgia, Kentucky, Louisiana, Mississippi, North Carolina, Oklahoma, South Carolina, Tennessee, Texas, Virginia, West Virginia)	Southern Early Childhood Association (www.southernearlychildhood.org/aff_map.asp)
Exit exam	0.66 (0.89)	0, if no exit testing conducted by 1999; 1, if exit testing by 1999; 2, if exit testing by 1992	*Digest of Education Statistics*, NCES (1995), table 146; *Digest of Education Statistics*, NCES (2001), table 155 (nces.ed.gov/programs/digest/d01/dt155.asp)

AYP = adequate yearly progress; NAEP = National Assessment of Educational Progress; SD = standard deviation.

a. All data refer to the mean and standard deviation of fifty observations (state means).

Appendix 9A-3. NCLB Activities in the States

Alabama
No action

Alaska
SJR30 introduced to receive waiver if academic achievement increases (April 11, 2004).

Arizona
House introduced proposals HB2696, HB2594 to opt out of NCLB.

Senate introduces two resolutions, SB1304 and SCM1006, that permit opting out, changes, and waivers.

Both sets of resolutions were defeated.

Arkansas
House introduced HB 2903 to implement "HQ (high quality)" rating provision of NCLB.

California
SJR27 introduced November 2004 to request full funding for NCLB.

AJR88 passed House on June 21, 2004, passed Senate on August 19, 2004: requested full funding and changes to accountability model and determination of HQ credential for teachers.

Colorado
On May 7, 2005, Governor Owens allowed SB50 to become law. It permits school districts to opt out of the NCLB and federal funding. Districts still must keep track of test scores so that the state as a whole is eligible for federal funding.

HJR05-1056, which calls upon the Congress to provide full funding, passed the House and is currently in the Senate.

Connecticut
State filed lawsuit against federal government claiming that state and local money cannot be used toward meeting federal testing goals. West Hartford school board voted without dissent to support the lawsuit. The Region board, in a 6-4 vote, also supports the suit.

Chelshire, Marlborough, and Somers districts rejected Title 1 funding to avoid compliance with NCLB.

The State Senate passed SJR40, which asked the federal government for several amendments to NCLB. State House introduced HJR30 that requests waivers for high-performing schools. SJR4 (2004) requested waivers for states such as Connecticut with overall high academic performance.

Delaware
No action

Florida
In HM877 (in 2005), the House urged Congress to reevaluate requirements of NCLB and funding levels. HM877 was defeated in committee.

HR1967 (2004), an earlier version of HM877, died in committee.

Georgia

Since it's being fined in 2003, Georgia requested and received permission to increase minimum number of children in subgroups before school is held accountable for those
subgroups.

Hawaii

HCR245 passed in House and Senate and was transmitted to the public as of May 6,
2005. It asks Congress to amend NCLB per the recommendations of the National
Conference of State Legislature's task force. HR178, SR124 had formerly made a similar request.

HR179 and SR122 asked for general amendments and adjustments in NCLB. State representatives and senators (in 2004 and 2003) introduced five more similar proposals to
amend NCLB.

HR118 was adopted in 2003 and transmitted to the public. It suggested reevaluating
Hawaii's participation in NCLB.

Idaho

State Senate passed SJM106 that expresses changes Idaho would like to see happen to
NCLB (referred to House on March 4, 2005).

SJM101 introduced in the Senate asks that cities of 1 million or less be exempt from
NCLB (referred to Education Council).

Passed in the House and Senate (as of March 2004), SJM108 suggests that changes be
made to AYP provisions.

Illinois

Governor Rod Blagojevich has signed HB3678 that changes testing provisions for special
education students.

Princeton and Ottowa school districts filed suit against the federal government on the
grounds that NCLB conflicts with IDEA.

Illinois State Board of Education announced several changes to NCLB: definition of failing and subgroups.

State Senate introduced SJR47 (in May 2004) that asks the Illinois delegation to review
and change NCLB (passed Senate, arrived in House).

In August 2004 two districts turned down Title I funding to avoid requirements of
NCLB.

Indiana

State Board of Education voted to add its name to a letter protesting NCLB (in March
2004).

State Senate introduced and passed SB258 (in January 2004) that authorizes state officials
to seek waivers from NCLB if the act conflicts with Indiana's accountability standards.

State NEA chapter filed suit against the government.

Iowa

HR11 requested the congressional delegation to secure funding mandates for NCLB
(filed February 10, 2005).

SCR105 sought waivers if programs increased student achievement (in April 2004).

Kansas

Chairman Steve Abrams wants the State Board of Education to consider opting out of NCLB (on October 12, 2005).

State Senate introduced SR1834 that urges Congress to reevaluate NCLB and provide full funding.

State Senate introduced SCR1621 and State House introduced HR6028; both asked for a waiver considering the overall quality of Kansas schools.

Kentucky

Two resolutions (SR172, HR 174—passed House) asking for full funding and more flexibility (in March 2004).

Louisiana

HCR88 redefines "highly qualified teacher" (in May 2004).

HCR20 asks for fully funded mandate (passed on to Congress in April 2004).

HCR13, 12 express the right of Louisiana not to comply with NCLB unless it is fully funded (sent to Congress in April 2004).

Maine

LD 676 passed in May 2005 in the State House and Senate. It directs the attorney general to sue the federal government if funding is insufficient to implement NCLB.

LD 1716 (signed by the governor April 2004) says that the state department may not use any state money to implement NCLB.

Maryland

State Senate introduced a bill that identifies a conflict between NCLB and IDEA, resolves that the act must be fully funded or that the legislature must seek a waiver (May 2005). It was defeated in committee.

Massachusetts

No action

Michigan

State Board of Education voted to seek changes that would make it easier for the state to comply with NCLB.

The Pontiac School District is a lead plaintiff in a case against the federal government on the grounds that NCLB is an unfunded mandate. NEA groups and school districts in Texas and Vermont have signed on.

Minnesota

SF1244 places conditions under which the state may continue implementing NCLB (referred to finance, May 2005).

SF1245 amends NCLB per a task force's recommendations (passed Senate, House version 1490 still in committee, March 2005).

SF1092 asks Congress not to extend NCLB to high schools (passed Senate, now referred to Education Reform committee in House in March 2005).

HF 23 directs commissioner to seek waivers for ineffective aspects of NCLB (referred to Education Reform January 2005). Senate version passed already.

Mississippi
HB 150 "School Testing Right to Know Act" to furnish the public and policymakers with accurate information with which to make decisions about the future of Mississippi's education.

Missouri
Asked for and received waiver on 2004–05 AYP goals.

Montana
Superintendent McCulloch requested waivers due to the difficulty of implementing NCLB in rural areas (May 2005).

Nebraska
LR 23 introduced to Senate, asks Congress to fully fund NCLB or modify the act to meet budget constraints (January 2005).

Nevada
AB 562 gives priority to state accountability system over NCLB where they conflict (passed House, currently in Senate).
In February 2005 state minority leader Reid called for Nevada to pull out of NCLB.

New Hampshire
Introduced HB786 (last action January 2004), which prohibited the use of state's funds to comply with NCLB—died in committee.

New Jersey
In June 2005, state assembly voted to place NJ education goals ahead of NCLB (bill requires that school officials give NJ goals precedence over federal mandates).
In May 2005, ACR236 endorses National Conference of States' Legislatures recommendations for altering NCLB and encourages Congress to do the same.
A267 (May 2005) urged the governor to follow Connecticut in filing a lawsuit against the federal government.
S2528, A3993 direct local officials on implementing NCLB.
ACR142 (February 2004) calls upon Congress to give more time to meet the highly qualified teacher standard.
Legislature has directed attorney general to file suit if NCLB is deemed an unfunded mandate.

New Mexico
HM 02 resolves that Congress should fully fund the mandate (passed February 2004).
SJM55 calls for a study of unfunded mandates (February 2004).
HJM09 notes that additional costs to implement NCLB far outweigh additional federal funds (February 2004).
SB513 (February 2004) would have allowed the state to opt out of compliance with NCLB.

New York
No action

North Carolina
No action

North Dakota

HB 1038 (would have established a state NCLB advisory committee), HB 1365 (allowing school districts to opt out of NCLB), and HCR 3012 (redefined highly qualified teacher) failed to pass.

Ohio

State Senator Mark Dann introduced a resolution to follow Connecticut in suing the federal government (SCR 20, referred to Committee on Education, September 2005).

SCR25 called for full funding and waivers from NCLB (March 2004), never left committee.

Oklahoma

HR1037 (March 2004) passed to Congress and asks for a waiver for high-achieving states.

HCR1052 (March 2004) stalled in the Senate, which called upon congressional delegation to alter NCLB.

Oregon

HB 2900 prohibits participation in NCLB if federal funds are not received (referred to Ways and Means Committee, March 2005).

HJM 27 urges Congress to provide full funding and requests waivers (Education Committee, March 2005).

Pennsylvania

Introduced June 2004, HR794 asks that Congress restore funding cuts.

Reading school district sued Pennsylvania's Department of Education on the grounds the district had not been given enough resources to meet AYP (adequate yearly progress) goals.

Rhode Island

S3129 asked Congress to fully fund NCLB (passed in the Senate May 2004).

South Carolina

HCR4891 (HCR4889, SCR1031 are companion legislation) calls for amendments to NCLB (last action March 2004).

South Dakota

HCR1018 calls for full funding (February 2004).

Tennessee

SJR694 (March 2004) notes the state is burdened by funding NCLB.

Texas

As of August 2005, a second Texas school district is joining districts in Michigan and Vermont in filing suit against the federal government to relieve schools for paying for NCLB.

State commissioner allowed state testing rule to take precedence over the requirements of NCLB.

Utah

HB 135 and HB 1001 allow state laws to trump provisions of NCLB on the grounds that the act violates section 9527 that prohibits state spending on federal mandates.

Vermont

HB 59, SB 38 (introduced January 2005) orders state to withdraw participation in NCLB.

Leicester, Neshobe, Otter Valley, Rutland Northeast Supervisory Union, Pittsford Town, Sudbury Town, and Whiting Town districts joined with the NEA and districts in Texas and Michigan.

HJR37 (in committee as of April 2005) would support the plaintiffs in a lawsuit related to funding for the No Child Left Behind Act of 2001.

Orleans Southwest, Southwest Vermont, and Windham Northeast are reallocating Title I funds so certain schools are not subject to AYP provisions.

Virginia

HB 1592, HB2602, HB2685, HJR 561, HJR 576, HJR 708, SB 948, SB1136, SJR 437: direct state Board of Education to seek waivers from NCLB or to urge Congress and the administration to grant waivers to states that maintain high academic standards.

Washington

SJM 8001 requests full funding for NCLB (in the Rules Committee April 2005). House's corollary legislation is HJM4010.

West Virginia

SCR32 passed Senate in February 2004. It outlines the difficulties of implementing NCLB.

HR6 asks Congress to pass waivers for states like West Virginia that show academic improvement.

Wisconsin

In May 2004 Attorney General Peggy Lautenschlager released an opinion letter on the constitutionality and appropriateness of the mandates and funding levels inherent in NCLB.

State Senate introduced SR33 that urges the state not to appropriate state funds for implementing NCLB (last action March 2004).

SR19 asks for full funding (last action March 2004).

SR32 asks for delegation to procure more money to implement NCLB (was adopted in the Senate).

Wyoming

HJR06 notes the impact of NCLB on the state of Wyoming (last action March 2004).

HB127 would have prohibited state participation in NCLB (died without being heard).

Appendix 9A-4. Resources Used for Creating State Resistance Scale

Baldwin, Tom. 2005. "Assembly Votes to Override No Child Left Behind." *Courier News,* June 27.

Billeaud, Jacques. 2004. "Lawmaker: Proposal to Opt Out of Bush Plan Unlikely to Succeed." Associated Press State and Local Wire, March 15.

Carrier, Paul. 2005. "Baldacci: No-Child Costs Justify Suit." *Portland Press Herald,* April 27, p. B1.

Clark, Korey. 2005. "States Rebel Against No Child Left Behind." *State Net Capitol Journal* 8, no. 21 (June 13).

Communities for Quality Education. "State Legislative Summaries." Washington (www.qualityednow.org/summaries/states/ [January 10, 2006]).

Dillon, Sam. 2005. "No Child Left Behind Law Flawed, Bipartisan Panel Says." *New York Times,* February 24, p. 18.

Dobbs, Michael. 2004. "More States Are Fighting 'No Child Left Behind' Law." *Washington Post,* February 19, p. A3.

————. 2005. "Connecticut Stands in Defiance on Enforcing 'No Child.'" *Washington Post,* May 8, p. A10.

Erwin, Erica. 2005. "Erie Board Backs No Child Left Behind Lawsuit." *Erie Times News,* November 13.

Gillespie, Noreen. 2005. "Conn. Challenges No Child Left Behind Law." Associated Press, August 23.

Higgins, A. J. 2005. "Maine Weighs Joining Federal No Child Suit." *Bangor Daily News,* April 27, p. A4.

Higgins, Lori. 2005. "Pontiac Sues over Funding." *Detroit Free Press,* April 21, p. 1B.

Hoff, David J. 2005. "Colorado Town Raises Taxes to Finance NCLB Withdrawal." *Education Week* 25, no. 16 (January): 3.

————. 2005. "NCLB Law Needs Work, Legislators Assert." *Education Week* 24, no. 25 (February 24): 1.

————. 2005. "Texas Stands Behind Own Testing Rule." *Education Week* 24, no. 26 (March 9): 1.

Hooper, Kim. 2004. "State Joins Protest of Education Law." *Indianapolis Star,* March 5, p. 1B.

Lambeck, Linda Conner. 2005. "'Outrage' over 'No Child' Suit Reply." *Connecticut Post,* December 6.

Milburn, John. 2005. "Corkins Willing to Explore Seeking Freedom from No Child Left Behind." Associated Press State and Local Wire, October 6.

National Conference of State Legislatures. 2005. "State Activity on No Child Left Behind: Quick Facts 2004–05." Washington (November 2).

National Education Association. "State Legislative Activity." Washington (www.nea.org/esea/chorus1.html#state [December 15, 2005]).

Okoben, Janet. 2005. "Lawmaker Introduces Resolution to Sue over No Child Left Behind." *Cleveland Plain Dealer,* September 13, p. B2.

Olson, Lynn. 2005. "Requests Win More Leeway under NCLB." *Education Week* 24, no. 42 (July 13): 1.

————. 2005. "Virginia Gets First-Ever Waiver to Reverse Order of NCLB Sanctions." *Education Week* (August 29).

PR Newswire. 2004. "State Education Officials Tell National Leaders—'States Need Full Funding for Special Education and More Flexibility in No Child Left Behind Reforms.'" New York, March 18.

Ravitz, Jessica. 2005. "Utahns Cheer as Guv Signs NCLB Protest." *Salt Lake Tribune*, May 11.

Results for America. "Revolt Against No Child Left Behind Spreads to 47 States." Newton Centre, Mass.: Civil Society Institute (www.nclbgrassroots.org/revolt.php [December 12, 2005]).

Ripley, Amanda, and Sonja Steptoe. 2005. "Inside the Revolt over Bush's School Rules." *Time*, May 9, p. 30.

Sykes, Shinika. 2005. "Utah Called Education 'Whipping Boy.'" *Salt Lake Tribune*, September 30, p. B8.

Toomer-Cook, Jennifer. 2005. "Utahns Give NCLB the Cold Shoulder." *Deseret Morning News*, April 20.

Welsh, John. 2004. "Senate Panel Snubs 'No Child Left Behind' Bill Exempts State from the Rules of Federal Act." *Saint Paul Pioneer Press*, February 18, p. B7.

Weyer, Jake. 2005. "Entenza Calls for End to Federal 'No Child' Act." *Duluth News Tribune*, September 7.

References

Americans for Better Education. 2004. *Americans for Better Education Survey on No Child Left Behind*. Arlington, Texas (January).

Cibulka, James. 1996. "The New Institutionalism and Education Politics: An Interpretative Analysis." In *The Politics of Education and the New Institutionalism: Reinventing the American School*, edited by Robert L. Crowson, William Lowe Boyd, and Hanne M. Mawhinney, pp. 7–22. New York: Routledge.

Dotterweich, Lisa, and Ramona McNeal. 2004. "State Compliance and the No Child Left Behind Act." Paper prepared for the Annual Meeting of the Midwest Political Science Association. Chicago, April 15–18.

Education Week. 2006. *Quality Counts at 10: "A Decade of Standards-Based Education."* vol. 25, no. 17 (www.edweek.org/ew/toc/2006/01/05/index.html).

Elazar, Daniel. 1966. *American Federalism: A View from the States*. New York: Thomas Crowell.

————. 1984. *American Federalism: A View from the States*, 3d ed. New York: Harper & Row.

[ETS] Educational Testing Service. 2005. *Ready for the Real World? Americans Speak on High School Reform*. Princeton, New Jersey (www.ets.org/Media/Education_Topics/pdf/2005highschoolreform.pdf).

Fusarelli, Lance D. 2005. "Gubernatorial Reactions to No Child Left Behind: Politics, Pressure, and Education Reform." *Peabody Journal of Education* 80, no. 2: 120–36.

Gray, Virginia, Russell Hanson, and Herbert Jacob. 1999. *Politics in the American States, A Comparative Analysis*, 7th ed. Washington: CQ Press.

Manna, Paul. 2004. "Management, Control, and the Challenge of Leaving No Child Behind." Paper prepared for the Annual Meeting of the Midwest Political Science Association, Chicago, April 15–18.

Mathis, William, Kevin Fleming, and Wendy Lecker. 2005. "The NCLB Rebellion: Money, Politics, and Student Learning." Paper presented at the American Education Finance Association's annual meeting. Louisville, Kentucky, March 18.

McDermott, Kathryn, and Laura Jensen. 2005. "Dubious Sovereignty: Federal Conditions of Aid and the No Child Left Behind Act. *Peabody Journal of Education* 80, no. 2: 39–56.

Moe, Terry M. 2001. *Schools, Vouchers, and the American Public.* Brookings.

[NCES] National Center for Education Statistics. 1995. *Digest of Education Statistics 1995,* by Thomas D. Snyder. NCES- 95-029. Washington: U.S. Department of Education, Institute of Education Sciences.

———. 2002. *Digest of Education Statistics 2001,* by Thomas D. Snyder. NCES-2000-130.

———. 2005. *Digest of Education Statistics 2004,* by Thomas D. Snyder. NCES-2006-005.

———. "Main NAEP (National Assessment of Educational Progress) Data Explorer" (nces.ed.gov/nationsreportcard/nde/).

———. "State Profiles" (nces.ed.gov/nationsreportcard/states/).

Olson, Lynn. 2005. "Room to Maneuver." *Education Week* 25, no. 15 (December 14): S1–S5 (ewdev.edweek.org/media/nclb_1214qualified.pdf).

Olson, Lynn, and David J. Hoff. 2005. "U.S. to Pilot New Gauge of 'Growth.'" *Education Week,* 25, no. 13 (November 16): 1.

Orfield, Gary, and Chungmei Lee. 2004. *Brown at 50: King's Dream or Plessy's Nightmare?* Harvard University, Civil Rights Project.

Results for America. 2004. *Poll of Parents on "No Child Left Behind": Summary of Survey Findings.* Prepared by Opinion Research Corporation. Newton Centre, Mass.: Civil Society Institute (www.resultsforamerica.org/education/).

Rose, Lowell C., and Alec M. Gallup. 2005. "The 37th Annual Phi Delta Kappa/Gallup Poll of the Public's Attitudes Toward the Public Schools. " *Phi Delta Kappan* 87, no. 1 (September): 41–57 (www.pdkintl.org/kappan/kpollpdf.htm).

Scoon, Karla Reid. 2005. "Civil Rights Groups Split over NCLB." *Education Week,* 25, no. 1 (August 31): 1.

Sharkansky, Ira. 1969. "The Utility of Elazar's Political Culture: A Research Note." *Polity* 2 (Fall): 66–83.

Sunderman, Gail L. 2003. "Implementing a Major Education Reform: No Child Left Behind and Federal-State Relations, First Impressions." Paper prepared for the Annual Meeting of the American Education Research Association. Chicago, April 21–25.

Sunderman, Gail, and James Kim. 2007. "The Expansion of Federal Power and the Politics of Implementing the No Child Left Behind Act." *Teacher's College Record* 109, no. 5 (ID 12227) (www.tcrecord.org/).

Wanker, William, and Kathy Christie. 2005. "State Implementation of the No Child Left Behind Act." *Peabody Journal of Education* 80, no. 2: 57–72.

Wirt, Frederick. 1980. "Does Control Follow the Dollar? School Policy, State-Local Linkages, and Political Culture." *Publius: The Journal of Federalism* 10, no. 2: 69–88.

Zehr, Mary Ann. 2005. "Bilingual Educators Ratchet Up Criticism of No Child Left Behind." *Education Week* 24, no. 21 (February 2): 13.

10

NCLB Lessons Learned: Implications for Reauthorization

ANDREW C. PORTER

After nearly forty years of watching Title I and consuming the results of its various evaluations, it was a treat to be given the assignment of serving as rapporteur for the February 2006 University of Wisconsin conference "Will Standards-Based Reform in Education Help Close the Poverty Gap?" Conference organizers Adam Gamoran and Maria Cancian asked me to go beyond reflecting on the findings of the conference to offer guidance about future directions for NCLB. What follows is my response.

In the spring of 2006, NCLB was in its infancy, too early for a direct test of its implementation and effects. Many of the provisions of NCLB had been in place in one state or another for a long enough period of time, however, to have a good sense for their promise. At the same time, NCLB is unique, thereby making direct inferences from earlier standards-based reform risky. With that in mind, I found the work in this volume thoughtful, careful, and methodologically sophisticated. I was pleased to see, across authors, disciplinary perspectives of psychology, economics, sociology, and public policy. The analyses contained within this volume are based almost exclusively on ingenious secondary analysis of existing databases. Not only does the volume represent important new work on timely questions about standards-based education reform, but each piece has an excellent summary and interpretation of other relevant literature. For the most part, the chapters are carefully tied to the provisions of NCLB, from the study of state accountability systems to teacher quality, from supplementary services to school choice. Although NCLB does not have provisions for student accountability, it might address them when it is reauthorized, making the chapters on grade retention and exit exams equally timely and relevant.

Given the politically charged terrain of standards-based reform with advocates of one position or another at every turn, I compliment the authors on their even-handed analyses. The collective goal was a careful analysis of the policies, their implementation, and their effects. Authors went where their results took them rather than forcing their results to fit preconceived notions. There are, to be sure, occasions where authors did not find what they expected and did not exactly give up their expectations, but that seems fair.

NCLB is ambitious, comprehensive legislation and, when printed, is nearly one foot thick. No conference or volume could adequately cover the breadth of issues it creates, and this volume is no exception. In addition to the material in this volume, it would be important to examine the quality of state content standards, state tests, professional development, and the degree to which these pieces are aligned. Similarly, it would be useful to know more about the technical assistance being provided by states to districts and by districts to schools, the effects on nontested subjects, and the implementation and effects of repeated calls for "research-based practices." These topics remain fertile ground for further work.

NCLB and Title I of the U.S. Department of Education had an allocation of nearly $13 billion out of a total department budget of $73 billion in 2006 (in contrast to the defense budget of $474 billion). Nevertheless, Title I is a substantial program that represented approximately 8 percent of K–12 education funding, and, by most accounts, it was the most substantial presence of the federal government in local schooling. As has been noted over the years, Title I is a funding stream, not a well-defined education program that can be replicated. While the law requires a great deal from states that accept funding, considerable discretion is left to states in its implementation. This foreshadows an important point missing from the earlier chapters but essential to assessing NCLB effects. The big story is the variation in state implementation of NCLB requirements. Early in what follows, I document differences among states in how they are implementing the law.

Figure 10-1 sketches a timeline on which I have placed some of the major requirements of NCLB and also the timing of the data collection of the various datasets analyzed in this volume. NCLB was passed in 2001 and implemented initially in 2002 with some provisions immediately put into effect.

Figure 10-1. *Timeline of NCLB Requirements and Volume Datasets*

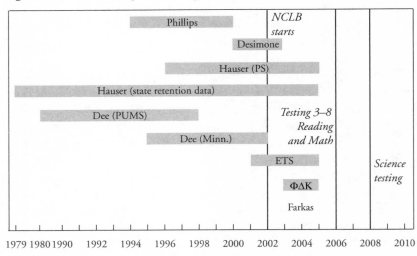

1979 1980 1990   1992   1994   1996   1998   2000   2002   2004   2006   2008   2010

ETS = Educational Testing Service; PUMS = Public Use Microdata Sample.

Most provisions, however, were phased in over time. For example, new teachers were required to be highly qualified as of the 2002–03 school year, but all teachers were to be highly qualified by the last day of the 2005–06 school year. In the spring of 2006 at the time the conference was held, the requirement of testing every grade third through eighth every year in reading and mathematics was just beginning to be implemented, and the requirement of science assessment was yet to come. As for school accountability, a school had to have failed making adequate yearly progress (AYP) for two consecutive years before "sanctions" went into effect (such sanctions as students being eligible to transfer to another public school that had not been identified as in need of improvement). A school must fail to make AYP three consecutive years before supplemental services are provided. Four consecutive years of failing to achieve AYP requires at least one corrective action, five years of failure requires a restructuring plan, and six years requires implementation of that plan. Thus, for states and schools starting in 2002, the final "sanction" for schools will not be in place until 2008, the same year that the science testing requirement goes into effect.

The datasets on which the chapters in this volume are based mostly predate NCLB; even those that cover the period since the 2002 baseline year of NCLB extend only to 2005. Clearly, a great deal will change over time in the implementation and effects of the NCLB provisions as states, districts, and schools gain experience and familiarity with the law and how best it might be implemented. Nevertheless, reauthorization is scheduled for 2007, which is not far off, as the conference organizers realized. Early experiences with NCLB have provided some data, and we did know quite a bit from earlier state-level implementations of various NCLB-like provisions. This volume is a useful and important compilation of what was known about NCLB as of 2006 and is a good source for thinking about where NCLB should be headed.

The discussion that follows is divided into four sections. First, I document state differences in interpretation and implementation of NCLB requirements to set a context for interpreting NCLB effects. This state variation may be an early effect of NCLB, or it may merely reflect previous between-state differences. In any event, state-to-state variation in implementation is clearly important to understanding the effects of the law. In this first section, I also document important methodological effects of NCLB on state practices that were also missing in the earlier chapters. Second, I address what is known about the poverty gap on which the conference focused and which NCLB targets to eliminate. Here, I draw from the chapters augmented by my own recent analysis of the gap.[1] Third, I provide a summary of what we know about the effects of NCLB or at least NCLB-like provisions based on the chapters in this volume plus a few selected other sources (for example, AIR-RAND's national evaluations of NCLB, the first phase of which had just been completed in spring 2006).[2] The fourth and final section is devoted to suggestions on how NCLB might be modified when reauthorized.

Some NCLB Effects Otherwise Missing from the Volume

Before getting into the details, it is worth taking a look at results from our nation's report card, the National Assessment of Educational Progress (NAEP). Although it would be folly to attribute to NCLB any jumps in student achievement on NAEP that correspond to the onset of NCLB, it is still worth knowing whether or not there were such jumps. Again, I hasten to add that, although NCLB began in 2002, its requirements are phased in over

---

1. Porter (2005).
2. The National Longitudinal Study of No Child Left Behind (NLS-NCLB), led by the American Institutes for Research (AIR) and RAND, will be the primary data source for the U.S. Department of Education on how districts and schools are addressing provisions of NCLB. First phase completed in spring 2006: Le Floch and others (2006); Yoon and others (2006).

time and some had not yet been in effect as of the spring of 2006. Given those caveats, the pattern of NAEP results for math is positive, while the pattern for reading is not. In mathematics at the fourth grade level, national NAEP student achievement was flat from 1992 to 2000. It jumped substantially from 2000 to 2003 and continued at this level in 2005. There was a similar, but less pronounced, pattern for eighth graders. Long-term trend NAEP provides yet another view. Again, from 1992 to 1999, the math achievement of nine-year-olds was fairly flat, but from 1999 to 2004, it increased notably. A similar pattern was evident with thirteen-year-olds. In reading, from 1992 to 2000, achievement of fourth graders declined slightly; but from 2000 to 2002, it jumped modestly to earlier levels of achievement that were maintained in 2003 and 2005. At the eighth grade level, reading achievement was constant from 1992 to 2005. In long-term trend NAEP, the patterns for reading are similar. There may have been a small increase from 1999 to 2004 for nine-year-olds, but reading achievement has been flat since 1992 for thirteen-year-olds.

Are the increases in math attributable to NCLB? Can one conclude that NCLB is not yet having a positive effect on reading, at least for thirteen-year-olds? These questions cannot be answered with certainty. Could the full effects of NCLB be seen by 2005? Almost certainly not.

State Variation in Implementation of Core NCLB Requirements

None of the chapters in this volume address what is already clearly one of the most important findings on the impact of NCLB. NCLB leaves considerable discretion to states in defining key provisions of the law, such as achievement level and what constitutes a highly qualified teacher. State discretion has resulted in large between-state variation in the implementation of the law. Whether or not state variation in implementation simply reflects already existing differences among states is less clear. What is clear is that these between-state differences have important implications for what constitutes acceptable performance from students and quality from teachers. These state differences surely translate into differences in the quality of instruction for students and are likely not in the best interests of closing the achievement gap.

NCLB requires that states set challenging content standards that are grade-level specific in reading and mathematics. States are required to have student achievement tests that are aligned to these challenging content standards and that must define achievement standards: two levels of high achievement, "proficient" and "advanced," and a third lower level, "basic" (these NCLB achievement standards match those of NAEP in number and terminology). Also, states must define "adequate yearly progress" for the performance of the school, district, and state. Annual measurable objectives will be set for each year, starting from the baseline of 2002 to the target of 2014, at which point 100 percent of students are to be proficient in reading and mathematics. In setting annual measurable objectives, states are given considerable latitude in determining the trajectory for increases from baseline to the year 2014, the minimum number of students required for reporting the results of disaggregated subgroups (NCLB requires that schools be held accountable not only for their entire group of students but also for disaggregated groups of students when there are sufficient numbers), and whether to use confidence intervals in deciding when an annual measurable objective has been met.[3] NCLB also requires that, as of the 2002–03 school year, all newly hired Title I teachers teaching core academic subjects must be highly qualified; by the 2005–06 school year, all public school teachers who teach core academic subjects must be highly qualified. To be *highly qualified*, NCLB specifies that teachers must have state certification or licensing and must have a bachelor's degree. They also must demonstrate competence in the subject matter in each of the academic subjects taught. However, setting the standard for subject matter competency is left to state discretion.

A good place to start looking at state variation in implementation of NCLB is in how states defined achievement levels. State reports of the percentage of students who are proficient are easily located on the web, and substantial variation across states is clearly evident.[4] But we know as well from state-by-state NAEP that states vary substantially in level of student achievement. It is not appropriate, therefore, to draw conclusions about state standards for proficiency by comparing the percentage of students proficient from state to state, because some of the variation reflects differences in levels of student achievement.[5] Consequently, I selected three states with the largest difference and three states with the smallest difference between percentage proficient reported on the state test and percentage proficient as defined on the state–by-state NAEP results (see tables 10-1 and 10-2). The difference columns in tables 10-1 and 10-2 show these contrasts. In table 10-1, Maine, Missouri, and Wyoming set relatively challenging proficiency achievement levels at the fourth and eighth grade levels. For example, 35 percent of Missouri students are proficient in reading at the fourth grade level on the state test, and 33 percent are proficient on the NAEP test. In contrast, in Georgia

---

3. Porter, Linn, and Trimble (2005).
4. Linn (2005).
5. Kingsbury and others (2003); Braun and Qian (2005); McLaughlin and de Mello (2002).

Table 10-1. *Percentage of Students Proficient on State and NAEP Tests in Reading, by Grade, 2005*

State	Fourth grade			Eighth grade		
	State test	NAEP test	Difference	State test	NAEP test	Difference
Maine	53	35	−18	44	38	−6
Missouri	35	33	−2	33	31	−2
Wyoming	47	34	−13	39	36	−3
Texas	79	29	−50	83	26	−57
Georgia	87	26	−61	83	25	−58
North Carolina	84	29	−55	89	27	−62

Source: Author's calculations.

Table 10-2. *Percentage of Students Proficient on State and NAEP Tests in Math, by Grade, 2005*

State	Fourth grade			Eighth grade		
	State test	NAEP test	Difference	State test	NAEP test	Difference
Maine	39	39	0	29	30	1
Missouri	43	31	−12	16	26	10
Wyoming	39	43	4	38	29	−9
Texas	81	40	−41	61	31	−30
Georgia	75	30	−45	69	23	−46
North Carolina	93	40	−53	85	32	−53

Source: Author's calculations.

87 percent of students are proficient on the fourth grade state test, but only 26 percent are proficient on NAEP. Table 10-2 shows similar results for math. In tables 10-1 and 10-2, the between-state variation is consistent across grade level, subject, and year (not presented in both tables are data for the year 2003 showing remarkably parallel results). Generally, states have set their achievement levels downward, from roughly comparable with NAEP to substantially less challenging than NAEP. The between-state variation is huge, with differences from as large as 60 percent more students being labeled proficient on the state test than on NAEP in Georgia to Missouri math at the eighth grade level where 10 percent fewer students were labeled proficient on the state test than on NAEP. In interpreting these contrasts between state proficiency and NAEP proficiency, it is well to keep in mind that NAEP is not a high-stakes test and may not be aligned equally well to

instruction across the states. These differences between NAEP and state tests could partially explain why, in general, the NAEP standards are higher than the state standards. However, differences in the nature of the two tests do not explain variation among states in the extent to which their achievement levels are challenging. Clearly, NCLB means very different things in Georgia than it does in Missouri.

There are also substantial differences among states in the percentage of schools failing to achieve AYP. Of the six states considered in tables 10-1 and 10-2, counterintuitively, there is no correlation between the challenge of the proficiency standard and percentage of schools failing AYP. Should not lower standards be easier to meet? In 2005 North Carolina had among the least challenging achievement levels (and the highest percentage of students proficient), yet 42 percent of its schools failed AYP, while Texas had nearly as many students proficient as North Carolina had, but only 10.7 percent of its schools failed AYP. Other factors are at play in determining the percentage of schools failing AYP, as was hinted at above. My colleagues and I examined the effects of state decisions about setting AYP targets using simulations based on Kentucky data.[6] States that back-loaded their trajectory and used wide confidence intervals and large minimum group size for disaggregated data identified substantially fewer schools that were failing to achieve AYP than states that did not do these things. In 2004 Kentucky's "design decisions" were to use a disaggregated group size of sixty, a two-tailed confidence interval of 99 percent, and no increase in AYP target until 2005. As a result, only 6 percent of Kentucky schools failed to achieve AYP in 2004. If Kentucky were to have cut their minimum group size by half (to thirty), the percentage of schools failing AYP in 2004 would have jumped to 11 percent. If they had dropped their confidence interval altogether, the number failing would have jumped to 28 percent. Dropping the confidence interval and using a straight line trajectory so that annual measurable objectives increased in 2003 and again in 2004, the number of schools failing AYP in 2004 would have been 41 percent. Combining all three design decisions to form the most stringent target for meeting AYP would have resulted in 56 percent of Kentucky schools failing AYP in 2004. Clearly, states vary in how they have made these design decisions, though over time most states have progressively moved toward more lenient design decisions leading to smaller percentages of schools failing AYP. Clearly, provision of school choice and supplemental services mean very different things in states with high percentages of schools failing AYP than they mean in states with few

6. Porter, Linn, and Trimble (2005).

schools failing AYP. Further, these state-to-state differences are not a function of school or student success so much as they are a function of differences among states in how they interpret and implement the law.

Obviously, it is still early in the game in terms of NCLB school accountability. For example, elementary schools tend to be small relative to middle schools and high schools, but in the 2005–06 school year, testing of student achievement must be in every elementary school grade third through eighth. At that point, essentially all elementary schools will meet the minimum number of students for reporting disaggregated data. Also, the first increase in AYP targets had to be in 2005, and the increases will continue to 2014. Obviously, the further into the full implementation of NCLB, the higher the standards and the greater the number of schools that will fail to make AYP. The National Education Association (NEA) projects that in Connecticut 93 percent of schools will fail AYP in 2014 and in California 99 percent will fail.[7] NEA tends to be negative about NCLB, so their projections may be biased high. As Bob Linn points out, there is no existence proof that schools can reach the 100 percent proficient level, and he has called repeatedly for more reasonable targets.[8]

The story of between-state variation and implementation of NCLB requirements plays out for highly qualified teacher as well. Thirty-seven states use the Educational Testing Service (ETS) PRAXIS II tests to determine teacher content knowledge. Each state sets its own minimum standard on PRAXIS for being highly qualified. Using mathematics at the secondary school level as an example, state cut scores vary from a high of 156 for Colorado to a low of 116 for Arkansas.[9] ETS reports that the median on the secondary school test of mathematics content knowledge is 143.[10] There is similar variability for the middle school test of mathematics content knowledge, with Virginia setting the highest cut at 163 (which is also the national median for the test) and Nevada and South Dakota tied for the lowest cut at 139. Clearly, being a highly qualified teacher depends on what state the teacher is in. Given the well-documented importance of teacher quality to student achievement, these seemingly arbitrary state-to-state differences are alarming. Students who are just on either side of a state line are subjected to substantially different qualities of teachers.

7. (www.nea.org/esea/greatlakesayp.html).

8. Linn (2005).

9. As shown on the two states' websites.

10. See "Understanding Your Praxis Scores 2005–06" by the Educational Testing Service (www.ets.org/Media/Tests/PRAXIS/pdf/09706PRAXIS.pdf).

A seldom discussed provision of NCLB is that states must determine the minimum number of days that a student is in a school before that student counts toward the accountability of that school. Again, NCLB leaves it to the state to define the minimum number of days. Most states appear to have set a date in the fall by which the student must be enrolled in the school. For students enrolled by that date and in the school at the time of the test, the student counts for accountability. Of the six states studied earlier in terms of state variance in achievement levels, Missouri specifies the last Wednesday in September; Maine and Wyoming, October 1; Georgia the first Tuesday in October; and Texas not until October 29. In contrast, North Carolina sets the limit at 140 days (with a typical school year being 180 days). These state decisions are important; the greater the number of days, the fewer students included in accountability. Mobile students tend to come from low-income families; to close the poverty gap, mobile students are the very students for which schools should be held accountable. However, that is not an NCLB requirement.

Methodological Effects of NCLB

Serving on a number of state technical panels for their assessment programs provides me an opportunity to observe firsthand how states have responded to NCLB requirements of testing and accountability. From my up close vantage point, I have seen a revolution in state practices that I attribute to NCLB.

Before NCLB, states typically tested reading and math at one grade level each at the elementary, middle, and high school levels. Because these assessments were spread across grades, there was no interest in measuring student growth. Many states discussed the need for a student identification number, but most did not implement that concept because the collection of longitudinal data on students was not a priority. As states anticipated the 2005–06 deadline for testing third through eighth grades every year in reading and math, most states decided to develop vertically equated scales so that student performance at one grade level could be compared with performance at earlier grade levels. This in turn led to implementing student identification numbers to enable setting up and maintaining longitudinal databases of students. Availability of student longitudinal datasets stimulated the consideration of estimating a school's value-added to student achievement.

Many psychometricians are skeptical about the feasibility of building vertical scales and the confusion they can create when, for example, a third grader has a scale score on the vertical scale equal to a sixth grader's score. The interpretation of such results is not clear, but this does not necessarily

mean that the third grader can do what the sixth grader can. Joseph Martineau has demonstrated that shifts in the constructs being measured from
grade to grade jeopardize the validity of inferences made from longitudinal
value-added models.[11] While Martineau argues that value-added accountability models require student data to be vertically scaled, William Sanders,
Arnold Saxton, and Sandra Horn argue that Sanders' value-added model
does not require a vertical scale.[12] States argue that a vertical scale can provide nonsophisticated value-added results since a student's performance at
fifth grade can be compared with his or her performance at fourth grade. In
fact, vertical scales make comparisons of differences across schools, or even
across teachers, easy. It is highly doubtful that the current enthusiasm among
states for creating student identification numbers so that they can produce
longitudinal datasets, measuring student achievement on scales vertically
equated across grades, and exploring the use of value-added for school
accountability would have happened without NCLB.

NCLB requires that parents be informed as to whether or not their child's
school has been identified as in need of improvement, thus making their
child eligible for school choice options. Feedback to parents is to be made in
a timely fashion, putting great pressure on states to return results of student
assessments more quickly than ever before. At the same time, states are moving to test later in the school year so that students' full value-added can be
measured. The push for quick turnaround of student achievement results has
worked against the use of performance assessment. States with historically
strong commitments to performance assessment (Kentucky, for example) are
moving toward more multiple choice testing, not out of a lack of commitment to performance assessments and their ability to test higher-order cognitive demand achievements, but out of the need to streamline assessments so
that they can be scored more quickly and results returned in a timely fashion.
Multiple choice testing is also less expensive; concerns about costs have
increased as the amount of testing has escalated. Curiously, in the face of
increased testing due to NCLB, a popular new reform is interim assessments
(that is, testing four times a year for diagnostic purposes).

NCLB requires that states provide "reasonable adaptations and accommodations" for testing students with a disability. In addition, students with significant cognitive disabilities may take an alternate assessment. NCLB
requires that the progress of students with disabilities be measured relative to

11. Martineau (2006).
12. Sanders, Saxton, and Horn (1997).

the state standards for the grade in which the student is enrolled. Thus students are not to be tested using an out-of-grade test. Nevertheless, states can develop alternate achievement standards, and it is to these alternate standards that the alternate assessment is to be aligned. For purposes of school accountability and AYP, up to 1 percent of a state's students can be reported as proficient on the alternate achievement test. In 2006 the U.S. Department of Education announced that an additional 2 percent could be reported as proficient on modified achievement standards.

There is great confusion among states as to how to implement these requirements of alternate standards, alternate assessments, modified standards, modified assessments, and accommodations. Nevertheless, all states have an alternate assessment and are using accommodations, and most states are in the process of designing a plan for a modified assessment. Obviously, for a student to be proficient on the alternate assessment is not comparable with proficiency on the regular assessment. Presumably, the same will be true for the modified assessments and the 2 percent. As for accommodations, the standard is that the accommodation should not alter the construct being assessed, the so-called construct irrelevant standard.[13] Demonstrating empirically that accommodations are construct irrelevant has proven challenging. NCLB has been a huge stimulant to research and development of various approaches to alternate standards and assessments. Where the field will be five years from now remains to be seen. Hopefully, the net effect will be better instruction for students with disabilities. Testing students with cognitive disabilities is the wild and woolly frontier of the test and measurement industry.

NCLB school accountability is based on the level of student achievement, not on value-added to student achievement. Value-added is a new name for the old problem of measuring change. Essentially the idea is to statistically estimate the effects of an intervention that would have been estimated from a high-quality randomized experiment. Historically, efforts to estimate value-added have been in the context of quasi-experiments (that is, intervention studies in which for one reason or another randomization did not occur). Since the inception of NCLB, researchers, policymakers, and even educators have been increasingly interested in estimating the effects on student achievement of attending one school compared with the effects of attending another.[14] The increased interest in value-added may be attributable to the

13. Messick (1989).

14. See, for example, the special 2004 issue (29, no. 1) of the *Journal of Educational and Behavioral Statistics*, which was devoted exclusively to value-added assessment; Martineau (2006).

NCLB requirement of testing reading and math achievement every year in every grade from third through eighth. Meeting this NCLB requirement generates a longitudinal database virtually crying out for value-added analysis, at least of schools if not of teachers.

The U.S. Department of Education recently offered states the possibility to experiment with value-added models in contrast to the AYP criterion. As indicated above, the two criteria for school accountability are fundamentally different, one from the other. AYP requires all students to reach a high minimum level, labeled proficient. In contrast, value-added models focus on student achievement growth, not level of achievement obtained. These distinctions are politically charged. Some fear that a value-added model allows schools to be judged as being effective for stimulating growth in student achievement even when all students in the school achieve at unacceptably low levels. Concern for this possibility surely was the motivation for establishing AYP targets solely in terms of level of achievement, not of growth. Others argue, however, that setting a target for level of achievement is unfair for schools serving high concentrations of extremely low-achieving students. The U.S. Department of Education finesses these differences by requiring that value-added growth targets be set so that students reach the goal of 100 percent proficient by 2014. The finesse requires, of course, that the lowest-achieving schools have substantially larger value-added than that of the highest-achieving schools. One could imagine a value-added target that is constant across schools. In comparison with the NCLB AYP target, such a constant value-added target might set a higher standard for schools serving high concentrations of high-achieving students and a lower standard for schools serving high concentrations of low-achieving students. The constant value-added target would not require a closing of the achievement gap, however.

Adopting a value-added approach to school accountability raises two problems. First, what is the right value-added model? Second, what is the right annual target for value-added? Should all schools be required to produce a constant minimum amount of value-added? Alternatively, should some schools be required to produce a bigger value-added than other schools? Presumably the two criteria, level and value-added, could be used in concert. Schools might be plotted in a two-dimensional graph with level of achievement on one axis and size of value-added on the other. Schools high on both criteria are doing well. Schools low on both criteria are doing poorly. Schools high on level but poor on value-added or vice versa would need to be evaluated more carefully. Perhaps a sufficiently high level of achievement would negate the need for a large value-added, and perhaps a large value-added despite a low level of achievement might be acceptable, at least for some period of years.

But what if the value-added for a student in, say, third grade does not remain fully in place to build upon in subsequent grades? What is the shelf life of one school year's value-added? The probability of less-than-complete retention raises questions about the appropriateness of NCLB requiring that 100 percent of first graders be proficient as well as 100 percent of twelfth graders. As will be seen later, the achievement gap is large even when defined on students at young ages who have yet to go to school. Thus NCLB puts schools in the role of eliminating achievement gaps for which schools are clearly not responsible. Recognizing that there are thirteen years of schooling before postsecondary education, should the school system be given all thirteen years to eliminate the achievement gap? Imagine a student from a low-income family whose achievement before starting kindergarten is substantially below the achievement of his or her more affluent counterparts. If every year the student goes to effective schools and is in classrooms with effective teachers, the level of the student's achievement should become acceptable, if not superior, over time. My analysis is complicated by the possibility that students who enter school as relatively high achievers might get an equally positive experience such that the achievement gap would not narrow, but put that aside for a moment. Might it not be acceptable to have schools with first grade experiences that produce large value-added but do not bring 100 percent of the students to proficiency, if by twelfth grade through repeated effective education experiences the students all reach proficiency? My analysis is based on the assumption that proficiency has a common meaning across grade levels (though what that common meaning might be is elusive).

What Do We Know about the Achievement Gap?

The focus of this volume is on standards-based reform closing the poverty gap. Actually, NCLB seeks to eliminate each of several different kinds of achievement gaps by requiring that 100 percent of students be proficient by the year 2014 including, in particular, gaps for students who are in various subgroups based on race or ethnicity, English proficiency status, migrant status, disability status, economic status, and gender. Given sufficient numbers, schools are to be held accountable on each of these six categories annually from the baseline year of 2002 to the target year of 2014.

In the United States, educators and the public have focused a great deal of attention on the achievement gap, at least since 1965 and President Lyndon

Johnson's War on Poverty (and, of course, the famous Coleman report of 1966).[15] Nevertheless, the achievement gap continues to be large regardless of definition, age group, and academic subject.

Perhaps the best data for monitoring the achievement gap in the United States come from long-term trend NAEP, which is a national assessment of a probability sample of students at ages nine, thirteen, and seventeen in reading, mathematics, and science that has been conducted periodically since the early 1970s. Student self-reports on their parents' education have been used to monitor the parents' education gap, a rough measure of the socioeconomic status (SES) gap. In reading, not much has changed since 1971, although generally, reading scores are slightly lower today than they were in the early 1970s. The gap may have narrowed slightly for thirteen- and seventeen-year-olds because there was no decrease in scores among students whose parents did not graduate from high school. For mathematics, data on the parents' education gap are available from 1978 to 1999. Generally, achievement has been flat for students in families with parents of the highest education, but there have been modest gains for students with parents of less education. It is important to note that there is some problem with defining the SES achievement gap in terms of parents' education; in 1999, 34 percent of nine-year-olds, 11 percent of thirteen-year-olds, and 3 percent of seventeen-year-olds were unable to report their parents' education.[16] In assessing the Black-White achievement gap using the same dataset, the gap appears to narrow to its smallest point in the late 1980s and has remained stable since then. Larry Hedges and Amy Nowell report the Black-White achievement gap as roughly 0.7 standard deviation in reading and 0.9 standard deviation in math on long-term trend NAEP.[17]

Several authors have looked at the question of whether achievement gaps increase among students as they progress through school. The results of these analyses are mixed and full of methodological complications. The general conclusion is that the Black-White gap increases during the K–12 education experience, perhaps by as much as one-third of a standard deviation.[18] More important, the achievement gap is substantial before students go to school. The National Longitudinal Survey of Youth shows a Black-White achievement gap for three- and four-year-olds of 1.2 standard deviations in favor of Whites on the Peabody Picture Vocabulary test.[19]

15. Coleman and others (1966).
16. NCES (2000).
17. Hedges and Nowell (1998).
18. Philips, Crouse, and Ralph (1998).
19. Jencks and Phillips (1998).

The achievement gap for poverty obviously varies according to the way in which poverty is defined. Sometimes poverty is defined as students receiving free and reduced price lunch compared with those who are not (the NCLB definition). Other times the gap is defined in terms of parents' education, as described above. Still other times, the gap is defined in terms of family income. Sometimes the gap is defined in a normative way by contrasting, for example, the 10 percent of students at the top of the distribution with the 10 percent at the bottom. Sometimes the gap is defined in criterion-referenced ways, such as the free and reduced price lunch standard. These different definitions make a single estimate of the poverty achievement gap impossible.

One consistent finding is that, regardless of the definition, the gap increases less during the school year than it does during the summer. Barbara Heyns was the first to estimate summer effects, studying sixth and seventh graders in Atlanta, Georgia.[20] She found that the gap between disadvantaged and advantaged children increased during the summer but not during the school year. Doris Entwisle and Karl Alexander followed Baltimore children beginning in first grade, and they too concluded that socioeconomic gaps occurred during the summer but not during the school year.[21] Douglas Downey, Paul von Hippel, and Beckett Broh, using the kindergarten cohort of 1998–99 from the Early Childhood Longitudinal Study, similarly concluded that the SES achievement gap grows faster during the summer than it does during the school year, but not the Black-White achievement gap when SES is held constant.[22] Harris Cooper and others conducted a meta-analysis of thirty-nine studies dating back to 1906 and concluded that summer losses are larger for students from low SES families than they are for students from higher SES families.[23]

To reiterate, the achievement gap is large and robust across time, grade level, and academic subject. Whether defined in terms of poverty or race and ethnicity, the gap is present at a very early age (before students have gone to school). If the gap does increase during the K–12 education experience, it increases substantially less while students are in school than while they are out of school. Clearly, schools are not primarily responsible for creating the achievement gap; this volume asks if they can be an important part of the solution.

---

20. Heyns (1978, 1987).
21. Alexander, Entwisle, and Thompson (1987); Alexander, Entwisle, and Olson (2001); Entwisle and Alexander (1992, 1994).
22. Downey, von Hippel, and Broh (2004).
23. Cooper and others (1996).

The literature reveals that the gap is not the same across academic subjects. The gap is smaller for reading than it is for mathematics. The gap
appears to increase less with age for reading than it does for math. Summer
loss is greater in math than it is in reading. There are, however, no consistent
results as to whether the achievement gap is more easily reduced in reading
than in mathematics.[24]

There have been countless reforms in education directed at reducing, if
not eliminating, the gap. Recently, I updated and extended Ronald Ferguson's reviews of six of the most popular strategies: preschool programs, grouping by student ability, instructional interventions for students at risk of failure, matching of students and teachers by race, selection of teachers with
strong test scores, and smaller class sizes.[25] From my analysis, I concluded
that the most promising strategies for reducing the achievement gap address
inequalities in students' opportunity to learn. For example, students from
low-income families and students of color are less likely to be taught by high-
quality teachers than are white and more affluent students. Teacher quality,
by most accounts, has strong and consistent effects on value-added to student
achievement. Students from low-income families are less likely to be taught
ambitious academic content that is aligned to challenging state content standards. NCLB provisions attempt to address inequalities in opportunity to
learn through such provisions as requiring that all teachers be highly qualified, through offering school choice to all students in Title I schools that fail
to meet their AYP targets for two consecutive years and providing supplemental services to low-income students in Title I schools that fail their AYP
target for three consecutive years.

Because the achievement gap appears to be in part a function of differential loss in the summer months, summer school interventions would appear
to be a promising remedy. Cooper and others conducted a meta-analysis of
ninety-three studies of summer school and found an average effect size of
0.2.[26] Instead of closing the achievement gap, they found that the effects
were larger for students from high-income families than they were for students from low-income families. It could be that students from low-income
families go to lower-quality summer programs than do students from high-
income families.

Recently, Geoffrey Borman and Maritza Dowling used a randomized field
trial to investigate the effects of the "Teach Baltimore" summer school pro-

24. Porter (2005).
25. Ferguson (1998); Nye, Hedges, and Konstantopoulos (2002); Porter (2005).
26. Cooper and others (2000).

gram.[27] For seven weeks each summer for three summers, students received three hours of intensive reading and writing instruction each morning followed by an hour and a half of hands-on math and science projects in the afternoon. College undergraduates received three weeks of training in how to implement the program before serving as tutors to the high school students.

Unfortunately, student attendance was a problem, with average attendance over three summers at 39 percent. Perhaps as a result, student achievement was no better for the treatment group than it was for the control group. Analyses using the instrumental variable approach sought to estimate the effect of the treatment for those who did attend in comparison with those in the control group who would likely have attended. The analyses found a 0.3 effect size on reading achievement in favor of the treatment. However, the question remains as to how to solve the attendance problem and whether or not attendance is correlated with poverty.

Anticipating the Effects of NCLB

In this section, I comment on what the chapters in the volume have to say about the NCLB provision of accountability, highly qualified teachers, and the rights of students in schools identified as in need of improvement (for example, school choice and access to supplemental services). I title the section anticipated effects because much of the volume addresses effects of NCLB-like provisions that were implemented by states before the passage of NCLB and because 2006 was too early in the existence of NCLB for all of the provisions to have reached maturity or, in several cases, been implemented. Where appropriate, I add results from the recently completed first phase of AIR-RAND's national evaluation of NCLB.[28]

School Accountability

Meredith Phillips and Jennifer Flashman in chapter 3 of this volume use data from the Council of Chief State School Officers and School and Staffing Survey to estimate the effects of changes in state school accountability policies in first through sixth grades for the period 1993–94 to 1999–2000. Although the period studied predates NCLB, the policies of student achievement testing and school and teacher accountability are very much a part of the NCLB structure. Phillips and Flashman also looked at student retention, which is

---

27. Borman and Dowling (2006).
28. Le Floch and others (2006).

not included in NCLB. As for their dependent variables, they investigated these effects on the number of hours per week teachers spent on school-related work, the amount of professional development, class size, teacher autonomy and stability, and teacher quality as measured by a number of proxies such as years of experience and having an advanced degree.

Using data from all fifty states, they looked at the effects of changes in policies on changes in practices using a state fixed-effects model. As with all secondary data analysis, they experienced some challenges obtaining all the data they wanted for their model. For example, their dataset lacked student achievement.

Like others before them, Phillips and Flashman found some evidence of positive effects of state accountability and little evidence of negative effects.[29] While the patterns were not always consistent, there was some evidence that accountability had its largest effects on schools serving high concentrations of students from low-income families and from families of color. Although these findings stop short of assessing these effects on student achievement, they do suggest that NCLB school accountability provisions may address inequalities in students' opportunity to learn and in so doing may reduce the poverty gap.

They found evidence of some reduction in teacher autonomy, which should not come as a surprise since increased accountability is meant to decrease teacher autonomy. Whether or not the loss in teacher autonomy is detrimental for student learning remains to be seen. For example, they found that strong accountability policies were associated with less teacher turnover in disadvantaged schools, but these policies had a modest negative effect on teacher experience that was most pronounced in non-White schools. Unfortunately, the size of policy changes from 1994 to 2000 was not large, and even though they used a state fixed-effects model, there was some covariation in changes in accountability and other reforms during the period investigated (for example, increases in accountability and decreases in class size were two of the most popular reforms during the course of the period of study).

Researchers using fixed-effects models to analyze natural variation data need to document that within-state (or within-district) variation over time in the independent variables under investigation is sufficient. Readers and researchers must guard against confusing the typically large between-state (between-district) variation within time with the typically much smaller within-state variation over time. Clearly, small variation in an independent variable prevents investigation of the potential of that independent variable.

29. Carnoy and Loeb (2002); Hanushek and Raymond (2005); Jacob (2005).

NCLB plows new ground in requiring that schools be held accountable for increasing the proficiency of students with disabilities. In chapter 2 of this volume, Barbara Foorman, Sharon Kalinowski, and Waynel Sexton place NCLB and IDEA into a historical context, noting that typically special education and its provisions have been kept separate from general education. Foorman, Kalinowski, and Sexton's parallel account of "equal education and right-to-education movements" is informative and certainly consistent with my earlier conclusion that the most promising way to reduce the achievement gaps is by addressing inequalities in student opportunity to learn. Referring to the most recent reauthorizations of NCLB and IDEA, they note that "the two acts work in concert to ensure high quality instruction that closes the achievement gap." According to the authors, the two laws "place an emphasis on prevention and early intervention and rely on whole-school approaches and multitiered instruction that incorporate scientifically based academic programs and positive behavioral interventions and supports. Both require highly qualified teachers as defined by federal law. Both require alignment of performance goals and indicators with states' definitions of adequate yearly progress. Both require progress monitoring, data collection, and data evaluation to inform the instructional process. Both mandate high expectations for students with disabilities." Their pointing out the parallels in the two laws was new information for me and helps me understand how the provisions are meant to work through mutual reinforcement.

While their chapter provides no new evidence on the implementation or effects of NCLB or IDEA, it does provide convincing arguments for the desirability of closing the achievement gap for students with disabilities. The underlying theme of the chapter is one with which I wholeheartedly agree: special education needs to be brought into the mainstream in terms of legislation, research, and education reform. Special education and general education need to be carefully articulated, one with the other, student by student, if their collective benefits are to be maximized.

Occasionally among the chapters in this volume, there is mild disagreement about the extent to which NCLB requires that the achievement gap be closed. Foorman, Kalinowski, and Sexton are clear in stating that NCLB and IDEA both require that the achievement gap be closed, first by requiring that all students be proficient by 2014 (and that 95 percent of the students be tested) and second by requiring that along the way schools and districts meet AYP targets for subgroups of students. Admittedly, an achievement gap can still exist even if the NCLB requirement of 100 percent proficiency is met, but at least 100 percent proficiency guarantees a floor below which no student is allowed to fall.

Going beyond this volume, in 2006 the National Longitudinal Study and the Study of State Implementation of No Child Left Behind had just completed the first phase of their work (conducted by a consortium of RAND, the American Institutes for Research, the National Opinion Research Center, the Council of Chief State School Officers, and the Regional Educational Data Aggregation Project). The two studies' main objectives are to describe the actions taken by states, districts, and schools to implement NCLB. The first wave of data collection was for the year 2004–05 and included telephone interviews of officials in all fifty states plus a nationally representative sample of 300 districts and 1,500 schools. The quality of the data obtained is especially impressive, with 100 percent response from states, 96 percent from districts, 89 percent from principals, 84 percent from teachers, and 60 percent from parents. Here, I draw selectively from the early results to augment what we know about NCLB school accountability. In 2003–04, 75 percent of schools and 71 percent of districts met AYP. A higher percentage of schools met AYP at the elementary school level than at the middle or high school level (perhaps, in part, because middle schools and high schools are larger and so a higher percentage are held accountable on disaggregated data). Only 23 percent of schools that failed AYP failed because they fell short of the target for a single group of students. Of schools that were held accountable for six or more disaggregated groups of students, only 61 percent met AYP, while for schools with only one group, 90 percent met AYP. Because of the newness of NCLB, only 13 percent of schools had failed AYP for two consecutive years and thus were identified as in need of improvement (this was true for 18 percent of Title I schools). There is evidence of a loosely coupled system in that 22 percent of the principals in schools identified as having failed AYP did not know that their school had failed AYP. One especially promising finding is that since 2002 over half of the states had revised their content standards in reading or mathematics or both. As will be argued later, the quality of state content standards is absolutely crucial to the success of NCLB.

Student Accountability

While student accountability is not part of the NCLB legislation, several states include student accountability as a part of their standards-based reform, especially at the high school graduation level. In 2006 more states were considering adding student accountability primarily because of the perception that middle and high school students were not trying their best on the student achievement tests used for school accountability and probably were not trying their best in school either. Robert Hauser, Carl Frederick, and Megan

Andrew in chapter five provide a careful and informative investigation of grade retention using the current population survey (CPS) dataset. They investigate retention in grade by looking at students who are above the modal age for the grade. For fourteen states, they augment these analyses with data on grade retention. The period of time investigated is 1994 to 2006.

Like others, Hauser, Frederick, and Andrew find that retention is highest: in central cities, in southern states, for boys, for Blacks and Hispanics, for students from low-income families, and for students from single parent homes. Further, retention is highest in first grade at 7 percent and next highest in kindergarten at 4.5 percent. After that, retention is highest in ninth grade at 3 percent. All of these grade levels are not targeted by NCLB for student achievement testing. The authors find no evidence that NCLB is causing an increase in grade retention. NCLB is quiet on student accountability, with respect to both grade-level retention and high school graduation tests. Thus, if NCLB were having an effect upon grade retention, it would be an indirect effect possibly operating through NCLB's policies on school accountability. The hypothesis would be that schools in danger of failing AYP might retain more students on the grounds that through retention they are more likely to meet the proficient criterion because students are older and have more years of schooling behind them when they take the test at a particular grade level. In contrast, grade-to-grade retention rates could be one of the "other academic indicators" identified by a state for use in determining AYP, which would work against the idea of initiating grade retention policies in response to NCLB.

Hauser, Frederick, and Andrew do not investigate the effects of retention on subsequent student performance and achievement, but there is a substantial literature on the effects of grade retention, most of which finds negative effects.[30] However, not all retention programs are the same. Melissa Roderick, Brian Jacob, and Anthony Bryk found positive effects of a Chicago retention program with the effects greatest for students in schools with high concentrations of Black students.[31] The results were complex, however, suggesting that the within-school achievement gap might be closed for reading but exacerbated for mathematics. Yet, the overall achievement gap was reduced for both subjects.

While Hauser, Frederick, and Andrew find no abrupt or sustained increases in levels of retention in the decade of accountability that foreshadowed NCLB or occurred after passage of NCLB, they did find substantially

30. Gampert (1987); Gottfredson, Fink, and Graham (1994); Grissom and Shepard (1989); Reynolds (1992); Roderick (1994); Holmes (1989); Jimerson (2001).
31. Roderick, Jacob, and Bryk (2002).

higher retention rates for students from low-income families and for Black students (as well as boys). Given that the bulk of the literature on the effects of retention in grade shows negative effects for those retained, it could be that differential retention is leading to an increase in the achievement gap and perhaps an increase in the dropout gap as well.

Thomas Dee and Brian Jacob in chapter 6 investigate the effects of high school exit exams and high school course requirements on student dropout and completion rates and achievement. NCLB requires that, for high schools, one of the "other academic indicators" must be the graduation rate. Thus states concerned about schools meeting AYP would appear to be ill advised to keep weak students in high school longer than they otherwise might be and to graduate fewer students because they are unable to pass an exit exam. Nevertheless, according to Dee and Jacob, high school exit exams are a popular reform, with nineteen states currently requiring an exit exam and seven more planning to do so in the near future.

Dee and Jacob do an excellent job of reviewing the literature on exit exams, which is essentially mixed as to the effects of exit exams on high school completion and achievement. When effects are found, they tend to be very small. Dee and Jacob also investigate course requirements, which tend to be blunt policy instruments specifying only number of courses in a subject area, not the type of course (such as a college prep course). Perhaps these mixed results from past research are explained by Dee and Jacob's careful analysis; as they work the reader through the possibilities, for every potential positive there appears to be a potential negative.

Dee and Jacob use data from the Public Use Micro Sample (PUMS) 2000, a 5 percent sample of the U.S. Census with 14 million respondents. From these data they assemble a subsample of approximately 3 million White, Black, and Hispanic respondents who were 18 years of age between 1980 and 1998. To the PUMS dataset, they add information as to whether at the time of graduation each state had an exit exam or course requirements: high requirements (at least 3 credits of English, 2 of social studies, 1 of science, and 1 in mathematics) and very high requirements (4 credits in English, 3 in social studies, 2 in math, and 2 in science).

Thirty-two percent of the state-by-year data points had an exit exam. Seventy-five percent had a high course requirement, and twenty-five percent a very high course requirement. Using state fixed effects to look at relationships between changes in policies and changes in outcomes, they used a variety of ingenious techniques to help ensure that their analyses controlled for important confounding.

They found no significant relationship between likelihood of dropping out and the introduction of either a state exit exam or a rigorous course requirement. When they considered the more difficult exit exam, they found a very small negative effect on the probability of completing high school (0.007 percentage point). Also using states as fixed effects, John Warren, Krista Jenkins, and Rachel Kulick reported lower regular graduation rates (2.1 percent) and higher GED rates associated with the introduction of more difficult state exit exams.[32] Dee and Jacob found a slight tendency for greater dropout for Black males and higher completion for Hispanics in the presence of exit exams. I am as puzzled as they were by the strange pattern of results. Not surprisingly, they found course requirements positively related to enrollment in college; the whole point of course requirements is to make students better prepared for college. Effects on employment and earnings are tiny and vary by race. Curiously, among Black males, high school graduates earn slightly more and dropouts slightly less when there is not an exit exam. These results must be tempered somewhat by the authors' not reporting the extent to which the state policies they examined varied substantially during the period under investigation, as they must if there is to be any chance of finding effects.

Dee and Jacob also analyze Minnesota data during the period when the state went from having no exit exam to having an exit exam. Their estimates of the consequences of initiating an exit exam indicate a reduction in dropout rates at tenth and eleventh grades and a comparable increase in twelfth grade. The effects were larger in districts with high concentrations of minorities (though there are relatively few minorities in Minnesota). As for poverty, the dropout effect for twelfth grade was largest for high-poverty districts. The improvements in retention at tenth and eleventh grades were highest for the low-poverty districts and, in fact, there was no rate increase in twelfth grade dropout for the low-poverty districts. Because the positive effects were largest for low-poverty districts and the negative effects were largest for high-poverty districts and districts with high concentrations of Black students, the policies actually exacerbated the achievement gap slightly.

In sum, student accountability is not a component of NCLB, and there is no evidence that NCLB is stimulating states to initiate student accountability. To the contrary, NCLB would appear to give states reasons to avoid high school exit exams, yet such policies appear to be popular anyway. The balance of evidence is that grade-to-grade retention as typically implemented has at

32. Warren, Jenkins, and Kulick (2006).

least short-term negative effects on students. Unfortunately, the research does not address the main hypothesis that grade retention policies over time force the education system to get better, thus providing long-term positive effects. As for exit exams, one thing seems clear: their effects are not large.

Highly Qualified Teacher

Laura Desimone, Thomas Smith, and David Frisvold investigate state policy and SES effects on teacher quality using state-by-state and national NAEP, as well as a database of state policies that they cleverly assembled from a variety of sources. They focus on mathematics data from middle schools from 2000 to 2003. They investigate the quality of instruction as well as more distal variables of class size and professional development. Again, while the time period is a bit early to see NCLB effects, they investigate variables that are a part of NCLB and therefore may be predictive of subsequent NCLB effects.

Like others before them, they find that teacher quality is better in low-poverty schools than it is in high-poverty schools (*low poverty* being defined as 10 percent or fewer students eligible for free lunch). They also find within-school differences to such an extent that an advantaged student in a high-poverty school is more likely to have a high-quality teacher than is a disadvantaged student in a low-poverty school. Almost surely, these differences contribute to the poverty gap. While they find relatively small changes in teacher quality from 2000 to 2003, they do find some modest effects of changes in NCLB-like policies on teacher quality. Unfortunately, the results are neither large nor consistent enough to suggest that they will solve the gap in teacher quality. Using a policy attributes theory, they find modest evidence that policies based in authority (for example, state-provided support to implement change) have larger effects on teacher quality than do state policies based in power (for example, rewards and sanctions).[33] According to the theory, the effects of authoritative policy may be longer lasting as well. Desimone, Smith, and Frisvold also find some evidence that policy initiatives in one area may offset the effects of policy initiatives in another. For example, resources spent on new curricula and tutoring may leave fewer resources to devote to improving teacher quality.

The AIR-RAND national evaluation of Title I results shed further light on NCLB and teacher quality. By 2004–05, forty-eight of the fifty states were testing the content knowledge of new teachers, but as documented ear-

---

33. Porter and others (1988); Desimone (2002).

lier, there was substantial variation from state to state in definitions of minimally accepted content knowledge. Seventy-five percent of elementary and middle school teachers and 69 percent of high school teachers reported they were considered by their state as highly qualified (although a full 20 percent did not know whether their state considered them highly qualified or not). The percentages of highly qualified special education teachers were substantially lower. Consistent with the results of Desimone and her coauthors, percentages of highly qualified teachers were lower in high-poverty schools and lower in schools failing AYP. Curiously, among high school teachers considered by their state as highly qualified, approximately half lacked a degree in the subject they taught (46 percent for English and 59 percent for mathematics). According to the websites for the six states reported earlier, all six had 87 percent or more highly qualified teachers in the 2005–06 school year, ranging from 87.4 percent in North Carolina to 97.2 percent in Missouri and Georgia. The discrepancy between these figures and the ones reported from the AIR-RAND study is surely explained by the percentage of teachers who did not know whether they were highly qualified or not. The main point seems to be that for most states, a very high percentage of teachers is labeled highly qualified. At the same time, the public perception is that a substantial fraction of teachers are not highly qualified. For some, this may suggest that the criteria for what constitutes highly qualified teacher need to be defined more rigorously by the states. Yet one might ask, what percentage of teachers who are not highly qualified could be tolerated? If, for example, a state had only half of its teachers highly qualified, what would be the implications? If the state needed to dramatically increase the percentage of highly qualified teachers, how could the state accomplish that goal? As for reducing the poverty gap, the key is to ensure that all teachers in schools with high concentrations of students from low-income families are truly highly qualified. At present, that would require taking many of the best teachers out of schools serving high concentrations of students from affluent families. So far that solution has not garnered sufficient political support. Although setting a low bar for highly qualified teachers has political support at least at the time of this writing, it will not reduce the poverty gap.

The Rights of Students in Schools Identified as in Need of Improvement

Two of the most controversial provisions of NCLB have to do with the rights of students attending schools failing their AYP targets for two or more consecutive years. First, for schools in this group, the district must permit students to transfer from the failing public school to another public school in the district that has not been identified for improvement. Second, for schools failing their AYP target for three consecutive years, the district must provide supplemental educational services for students from low-income families.

In chapter 8 of this volume, Paul Hill addresses the school choice requirement. Hill writes about choice with the wisdom of someone who has been watching the success and failures of Title I for even longer than I have been. He headed a Title I study for the National Institute of Education back in the mid-1970s (NIE was the government's first version of what is now the Institute of Education Sciences [IES]). Hill sees the choice provision of NCLB as a typical legislative compromise, concluding, "It is [hard] to say exactly how much choice NCLB was intended to create or to estimate how much, for whom, and in what forms choice will ultimately emerge as a result of NCLB." Nevertheless, he notes (as have others) that the amount of choice being exercised as a function of NCLB is relatively small. In some districts there are no schools to which a student might transfer. This is, not surprisingly, especially true at the high school level where many districts have only one high school. In most districts, parents were not informed in a timely fashion that their child was eligible for school choice. The AIR-RAND national evaluation found that in the 2004–05 school year only fifteen states had reported school AYP status by the start of school (already too late for parents to exercise meaningful choice). While 6.3 million students were eligible for choice, less than 1 percent actually exercised their choice option. Thirty-nine percent of districts required to offer choice did not. Of course, knowing that choice is an option is not sufficient to exercise meaningful choice. Parents must be armed with information about the quality of the various schools from which they might select. Providing this information in an accessible and timely fashion was a challenge not yet met by the spring of 2006.

Hill provides an even-handed analysis of the costs and benefits of school choice. Just as some students might benefit by transferring to a better school, other students might be left behind in a school that is all the worse for having lost some of its students. The hope is that through competition, schools will get better across the board (at least the schools that survive). Reviewing the evidence, Hill reports mixed findings with no clear pattern of evidence for or against the benefits of school choice. He characterizes the research on charter schools in a similar vein; charter schools obviously vary in quality.

Just as Hill finds it difficult to argue conclusively for the benefits of choice (and charter schools), he does a good job of addressing some of the most serious criticisms. In addressing fears of segregation, he reports lotteries as being run in an unbiased way and that creaming is unlikely in central cities where families exercising choice are mainly African American. As for the contention that the loss of students to choice causing districts to fail, Hill argues that many urban districts have steadily lost students for years because of a variety of factors and that loss of students due to NCLB choice is likely to be small.

Until choice is exercised by a considerably larger number of families and students, the effect of the NCLB choice option will remain small. For NCLB choice to work to the benefit of students and families, Hill argues that the following are needed: funding must follow students in sufficient amounts to encourage formation of quality choice options, better information must be provided to parents so that they can exercise informed choice, and the admissions process must be monitored to ensure fairness. Still, as Hill notes, even if NCLB does in the long term stimulate a significant amount of choice, whether the effects on the level of student achievement and on the poverty gap will be positive, negative, or neutral remain to be seen. According to current research, the results are likely to be mixed.

Drawing from a variety of sources, George Farkas and Rachel Durham describe supplemental services as services focusing on reading that are delivered to small groups of students, provided after school several times a week for one to two hours, and are typically offered at the student's school by certified teachers. More than half of the providers are private nonprofit organizations, but a substantial number are school districts (school districts identified as in need of improvement cannot provide supplemental services). Farkas and Durham report that student attendance is poor and the number of hours of participation per student is highly variable, with a mean of sixty hours a year.

In contrast to the more than 6 million students eligible for school choice in the 2004–05 school year, fewer than 2 million students were eligible for supplemental services. Farkas and Durham report that somewhere between 10 and 15 percent of eligible students participate, a percentage that is almost sure to increase as the option matures.

Farkas and Durham express considerable concern about the quality of the services provided. They would like the bulk of the services to be one-on-one tutoring, not those provided in a small group format. They want better competition among providers, in part achieved through better-informed parents, and they want efforts to improve student participation rates. In reviewing the literature, they find little evidence for the effects of supplemental services on student achievement and grades. Without a change in the provision of supplemental services, Farkas and Durham are doubtful of seeing any positive effects. High-quality supplemental services targeted to students from low-income families would likely reduce the poverty gap, however.

Challenges to What We Know about NCLB Effects

Clearly, there is a great deal known about the early effects of NCLB and a great deal known from analyses of earlier implementation of NCLB-like policies and practices. While this volume is immensely useful in presenting what is known thus far, at the same time, it is clear that state implementations of NCLB requirements will change over time. In 2006 not all of the provisions of NCLB had yet taken effect, and those that had were in their infancy. Change is difficult, and initial reactions tend toward the negative. Further, NCLB requires states to do a great deal in a short period of time. While I am amazed at the extent to which states have been able to implement most of the NCLB requirements, I am certain that the depth and quality of implementation will improve with time. More than half of the states have already revised their academic subject content standards at least once. States are also moving to cut the turnaround time on returning results of student achievement, which should help parents exercise their choice option.

As for the chapters in this volume, authored by bright and talented researchers, the negative consequences of NCLB that many anticipated did not emerge. The pattern of results is more positive than negative. At the same time, for those who would champion NCLB, the effects are disappointingly small. The results are based on secondary analyses of natural variation using states as fixed effects. These state-of-the-art analyses are efficient and excellent for controlling pesky confounding variables. However, they are dependent upon there being substantial within-state variation over time in the policies being investigated and good measures of independent and dependent variables. Better measures of variables and greater policy variance over time might have led to bigger effects.

As one might expect in such a politically charged terrain, some authors worry especially about negative effects. For example, Phillips and Flashman worry that NCLB might be reducing teacher autonomy. Desimone, Smith, and Frisvold worry that NCLB might be driving good teachers from the field. Hauser, Frederick, and Andrew worry that NCLB is causing an increase in student retention. I find no evidence to support these worries. As for teacher autonomy in particular, NCLB's focus on outcomes leaves great freedom in how those outcomes might be pursued. Moreover, it is not clear that loss of autonomy in deciding what to teach is harmful for student achievement.[34]

---

34. Porter and others (1988).

Suggestion for the Reauthorization of NCLB

To some extent, the reauthorization of NCLB will be a function of its political support. In his chapter, Tom Loveless explores the resistance to and enthusiasm for NCLB, both among the public and the states. Drawing on a Phi Delta Kappan poll and a poll by the Educational Testing Service (ETS), he finds that from 2001 to 2005 public opinion of NCLB went from positive to evenly divided. In the ETS poll, an ingenious experiment manipulated the amount of information that respondents had on the provisions of NCLB. The more-informed respondents were less certain of how they felt about the law. Given the complexity of the law, this finding of less certainty with more information is understandable. In any event, as of 2006 there was no evidence of a majority opposition to NCLB among the public. Those most favorable toward NCLB are Republicans, persons of color, poor people, and people residing in rural areas. Responses to questions about specifics of the law reveal some troubling confusions. People like that the law holds students accountable, but it does not. They do not like that the law relies on a single test, withholds funds from failing schools, and holds special education students to the same standards as other students, but the law has none of these requirements.

There is less systematic evidence about state views of NCLB. Loveless assembles a useful summary of state-by-state resistance in appendix 9A-3. He also creates a six-point scale of state resistance against which he runs a number of bivariate correlations to identify predictors of state resistance. As Loveless notes, it is difficult to interpret the bivariate correlations because of collinearity among the predictors. One pattern that seems to hold, however, is that the states most in need of improving the quality of their education system are the states least resistant to NCLB. The one possible exception is states with large populations of Hispanics, but their resistance may be to the NCLB testing in English requirements. On Loveless' six-point scale of state resistance, only two states had taken strong negative reactions to NCLB (Utah and Connecticut), and only an additional nine had taken what I would judge to be mildly resisting action. In short, the bulk of the states seem to be going along with NCLB.

As Loveless notes, "the future of NCLB, and its reauthorization in 2007, hinges on holding that (left-right) coalition together." Holding the coalition together and maintaining support for NCLB will, of course, be a function of reactions to the law as it was originally written and implemented. At the same time, the reauthorization provides an opportunity to reconsider and revise the provisions of the law in ways that might make it more effective and popular.

By most, if not all, accounts the main idea behind NCLB is one for which there remains considerable support: to close the achievement gaps, education reform should continue its focus on accountability for the outputs of education. None of the professional organizations, not even the highly resistant teachers unions, are calling for a return to regulating inputs. Nevertheless, there are a number of possibilities for adjusting NCLB provisions in response to the considerable amount of insight provided in this volume.

A Theory for Doing High-stakes Testing Right

To organize my thinking about NCLB reauthorization, I turned to a "theory" I created for doing high-stakes testing right.[35] The simple three-part theory hypothesizes that education accountability, in terms of student achievement, should meet three criteria: set a good target, make accountability symmetric, and make accountability fair. As will be seen, the initial version of NCLB looks pretty good against these three criteria, but there is room for improvement.

SET A GOOD TARGET. It is an old cliché to say that teachers teach what is tested. NCLB responds to this maxim by requiring states to have ambitious content standards for core academic subjects, especially reading and mathematics, with aligned student achievement tests. The content standards and aligned tests are to be the target for teachers' decisions about what to teach. There is considerable research that shows that what teachers teach is the strongest school-controlled explanation for student achievement gains.[36] NCLB requires grade-level-specific content standards and testing at every grade, third through eighth, in reading and mathematics. In 2008 science must be tested at three grade levels across the K–12 spectrum. These provisions help to set a good target in that the focus is on more than just one subject and more than just a few selected grades. NCLB also requires that at least 95 percent of the students be tested and that data be disaggregated to report results by subgroups of students where there are sufficient numbers. Again, these provisions set a good target in the sense of calling for reductions in the achievement gaps.

MAKE ACCOUNTABILITY SYMMETRIC. Here, NCLB is not consistent with the theory. Making accountability symmetric means that schools and

---

35. Porter, Chester, and Schlesinger (2004).
36. Gamoran and others (1997).

students are both held accountable for what they collectively produce. With NCLB, schools are held accountable but not students. Surprisingly, most accountability systems are not symmetric. In the past, there have been states that held students accountable but not schools, and there are states now that hold schools accountable but not students. When education is effective, however, students and schools work together. Neither leaves the other "hanging out to dry." A common complaint about NCLB, especially at the middle and high school levels, is that students do not try their best on the test used for school accountability because students are not held accountable for their performance. The evidence is anecdotal, but the possibility makes sense. As further support, when states set their achievement level standards on field test data, the percentage proficient estimated on the field test data is typically lower than the percentage proficient on the first operational administration of the test, especially at the upper grades. The increase is not in response to student accountability, but it does imply that student effort may be a problem. In this volume, two chapters focus on two measures of student accountability: high school exit exams and grade-to-grade promotion. There are other possibilities for student accountability that are less draconian. For example, performance on the state test might be placed on the student's transcript or might count toward a student's grades.

DEVELOP A FAIR SYSTEM OF ACCOUNTABILITY. There are three components to fairness. First, students must be provided the support that they need to be successful. Here, the central concept is opportunity to learn. Courts have ruled repeatedly that students cannot be held accountable for achievement of content that they have not had an adequate opportunity to learn.[37] Further, I hypothesized earlier that addressing inequities in student opportunity to learn is the key to reducing the poverty gap. The second component is support for schools. If schools are to be held accountable, they must be given the resources they need to be successful. This is, of course, a slippery slope and one that many will use to argue for increased expenditures. But it is becoming increasingly clear that money alone is not a solution; the money must be spent wisely.[38] NCLB provides supports for students in the form of supplemental services and the option for school choice. NCLB requires support for schools in the sense that state and district services are to be provided to schools identified in need of improvement and in the requirement that

37. Heubert and Hauser (1999).
38. Hanushek (1989); Hedges, Laine, and Greenwald (1994).

teachers be highly qualified teachers and that they receive high-quality professional development. The third component of a fair accountability system is the accuracy of the data on which accountability decisions are made—the typical psychometric requirements of reliability and validity. NCLB requires tests that are aligned, and alignment is a key component of validity. Beyond that, NCLB is largely silent. Nevertheless, in my experience states are struggling mightily to build the best student achievement tests possible, documenting their psychometric properties and guarding against cheating, errors of scoring, and the like, as is called for in the Standards for Educational and Psychological Testing developed by the American Educational Research Association, the American Psychological Association, and the National Council on Measurement in Education.[39]

Thoughts on Reauthorization

My simple three-part theory for doing high-stakes testing right can be used to organize thinking about suggestions for the reauthorization of NCLB.

SET A GOOD TARGET. State variation in implementation of NCLB brings to light whether or not it is time to set national content and performance standards and have an aligned national test of student achievement and a national definition of a highly qualified teacher. State-to-state variation is troubling, not to mention expensive and difficult to manage. National content standards and a national achievement test would greatly simplify the provision of high-quality curriculum materials, professional development for teachers, and preservice teacher education. National content standards and a national achievement test would focus reform energies, reduce expensive redundancies, and allow a pooling of resources to produce the best products and supports possible. There would be enormous resistance to such a move, with people arguing that it infringes on state rights; the reaction to President Clinton's call for a national test is a case in point. I am not saying it is time for national standards and a national test; I am saying it is time to give serious consideration to that possibility, with arguments presented pro and con before a decision is made. Why should states have different standards such that a student labeled proficient in one state would be labeled advanced in another and only basic in yet a third? Why should students in one state be subjected to teachers who are found unacceptable in another?

39. Heubert and Hauser (1999).

Does NCLB's focus on reading and mathematics divert attention from other academic subjects and is this a problem? Perhaps NCLB should require content standards, student achievement testing, and school accountability equally in science and social studies as it does in reading and mathematics. Similarly, should NCLB require more testing at the high school level? One option to consider, as some states are, is end-of-course testing. A move to end-of-course testing would help ensure that college prep courses maintain their integrity, since these courses are increasingly required of all students.

Almost certainly some revision of AYP targets is needed. As Robert Linn has pointed out repeatedly, there is no existence proof that schools can meet the AYP targets that they will be required to meet in the not-too-distant future.[40] I am a proponent of both school and student accountability, but I recognize that standards for accountability have to be set reasonably. Given informed effort, there must be a good possibility of meeting and exceeding the target. If the AYP targets of NCLB become completely unreasonable, they will become irrelevant.

School accountability should be a function of how well all students achieve. NCLB is to be commended for requiring that 95 percent of students be tested and that accountability of schools be based on disaggregated data, but there are at least two problems yet to be solved. First, AYP targets are based only on the percentage of students who are proficient. The only students that matter in terms of accountability and meeting targets are those that in a given year can be moved from the level of below proficient to that of proficient; the rest of the students do not count. Why not develop an accountability index that is based on the performance of all students? After all, schools serve all students. Besides, an index based on all students would be more stable in a statistical sense. Second, NCLB requires school accountability on student achievement of only those students who are in the school for the school year. This leaves out the very students who are most in need of a quality education: mobile students. NCLB school accountability could be a function of every student if a student's achievement were allocated to each school he or she attended, with the achievement weighted by the amount of time the student was in each school.

While NCLB requires that tests be aligned to ambitious content standards and the U.S. Department of Education requires that each state document that its tests are aligned, alignment is clearly a continuous variable ranging from highly aligned to not aligned at all. Not enough is currently

40. Linn, Baker, and Betebenner (2002); Linn, Baker, and Herman (2005).

known about the quality of alignment. An area of investigation that has shown good early progress deals with measuring alignment and setting standards to meet alignment requirements. Should NCLB set a standard for minimal alignment?

MAKE ACCOUNTABILITY SYMMETRIC. NCLB accountability is not symmetric, and not much more can be said. School accountability is in place, but student accountability is not. As seen in this volume, the literature on student accountability is mixed, but it is more negative than positive, at least for students in the short run. The ideal is for students to be intrinsically motivated to achieve, yet it is far from being realized. One suggestion is that a little external motivation could be applied, if done correctly.

DEVELOP A FAIR SYSTEM OF ACCOUNTABILITY. Thus far the big areas for consideration in the reauthorization of NCLB are supplemental services and highly qualified teachers. Neither of these two provisions of the law appears to be working well; exactly how each could be fixed remains unclear. Perhaps a standard definition of a highly qualified teacher should be implemented across states. How demanding that criterion should be is difficult to determine. If the standard were made too demanding, an unacceptable number of teachers would be judged as not being highly qualified. Alternatively, the requirement would become a sham if it were set too leniently. In most states as of 2006, we seem closer to the latter situation than to the former. As for supplemental services, perhaps NCLB should insist upon one-on-one tutoring as called for by Farkas and Durham and shown by research to be more effective than the currently favored method of small group instruction.

Another area that appears to need work concerns alternate standards, alternate assessments, and accommodations for students with disabilities. Again, I am uncertain of the solutions, but I am certain that substantial problems in this area need to be addressed. At the time of this writing, states are scrambling to implement the provision concerning students with disabilities, but, at least, the states with which I am working are far from certain that what they are doing is the best that can be done. The goal has to be on how to provide the best quality instruction to students with disabilities. Individual Education Plans were meant to do that, but they have largely failed.

As was seen in defining school accountability, states' decisions about disaggregated group size, confidence intervals, and trajectories vary considerably. Should some of this be tightened up? Is this another place for a national decision?

NCLB is the most ambitious U.S. government education reform, at least since the 1960s. The law is comprehensive and complex. This volume contributes greatly to what is known about the early effects of NCLB and NCLB-like provisions. NCLB will be strengthened and improved as states gain experience with implementation. Just as the law mentions research-based practice 111 times, I am hopeful that revisions to the law will also be based on research.

References

Alexander, Karl L., Doris R. Entwisle, and Linda S. Olson. 2001. "Schools, Achievement, and Inequality: A Seasonal Perspective." *Educational Evaluation and Policy Analysis* 25, no. 2: 171–91.

Alexander, Karl L., Doris R. Entwisle, and Maxine S. Thompson. 1987. "School Performance, Status Relations, and the Structure of Sentiment: Bringing the Teachers Back In." *American Sociology Review* 52, no. 5: 665–82.

American Educational Research Association, American Psychological Association, and National Council on Measurement in Education. 1999. *The Standards for Educational and Psychological Testing*. Washington.

Borman, Geoffrey D., and Maritza Dowling. 2006. "Longitudinal Achievement Effects of Multiyear Summer School: Evidence from the Teach Baltimore Randomized Field Trial." *Educational Evaluation and Policy Analysis* 28, no.1: 25–48.

Braun, Henry, and Jianling Qian. 2005. *Mapping State Performance Standards on to the NAEP Scale*. Princeton, N.J.: Educational Testing Service.

Carnoy, Martin, and Susanna Loeb. 2002. "Does External Accountability Affect Student Outcomes: A Cross-State Analysis." *Educational Evaluation and Policy Analysis* 24, no. 4: 305–31.

Coleman, James, and others. 1966. *Equality of Educational Opportunity*. Washington: Department of Health, Education and Welfare.

Cooper, Harris, and others. 1996. "The Effects of Summer Vacation on Achievement Test Scores: A Narrative and Meta-Analytic Review." *Review of Educational Research* 66, no. 3: 227–68.

Cooper, Harris, and others. 2000. "Making the Most of Summer School: A Meta-Analytic and Narrative Review." *Monographs of the Society for Research in Child Development* 65, no. 1 (Serial No. 260): 1–118.

Desimone, Laura. 2002. "How Can Comprehensive School Reform Models Be Successfully Implemented?" *Review of Education Research* 72, no. 3: 433–79.

Downey, Douglas B., Paul T. von Hippel, and Beckett A Broh. 2004. "Are Schools the Great Equalizer? Cognitive Inequality during the Summer Months and the School Year." *American Sociological Review* 69, no. 5: 613–35.

Entwisle, Doris R., and Karl L Alexander. 1992. "Summer Setback: Race, Poverty, School Composition, and Mathematics Achievement in the First Two Years of School." *American Sociological Review* 57, no. 1: 72–84.

———. 1994. "The Gender Gap in Math: Its Possible Origins in Neighborhood Effects." *American Sociological Review* 59, no. 6: 822–38.

Ferguson, Ronald F. 1998. "Can Schools Narrow the Black-White Test Score Gap?" In *The Black-White Test Score Gap*, edited by Christopher Jencks and Meredith Phillips, pp. 318–74. Brookings.

Gamoran, Adam, and others. 1997. "Upgrading High School Mathematics Instruction: Improving Learning Opportunities for Low-Achieving, Low-Income Youth." *Educational Evaluation and Policy Analysis* 19, no. 4: 325–38.

Gampert, Richard D. 1987. *A Follow-Up Study of the 1982–83 Promotional Gates Students*. New York: New York City Public Schools, Office of Educational Assessment.

Gottfredson, Denise C., Carolyn M. Fink, and Nanette Graham. 1994. "Grade Retention and Problem Behavior." *American Educational Research Journal* 31, no. 4: 761–84.

Grissom, James B., and Lorrie A. Shepard. 1989. "Repeating and Dropping Out of School." In *Flunking Grades: Research and Policies on Retention*, edited by Lorrie A. Shepard and Mary Lee Smith, pp. 34–63. New York: Falmer Press.

Hanushek, Eric A. 1989. "The Impact of Differential Expenditures on School Performance." *Educational Researcher* 18, no. 4: 45–51.

Hanushek, Eric, and Margaret Raymond. 2005. "Does School Accountability Lead to Improved Student Performance?" *Journal of Policy Analysis and Management* 24, no. 2: 297–327.

Hedges, Larry V., Richard D. Laine, and Rob Greenwald. 1994. "Does Money Matter: A Meta-Analysis of Studies of Effects of Differential School Inputs on Student Outcomes." *Educational Researcher* 23, no. 3: 5–13.

Hedges, Larry V., and Amy Nowell. 1998. "Black-White Test Score Convergence Since 1965." In *The Black-White Test Score Gap*, edited by Christopher Jencks and Meredith Phillips, pp. 149–81. Brookings.

Heubert, Jay P., and Robert M. Hauser, eds. 1999. *High Stakes Testing for Tracking, Promotion, and Graduation*. Washington: National Academy Press.

Heyns, Barbara. 1978. *Summer Learning and the Effects of Schooling*. New York: Academic Press.

———. 1987. "Schooling and Cognitive Development: Is There a Season for Learning?" *Child Development* 58, no. 5: 1151–160.

Holmes, C. Thomas. 1989. "Grade Level Retention Effects: A Meta-Analysis of Research Studies." In *Flunking Grades: Research and Policies on Retention*, edited by Lorrie Shepard and Mary L. Smith, pp. 16–33. London: Falmer Press.

Jacob, Brian. 2005. "Accountability, Incentives, and Behavior: The Impact of High Stakes Testing in the Chicago Public Schools." *Journal of Public Economics* 89, no. 5: 761–96.

Jencks, Christopher, and Meredith Phillips, eds. 1998. *The Black-White Test Score Gap*. Brookings.

Jimerson, Shane R. 2001. "Meta-Analysis of Grade Retention Research: Implications for Practice in the 21st Century." *School Psychology Review* 30, no. 3: 420–37.

Kingsbury, Gage G., and others. 2003. *The State of State Standards: Research Investigating Proficiency Levels in Fourteen States*. Lake Oswego, Oreg.: Northwest Evaluation Association.

Le Floch, Kerstin, and others. 2006. "No Child Left Behind in 2004: Results from the National Longitudinal Study of NCLB and Study of State Implementation of NCLB. Implementation of the Accountability Provisions of No Child Left Behind." Presentation at the Annual Meeting of the American Educational Research Association. San Francisco, April 7–11.

Linn, Robert L. 2005. "Test-Based Educational Accountability in the Era of No Child Left Behind." Center for the Study of Evaluation Report 651. Los Angeles: National Center for Research on Evaluation, Standards, and Student Testing.

Linn, Robert L., Eva L. Baker, and Damian W. Betebenner. 2002. "Accountability Systems: Implications of Requirements of the No Child Left Behind Act of 2001." *Educational Researcher* 31, no. 6: 3–16.

Linn, Robert L., Eva L. Baker, and Joan L. Herman. 2005. "Chickens Come Home to Roost." *Newsletter of the National Center for Research on Evaluation, Standards, and Student Testing.* Los Angeles, Fall.

Martineau, Joseph A. 2006. "Distorting Value-Added: The Use of Longitudinal, Vertically Scaled Student Achievement Data for Growth-Based, Value-Added Accountability." *Journal of Educational and Behavioral Statistics* 31, no. 1: 35–62.

McLaughlin, Don, and Bandeira V. de Mello. 2002, April. "Comparison of State Elementary School Mathematics Achievement Standards Using NAEP 2000." Paper presented at the Annual Meeting of the American Educational Research Association. New Orleans, La., April 1–5.

Messick, Samuel. 1989. "Validity." In *Educational Measurement*, 3d ed., edited by Robert L. Linn, pp. 13–103. New York: American Council on Education and Macmillan.

National Center for Education Statistics. 2000. *NAEP 1999 Trends in Academic Progress: Three Decades of Student Performance.* NCES 2000-469. Washington: U.S. Department of Education, Office of Educational Research and Improvement. (http://nces.ed.gov/nationsreportcard/pdf/main1999/2000469.pdf [August 7, 2003]).

Nye, Barbara A., Larry V. Hedges, and Spyros Konstantopoulos. 2002. "Do Low-Achieving Students Benefit More from Small Classes? Evidence from the Tennessee Class Size Experiment." *Educational Evaluation and Policy Analysis* 24, no. 3: 201–17.

Phillips, Meredith, James Crouse, and John Ralph. 1998. "Does the Black-White Test Score Gap Widen after Children Enter School?" In *The Black-White Test Score Gap*, edited by Christopher Jencks and Meredith Phillips, pp. 229–72. Brookings.

Porter, Andrew C. 2005. "Prospects for School Reform and Closing the Achievement Gap." In *Measurement and Research in the Accountability Era*, edited by Carol Anne Dwyer, pp. 59–95. Mahway, N.J.: Lawrence Erlbaum Associates.

———. 2006. "Curriculum Assessment." In *Handbook of Complementary Methods in Education Research*, edited by Judith L. Green, Gregory Camilli, and Patricia B. Elmore, pp. 141–59. Washington: American Educational Research Association.

Porter, Andrew C., Mitchell D. Chester, and Michael D. Schlesinger. 2004. "Framework for an Effective Assessment and Accountability Program: The Philadelphia Example." *Teachers College Press* 106, no. 6: 1358–400.

Porter, Andrew C., Robert L. Linn, and C. Scott Trimble. 2005. "The Effects of State Decisions about NCLB Adequate Yearly Progress Targets." *Educational Measurement: Issues and Practice* 24, no. 4: 32–39.

Porter, Andrew C., and others. 1988. "Content Determinants in Elementary School Mathematics." In *Perspectives on Research on Effective Mathematics Teaching*, edited by Douglas A. Grouws and Thomas J. Cooney, pp. 96–113. Hillsdale, N.J.: Lawrence Erlbaum Associates.

Reynolds, Arthur J. 1992. "Grade Retention and School Adjustment: An Explanatory Analysis." *Educational Evaluation and Policy Analysis* 14, no. 2: 101–21.

Roderick, Melissa. 1994. "Grade Retention and School Dropout: Investigating the Association." *American Educational Research Journal* 31, no. 4: 729–59.

Roderick, Melissa, Brian A. Jacob, and Anthony S. Bryk. 2002. "The Impact of High-Stakes Testing in Chicago on Student Achievement in Promotional Gate Grades." *Educational Evaluation and Policy Analysis* 24, no. 4: 333–57.

Sanders, William L., Arnold M. Saxton, and Sandra P. Horn. 1997. "The Tennessee Value-Added Assessment System: A Quantitative, Outcomes-Based Approach to Educational Assessment." In *Grading Teachers, Grading Schools: Is Student Achievement a Valid Evaluation Measure?* edited by Jason Millman, pp. 137–62. Thousand Oaks, Calif.: Corwin Press.

Warren, John R., Krista N. Jenkins, and Rachel B. Kulick. 2006. "High School Exit Examinations and State-Level Completion and GED Rates, 1975 through 2002." *Educational Evaluation and Policy Analysis* 28, no. 2: 131–52.

Yoon, Kwang S., and others. 2006. "No Child Left Behind in 2004: Results from the National Longitudinal Study of NCLB and Study of State Implementation of NCLB. Implementation of the Accountability Provisions of No Child Left Behind." Presentation at the Annual Meeting of the American Educational Research Association. San Francisco, April 7–11.

About the Editor and Authors

Editor

Adam Gamoran is professor of sociology and educational policy studies, faculty affiliate at the Institute for Research on Poverty, and director of the Wisconsin Center for Education Research at the University of Wisconsin–Madison. A member of the National Academy of Education, Gamoran has published widely on educational inequality and school reform. He has coedited four books on education policy and is the lead author of *Transforming Teaching in Math and Science: How Schools and Districts Can Support Change* (Teachers College Press, 2003).

Authors

Megan Andrew is a doctoral student in sociology at the University of Wisconsin–Madison. Her research interests are in social stratification, the life course, education and work transitions, and social policy.

Thomas S. Dee is an associate professor of economics at Swarthmore College and a faculty research fellow at the National Bureau of Economic Research. His research interests focus largely on the economics of health and education. Examples of his recent research include studies that examine the effects on student outcomes of racial and gender matches of students and teachers and a study that examines the effects of graduated licensing policies on youth traffic fatalities.

Laura M. Desimone is associate professor at the Graduate School of Education at the University of Pennsylvania. Her research focuses on policy effects on teaching and learning; policy implementation; and the improvement of instruments and methods for studying education policy, such as improving the quality of surveys and the appropriate use of multiple methodologies.

Rachel E. Durham is assistant research scientist with the Baltimore Education Research Consortium at Johns Hopkins University. Her research interests include educational policy, school processes, immigration, English language acquisition, and school readiness.

George Farkas is professor of sociology, demography, and education at Pennsylvania State University. An expert in studies of poverty, inequality, and the sociology of education, he has written or edited four books and numerous articles on these and related topics. His current work includes research on the acquisition of cognitive skills among at-risk students. He also developed a one-on-one reading instructional program that helped invent President Clinton's "America Reads" initiative.

Jennifer Flashman is a doctoral student in sociology at UCLA. Her research interests are in social stratification, social demography, and quantitative methods.

Barbara R. Foorman is the Francis Eppes Professor of Education and director of the Florida Center for Reading Research at Florida State University. She is internationally known for her research on language and reading development. Her extensive record of national leadership includes service during 2005 as the nation's first commissioner of education research in the Institute of Education Sciences, U.S. Department of Education.

Carl B. Frederick is a doctoral student in sociology at the University of Wisconsin–Madison. His research interests are in education and social policy.

David Frisvold is a Robert Wood Johnson Scholar in health policy research at the University of Michigan. His research focuses on health policy, policy evaluation, early childhood education, and the economics of education.

Robert M. Hauser is Vilas Research Professor and Samuel A. Stouffer Professor of Sociology, faculty affiliate and former director of the Institute for Research on Poverty, and director of the Center for the Demography of Health and Aging at the University of Wisconsin–Madison. Among his many honors are membership in the National Academy of Education and the National Academy of Sciences. He has published widely on social stratification, education, aging, and social statistics.

Paul T. Hill is John and Marguerite Corbally Professor of public affairs and director of the Center on Reinventing Public Education at the University of Washington–Seattle, and a nonresident senior fellow of the Brookings Institution. He is the author or editor of seven books on educational policy including his most recent work, *Charter Schools against the Odds* (Hoover Press, 2006).

Brian A. Jacob is the Walter H. Annenberg Professor of education policy and professor of economics at the University of Michigan. He also serves as the director of the Center on Local, State, and Urban Policy and is a faculty research fellow at the National Bureau of Economic Research. He has previously served as a policy analyst in the New York City mayor's office and taught middle school in East Harlem. His primary fields of interest are labor economics, program evaluation, and the economics of education. His current research focuses on urban school reform and teacher labor markets. In recent work, he has examined school choice, education accountability programs, housing vouchers, and teacher labor markets.

Sharon J. Kalinowski is a program manager at the University of Texas Health Science Center at Houston where she works on the Texas Reading First Initiative. She was executive director of special services in the Alief Independent School District for twenty years.

Tom Loveless is a senior fellow and director of the Brown Center on Education Policy at the Brookings Institution. He is an expert on U.S. education reform, serves as the U.S. representative to the International Association for the Evaluation of Educational Achievement (IEA), and is the author of *The Brown Center Report on American Education* and editor of seven books on education policy

Meredith Phillips is associate professor of policy studies and sociology at UCLA. She coedited *The Black-White Test Score Gap* (with Christopher Jencks, Brookings, 1998), and her research focuses on social inequality, ethnicity, and educational policy. Among her current projects is a nationwide study of teacher, school, and neighborhood quality.

Andrew C. Porter is Dean of the Graduate School of Education at the University of Pennsylvania. He is an elected member and vice president of the National Academy of Education, a Lifetime National Associate of the National Academies, and past president of the American Educational Research Association. He has published widely on psychometrics, student assessment, education indicators, and research on teaching.

Waynel L. Sexton is an assistant professor at the University of Texas Health Science Center at Houston, where she directs the Texas Reading First

Initiative. She was an elementary teacher, coach, and Associate Reading Manager in the Houston Independent School District for thirty years.

Thomas M. Smith is assistant professor of public policy and education at Peabody College of Education at Vanderbilt University. He is an expert on school organization and teacher quality whose current research focuses on the relations between educational policy and school organization, teacher commitment, and classroom instruction.

Index